College Mathematics Review

Fourth Edition

Robert Blitzer
Miami-Dade Community College

Jack C. Gill

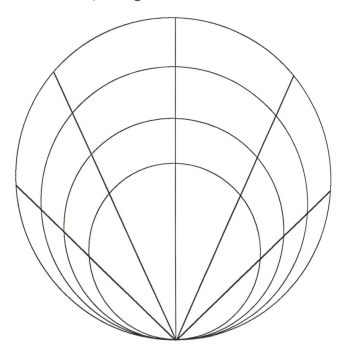

H&H Publishing Company, Inc.
Clearwater, Florida

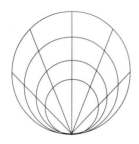

College Mathematics Review, 4th Edition
Robert Blitzer, Jack Gill

Copyright 1992
H&H Publishing Company, Inc.
1231 Kapp Drive
Clearwater, FL 33765
(727) 442-7760
hhservice@hhpublishing.com
www.hhpublishing.com

ISBN 0-943202-40-X

Library of Congress card catalog number 92-072450

Printing is the lowest number: 10 9 8

Preface

Many states and university systems are now mandating that students and teachers achieve a mastery of fundamental mathematics competencies. As these mandates have developed, there is an increasing consensus toward a knowledge of topics associated with courses in liberal arts mathematics, general college mathematics, algebra, and arithmetic, with emphasis on problem solving and critical thinking. Using this perspective, *College Mathematics Review, 4th Ed.*, covers the vast gamut of these topics in the areas of sets-logic (Chapter 1), probability-statistics (Chapter 2), informal geometry (Chapter 3), and algebra (Chapter 4). Also included is a fundamental review of basic arithmetic (appendix 1). The content of the text is appropriate for a traditional general education (liberal arts) course as well as a course specifically designed to meet competency requirements in higher education.

Chapter 1 introduces the major concepts of logic, with emphasis on both formal and informal methods for considering all evidence to arrive at conclusions. Also accentuated is the use of symbolic logic to increase students' proficiency with the English language.

The focus in Chapter 2 is on basic concepts of probability theory, with consideration given to the role of probability in real-world situations and in the statistical research method.

Chapter 3 utilizes fundamental Euclidean axioms involving angles, parallel lines, and congruent triangles to establish basic properties of triangles, quadrilaterals, and polygons, with emphasis on the use of these properties in logical reasoning based upon a geometric figure. Also stressed is measurement and real-world situations involving perimeter, area, and volume.

Chapter 4 is intended for students who have already taken an introductory algebra course. Basic algebraic topics (real numbers, exponents, equations, inequalities, factoring, graphing, systems of equations) are reviewed, although as with all chapters of the text the intent is to foster critical thinking, problem solving, generalizing knowledge, and applying knowledge. Challenging algebraic verbal problems that cannot be solved mechanically and through rote imitation, but that require thoughtful ingenuity, are included.

All four chapters can be covered in a one-semester course. Only the algebra chapter assumes prior knowledge on the part of the student and it is suggested that this chapter be handled as a review chapter at an accelerated pace.

We would like to draw your attention to the format of this text. Each chapter opens with an interdisciplinary or historical introduction that sets the stage for the material covered in that chapter. The chapters are divided into topics, with a brief introduction in each topic leading to a statement of specific behavioral objectives that prepare students for the material covered under that topic. Each topic contains concise explanations, a wealth of solved problems, and a problem set. Boxes are used throughout expository sections to set forth important definitions, formulas, and theorems. A chapter summary follows each chapter, making it easier for students to synthesize their knowledge once they have worked the entire chapter. Each chapter concludes with a sample examination ranging from 55 to 93 multiple-choice questions that review all important ideas presented in the chapter. An appendix is provided (Appendix 1) that reviews frequently-tested arithmetic skills in the context of solved problems, offering the student a collection of 50 basic skills questions, including applied word problems. A cumulative 130-item multiple-choice examination (Appendix 2) gives the student reader an opportunity to simulate the demands of a non-trivial test developed on the foundation of the text's mathematical competencies. Also included are answers and brief explanations. Answers to all problems appear at the back of the book.

Suggestions for improvements from instructors and changing state-mandated mathematical competencies resulted in both rewriting and reorganization for the fourth edition. The major changes are highlighted in the following list.

Chapter 1

a. Truth tables are carefully used to establish equivalences, non-equivalences, and negations of statements.
b. Almost all English examples are changed to bridge the gap between students' intuitive understanding of logic and formal symbolic logic.
c. More emphasis is placed (both intuitively and formally) on equivalences, non-equivalences, and negations.
d. Discussions and examples are included to increase students' proficiency with the English language.
e. A section is added on logic in everyday life. This section requires students to use more informal methods of reasoning to deduce logical conclusions.
f. The sample examination is rewritten and expanded (45 multiple-choice items).

Chapter 2

a. Arrangements and combinations are introduced before considering probability.
b. More emphasis is placed on real-world problems that utilize the fundamental counting principle and basic concepts of probability.
c. A section on the role of probability in the statistical research method, with emphasis on null hypotheses, sampling, sample and population statistics, and sampling error, is added.
d. Problems on interpreting real-world data involving frequency and cumulative frequency tables are added.
e. Problems and graphs, including plot diagrams, requiring students to infer relations and make accurate predictions from studying statistical data are now included.

f. There are more illustrative examples and problems dealing with properties and interrelations among the mean, median, and mode in a variety of distributions.

g. The sample examination is rewritten and expanded (65 multiple-choice items).

Chapter 3

a. Basic Euclidean concepts involving angles, parallel lines, and congruent triangles are used to establish angle relationships for triangles and properties of quadrilaterals.

b. In order to derive basic Euclidean theorems, a section on congruent triangles is added.

c. Numerous problems emphasizing logical reasoning based upon a geometric figure are added.

d. Notations for parallel and perpendicular lines, congruent line segments, and a more precise definition of polygon are included.

e. A proof for the Pythagorean Theorem is included.

f. The sample examination is rewritten and expanded (50 multiple-choice items).

Chapter 4

a. Problems are added that go beyond students merely recognizing the names of properties of operations. These problems require students to use the properties correctly and recognize when they are not used correctly.

b. More detail on exponential simplification is presented in an expanded section.

c. Problems on base 10 numerals are expanded.

d. Problems are added that require students to use applicable properties to select equivalent equations and inequalities.

e. A section on verbal problems is added. The section covers traditional number problems, consecutive integer problems, and digit problems, but also includes contest problems to enhance problem solving skills and critical thinking.

f. Real-world applied problems are added throughout.

g. A section is added on solving a system of two linear equations in two variables by substitution and elimination methods.

h. The sample examination is rewritten and expanded (93 multiple-choice items).

Also new are the chapter introductions and the 130-item review in Appendix 2. This cumulative all-inclusive review should be useful to students preparing for a final course examination as well as for state-mandated competency examinations.

We are indebted to the staff of H & H Publishing Company, Inc. which has improved the technical quality of this book, delivered this edition in a timely manner, while maintaining a reasonable book price for our students. Special thanks go to Tom Howland, and, above all, to our ever-efficient and helpful editor, Karen H. Davis.

Robert F. Blitzer   Jack C. Gill
Miami-Dade Community College
July, 1992

Contents

Sets and Logic

"Elementary, my dear Watson!" Many have been thrilled by Sherlock Holmes' famous utterance. Every faithful reader knew he or she was to be treated to a marvelously logical explanation of some mysterious phenomena.

This chapter contains some of the basic principles of logic, namely, the language, the symbols, and some applications. Naturally this brief exposure cannot make you another Sherlock Holmes. Indeed, Lord Dunsany, an Irish poet, contended that logic, like whiskey, can lose its beneficial effect when taken in too large quantities. Still, this discussion might emphasize the need for clear thinking as well as increase your proficiency with the English language.

The study of mathematics can nurture the ability to reason. It can also focus attention on the importance of thinking logically. In all disciplines the ability to reason abstractly in solving problems is an important tool. One must be able to understand the written and spoken word of reasonable people, to analyze problems objectively, and to avoid arriving at conclusions hastily without considering all the evidence. Surely, intolerance and prejudice thrive in the absence of clear-thinking individuals.

Since the reasoning process is often expressed in terms of declarative English sentences, we begin our discussion by considering these sentences (called simple statements) and the ways in which they can be combined.

One method for arriving at logical conclusions is through the use of set diagrams as a way of communicating information that is given in an argument. Before defining precisely what we mean by a valid argument, we begin this chapter with some basic concepts involving sets and their operations.

Sets – Union, Intersection, Complement

In this section the basic idea of a set is presented and the operations of union, intersection and complement are defined. The idea of subset is explained. At the end of this topic you need to be able to find the union, intersection and complement of given sets. You should also be able to list all subsets for a given set.

◊ **Definition**

A **set** is a collection of objects. The objects in a set are called the **elements** or **members** of the set.

E X A M P L E

The set of whole numbers from 1 to 5 inclusive may be shown as {1,2,3,4,5} where the braces indicate that the collection is to be considered a set and each of the numbers listed inside the braces is to be considered an element or member of the set.

Sometimes a capital letter is used to denote a set. For example, A = {1,2,3,4,5}.

Notation

The symbol ∈ is used to indicate that an object is an element of a set, and the symbol ∉ is used to indicate that an object is not an element of a set.

E
X
A
M
P
L
E
S

1. It is correct to write: a ∈ {a,b,c,d} because the letter a is certainly an element of this set.

2. It is correct to write: e ∉ {a,b,c,d} since element e is not an element of this set.

3. It is not correct to write: {b} ∈ {a,b,c,d}. However, it is correct to write: b ∈ {a,b,c,d}.

4. It is correct to write {b} ∈ {{a}, {b}, {c}, {d}}.

◊ Definition

A set with no elements is called the **empty set** or the **null set** and represented by { } or Ø, but not {Ø}.

There are three important operations involving sets.

◊ Definitions

1. Union
   A ∪ B (**A union B**) is a set consisting of elements in A or in B or in both A and B.

2. Intersection
   A ∩ B (**A intersection B**) is a set consisting of elements in both A and B.

3. Complement
   A' (the **complement of A**) is the set of elements that are not in A, but that are in a given universal set U. The universal set contains all possible elements under consideration in a problem.

Problem 1

If A = {3,4,5}, B = {4,5,6,7} and C = {5,7,8,9}, find:

a.   A ∪ B
b.   A ∩ B
c.   (A ∩ C) ∪ B
d.   (A ∪ B) ∩ C

Solutions

a.   A ∪ B = {3,4,5,6,7}. This is the set of elements in A or B or both. Notice that 4 and 5 are not listed twice.

b.   A ∩ B = {4,5}. This is the set of elements in both A and B.

c.   (A ∩ C) ∪ B = {4,5,6,7}. First perform the operation in parentheses: A ∩ C = {5}.
     Then the problem is {5} ∪ {4,5,6,7}.

d.   (A ∪ B) ∩ C = {5,7}. Again, first do the operation inside the parentheses: A ∪ B = {3,4,5,6,7}. Then complete {3,4,5,6,7} ∩ {5,7,8,9}.

Problem 2

Let A = {a,b}, B = {c,d}, and C = {d,e,f}. Find:

a.   A ∪ B
b.   A ∩ B
c.   (A ∩ B) ∪ C
d.   (B ∩ C) ∪ A

Solutions

a.   A ∪ B = {a,b,c,d}
b.   A ∩ B = ∅. There are no elements in both A and B.
c.   (A ∩ B) ∪ C = ∅ ∪ {d,e,f} = {d,e,f}. Notice that the union of the empty set with any other set always gives that second set.
d.   (B ∩ C) ∪ A = {d} ∪ {a,b} = {a,b,d}

Sometimes it is tedious to list all the elements of large sets. Thus, another notation is used. We could describe the set of books in the library of Congress by using a letter, say x, to obtain:

{x | x is a book in the Library of Congress}

We read this as:

"The set of all elements x such that x is a book in the Library of Congress." The vertical line is read "such that." The remaining notation defines the conditions necessary for a candidate to be a member of the set. By substituting specific books for the letter x we are able to build a set. We refer to this as the **set-builder notation**.

As another example: {x | x is an even whole number greater than 3 and less than 200} implies the following set: {4,6,8,...,198}

It will be helpful to remember the word "or" is associated with the union operation, and the word "and" is associated with the intersection operation. Using set-builder notation it is possible to define the union of set A and set B as: $A \cup B = \{x \mid x \in A \text{ or } x \in B\}$. Using set-builder notation it is possible to define the intersection of set A and set B as: $A \cap B = \{x \mid x \in A \text{ and } x \in B\}$.

◊ **Definition**

Two sets that have no elements in common are called **disjoint sets**. Their intersection is the null set.

E
X
A
M
P
L
E

If set A = {1,2} and set B = {a,b}, then set A and set B are disjoint sets because there are no elements that are common to both sets.

$$A \cap B = \emptyset$$

Problem 3

Let A = {1,2,3}, B = {2,3,4}, and U = {1,2,3,4,5}.
Find:

a.   A'
b.   B'
c.   A' ∪ B'
d.   (A ∩ B)'
e.   A' ∩ B'
f.   (A ∪ B)'

Solutions

a.   A' = {4,5}. The complement of A is the set of all elements in U that are not in A.

b.   B' = {1,5}

c.   A' ∪ B' = {1,4,5}. The answer is the union of the two sets listed in parts a and b.

d.   (A ∩ B)' = {1,4,5}. First find A ∩ B.
A ∩ B = {1,2,3} ∩ {2,3,4} = {2,3}
Now find the complement of {2,3}.

e.   A' ∩ B' = {5}. First find the complement of A and the complement of B. Then find the intersection of those two sets.

f.   (A ∪ B)' = {5}. First find the union of A and B. Then find the complement of that union. -

It is no coincidence that problems c and d above had the same answer. For any two sets A and B it is always true that:

$$(A \cap B)' = A' \cup B'$$

It is also no coincidence that problems e and f above had the same answer. For any two sets A and B it is true that:

$$(A \cup B)' = A' \cap B'$$

We often encounter situations in which all the elements of one set are also elements of another set. This leads us to the following.

◊ **Definition**

Set A is said to be a **subset** of set B if every
element in set A is also in set B. Symbolically,
this is expressed as: $A \subseteq B$. $A \not\subseteq B$ means that
set A is not a subset of set B.

E
X
A
M
P
L
E
S

1. If set A = {1,2,3} and set B = {1,2,3,4,5,6}, we see that every
   element in set A is also an element of set B. Thus we can write:
   $A \subseteq B$. Notice that set B is not a subset of set A. We write: $B \not\subseteq A$.

2. If set X = {a,b,c} and set Y = {a,b,c}, we see that every element
   in set X is also an element in set Y. Thus, we write $X \subseteq Y$. In fact,
   X = Y. Notice that when X = Y, both $X \subseteq Y$ and $Y \subseteq X$ are true.
   This example illustrates that a set is a subset of itself.

An interesting property of the null set is the fact that <u>the null set is a subset of
every set</u>, expressed symbolically as $\emptyset \subseteq A$.

E
X
A
M
P
L
E

The list of all subsets of {a,b,c} must include the three-element set {a,b,c}
and the empty set, Ø. Other subsets will be all possible two-element and
one-element sets.

The set itself is a subset	Two element subsets	One element subsets	Empty set
{a,b,c}	{a,b}	{a}	Ø
	{a,c}	{b}	
	{b,c}	{c}	

Notice that there are 8 subsets that can be formed from the set {a,b,c}.

Sets and Logic

The **number of subsets** that can be formed from a given set is given by the expression 2^n in which n represents the number of elements in the given set.

Consequently, the number of subsets of {a,b,c} is given by $2^3 = 2 \cdot 2 \cdot 2 = 8$, verified by the previous example.

Problem Set 1

1. Let A = {5,7,9}, B = {3,7,9,10}, and C = {5,10,11}. Find:
   a. $A \cup B$ b. $A \cap B$
   c. $(A \cap C) \cup B$ d. $(A \cup B) \cap C$

2. Let A = {d,i,c,e}, B = {r,i,c,e}, and C = {e}. Find:
   a. $A \cup C$ b. $A \cap C$
   c. $(A \cup B) \cap C$ d. $(A \cap B) \cup C$

3. Let A = {2,4,6}, B = {1,2,3}, and C = {3,4,6}. Find:
   a. $A \cap B$ b. $B \cap C$
   c. $(A \cap C) \cap B$ d. $A \cap (B \cap C)$

4. Let A = {3,5,7}, B = {1,6,7} and U = {1,2,3,4,5,6,7,8,9,10}. Find:
   a. A' b. B'
   c. $A' \cup B'$ d. $(A \cap B)'$
   e. $A' \cap B'$ f. $(A \cup B)'$
   g. $A \cup B'$ h. $A' \cap B$

5. Let X = {a,b,c}, Y = {b}, and U = {a,b,c,d}. Find:
   a. X' b. Y'
   c. $X' \cup Y'$ d. $(X \cap Y)'$
   e. $X' \cap Y'$ f. $(X \cup Y)'$
   g. $X \cup U$ h. $X \cap U$
   i. $X \cup X'$ j. $X \cap X'$

6. List the elements in the following sets.
   a. {x | x is a whole number greater than 10}
   b. {x | x is a whole number between 4 and 20}

7. Find a subset of M = {1,2,3,4,5,6,7,8} that contains:
   a. all the odd numbers in M
   b. the numbers in M whose triples are in M
   c. the numbers in M that are divisible by 2

8. Label each of the following as true or false.
   a. {1,3} $\subseteq$ {2,4,9,3}
   b. {0,1,5} $\nsubseteq$ {1,5,7,9}
   c. {4,6} $\subseteq$ {x | x is a whole number}
   d. {1,2,3,4} $\subseteq$ {1,2,3}

9. Write all the subsets that can be formed from each of the following.
   a. {x,y}   b. {x,y,z}
   c. {0}   d. {x,y,∅}
   e. ∅

10. Use the results from problem #9 to complete the following.
    a.

Number of elements in a set	1	2	3	4
Number of subsets that can be formed				

   b. How many subsets can be formed from a set containing 4 elements? 5 elements?

11. Is the following true? $\emptyset \cap \emptyset = \emptyset$

12. $\{x \mid x$ is an even whole number$\} \cap \{x \mid x$ is an odd whole number$\} = $?

13. Consider the following sets:
    U = {all citizens}
    A = {all citizens of Florida}
    B = {all employed citizens of Florida}
    C = {all registered Democrats in Florida}
    Express each of the following sets in words.
    a. $A \cap B$ b. $B \cap C'$
    c. $(A \cap B) \cap C$

14. Let $A = \{1,2,3,4,5,6\}$, $B = \{2,4,5,6,7,8\}$, and $C = \{1,3,5,6,7,8\}$. Verify the following.
    a. $A \cup B = B \cup A$ (The Commutative Property for set union)
    b. $A \cap B = B \cap A$ (The Commutative Property for set intersection)
    c. $(A \cup B) \cup C = A \cup (B \cup C)$ (The Associative Property for set union)
    d. $(A \cap B) \cap C = A \cap (B \cap C)$ (The Associative Property for set intersection)
    e. $A \cup (B \cap C) = (A \cup B) \cap (A \cup C)$ (The Distributive Property for set union over set intersection)
    f. $A \cap (B \cup C) = (A \cap B) \cup (A \cap C)$ (The Distributive Property for set intersection over set union)

Topic 2

Venn Diagrams

Set diagrams provide a convenient way to show relationships among sets, as well as a useful tool in deducing logical conclusions from given information. In this section we consider the basic ideas of set diagrams. At the end of this section, given a diagram of sets, you should be able to identify correct statements of relationship among sets and set membership.

It is possible to obtain a more thorough understanding of sets and their operations by considering graphic illustrations that allow visual analyses. Venn diagrams, named for the nineteenth century British mathematician John Venn, are used to show the visual relationships among sets.

Sets and Logic

There are six basic ideas that are used to construct Venn diagrams:

1. In a Venn diagram the **universal set** U will always be represented by an area inside a rectangle. The figure at the right represents the universal set U.

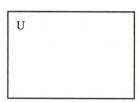

2. Any **subset** of U must be completely within the rectangle representing U. In the figure at the right, the set A is represented by the area inside the circle. Set A is a subset of U because the circle is inside the rectangle. Any subset of A must be a figure inside the circle of A.

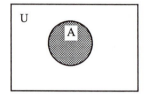

3. The **complement** of set A with respect to U is shown in the figure at the right. The area outside the circle, but within the rectangle, represents the set of elements in U that are not in set A. Thus, the shaded area represents the complement of A which is A'.

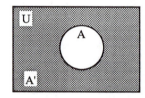

4. Two sets that have no elements in common are **disjoint sets**. Two disjoint sets A and B are shown in the figure at the right. Disjoint sets appear as circles which do not overlap.

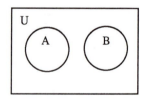

5. If two sets have some common elements, then the circles representing them must overlap. The figure at the right shows a shaded area where sets A and B overlap. This shaded area represents the **intersection** of sets A and B.

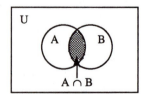

6. The **union** of sets A and B includes elements in A or in B or in both A and B. The shaded area of the figure at the right includes all of the two circles. This shaded area is the union of the two sets.

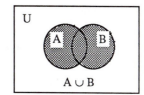

The following table illustrates three common relationships among sets.

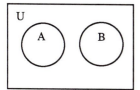

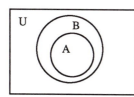

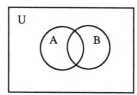

No elements of set A are elements of set B.

$(A \cap B = \emptyset)$

All elements of set A are elements of set B.

$(A \subseteq B)$

Some elements of set A are elements of set B. (At least one element of set A is an element of set B.)

We can use a shading technique to determine specified regions of a Venn diagram, as illustrated by the following problem.

Problem 1

Draw a Venn diagram and determine the region represented by $A' \cap B$ in which A and B are overlapping sets. Use the shading technique.

Solutions

Step I

Because A and B are overlapping sets they can be represented by circles like those shown at the right. Note: The circles will always overlap unless the directions state that A and B are disjoint sets or that there is a subset relationship between A and B.

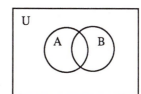

Step 2

The area representing A' is shaded. A' is the region of U that is outside circle A. This region is shaded using vertical lines.

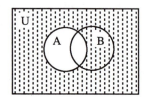

Step 3

The area representing B is shaded. This is the region inside circle B. Horizontal lines are used to shade set B.

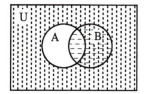

Step 4

The intersection of set A' and set B is the region where the two shaded areas overlap. This cross-hatched area is shaded heavily and is the region representing A' ∩ B. This region represents the set of elements that are **not** in A, but that **are** in B.

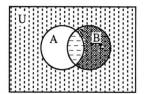

As illustrated in the previous problem, two sets A and B separate the universal set into four distinct regions. These four regions are shown in the figure below. The numbering is arbitrary.

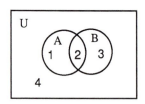

region 1   Elements of A, but not B: A ∩ B'

region 2   Elements of both A and B: A ∩ B

region 3   Elements of B, but not A: B ∩ A'

region 4   Elements of neither A nor B: A' ∩ B'

Three sets separate the universal set U into the **eight** regions shown in the figure below. The numbering is arbitrary.

region 1	Elements of A but not B or C
region 2	Elements of A and B but not C
region 3	Elements of B but not A or C
region 4	Elements of A and C but not B
region 5	Elements of A, B, and C
region 6	Elements of B and C but not A
region 7	Elements of C but not A or B
region 8	Elements of U that are not in A, B, or C

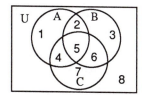

Problem 2

Use the Venn diagram shown above. Assume that no region is empty (there is at least one element in every region numbered 1 through 8). Determine if each of the following statements is true or false.

a. Any element of set A is also a member of set U.

Solution

This is true since set A is within the rectangular region U. If you place an x anywhere in circle A, the x also appears in U.

b. No element is a member of all three sets, A, B, and C.

Solution

This is false. In the Venn diagram, Region 5 represents the set of all elements in A, B and C (A ∩ B ∩ C).

c. Any element of set U is also a member of set C.

Solution

This is false. An x can be placed in Regions 1, 2, 3, or 8 which belong to U, but are not in C.

d. Any element belonging to set B is a sufficient guarantee that the element belongs to U.

Solution

This is true. Any element in B must also be in U. The use of the word "sufficient" in the statement is of special importance in mathematical situations.

Problem 3

Which statement listed below is true for the Venn diagram shown at the right? Assume that no region is empty.
a. No element is a member of both sets A and B.
b. There are fewer than four elements that are shared by both set B and set C.
c. Any element belonging to set U is also an element in set C.
d. $A \cap U = U$

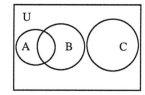

Solution

Let us consider each statement in the list above.

Statement **a** is false. If an x is placed in the region where circles A and B overlap, x is an element of both sets A and B. The x indicates that some elements belong to all three sets A, B and U.

Statement **b** is true. Since $B \cap C = \emptyset$, there are no elements that are shared by both set B and set C. Since they share zero elements, they certainly have fewer than four elements in common.

Statement **c** is false. An x may be placed anywhere in the rectangular region except inside circle C to show a counter-example for this statement. Although membership in set U is not a sufficient condition for membership in set C, observe that all elements belonging to set C are also members of set U.

Statement **d** is false. Set A intersected with set U is the set of elements in both A and U. Thus $A \cap U = A$ is true, but $A \cap U = U$ is false.

Problem Set 2

1. Sets A, B, C, and U are related as shown in the diagram. Which one of the following is true assuming that no region is empty?

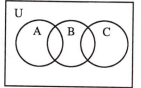

   a. Some elements are common to all four sets A, B, C, and U.
   b. Some elements belong to both sets B and C but not to set A.
   c. There are more than four elements that are shared by both set A and set C.
   d. All elements in set U are elements belonging to set C.

2. Sets A, B, C, D, and U are related as shown in the diagram. Which one of the following is true assuming that no region is empty?

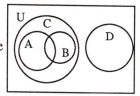

   a. All elements in A ∩ B are also elements in set C.
   b. All elements of set U are elements of set D.
   c. Some elements are common to all three sets A, B, and D.
   d. Some elements belong to set A but not to set C.

3. Sets A, B, C, D, and U are related as shown in the diagram. Which one of the following is true assuming that no region is empty?

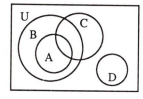

   a. Some elements are common to all three sets B, C, and D.

   b. Some elements of set A are not elements of set B.
   c. All elements of A ∩ C are elements of set B.
   d. All elements of set U are elements of set D.

4. The diagram at the right shows sets A, B, C, and U. Each bounded region in the diagram is also given a lower case letter. None of these regions is empty. Which one statement listed below is true?

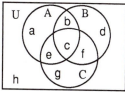

   a. Regions f and d make up all of set B.
   b. B ∪ C is represented by regions c and f.
   c. Region g represents the set of elements belonging to set C that do not belong to set A or set B.
   d. Region b represents the set of elements belonging to all three sets A, B, and C.

5. Sets A, B, C, and U are related as shown in the diagram. Which one of the following is true assuming that no region is empty?

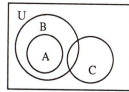

   a. All elements of set B are elements of set A.
   b. Some elements are common to all three sets A, B, and C.
   c. A ∩ B = B
   d. Some elements are common to all three sets B, C, and U.

Sets and Logic

6. Sets A, B, C, and U are related as shown in the set diagram. Which one of the following is true assuming none of the regions is empty?

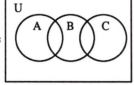

   a. All elements of set B are elements of set C.
   b. Some elements belong to all three sets A, B, and U.
   c. All elements of set U are elements of set B.
   d. A ∩ C is not the empty set.

7. Sets A, B, C, and U are related as shown in the set diagram. Which one of the following is true assuming none of the regions is empty?

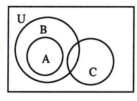

   a. All elements of set A are elements of set B.
   b. Some elements are common to all four sets A, B, C, and U.
   c. At least one element of set U is a member of both sets A and C.
   d. There are more than two elements that belong to B ∩ C.

8. Sets A, B, C, and U are related as shown in the set diagram. Which one of the following is true assuming none of the regions is empty?

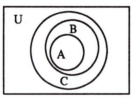

   a. No element is a member of all four sets A, B, C, and U.
   b. Any element that is a member of set B is also a member of set A.
   c. Some elements belong to set B but not to set C.
   d. A ∩ B = A

9. The diagram at the right shows sets A, B, C, and U. It also shows the number of elements that belong to each region in the set diagram. (For example, set B contains 2 + 1 + 4 + 5 = 12 elements.) Which one statement listed below is true?

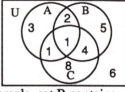

   a. Set A contains 3 elements.
   b. There are 2 elements belonging to A ∩ B.
   c. Set U contains 6 elements.
   d. There are 4 elements in common to sets B and C that do not belong to set A.

10. Use the set diagram at the right to select a statement equivalent to:
   All elements of set A are elements of set B.

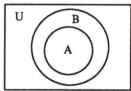

   Again, assume that no region is empty.
   a. All elements of set B are elements of set A.
   b. There are no elements of set A that are not elements of set B.
   c. There are no elements of set B that are not elements of set A.
   d. There are some elements of set A that are not elements of set B.

11. Use the previous problem to write a statement that is equivalent to:
   All quadrilaterals are polygons.

12. Use the set diagram at the right to select a statement equivalent to: *No elements of set A are elements of set B.* Assume that no region is empty.

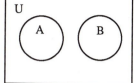

a. All elements of A are not elements belonging to B.

b. Some elements are shared by both sets A and B.

c. $A \cup B = \emptyset$

d. $A \cap B = U$

13. Use the previous problem to write a statement that is equivalent to: *No triangles are squares.*

Topic 3

Valid Arguments Using Set Diagrams

In this section the idea of a valid argument is introduced. At the end of this topic you should know what is meant by a valid argument. You should be able to use set diagrams to show that an argument is valid or invalid. You should also be able to use set diagrams to draw a logical conclusion that will result in a valid argument.

◊ Definitions

Forms of reasoning are known as **arguments**. Arguments contain statements assumed to be true which are called **premises**. Arguments also contain statements called **conclusions** which are derived from the premises. An argument is said to be **valid** if the conclusion follows logically from the premises. An argument that is not valid is called an **invalid argument**, a **fallacy**, or a **fallacious argument**.

Sets and Logic

Many arguments that we shall consider consist of two given premises and a conclusion. These statements can be arranged as shown below.

given premises	Statement 1 (is true)
	<u>Statement 2 (is true)</u>
conclusion	Statement 3

E X A M P L E

Consider the following argument:

All birds have feathers and all parrots are birds. Therefore, all parrots have feathers.

This argument can be arranged formally as:

premise	All birds have feathers.
premise	<u>All parrots are birds.</u>
conclusion	∴All parrots have feathers.

(The symbol ∴ is read "thus" or "therefore." This symbol is written preceding the conclusion of an argument.) This argument contains two premises which imply its conclusion. The argument is **valid** because the conclusion follows directly from the premises. If the two premises are assumed true, then this particular conclusion must be true also.

E X A M P L E

Consider the following argument:

Some Americans are Democrats. Henry is an American. Therefore, Henry is a Democrat.

This argument can be arranged formally as:

premise	Some Americans are Democrats.
premise	<u>Henry is an American.</u>
conclusion	∴Henry is a Democrat.

Assuming that both premises are true, observe that the conclusion might be true, but might be false. The argument is invalid because the conclusion does not follow directly from the premises. If the two premises are assumed true, then this particular conclusion is not necessarily true.

These examples illustrate that it is sometimes obvious whether an argument is valid or invalid by simply reading the premises and the conclusion. However, as we add more premises to an argument, we might not be able to use our intuitive sense of validity to determine whether or not a conclusion can be deduced from numerous premises.

It is possible to determine the validity of arguments whose premises involve words such as "all," "some," and "no," by using four basic set diagrams known as Euler circles. These are attributed to the Swiss mathematician Leonard Euler who used diagrams to study the validity of arguments. In these diagrams, circles are used to indicate relationships of premises to conclusions just as circles are used in Venn Diagrams to visualize set relationships.

All A are B.	Some A are B.	No A are B.	x belongs to A.
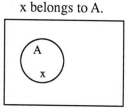	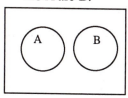		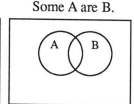

Use the following procedure to determine the validity or fallaciousness of an argument.

1. Make a set diagram of the first premise.
2. Make a set diagram of the second premise on top of the set diagram for the first premise.
3. Continue making set diagrams as in steps 1 and 2 until all the premises are diagrammed.
4. The argument is valid only if the final diagram uniquely illustrates the conclusion of the argument. If there is even *one* possible set diagram that contradicts the conclusion, then the argument is **invalid** (fallacious).

Problem 1

Is the following argument valid?

given premises: All birds have feathers.
                      All parrots have feathers.
conclusion: All parrots are birds.

Solution

First make a set diagram of the first premise. The diagram at the right is the only possible way of diagramming "All birds have feathers" (allowing for other equivalent ways of positioning the "bird" circle inside the "feather" circle).

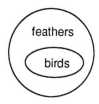

Second, make a set diagram of the second premise (all parrots have feathers) and impose it over the diagram for the first premise. In this case, there are three different ways to place the "parrot" circle.

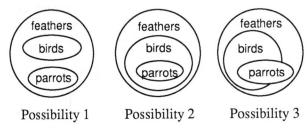

Possibility 1   Possibility 2   Possibility 3

Only Possibility 2 justifies the conclusion "All parrots are birds" and, consequently, the argument is **not valid (fallacious).** The conclusion does not necessarily follow from the premises.

In the previous sample problem, the conclusion "All parrots are birds" is obviously true. However, this is irrelevant when determining whether the argument is valid. In essence, what counts is whether or not the conclusion follows logically from the premises and not whether the conclusion is true as a statement by itself.

Problem 2

Is the following argument valid?

All birds have feathers and all parrots are birds. Therefore, all parrots have feathers.

Solution

First, notice that two premises are contained in the first sentence of the argument. The conclusion is the second sentence of the argument.

Draw a set diagram of the first premise
"All birds have feathers."
This drawing is shown at the right.

Now draw a set diagram of the second premise "All parrots are birds." That drawing is shown at the right. Notice that there is only one way to place the "parrot" circle and that is inside the "bird" circle.

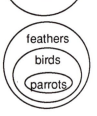

The conclusion "All parrots have feathers" can immediately be seen from the set diagram. Since this is the only possible set diagram and it justifies the conclusion, the argument is **valid**.

From the two sample problems, notice that both invalid and valid arguments can both have conclusions that are true. Validity, however, depends upon the relationship of the premises and the conclusion.

Problem 3

Use Euler circles to determine the validity of the following argument.
All insects have six legs and horses have four legs.
Accordingly, horses are not insects.

This argument may be stated in the following form:
premise   All insects have six legs.
premise   <u>Horses have four legs.</u>
conclusion   Horses are not insects.

Solution

Step 1
Since *all insects have six legs*, the circle representing insects is placed completely inside the circle representing six-legged creatures, as shown at the right.

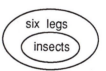

Step 2
The second premise (*Horses have four legs*) implies that no horses have six legs. This means that the circle representing horses must be drawn outside the circle representing six-legged creatures, as shown at the right.

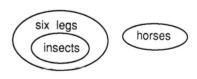

We have only one possible diagram, showing the "horses" as a circle drawn separately from the "insect" circle. This one possible diagram shows that *horses are not insects*. (Equivalently, no horses are insects.) This Euler circle demonstration makes the argument **valid**.

Problem 4

Use Euler circles to determine the validity of the following argument.
No parrots have four legs. This can be concluded because dogs have four legs and parrots are not dogs.

The argument may be stated in the following form:

premise	All dogs have four legs.
premise	<u>Parrots are not dogs.</u>
conclusion	No parrots have four legs.

Solution

Step 1

The first premise (*All dogs have four legs*) is diagrammed at the right.

Step 2

We now construct Euler circles for the second premise (*Parrots are not dogs*). Since no parrots are dogs, the "parrot" circle must be drawn outside the "dog" circle. There are at least three possible ways to do this, as shown in the accompanying diagram.

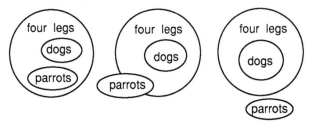

Only the last set diagram justifies the conclusion "*No parrots have four legs.*" Since the conclusion does not necessarily follow from the premises, as seen in the first two set diagrams, the argument is **invalid** (a fallacy).

Problem 5

Use Euler circles to determine the validity of the following argument.
Jill is either a poet or a journalist. I know this because all poets are writers, all journalists are writers, all writers appreciate language, and Jill is a writer.

This argument may be stated in the following form:

premise	All poets are writers.
premise	All journalists are writers.
premise	All writers appreciate language.
premise	<u>Jill is a writer.</u>
conclusion	Jill is either a poet or a journalist.

Solution

Step 1

Since the word "all" appears in the first premise (*All poets are writers*), the circle representing poets is placed completely inside the circle representing writers. The diagram at the right shows this relationship.

Step 2

The second premise (*All journalists are writers*) contains the word "all" and another circle representing journalists must be placed completely inside the circle representing writers. As shown in the accompanying diagrams, numerous possibilities exist.

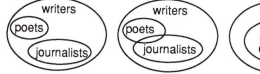

Step 3

The third premise (*All writers appreciate language*) again contains the word "all" and the circle representing writers must be placed within another circle representing the set of people who appreciate language. Each of the four possible diagrams in step 2 must show the "writers" circle inside the "appreciate language" circle. This is shown in the accompanying diagrams.

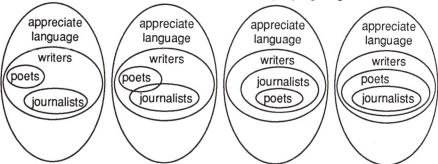

Step 4

The last premise (*Jill is a writer*) means that Jill will be shown as a point in the writer circle. We will take the four possible diagrams shown so far and in each diagram we will place Jill in as many different positions as possible within the writer circle.

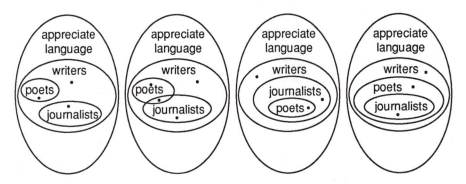

If just one possible diagram does not illustrate the conclusion (*Jill is either a poet or a journalist*), this means that the conclusion might be false relative to the premises, and therefore the argument is invalid. If you focus on the one possible diagram shown at the right, we see that in this case Jill is a writer but is neither a poet nor a journalist. This diagram contradicts the conclusion and the argument is **invalid**.

On the other hand, if you study the many diagrams shown in step 4, observe that in every case both the circles representing poets and journalists fall within the "appreciate language" circle. Furthermore, Jill always is contained within this outermost circle. Consequently, we can logically (validly) conclude that:

> All poets appreciate language.
> All journalists appreciate language.
> Jill appreciates language.

Problem 6

Use Euler circles to determine the validity of the following argument.

> *Some teachers are clowns. I know this because all teachers are funny people, and some clowns are funny people.*

This argument may be stated in the following form:

premise	All teachers are funny people.
premise	<u>Some clowns are funny people.</u>
conclusion	Some teachers are clowns.

Solution

Step 1

Diagram the first premise *All teachers are funny people* by a circle representing the set of teachers completely contained in a circle representing the set of funny people. The diagram would appear as shown at the right.

Notice that the premise *All teachers are funny people* is equivalent to: *There are no teachers who are not funny people.* It is also equivalent to: *Teachers are funny people.*

Step 2

The word "some" in the premise *Some clowns are funny people* claims that there is **at least one** clown who is a funny person. Furthermore, the premise *Some clowns are funny people* states no relationship between clowns and teachers. Two possibilities exist for diagramming the information of this premise.

i. Diagram statements involving the word "some" by using **intersecting** circles. The premise *Some clowns are funny people* diagrams as two intersecting circles for clowns and funny people. In the possibility shown at the right, the clown and teacher circles do not intersect, which translates as *No clowns are teachers*.

ii. Again, the clown and funny people circles intersect because *Some clowns are funny people.* However, in the possibility shown at the right, the clown and teacher circles also intersect, which translates as *At least one clown is a teacher.*

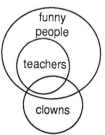

It is important to note that whenever the word "some" occurs in the second premise of an argument, more than one diagram must be drawn that will support the premise.

Step 3
Finally, consider the conclusion: *Therefore, some teachers are clowns.*
Notice that one of the two possibilities for drawing the diagrams does not
agree with this conclusion, namely case (i). Since it is not correct to select
only the diagram that does agree, this argument is **fallacious**.

A common misimpression with Euler diagrams is that if there is more than one
possible way to diagram the premises, an argument is invalid. Our next problem
shows that this is not the case.

Problem 7

Use Euler circles to determine the validity of the following argument.
> *All dogs have fleas and some dogs have rabies. Consequently,
> all dogs with rabies have fleas.*

Solution

Step 1
Diagram the first premise
(*All dogs have fleas*) as shown
at the right.

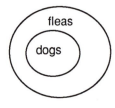

Step 2
Diagram the second premise (*Some dogs have rabies*) by showing the set
of dogs intersecting the set of creatures that have rabies. Two possibilities
exist, as shown in the accompanying Euler diagrams.

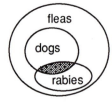 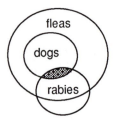

In both Euler diagrams, the shaded region represents dogs with rabies. In
both diagrams this region falls inside the circle representing animals with
fleas. Both diagrams illustrate that *all dogs with rabies have fleas* and the
argument is **valid**.

Problem 8

Is the following argument valid?

Some houses have two stories.
<u>Some houses have air-conditioning.</u>
Some houses with air-conditioning have two stories.

Solution

The diagram for the first premise (Some houses have two stories) must have two circles which intersect like the ones shown at the right.

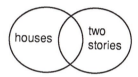

Two possibilities for the second premise (Some houses have air-conditioning) are shown below.

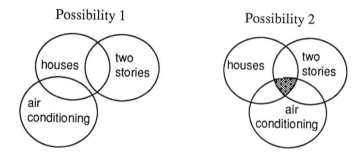

In Possibility 1 there are no points common to all three circles. In Possibility 2 the shaded region represents the two-storied houses with air-conditioning.

Since all possibilities (Possibility 1) do not illustrate the conclusion, the argument is **invalid**. Notice that Possibility 1 illustrates that no houses with air-conditioning have two stories.

In our next two problems we will use Euler circles to draw logical (valid) conclusions.

Problem 9

All spies have trenchcoats. Every Londoner has a trenchcoat. Sean is a spy. What can we logically conclude?

a. Some Londoners are spies.
b. Sean is a Londoner.
c. Sean has a trenchcoat.
d. None of the above is warranted.

Solution

We construct set diagrams to illustrate the premises. "All spies have trenchcoats" is illustrated at the right.

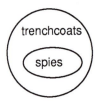

"Every Londoner has a trenchcoat" can be shown in at least three ways.

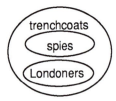 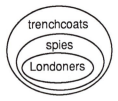 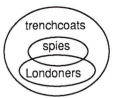

If we let x represent Sean, the statement "Sean is a spy" indicates that x must be shown inside the circle representing the set of spies. Numerous possibilities exist.

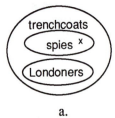 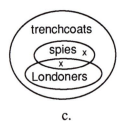

a.   b.   c.

Since the conclusion must be illustrated in all possible set diagrams to be valid, we see that x always falls within the circle of people who wear trenchcoats. The valid conclusion is: Sean has a trenchcoat, choice c.

Problem 10

No polite people talk at live theater. No theater-lovers talk at live theater. Jerry loves theater. Therefore,

a. Jerry is polite and does not talk at live theater.
b. Jerry is polite and talks at live theater.
c. Jerry does not talk at live theater.
d. None of the above is warranted.

Solution

"No polite people talk at live theater" is shown below.

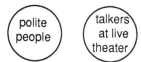

"No theater-lovers talk at live theater" can be shown in a number of ways.

If we let x represent Jerry, "Jerry loves theater" indicates that x must be placed within the circle of theater-lovers. Once again, numerous possibilities exist.

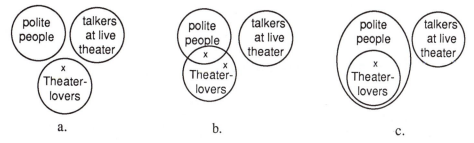

a.   b.   c.

We now see that in all possible diagrams x falls outside the circle of talkers at live theater. A valid conclusion is: Jerry does not talk at live theater, choice c.

Problem Set 3

Use Euler circles to determine if each of the following arguments is valid or invalid.

1. Stan is a dancer. I know this because all dancers are athletes, and all athletes are in good shape. Stan is in good shape.

2. All dogs have hair and all dalmatians are dogs. Therefore, all dalmatians have hair.

3. Buzzards have wings. I know this because birds have wings and buzzards are birds.

4. All Londoners wear trenchcoats and all spies wear trenchcoats. Therefore, all Londoners are spies.

5. All birds have feathers and dogs do not have feathers. Thus, no dogs are birds.

6. All birds have feathers and no dogs are birds. Thus, no dogs have feathers.

7. No good students talk during lecture. Zane, based upon his 4.0 grade point average, is certainly a good student. We can conclude that Zane does not talk during lecture.

8. All moccasins hurt when they strike. I know this because all moccasins are poisonous snakes and all poisonous snakes hurt when they strike.

9. Citrus is rich in vitamin C and grapefruit is rich in Vitamin C. Thus, grapefruit is citrus.

10. All horses have legs and snakes are not horses. Thus, no snakes have legs.

11. All multiples of 6 are multiples of 3. Seventeen is not a multiple of 3. Consequently, 17 is not a multiple of 6.

12. All clocks keep time accurately. All time-measuring devices keep time accurately. Therefore, all clocks are time-measuring devices.

13. Plants that are native to the Florida Keys can withstand prolonged droughts. The gumbo limbo is native to the Florida Keys. Therefore, the gumbo limbo can withstand prolonged droughts.

14. All logic problems make sense and some jokes make sense. Therefore, some logic problems are jokes.

15. Some immoral acts are justifiable. I know this because all thefts are immoral acts and some thefts are justifiable.

16. Flight attendants are pleasant. Some people with beards are pleasant. Therefore, some people with beards are flight attendants.

17. Some people enjoy reading and some people enjoy television. Therefore, some people who enjoy reading enjoy television.

18. All mathematicians are human beings and all physics teachers are human beings. Therefore, some physics teachers are mathematicians.

19. All philosophers are wise and some Greeks are philosophers. Therefore, some Greeks are wise.

20. No philosophers are wicked. Some Greeks are philosophers. Therefore, some Greeks are not wicked.

21. Some philosophers are wicked. Some Greeks are philosophers. Therefore, some Greek philosophers are wicked.

22. All parrots have feathers and some parrots talk. Therefore, all parrots that talk have feathers.

For each of the following examples, use Euler circles to select a logical conclusion that will result in a valid argument.

23. *All physicists are scientists. All biologists are scientists. All scientists are college graduates. Florence is a scientist. Therefore,*
    a. Florence is a physicist or a biologist.
    b. All biologists are college graduates.
    c. Florence is not a college graduate.
    d. None of the above is warranted.

24. *All logicians are strange and all strange people are unexciting. Phil is exciting. Therefore,*
    a. Phil is strange but is not a logician.
    b. Phil is a strange logician.
    c. Phil is neither strange nor a logician.
    d. None of the above is warranted.

25. *No creatures that eat meat are vegetarians. No cat is a vegetarian. Avram is a cat. Therefore,*
    a. Avram eats meat.
    b. All creatures that do not eat meat are vegetarians.
    c. Avram is not a vegetarian.
    d. None of the above is warranted.

26. *All poets appreciate language and all writers appreciate language. Therefore,*
    a. All poets are writers.
    b. Some poets are writers.
    c. No poets are writers.
    d. None of the above is warranted.

27. *All politicians make promises, but some politicians are liars. Therefore,*
    a. Some people who make promises are politicians.
    b. All liars make promises.
    c. All people who make promises are liars or politicians.
    d. None of the above is warranted.

28. *All timid creatures are bunnies, some timid creatures are dumb, and some students are timid creatures.* Select the conclusion(s) that makes the argument valid.
    a. Some bunnies are dumb.
    b. Some students are bunnies.
    c. Some students are dumb-bunnies.
    d. None of the above is warranted.

29. All of the following arguments have true conclusions, but one of the arguments is not valid. Select the argument that is **not** valid.
    a. All biologists are scientists. All scientists attended college. Thus, people who did not attend college are not biologists.
    b. Poets appreciate language and writers appreciate language. Therefore, poets are writers.
    c. No democracies are an outgrowth of a military coup. In October, 1991, Haiti's president was overthrown by a military coup. Therefore, the government that took over Haiti in October, 1991, was not a democracy.
    d. All babies are illogical. No illogical being can manage a crocodile. Therefore, babies cannot manage a crocodile.

The Connectives of Symbolic Logic

This section describes simple and compound statements. The symbols for connecting simple statements are introduced. At the end of this section you should be able to use these connectives to translate statements and arguments that are given in English into symbolic notation. You should also be able to change the wording of a conditional statement to the familiar "if . . . then" form.

◊ Definition

A **simple statement** in logic is one which is either true or false. A simple statement contains no parts that are also simple statements.

E
X
A
M
P
L
E
S

1. The following is a simple statement: *Today is Sunday.*
   It certainly would be possible to determine whether this statement is true or false on any given day.

2. The following is a simple statement:
   There are ten billion grains of sand on the beaches of Daytona Beach, Florida.
   This statement is true or false, although it would not be easy to determine!

3. The following is not a simple statement: *Is logic illogical?*
   This is a question, and questions are not simple statements.

4. The following is not a simple statement: *Take a long walk on a short pier!*
   This exclamatory statement is in the form of a command and is not a declarative sentence.

5. The following is not a simple statement: *Logic is fascinating.*
    This declarative sentence is a matter of opinion and cannot clearly be
    labeled as true or false.

6. The following is not a simple statement:
    Carter was the second American President and
    Orlando is a city in Florida.
    This statement has two parts which are both simple statements.

Now we will see that it is possible to combine simple statements.

◊ **Definitions**

A **compound statement** is one that is formed
by combining two or more simple statements. A
compound statement consisting of two simple
statements joined by the connective "and" is called
a **conjunction**. A compound statement consisting
of two simple statements joined by the connective
"or" is called a **disjunction.** A compound
statement consisting of two simple statements
joined by the connective "if . . . then" is called an
implication or a **conditional statement**.

E
X
A
M
P
L
E
S

1. The following is a compound statement:
    Today is Sunday and this is the month of May.
    This statement is a conjunction.

2. The following is a compound statement:
    Today is Sunday or this is the month of May.
    This statement is a disjunction.

3. The following is a compound statement (conjunction):
    Thelma and Mary are both passing the course.
    What is implied is that "Thelma is passing the course and Mary
    is passing the course."

Sets and Logic

The connectives "and" and "or" are two connectives that we frequently use in English. From the standpoint of English, there are certain equivalent connectives that imply the idea of "and":

a. Today is Sunday, **but** this is the month of May.
b. Today is Sunday, **even though** this is the month of May.
c. Today is Sunday, **yet** this is the month of May.
d. Today is Sunday, **although** this is the month of May.

Of these equivalent connectives the word "but" will be of particular interest to us.

Notations

Simple statements and connectives may be expressed using symbols. The letters p and q are often used to represent simple statements. The symbol $\wedge$ is used to mean "and" and $\vee$ is used to mean "or."

E
X
A
M
P
L
E
S

The letter p can be used to represent the simple statement
  Today is Monday.

The letter q can be used to represent the simple statement
  I am falling asleep.

The compound statement,
  Today is Monday and I am falling asleep.
is represented symbolically as $p \wedge q$.

Let p represent: *Today is Monday.*
Let q represent: *I am falling asleep.*
The compound statement,
  Today is Monday or I am falling asleep.
is written symbolically as $p \vee q$.

E
X
A
M
P
L
E
S

Let p be: *Today is Monday.*
Let q be: *I am falling asleep.*
Translate each of the following into an English statement.

1. ~p: *Today is not Monday.* This may equivalently be translated as:
    a. *It is **not true** that today is Monday.*
    b. *It is **not the case** that today is Monday.*
    c. *It is **false** that today is Monday.*

2. ~(~p): *It is false that today is not Monday.*
    This may be equivalently translated as: *Today is Monday.*

3. ~p ∧ q: *Today is not Monday and I am falling asleep.*

4. p ∨ ~q: *Today is Monday or I am not falling asleep.*

5. ~(p ∧ q): *It is not true that both today is Monday and I am falling asleep.*
    Notice that the compound statement is enclosed in parentheses and preceded
    by the negation symbol. The translation "*it is not true that **both**...* " is used
    to convey the idea of negating the entire expression (p ∧ q). The translation
    is a bit more precise than:
    It is not true that today is Monday and I am falling asleep.
    which could be the translation for either ~(p∧ q) or ~p ∧ q. Observe that
    ~(p∧ q) and ~p ∧ q convey quite different meanings.

6. Let p be: *Today is not Monday.*
    The statement ~p is: *Today is Monday.*

Sets and Logic

There are statements in logic that depend upon some given condition. Consider the following statement:

If the team wins the game, then I will be very happy.

Observe that the condition is the team's winning the game, which implies that I will be very happy. If that condition is met, then I will be very happy. Observe also that this statement involves the use of the connective words "if" and "then."

This conditional statement can also be stated as follows:

1. *If the team wins the game, I will be very happy.*
2. *I will be very happy if the team wins the game.*
3. *When the team wins the game, I will be very happy.*
4. *I will be very happy when the team wins the game.*
5. *The team winning the game implies my being very happy.*
6. *The team wins the game only if I am very happy.*
7. *Only if I am very happy does the team win the game.*
8. *The team winning the game is a sufficient condition for my being very happy.*
9. *My being very happy is a necessary condition for the team winning the game.*
10. *The team does not win the game unless I am very happy.*

These statements can be expressed symbolically:

Let statement p be: *The team wins the game.*

Let statement q be: *I will be very happy.*

The statement could be written as: If p, then q   or   p implies q   or $p \rightarrow q$

> **Notation**
>
> The symbol $\rightarrow$ is translated as "if... then."

◊ **Definitions**

Statements of the form $p \rightarrow q$ are called **conditional statements** or **implications**. In such a statement, p is called the **hypothesis** or **antecedent**, and q is called the **conclusion** or **consequent**.

Remember that the hypothesis always follows "if" or "when."

E X A M P L E S

1. Consider the following statement:

    If you bring the teacher an apple, then you will make an A.
    The hypothesis (p) is the statement: *You bring the teacher an apple.*
    The conclusion (q) is the statement: *You will make an A.*

2. Consider the following simple statements:

    p: *You speak loudly.*   q: *I can hear you.*

    Express the following symbolic statements as sentences.

    a. ~p → ~q is: *If you do not speak loudly, then I cannot hear you.*
    b. q → p is: *If I can hear you, then you speak loudly.*
    c. ~q → ~p is: *If I cannot hear you, then you do not speak loudly.*

Conditional statements can appear in many forms. To express them in the familiar
"if ... then" form it is often necessary to change the wording.

E X A M P L E S

1. Consider the statement: *It pours when it rains.*
    This statement can be expressed as: *If it rains, then it pours.*

2. Consider the statement:

    Michelle experiences anxiety when she does not tell the truth.
    This statement can be expressed as:
    If Michelle does not tell the truth, then she experiences anxiety.

3. Consider the statement: *No dogs have wings.*
    This statement can be expressed as:
    If it is a dog, then it does not have wings.

4. Consider the statement: *Jane always eats dinner at a cafeteria.*
    This statement can be expressed as:
    If Jane eats dinner, then she eats at a cafeteria.

Sets and Logic

The ability to change the wording of a conditional statement to the familiar "if…then" form frequently depends upon understanding the English syntax, the way in which the words are put together to form phrases, clauses, and sentences. However, you may find the following table helpful.

> ### Equivalent Ways Of Translating $p \rightarrow q$ Into English
>
> a. If p, then q.
> b. If p, q.
> c. p implies q.
> d. p only if q.
> e. Only if q, p.
> f. p is a sufficient condition for q.
> g. q is a necessary condition for p.
> h. Not p unless q.

E
X
A
M
P
L
E

Consider the statement: *If you live in New York, then you live in America.* In terms of sets, the set of New Yorkers is a subset of the set of Americans. Notice that living in New York is a **sufficient condition** (a guarantee) for living in America. This can be seen in the Venn Diagram shown below. However, living in America is certainly not a guarantee (not a sufficient condition) for living in New York.

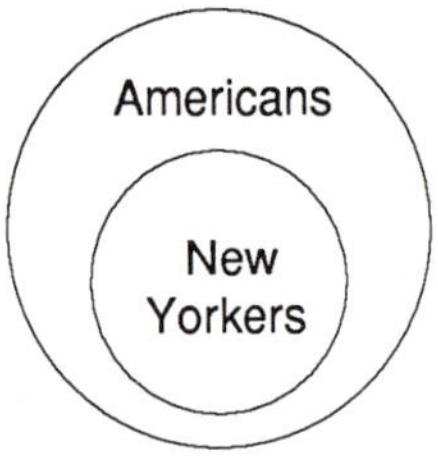

Living in America is not a sufficient condition for living in New York, but it is a **necessary condition** because you do not live in New York unless you live in America. An x cannot be placed in the New Yorker circle unless it is also placed in the American circle. Living in America is a necessary prerequisite for living in New York. Obviously, if you don't live in America, then you can't possibly live in New York. You live in New York only if you live in America.

Let us use the previous table, with:
>   p: *You live in New York.*
>   q: *You live in America.*

We translate p → q into English as follows:
- a.   *If you live in New York, then you live in America.*
- b.   *If you live in New York, you live in America.*
- c.   *Living in New York implies living in America.*
- d.   *You live in New York only if you live in America.*
- e.   *Only if you live in America do you live in New York.*
- f.   *Living in New York is a sufficient condition for living in America.*
- g.   *Living in America is a necessary condition for living in New York.*
- h.   *You do not live in New York unless you live in America.*

Problem 1

Let p be: It snows.
Let q be: We stay home.
Let r be: We study.
Write the following argument in symbolic form.
If it snows, we stay home or study. It's snowing and we're not staying home. Thus, we're studying.

Solution

Translate the first statement symbolically.
If it snows then we stay home or we study.

>   p   →   (q   ∨   r)

Write the symbolic form for the second statement.

>   It's snowing   and   we're not staying home.

>   p   ∧   ~q

Finally, translate the conclusion.
>   We're studying.

>   r

The argument appears in symbolic form as $p \rightarrow (q \vee r)$
$$\underline{p \wedge \sim q}$$
$$\therefore r$$

Problem Set 4

1. Translate each of the following into English using:

     p to represent : *Mary has it.*
     q to represent: *Alice has had it.*

   a. p ∨ ~q   b. ~p ∨ q
   c. ~p ∧ ~q   d. ~(p ∨ q)
   e. ~(p ∧ ~q)   f. ~(~q)

2. Represent each of the following statements symbolically using:

     p to represent: *I study hard.*
     q to represent: *I pass the test.*

   a. *I do not study hard or I pass the test.*
   b. *It is not true that both I study hard and I do not pass the test.*
   c. *I do not study hard and I do not pass the test.*
   d. *Neither do I study hard nor do I pass the test. (careful!)*

3. Identify the hypothesis (antecedent) and conclusion (consequent) in each of the following conditional statements.

   a. If I work hard, I will pass the course.
   b. If a polygon is a quadrilateral, then the polygon has four sides.
   c. It is not raining if the sky is not overcast.

4. Consider the following simple statements:
   p: *You have long hair.*
   q: *You will get dandruff.*
   Express the following symbolic statements as sentences.

   a. p → q   b. q → p
   c. ~p → ~q   d. ~q → ~p

5. Express the following using the "if ... then" form.

   a. George always buys a Sony television.
   b. No soldier is afraid.
   c. The class is over when the bell rings.
   d. All students will pass this test.
   e. A Corvette won't enter this race.
   f. Criminals will be punished.
   g. None of your teachers is dull.
   h. Every tall person should play basketball.
   i. No one remains standing when the National Anthem is not being played.
   j. All members are required to attend the meeting unless excused.

6. Select the statement that is equivalent to:
   My throat is tense when I am not telling the truth.

   a. If my throat is tense, then I am not telling the truth.
   b. If I am telling the truth, then my throat is not tense.
   c. If I am not telling the truth, then my throat is tense.
   d. I am not telling the truth and my throat is not tense.

7. Express each of the following statements in "if ... then" form.

   a. You avoid a ticket only if you observe the speed limit.
   b. Watering the flowers is a necessary condition for making them grow.
   c. Attending class regularly is a sufficient condition for passing the course.
   d. I can live in the North only if I can endure the winters.

e. Turning on the ignition is a necessary condition for starting the car.

f. Missing the bus is a sufficient condition for being late to class.

8.   Let p be: There is a flood.
        Let q be: There is a windstorm.
        Let r be: The company reimburses you.
Write the following argument in symbolic form. If there is a flood or windstorm, the company reimburses you. The company reimbursed you and there was no windstorm. Thus, there was a flood.

9.   Let p be: Mary stars.
        Let q be: Ethel stars.
        Let r be: The musical is a success.
Write the following argument in symbolic form. If both Mary and Ethel star, then the musical is a success. The musical was not a success. Thus, Mary did not star or Ethel did not star.

10. Select the symbolic form of reasoning pattern for the following argument. If the air conditioner and the microphone fail, the class is cancelled. The class was not cancelled on Wednesday and the microphone failed. Therefore, the air conditioner did not fail on Wednesday.

a. $(r \wedge p) \to q$
    $\dfrac{\neg q \wedge p}{\therefore r}$

b. $(r \wedge p) \to q$
    $\dfrac{\neg q \wedge p}{\therefore \neg r}$

c. $(r \vee p) \to q$
    $\dfrac{\neg q \vee p}{\therefore r}$

d. $(r \vee p) \to q$
    $\dfrac{\neg q \vee p}{\therefore \neg r}$

11. Select the symbolic form of reasoning pattern for the following argument. You will gain weight if you eat cookies or junk food. (Equivalently, if you eat cookies or junk food, then you will gain weight.) You ate cookies but you didn't eat junk food. (Equivalently, you ate cookies and you didn't eat junk food.) Consequently, you gained weight.

a. $(q \wedge p) \to r$
    $\dfrac{q \vee \neg p}{\therefore r}$

b. $r \to (q \wedge p)$
    $\dfrac{q \vee \neg p}{\therefore r}$

c. $(q \vee p) \to r$
    $\dfrac{q \wedge \neg p}{\therefore r}$

d. $r \to (q \vee p)$
    $\dfrac{q \wedge \neg p}{\therefore r}$

12. Select the symbolic form of reasoning pattern for the following argument. Maggie has a good time when she attends the opera. Maggie is not having a good time. Accordingly, Maggie is not attending the opera.

a. $p \to q$
    $\dfrac{\neg p}{\therefore \neg q}$

b. $p \to q$
    $\dfrac{q}{\therefore p}$

c. $p \to q$
    $\dfrac{\neg q}{\therefore \neg p}$

d. $p \to q$
    $\dfrac{q \to r}{\therefore p \to r}$

The Definitions of Symbolic Logic

In this section we present the four basic definitions of symbolic logic. (In the previous topic, we introduced the notation for these definitions.) At the end of this section you need to know (by memory) the definitions of negation, conjunction, disjunction, and implication/conditional. You should understand the difference between "or" in the inclusive and exclusive sense. Furthermore, you should be able to use these definitions to decide whether a given English statement is true or false.

◊ **Definition**

Negation (not)
The negation of a true statement is a false statement.
The negation of a false statement is a true statement.

The table at the right shows
the negation definition.

p	~p	
T	F	(When p is true, ~p is false.)
F	T	(When p is false, ~p is true.)

Let us consider a double negation, namely ~(~p).

The negation of the negation of a statement is equivalent to the statement itself. That is, both ~(~p) and p have the same truth value.

> **~(~p) is equivalent to p**

Symbolically, we may write: $\sim(\sim p) \equiv p$. The symbol " $\equiv$ " means "is equivalent to." We will encounter this symbol again in later sections.

E
X
A
M
P
L
E
S

1. If statement p is a true statement, then ~p is a false statement. Consider each of the following statements:

> p: *Tallahassee is the capital of Florida.* (True)
>
> ~p: *Tallahassee is not the capital of Florida.* (False)

Notice that ~(~p) is: It is false that Tallahassee is not the capital of Florida. This is a true statement and has the **same** truth value as statement p. Thus, ~(~p) is equivalent to p.

2. If statement p is a false statement, then ~p is a true statement. Consider each of the following statements:

> p: *Florida is located in Canada.* (False)
>
> ~p: *Florida is not located in Canada.* (True)

Notice that ~(~p) is: *It is false that Florida is not located in Canada.* This is a false statement and has the same truth value as p. ~(~p) is equivalent to p.

If a compound statement is constructed using connectives and two simple statements, p and q, then **four** possibilities can occur:

		p	q
Case 1	p could be true and q could be true.	T	T
Case 2	p could be true and q could be false.	T	F
Case 3	p could be false and q could be true.	F	T
Case 4	p could be false and q could be false.	F	F

Recall that a compound statement in the form $p \wedge q$ is called a conjunction. It is possible to determine the truth values of the conjunctions in terms of the four possibilities of p and q by using the following table:

Conjunction Table

	p	q	$p \wedge q$
(1)	T	T	T
(2)	T	F	F
(3)	F	T	F
(4)	F	F	F

E
X
A
M
P
L
E
S

1. The statement "2 + 2 = 4 (T) and 3 + 2 = 5 (T)" is true.
2. The statement "2 + 2 = 4 (T) and 3 + 2 = 6 (F)" is false.
3. The statement "2 + 2 = 5 (F) and 3 + 3 = 6 (T)" is false.
4. The statement "2 + 2 = 5 (F) and 3 + 3 = 7 (F)" is false.

We can summarize this discussion with the following definition:

◊ **Definition**

Conjunction (and)
A compound statement made with the connective "and" is true only when all component simple statements are true.

Let us now turn to the definition of disjunction.

◊ **Definition**

Disjunction (or)
A compound statement made with the connective "or" is true when at least one simple statement is true.

This definition can be presented by means of the following table.

Disjunction Table

	p	q	p ∨ q
(1)	T	T	T
(2)	T	F	T
(3)	F	T	T
(4)	F	F	F

E
X
A
M
P
L
E
S

1. *Clearwater is in Florida or Jacksonville is in Florida.*
    This statement is true since both statements are true.
2. *Clearwater is in Florida or Jacksonville is in Texas.*
    This statement is true since one statement is true.
3. *Clearwater is in Georgia or Jacksonville is in Florida.*
    This statement is true since one statement is true.
4. *Clearwater is in Georgia or Jacksonville is in Texas.*
    This statement is false since both statements are false.

Observe that a disjunction is true when at least one of its simple statements is true (cases (1) through (3) in the disjunction table).

The word "or" in everyday English is commonly given either of two possible meanings. Consider the following statement:
    Jose studies English or mathematics.

This statement is considered true if Jose studies English, if he studies mathematics, or if he studies both subjects. In this situation the word "or" is used in the **inclusive** sense and implies "one or the other or both." Consequently, we cannot conclude that:
    If Jose studies English, then he does not study mathematics.
    (He can be studying both disciplines.)

Similarly, the original statement does not tell us that:
    If Jose studies mathematics, then he does not study English.

Notice, however, that when we are told that Jose studies English or mathematics, if we know with certainty that Jose does not study one of the subjects, we can conclude that he does study the other subject. Consequently, the original statement enables us to say:
    If Jose does not study English, then he studies mathematics.
    If Jose does not study mathematics, then he studies English.

Later in this chapter we will verify these informal observations with the principles of formal logic.

There is another, different, interpretation for the word "or." Consider the following statement:
    The person in the distance is a man or a woman.

In this situation the truth of one of the possibilities excludes the truth of the other

Sets and Logic

possibility. In the **exclusive** sense "or" implies "one or the other, but not both."

The ambiguity of "or" is resolved in English by adding the words "or both" or "but not both." Thus the inclusive sense is expressible in the unambiguous fashion:

Jose studies English or mathematics or both.

The exclusive sense is expressed as:

Jose studies English or mathematics, but not both.

In this chapter the word "or" is used in the inclusive sense. Thus, the **inclusive** disjunction, p ∨ q, is true if p alone is true or if q alone is true or if both p and q are true.

> **Note**
> Each of the basic tables (giving the definitions of negation, conjunction and disjunction) is an example of a **truth table.**

We now wish to construct a truth table for the basic conditional statement. Consider the following conditional statement:

If it is a nice day, then I will go swimming.

Notice that the simple statements are:

p: *It is a nice day.*　　　q: *I will go swimming.*

There are four possibilities that could occur with this conditional statement:

				p	q
Case 1	*It is a nice day*	and	*I go swimming.*	T	T
Case 2	*It is a nice day*	and	*I do not go swimming.*	T	F
Case 3	*It is not a nice day*	and	*I go swimming.*	F	T
Case 4	*It is not a nice day*	and	*I do not go swimming.*	F	F

Let us consider the truth values of the statement under each of these four possible situations.

Case 1

It is a nice day, and I go swimming. Notice that both statements p and q are true in this case. Since I am doing what I said I would do if it were a nice day, this conditional statement is **true.**

p	q	p → q
T	T	T

46

Case 2

It is a nice day, and I do not go swimming. In this case
p is true and q is false. Since I am not doing what I said
I would do if it were a nice day, the original conditional
statement is **false**.

p	q	p → q
T	F	F

Case 3

It is not a nice day, and I go swimming. In this case,
p is false and q is true. Notice that this situation has
nothing whatsoever to do with the original statement.

p	q	p → q
F	T	T

The original statement is not affected at all. Nothing was said about what I
would do if it were not a nice day. Under these conditions the original statement is still **true** since it certainly has not been proven false.

Case 4

It is not a nice day and I do not go swimming. In this
case p is false and q is also false. Here again, this
situation has nothing to do with the original statement.

p	q	p → q
F	F	T

Since it certainly has not been proven false, the original statement is still
considered **true**.

These results may be summarized in a basic table for the conditional statement. Since
a conditional statement is also called an implication, the basic table is generally
referred to as the implication table.

Implication Table		
p	q	p → q
T	T	T
T	F	F
F	T	T
F	F	T

Observe that **an implication is false only when the hypothesis is true and the
conclusion is false,** case (2) in the table.

Sets and Logic

Each of the following compound statements is an implication.

If $2 + 2 = 4$ then $3 + 2 = 5$ is true because $\quad$ T $\rightarrow$ T = T.
If $2 + 2 = 4$ then $3 + 2 = 7$ is false because $\quad$ T $\rightarrow$ F = F.
If $2 + 2 = 5$ then $3 + 2 = 5$ is true because $\quad$ F $\rightarrow$ T = T.
If $2 + 2 = 5$ then $3 + 2 = 7$ is true because $\quad$ F $\rightarrow$ F = T.

Problem Set 5

Determine the truth values of:

1. $3 + 2 = 5$ and the fir tree gives us fur coats.

2. $3 + 2 = 5$ or the fir tree gives us fur coats.

3. $3 + 2 = 5$ and $2 + 5 = 7$.

4. $3 + 2 = 5$ or $2 + 5 = 7$.

5. Three is an even number or 4 is divisible by 2.

6. Three is an even number or 4 is not divisible by 2.

7. All birds have eyes and all dogs are mammals.

8. All birds have eyes and some dogs are not mammals.

9. Consider the statement: *Gill wrote the book or Blitzer wrote the book.*
   Which one of the following can we not conclude based upon using "or" in the inclusive sense?
   a. If Gill wrote the book, then Blitzer did not write the book.
   b. If Gill did not write the book, then Blitzer wrote the book.

c. If Blitzer did not write the book, then Gill wrote the book.

Based upon the implication table, determine the truth or falsity of each of the following.

10. If $3 + 5 = 8$, then $6 \cdot 6 = 42$.

11. If $4 + 4 = 32$, then $5 + 5 = 10$.

12. If $3 + 5 = 8$, then $5 + 5 = 10$.

13. If $3 \cdot 9 = 28$, then $6 \cdot 5 = 35$.

14. Consider the statement:
    If you see the concert, then you have a ticket.
    Determine if the statement is true or false under each of the following conditions.
    a. You see the concert. You also have a ticket.
    b. You see the concert. However, you do not have a ticket.
    c. You do not see the concert even though you do have a ticket.
    d. You do not see the concert. You also do not have a ticket.

Topic 6

Constructing Truth Tables
For Compound Statements

In this section we shall use the four basic definitions of symbolic logic to construct truth tables for compound statements. At the end of this section you should be able to use the procedure that we present in order to construct truth tables.

The four basic truth tables (negation, conjunction, disjunction, implication) can be used to construct truth tables for a variety of other statements. It is important for you to memorize these basic definitions. They can be remembered in table form or as compact rules.

1.	**Negation**	The negation of a statement has the opposite truth value as the statement.
2.	**Conjunction**	A conjunction is true only when all simple statements are true.
3.	**Disjunction**	A disjunction is true when at least one simple statement is true.
4.	**Implication**	A conditional statement is false only when the hypothesis is true and the conclusion is false.

Problem 1

Construct a truth table for p ∨ ~q.

Solution

Step 1

List the four possible truth values for p
and q. It is not necessary to list the
possibilities in this order, but it is standard
and makes for a consistent presentation.

p	q
T	T
T	F
F	T
F	F

Step 2

Observe that the statement (p ∨ ~q) contains
~q. A column of truth values for ~q is
constructed next to the q column. The ~q
column is filled in by taking the opposite of
the truth values in the q column.

p	q	~q
T	T	F
T	F	T
F	T	F
F	F	T

Step 3

The statement (p ∨ ~q) calls for the
disjunction of p and ~q. Another
column for p ∨ ~q is constructed
using the values in the p and ~q
columns. The p ∨ ~q column is
filled in by looking back at columns

p	q	~q	p ∨ ~q
T	T	F	T
T	F	T	T
F	T	F	F
F	F	T	T

1 (p) and 3 (~q) and remembering that a disjunction is true when at least
one simple statement is true. This occurs in all but the third row.

This completes the truth table for p ∨ ~q. The column at the far right shows the values
of p ∨ ~q for the four possibilities of the table. The final column constructed is the
"answer" column. Thus, the statement p ∨ ~q is false only when p is false and q is
true.

Problem 2

Construct a truth table for ~(p ∧ q).

Solution

Step 1

As with all truth tables, first list
all possible truth values for the
letters representing statements. In
this case there are two letters
and four possibilities.

p	q
T	T
T	F
F	T
F	F

Step 2

Make a column for the expression
within the parentheses, using the
truth values from the conjunction
definition. A conjunction is true
only when all simple statements are
true (case 1).

p	q	p ∧ q
T	T	T
T	F	F
F	T	F
F	F	F

Step 3

Construct one more column for ~(p ∧ q).
Fill in this last column by negating the values
in the p ∧ q column. Use the negation
definition, taking the opposite of the truth
values in column 3.

p	q	p ∧ q	~(p ∧ q)
T	T	T	F
T	F	F	T
F	T	F	T
F	F	F	T

This completes the truth table for ~(p ∧ q).

It is helpful to remember to first construct the column of truth values of the compound statement that appears within the parentheses. After doing this, negate each truth value for the expression in parentheses.

The final column in this table tells us that the statement ~(p ∧ q) is false only when both p and q are true. For example, using p: *Miami is a city.* (true), q: *Jacksonville is a city.* (true), we see that ~(p ∧ q) translates as: *It is not true that both Miami and Jacksonville are cities.* This statement is false.

Problem 3

Construct a truth table for $(\sim p \vee q) \wedge \sim q$.

Solution

The completed truth table is shown below. The first two columns on the left show the four possible truth values for p and q. The next three columns are successively completed for the expressions $\sim p$, $(\sim p \vee q)$, and $\sim q$. The final column for $(\sim p \vee q) \wedge \sim q$ is completed by applying the conjunction to the columns labeled $(\sim p \vee q)$ and $\sim q$.

p	q	$\sim p$	$(\sim p \vee q)$	$\sim q$	$(\sim p \vee q) \wedge \sim q$
T	T	F	T	F	F
T	F	F	F	T	F
F	T	T	T	F	F
F	F	T	T	T	T

Problem 4

Construct a truth table for the implication $q \rightarrow \sim p$.

Solution

Step 1

List the four truth possibilities p and q in the table in the same way as in previous truth tables.

p	q
T	T
T	F
F	T
F	F

Step 2

Complete the table by constructing columns for $\sim p$ and $q \rightarrow \sim p$. The $\sim p$ column is completed by negating the entries in the p column. The $q \rightarrow \sim p$ column is completed by applying the

p	q	$\sim p$	$q \rightarrow \sim p$
T	T	F	F
T	F	F	T
F	T	T	T
F	F	T	T

implication definition to the q and $\sim p$ columns. Since an implication is false only when the hypothesis (column 2) is true and the conclusion (column 3) is false, the first row in the table is the only false entry.

Problem 5

Construct a truth table for the statement $(p \lor q) \to q$.

Solution

Step 1

As always, list the four truth
possibilities for p and q in the
customary order.

p	q
T	T
T	F
F	T
F	F

Step 2

Construct a column for the
statement $(p \lor q)$. Use the values in
the p and q columns along with the
definition of the disjunction to
complete this column.

p	q	$(p \lor q)$
T	T	T
T	F	T
F	T	T
F	F	F

Step 3

Construct a column for the entire
implication statement, $(p \lor q) \to q$.
Use the values in the $(p \lor q)$ column
as the hypotheses and the values in
the q column as conclusions to
complete the final column.

p	q	$(p \lor q)$	$(p \lor q) \to q$
T	T	T	T
T	F	T	F
F	T	T	T
F	F	F	T

Problem Set 6

Construct truth tables for:

1. ~p ∨ q

2. p ∧ ~q

3. ~p ∨ ~q

4. ~p ∧ ~q

5. ~(p ∨ q)

6. ~(p ∨ ~q)

7. ~(p ∧ ~q)

8. ~(~p ∨ ~q)

9. ~p ∨ (p ∧ ~q)

10. (~p ∨ ~q) ∧ (p ∧ q)

11. ~(p ∨ q) ∧ ~(~p ∧ q)

12. Construct a truth table for ~p ∧ (q ∨ ~r). This compound statement involves three simple statements: p, q, and r. In this case there are **three** letters and **eight** combinations of truth values. A truth table showing the eight possibilities appears below. Complete each of the required columns.

p	q	r	~p	~r	(q ∨ ~r)	~p ∧ (q ∨ ~r)
T	T	T				
T	T	F				
T	F	T				
T	F	F				
F	T	T				
F	T	F				
F	F	T				
F	F	F				

A convenient way to remember the order for the possibilities is as follows. Let the p column contain four T's and four F's (TTTT,FFFF). Let the q column contain alternating groups of two T's and two F's (TT,FF,TT, etc.). Finally, let the r column contain alternating T's and F's (T,F,T,F, etc.).

Construct truth tables for each of the following.

13. ~p → q

14. q → p

15. ~p → ~q

16. ~q → ~p

17. Construct truth tables for p → q and ~q → ~p and compare the final columns.

18. (p ∧ q) → p

19. ~p → (p ∨ q)

20. ~(p → q) ∨ (q → p)

21. ~q → (p ∧ ~q)

22. (~p ∧ q) → (p ∧ q)

23. [(p → q) ∧ ~p] →~q

Topic 7

Conditional Statements: Equivalences, Non-Equivalences, Negation

In Lewis Carroll's *Alice's Adventures in Wonderland*, Alice, confused by the strange occurrences around her, questions her very identity. She reasons that her friend Mabel knows very little, and after determining that she too knows very little, concludes that she must be Mabel!

It is certainly true that: If one is Mabel, then one knows very little. However, it is not necessarily true that: If one knows very little, then one is Mabel. This common error in logic is discussed in this section, where we consider equivalences, non-equivalences, and a negation for conditional statements. At the end of this section you need to be able to formulate the equivalences, non-equivalences, and negation of a conditional statement presented in English.

It is possible to classify conditional statements according to the form they assume.

◊ Definition

If $p \rightarrow q$ is a conditional statement, then $q \rightarrow p$ is the **converse** of that conditional statement.

Recall that in $p \rightarrow q$, p is the hypothesis and q is the conclusion. **The converse of a conditional statement is obtained by reversing the hypothesis and the conclusion.**

E
X
A
M
P
L
E

Consider the following conditional statement of the form p → q:

If Tony is in Seattle, then he is in the West. (true)

Statement p is: *Tony is in Seattle.*

Statement q is: *Tony is in the West.*

The converse (q → p) of this statement is:

If Tony is in the West, then he is in Seattle.

Notice that the converse could be true, but could also be false. If Tony is in the West, he might or might not be in Seattle. This suggests that the converse of a conditional statement is not logically equivalent to the conditional statement.

◊ **Definition**

If p → q is a conditional statement, then ~p → ~q is the **inverse** of the conditional statement.

The inverse of a conditional statement is obtained by negating both the hypothesis and the conclusion.

E
X
A
M
P
L
E

Consider the following conditional statement of the form p → q:

If Tony is in Seattle, then he is in the West. (true)

Statement p is: *Tony is in Seattle.*

Statement q is: *Tony is in the West.*

The inverse (~p → ~q) of this statement is:

If Tony is not in Seattle, then he is not in the West.

Notice that the inverse could be true, but could also be false. If Tony is not in Seattle, he might or might not be in the West. Not only does this suggest that the inverse of a conditional statement is not logically equivalent to the conditional statement, but it also brings forth the idea that the inverse is not the negation of the conditional statement. If a statement is true, its negation must be false, and the inverse (If Tony is not in Seattle, then he is not in the West) is not necessarily false. The inverse does not contradict the original conditional statement.

═══════════════════════════

◊ Definition

If p → q is a conditional statement, then ~q → ~p is the **contrapositive** of that conditional statement.

═══════════════════════════

The contrapositive of a conditional statement is obtained by reversing the hypothesis and the conclusion and negating both of them.

E
X
A
M
P
L
E

Consider again the following conditional statement of the form p → q:

If Tony is in Seattle, then he is in the West. (true)

Statement p is: *Tony is in Seattle.*

Statement q is: *Tony is in the West.*

The contrapositive (~q → ~p) of this statement is:

If Tony is not in the West, then he is not in Seattle. (true)

Observe that the contrapositive must be true. If Tony is not in the Western United States, he cannot possibly be in Seattle. This suggests that the contrapositive of a conditional statement is logically equivalent to the conditional statement.

Below are shown truth tables for the conditional (p → q), its contrapositive (~q → ~p), its converse (q → p) and its inverse (~p → ~q).

Conditional Statement

p	q	p → q
T	T	T
T	F	F
F	T	T
F	F	T

Contrapositive

p	q	~q	~p	~q → ~p
T	T	F	F	T
T	F	T	F	F
F	T	F	T	T
F	F	T	T	T

Converse

p	q	q → p
T	T	T
T	F	T
F	T	F
F	F	T

Inverse

p	q	~p	~q	~p → ~q
T	T	F	F	T
T	F	F	T	T
F	T	T	F	F
F	F	T	T	T

Observe that the conditional (p → q) and the contrapositive (~q → ~p) have the same truth values in the final column and thus are **logically equivalent**.

$$p \rightarrow q \ \equiv \ \sim q \rightarrow \sim p$$

This means that the contrapositive can replace any conditional without changing its meaning. Notice that the converse (q → p) and the inverse (~p → ~q) also have the same truth values and are logically equivalent. However, a conditional statement is not equivalent to its converse or its inverse.

> **Equivalent and Non-Equivalences for a Conditional Statement**
> 1. p → q is logically equivalent to ~q → ~p.
> 2. p → q is not logically equivalent to q → p (its converse) and ~p → ~q (its inverse).

Problem 1

Write two statements that are **not** logically equivalent to:
> *If one is a biologist, then one is a scientist.* (true)

Solution

Both the converse and the inverse are not logically equivalent to the original conditional statement.

Let p be: *One is a biologist.*
Let q be: *One is a scientist.*
The non-equivalences are:

q → p (the converse): *If one is a scientist, then one is a biologist.* (not necessarily true)

~p → ~q (the inverse): *If one is not a biologist, then one is not a scientist.* (not necessarily true)

Problem 2

Write a statement that is logically equivalent to:
> *If a bill does not receive majority approval, then it does not become law.*

Solution

The contrapositive is logically equivalent to the original conditional statement.

Let p be: *A bill does not receive majority approval.*
Let q be: *The bill does not become law.*
The equivalence is: ~q → ~p (the contrapositive): *If a bill becomes law, then it does receive majority approval.*

We have seen that if a conditional statement is true, its converse is not necessarily true. However, there are certain English statements that are true in both directions.

Let us now consider a "two-way" conditional.

Let p be: *A set contains no elements.*
Let q be: *It is the null set.*

Notice that both of the following conditionals are true.

p → q: *If a set contains no elements, then it is the null set.*
q → p: *If a set is the null set, then it contains no elements.*

The conjunction of these two statements will therefore also be true and is the basis for defining the **biconditional** with symbol ↔.

$$p \leftrightarrow q \quad \text{is equivalent to} \quad (p \rightarrow q) \wedge (q \rightarrow p)$$

The choice of the two-way arrow (↔) is appropriate since, notationally speaking, this new connective indicates that the conditional can be considered in **both** directions. Furthermore, depending on the direction, both p and q are hypotheses and conclusions.

There are a number of ways of translating p ↔ q into English.

Translations for p ↔ q

a. p is equivalent to q.
b. p implies q and q implies p.
c. p if and only if q. (abbreviated: p iff q)
d. q if and only if p. (abbreviated: q iff p)
e. p is both necessary and sufficient for q.
f. q is both necessary and sufficient for p.

E
X
A
M
P
L
E

Let p be: *A set contains no elements.*

Let q be: *It is the empty set.*

p ↔ q can be translated as:

a.   A set contains no elements is equivalent to it is the empty set.

b.   A set contains no elements implies that it is the empty set and a set is the empty set implies that it contains no elements.

c.   A set contains no elements if and only if it is the empty set.

d.   A set is the empty set if and only if it contains no elements.

e.   A set contains no elements is both necessary and sufficient for the set being the empty set.

f.   A set is the empty set is both necessary and sufficient for the set to contain no elements.

Problem 3

Consider the following simple statements:

p: You live in Florida.   q: You live in America.

Does the biconditional connective, ↔ , relate these two statements?

Solution

The answer is no. The conditional does not work in both directions. If you live in Florida, then you do live in America. However, it is not necessarily true that if you live in America, then you live in Florida. Since the conditional does not work in both directions, it is incorrect to claim that living in Florida is both necessary and sufficient for living in America.

When a statement is formulated with "necessary and sufficient" or "if and only if" (iff), the statement is immediately the biconditional. This means that the first portion implies the second portion and, conversely, the second portion implies the first portion. The truth table for the biconditional is shown below. Notice that p ↔ q is true only when both statements have the same truth value.

Biconditional Table

p	q	p ↔ q
T	T	T
T	F	F
F	T	F
F	F	T

In addition to the contrapositive (~q → ~p), we can formulate another statement that is logically equivalent to p → q. Compare the final columns in the truth tables of p → q and ~p ∨q shown below.

p	q	p → q
T	T	T
T	F	F
F	T	T
F	F	T

p	q	~p	~p ∨ q
T	T	F	T
T	F	F	F
F	T	T	T
F	F	T	T

The final two columns of the two tables are identical, and these statements are equivalent. As we saw earlier, equivalent statements have the same truth values for corresponding values of the simple statements.

> Notice that we now have two statements that are logically equivalent to p → q:
> 1. p → q ≡ ~q → ~p (the contrapositive)
> 2. p → q ≡ ~p ∨ q

Problem 4

Use the second equivalence in the table to write a statement that is logically equivalent to: If a bill does not receive majority approval, then it does not become law.

Solution

Let p be: A bill does not receive majority approval.
Let q be: The bill does not become law.
The equivalence is: ~p ∨ q: A bill does receive majority approval or it does not become law.

Let us now turn our attention to the negation of a conditional statement, namely ~(p → q). Compare the final columns in the truth tables of ~(p → q) and p ∧~q shown below.

p	q	p →q	~(p → q)
T	T	T	F
T	F	F	T
F	T	T	F
F	F	T	F

p	q	~q	p ∧~q
T	T	F	F
T	F	T	T
F	T	F	F
F	F	T	F

The final columns of the two tables are identical, telling us that the negation of p → q is p ∧~q.   ~(p → q) ≡ p ∧ ~q

Let p be: *I work hard.* Let q be: *I will succeed.*

p → q is: *If I work hard, then I will succeed.*

The negation (p ∧ ~q) is: *I work hard and I will **not** succeed.*

Problem 5

Write the negation of: If a bill does not receive majority approval, then it does not become law.

Solution

Let p be: A bill does not receive majority approval.

Let q be: The bill does not become law.

The negation is:

(p ∧ ~q): A bill does not receive majority approval and it does become law.

Imagine if a professor made both of the following statements to a class:

If a bill does not receive majority approval, then it does not become law.

A bill does not receive majority approval and it does become law.

Students would immediately be aware that the second statement **contradicts** the first statement. This, of course, is the case because the second statement is the negation of the first statement. Whenever we utter a negation immediately after a statement, we wind up contradicting ourselves (as well as confusing our listeners). This observation is reinforced in the following example.

Consider the statement: p ∧ ~p. Let us construct a truth table for this compound statement.

Step 1

Since the statement is composed only of variations of simple statement p, there are only two cases for this table.

p can be true or false.

p
T
F

Step 2

Construct another column of values for ~p. Complete the ~p column by negating the values in the p column.

p	~p
T	F
F	T

Step 3

Construct a column for p ∧ ~p. Complete this column by applying the conjunction to the values in the p column with those in the ~p column.

p	~p	p ∧ ~p
T	F	F
F	T	F

The final column shows that p ∧ ~p is false in all cases. A compound statement that is false in all cases is called a **contradiction** and the two simple statements p and ~p are said to be contradictory. In short, the negated statement will always contradict the original statement. If the original statement is true, the negated statement will be false and vice-versa.

The equivalences, non-equivalences, and negation of a conditional statement are summarized below.

> **The Conditional Statement: p → q**
> Equivalences: ~q → ~p (contrapositive)
> ~p ∨ q
> Non-Equivalences: q → p (converse)
> ~p → ~q (inverse)
> Negation: p ∧ ~q

Problem Set 7

Write two non-equivalences (the converse and inverse) and the equivalent contrapositive for each of the following conditional statements.

1. *If Nigel is in London, then he is in England.*

2. *If it is a banana, then it is yellow.*

3. *If Joan is at the movies, then she is having a good time.*

4. *If it's St. Patrick's Day, then Erin does not wear red clothing.*

5. *If one advocates censorship, then one does not advocate freedom.*

6. p → ~q

7. ~p → ~q

8. *No animals are allowed in the restaurant.* (First write the statement in the "if...then" form.)

9. *All chemists are scientists.* (First write the statement in the "if...then" form.)

10. Consider the following simple statements:
    p: *Sherry lives in Palm Beach.*
    q: *Sherry lives in Florida.*
    Express each of the following in English. Determine also whether each is always true or not necessarily true.
    a. $p \rightarrow q$ b. the converse of $p \rightarrow q$
    c. the inverse of $p \rightarrow q$
    d. the contrapositive of $p \rightarrow q$

Write two statements that are not logically equivalent to each of the following.

11. *If I pass the test, then I am happy.*

12. *If it is St. Patrick's Day, then Erin wears green.*

13. *If one is a poet, then one is a writer.*

14. *If a number is divisible by 6, then it is divisible by 3.*

15. *If it's a banana, then it is not blue.*

Write two statements that are logically equivalent to each of the following.

16. *If a person does not work hard, then that person does not succeed.*

17. *If the temperature is above 32°, it does not snow.*

18. Select the statement that is logically equivalent to: *If the play is Othello, then Shakespeare is the author.*
    a. *If Shakespeare is the author, then the play is Othello.*
    b. *If the play is not Othello, then Shakespeare is not the author.*
    c. *If Shakespeare is not the author, then the play is not Othello.*
    d. *The play is Othello and Shakespeare is not the author.*

19. Select the statement that is **not** logically equivalent to:
    If the road is not repaired, then traffic problems will occur.
    a. *The road must be repaired or traffic problems will occur.*
    b. *Traffic problems will occur or the road is repaired.*
    c. *If traffic problems occur, the road was not repaired.*
    d. *If traffic problems do not occur, the road was repaired.*

20. Express the negations of:
    a. *If Barbara wins the election, then I will be sorry.*
    b. *If you speak loudly, then I can hear you.*
    c. *If it is a nice day, then I will go to the beach.*
    d. *If John is a criminal, then he will be punished.*
    e. *If Bill is 18, then he is eligible to vote.*

21. Consider the following simple statements:
    p: *A number is a multiple of 2.*
    q: *A number is even.*
    Translate $p \leftrightarrow q$ into English using the six ways indicated in this section.

22. Is the following statement true? *You are Albert Einstein if and only if you are a brilliant physicist.*

    Asked in another way, does the biconditional connective ↔ relate the two statements below?
    p: *You are Albert Einstein.*
    q: *You are a brilliant physicist.*

23. Is the following statement true? *x not being greater than 5 is both necessary and sufficient for x being less than or equal to 5.*

24. Is the following statement true?
    (a = b) iff (b = a)

25. Is the following statement true? *a is less than b iff b is greater than a.*

26. Is the following statement true? *x being greater than 5 is both necessary and sufficient for x being greater than 3.*

27. Is the following statement true? *x is greater than 0 iff x is positive.*

28. Is the following statement true? *x being divisible by 5 is both necessary and sufficient for x being divisible by 10.*

Topic 8

Equivalences And Negations For Statements Involving The Words "All," "Some," and "No"

In this section we present logical equivalences and negations for statements in the
form: All A are B.
       Some A are B.
       No A are B.
At the end of this section you need to be able to correctly write these equivalences and negations.

In a statement the word "some" means the existence of "at least one." The word "all" does not imply existence.

Sets and Logic

"Some people have blonde hair" means there exists at least one person with blonde hair.

In terms of the Venn diagram at the right, it means that at least one person is in the shaded region.

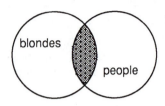

"All people with four heads have IQs over 180" does not mean that there exists any person with four heads.

If circles A and B at the right stand for:
A: People with four heads
B: People with IQs over 180
the relationship between A and B is indicated by the fact that A is inside B. However, there is no claim that any person is actually in circle A. Circle A is a subset of circle B, but it may be the empty set (Remember, the empty set is a subset of every set).

Let us begin with "all A are B" (equivalently: there are no A that are not B).

All A are B means that:
> *If x is in A, then x is in B.*
> Let p be: x is in A.
> Let q be: x is in B.

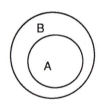

The negation is p ∧ ~q, which translates as:
> *x is in A and x is not in B.*

This means that something is in A and not in B. Thus, the negation of "all A are B" is "some A are not B."

Notice that when we assert "some A are not B" we are equivalently saying that "not all A are B."

E
X
A
M
P
L
E

Consider the following simple statement:

All professors are wealthy. (False)

Notice that the English equivalent is:

*There are **no** professors who **are** **not** wealthy.*

The negation could be stated in any one of the four following ways.

*Some professors are **not** wealthy.* (True)

***Not all** professors are wealthy.* (True)

***At least one** professor is not wealthy.* (True)

It is not true that all professors are wealthy. (True)

Now consider a statement in the form "some A are B."

The following simple statement is true because "some" means "at least one."

***Some** professors are wealthy.* (True)

Notice that the English equivalent is:

*There **is at least one** professor who is wealthy.*

The negation of this simple statement is:

***No** professors are wealthy.* (False)

By negating the original statement, we are saying that the statement is not true for even one professor. The negation is also:

It is not true that some professors are wealthy.

This statement is also false.

Notice that the negation is not: *Some professors are not wealthy.* This statement is true and is not the negation because both the original statement and this particular statement are true. **A statement and its negation can never have the same truth value.**

The fact that the negation of "all A are B" is "some A are not B" also tells us that the negation of "some A are not B" is "all A are B." Similarly, the negation of "some A are B" is "no A are B" and vice-versa.

Sets and Logic

The following table summarizes the negations of statements involving such words as "all," "no," "some" and "some...not."

Original Statement	Negation
All...	Some...not...
Some... not...	All...
Some...	No...
No...	Some...

All...   No...

Negation

Some...   Some...not

In English we frequently encounter statements involving "all," "some," and "no." You should be able to express each of these statements in equivalent ways.

Statement	Equivalent Statement
All A are B.	There are no A that are not B.
Some A are not B.	Not all A are B.
Some A are B.	At least one A is a B.
No A are B.	All A are not B.

Problem 1

Write the contrapositive of the conditional statement:
If it snows, then at least one road is open.

Solution

Let p be: *It snows.*
Let q be: *At least one road is open.* (Equivalently: *Some road is open.*)
The given statement (p → q) has as its contrapositive: ~q → ~p.
Since the negation of "some" is "no," the contrapositive is:
If no road is open, then it is not snowing.
Because "no road is open" means that all roads are closed, we can also express the contrapositive as:
If all roads are closed, then it is not snowing.

Problem 2

Write the logical equivalent of:
If all people take exams honestly, then no supervision is needed.

Solution

The logical equivalent is the contrapositive.
Let p be: *All people take exams honestly.*
Let q be: *No supervision is needed.*
The logical equivalent is ~q → ~p. Since the negation of "all" is "some...not"
and the negation of "no" is "some," the contrapositive is:
If some supervision is needed, then some people do not take exams honestly.

Problem 3

The city council of a northern city asserted that: *If it snows, then at least one
major road will remain open.*
The council was wrong. What can we conclude?

Solution

Since the council was wrong, we can conclude the negation of their statement.
Let p be: *It snows.*
Let q be: *At least one major road will remain open.*
Since the negation of "at least one" (which means "some") is "no," the nega-
tion (p ∧ ~q) is:
It snows and no major road remains open.
Equivalently, we can conclude that:
It snows and all major roads are closed.

Problem Set 8

1. Write the negation of:
   Some people like baseball.

2. Write the negation of:
   All Floridians are nice people.

3. Write the negation of:
   No parakeets weigh fifty pounds.

4. Write the negation of: *All books have titles.*

5. Write the negation of:
   Some teachers are not interesting.

Write the logical equivalent (the contrapositive) for each of the following conditional statements:

6. *If there is a hurricane, then all schools are closed.*

7. *If the review session is successful, then no students fail the test.*

8. *If all corporations place profit above human need, then some people suffer.*

9. Suppose that each statement listed below turns out to be false. What can we conclude in each case?
   a. *If a person studies Latin, then that person has an excellent vocabulary.*
   b. *If it's hot, then at least one of the city's pools will be open.*
   c. *If there is a lottery, then all schools will receive increased funding.*

10. The mechanic told me, "All parts were replaced." I later learned that the mechanic never tells the truth. What can I conclude?
    a. No parts were replaced.
    b. Some part was replaced.
    c. There was no part that was not replaced.
    d. At least one part was not replaced.

Topic 9

Conjunctions and Disjunctions: Equivalences, Non-Equivalences, Negations

In this section we consider equivalences, non-equivalences, and negations of conjunctions and disjunctions. At the end of this section you should be able to use DeMorgan's Laws to write negations of conjunctions and disjunctions. You should be able to formulate two statements that are equivalent to English statements whose form is $\sim(p \wedge q)$. You should understand the word "or" in the inclusive sense to write equivalences and non-equivalences for English statements in the form $p \vee q$.

A comparison of the final columns in the truth tables of $\sim(p \wedge q)$ and $\sim p \vee \sim q$ illustrates an important idea of logic. The tables are shown below.

p	q	p∧q	~(p∧q)
T	T	T	F
T	F	F	T
F	T	F	T
F	F	F	T

p	q	~p	~q	~p∨~q
T	T	F	F	F
T	F	F	T	T
F	T	T	F	T
F	F	T	T	T

The final columns of the two tables are identical, and these statements are said to be **equivalent.**

> **First De Morgan Law for Logic**
> $\sim(p \wedge q) \equiv \sim p \vee \sim q$

Observe that **the negation of a compound statement containing "and" is equivalent to negating each of the simple statements and changing "and" to "or."**

This law is the basis for expressing the negation of certain compound statements. For example, consider the compound statement:

Canada is a country and Africa is a country.

Sets and Logic

If p represents *Canada is a country* and q represents *Africa is a country*, the compound statement is of the form p ∧ q. The negation of this statement, ~(p ∧ q), is equivalent to

~p ∨ ~q since ~(p ∧ q) ≡ ~p ∨ ~q.

Thus, the negation is:

*Canada is **not** a country or Africa is **not** a country.*

We can summarize this result in two ways:
1. The **negation** of *Canada is a country and Africa is a country* is: *Canada is not a country or Africa is not a country.*
2. *It is not true that both Canada and Africa are countries* is **logically equivalent** to *Canada is not a country or Africa is not a country.*

Observe that the second result tells us that if it is not true that both places are countries, then one is not a country **or** the other is not a country. The result does **not** assert that Canada is not a country and Africa is not a country. This can be reinforced by comparing the truth values for ~(p ∧ q) with those for ~p ∧ ~q.

p	q	p ∧ q	~(p ∧ q)		p	q	~p	~q	~p ∧ ~q
T	T	T	F		T	T	F	F	F
T	F	F	T		T	F	F	T	F
F	T	F	T		F	T	T	F	F
F	F	F	T		F	F	T	T	T

The final columns of the two tables are not identical, and these statements are not logically equivalent.

A comparison of the final columns in the truth tables of ~(p ∧ q) and p → ~q gives us a second equivalent for ~(p ∧ q).

p	q	p ∧ q	~(p ∧ q)		p	q	~q	p → ~q
T	T	T	F		T	T	F	F
T	F	F	T		T	F	T	T
F	T	F	T		F	T	F	T
F	F	F	T		F	F	T	T

> Notice that we now have two statements that are logically equivalent to ~(p ∧ q):
> 1. ~(p ∧ q) ≡ p → ~q
> 2. ~(p ∧ q) ≡ ~p ∨ ~q   (A De Morgan Law)

Problem 1

Write two statements that are logically equivalent to:
It is not true that both <u>Moby Dick</u> and <u>I Love Lucy</u> are novels.

Solution

Let p be: *<u>Moby Dick</u> is a novel.*
Let q be: *<u>I Love Lucy</u> is a novel.*
The two equivalences for ~(p ∧ q) are:
1. <u>Moby Dick</u> is not a novel or <u>I Love Lucy</u> is not a novel. (~p ∨ ~q)
2. If <u>Moby Dick</u> is a novel, then <u>I Love Lucy</u> is not a novel. (p → ~q)

Problem 2

Write the contrapositive of the conditional statement:
If Mary and Ethel star, then the musical is a success.

Solution

Let p be: *Mary stars.*
Let q be: *Ethel stars.*
Let r be: *The musical is a success.*
The given conditional statement translates as: (p ∧ q) → r
With (p ∧ q) as the hypotheses and r as the conclusion, we form the contrapositive by reversing the hypothesis and the conclusion and negating both of them. The contrapositive is: ~r → ~(p ∧ q)

Using one of De Morgan's Laws, we obtain:
~r → (~p ∨ ~q)

This translates as:
If the musical is not a success, then Mary does not star or Ethel does not star.

Problem 3

Express the negation of the following statement as a conditional statement.
Bob plans to both pay his bills and write a letter.

Solution

Let p be: *Bob plans to pay his bills.*
Let q be: *Bob plans to write a letter.*
$p \wedge q$ is: *Bob plans to both pay his bills and write a letter.*

Since $\sim(p \wedge q) \equiv p \rightarrow \sim q$, the negation is: *If Bob plans to pay his bills, then he does not plan to write a letter.*

We now compare the final columns in the truth tables of $\sim(p \vee q)$ and $\sim p \wedge \sim q$ which are shown below.

p	q	p ∨ q	~(p ∨ q)		p	q	~p	~q	~p ∧~q
T	T	T	F		T	T	F	F	F
T	F	T	F		T	F	F	T	F
F	T	T	F		F	T	T	F	F
F	F	F	T		F	F	T	T	T

Since the final columns are identical in each truth table, these statements are **equivalent**.

> ### Second De Morgan Law for Logic
> $\sim(p \vee q) \equiv \sim p \wedge \sim q$

In other words, **the negation of a compound statement containing "or" is equivalent to negating each of the simple statements and changing "or" to "and."**

E
X
A
M
P
L
E

Consider the statement:

> *A majority of legislators must vote for a bill or the bill does not become law.*

Observe that the two simple statements are:

> *A majority of legislators must vote for a bill* (p). *The bill does not become law* (q).

Thus, the statement is expressed as:

> *A majority of legislators must vote for a bill or the bill does not become law.* (p ∨ q)

Since ~(p ∨ q) ≡ (~p ∧ ~q), the negation is:

> *A majority of legislators do not vote for a bill* **and** *the bill does become law.* (~p ∧ ~q)

Imagine if a professor made both of the following statements to a class:

> A majority of legislators must vote for a bill or the bill does not become law. A majority of legislators do not vote for a bill and the bill does become law.

Notice, once again, how the second statement (the negation) contradicts the original statement.

An important equivalence relating the disjunction and the conditional statement is shown below.

$$p \lor q \equiv {\sim}p \to q$$

In words, this says that **a disjunction may be expressed as a conditional statement by letting the negation of the first statement serve as the hypothesis and the second statement serve as the conclusion.**

To verify this equivalence we construct truth values for p ∨ q (the basic disjunction) and ~p → q:

p	q	p ∨ q		p	q	~p	~p → q
T	T	T		T	T	F	T
T	F	T		T	F	F	T
F	T	T		F	T	T	T
F	F	F		F	F	T	F

Since the final columns are identical in each truth table, we have verified the equivalence: $p \lor q \equiv {\sim}p \to q$.

E	Let p be: *Joe studies English.*
X	Let q be: *Joe studies mathematics.*
A	p ∨ q is: *Joe studies English or mathematics.*
M	This statement is logically equivalent to ~p → q which says:
P	*If Joe does not study English, then he studies mathematics.*
L	This new statement is equivalent to its contrapositive, obtained by reversing
E	and negating hypothesis and conclusion, which says:

If Joe does not study mathematics, then he studies English.

Both of these equivalences make sense, for if Joe studies one discipline or the other, if he does not study one, he must study the other. On the other hand, since we are dealing with the inclusive "or," the original statement (p ∨ q: *Joe studies English or mathematics.*) is **not** logically equivalent to:

If Joe studies English, then Joe does not study mathematics. (He might be studying both.)

To verify that p ∨ q is **not** equivalent to p → ~q, we once again construct truth tables.

p	q	p ∨ q		p	q	~q	p → ~q
T	T	T		T	T	F	F
T	F	T		T	F	T	T
F	T	T		F	T	F	T
F	F	F		F	F	T	T

The final columns of the two tables are not identical, and these statements are not logically equivalent.

We can now summarize the equivalences and nonequivalences of various statements in logic.

Statement	Equivalences	Nonequivalences
p → q	~q → ~p ~p ∨ q	q → p (converse) ~p → ~q (inverse)
p ∨ q	~p → q ~q → p	p → ~q q → ~p
~(p ∧ q)	p → ~q ~p ∨ ~q	~p ∧ ~q
~(p ∨ q)	~p ∧ ~q	~p ∨ ~q

Problem Set 9

Express the negations of:

1. *Jim is tall and John is an athlete.*

2. *Mary lives in Florida and Nancy lives in Georgia.*

3. *Estelle is both loud and abrasive.*

4. *Both the Dolphins and the Buccaneers are in the playoffs.*

5. *Clearwater is in Georgia and Atlanta is not in Florida.*

6. *The Strikers are not Jacksonville's team and the Bandits are Tampa's team.*

7. *Some movies are not exciting and no jokes are funny.*

8. *Vince is not tall and Mike is not wise.*

9. *All dogs are faithful and some cats are cute.*

10. Consider the statement:
    It is not true that both Frank and Judy appreciate rock music.
    Use De Morgan's Law to express the statement's logical equivalent.

11. Find the statement below which is not the logical equivalent of :
    It is not true that both Karen and Jim are students.
    a. Karen is not a student or Jim is not a student.
    b. Karen is not a student and Jim is not a student.

Express the negations of:

12. *London is in England or Paris is in France.*

13. *The bill passes or it's not a law.*

14. *Dave visits San Francisco or London.*

15. *It is not hot or it is not humid.*

16. *All mathematics books have sample tests or they do not get published.*

17. *Antonio is not Prospero's brother or Romeo is Juliet's lover.*

18. *All people carry umbrellas or some people get wet.*

Write the contrapositive for each of the following conditional statements:

19. *If lines are parallel, then they do not share a common point.*

20. *If both Jose and Marsha play, then the team wins.*

21. *If one is in Atlanta or New Orleans, then one is in the South.*

22. $\sim p \rightarrow (\sim q \vee r)$

23. $(p \wedge \sim q) \rightarrow \sim r$

24. Express the negations of each of the following statements as conditional statements.
    a. *Joan is both nervous and tense.*
    b. *Pete is going to the movies and the beach.*
    c. *Richard is rich and famous.*
    d. *Joe is our driver and our guide.*

Sets and Logic

25. Select the statement that is logically equivalent to: *It is not true that both Johnson and Eisenhower were Democrats.*
    a. *If Johnson was a Democrat, then Eisenhower was not a Democrat.*
    b. *Johnson was not a Democrat and Eisenhower was not a Democrat.*
    c. *Johnson was a Democrat and Eisenhower was a Democrat.*
    d. *Johnson was a Democrat or Eisenhower was not a Democrat.*

26. Select the statement that is **not** logically equivalent to: *It is not true that both the Rolling Stones and De Morgan's Laws are rock groups.*
    a. *The Rolling Stones are not a rock group or De Morgan's Laws are not a rock group.*
    b. *If the Rolling Stones are a rock group, then De Morgan's Laws are not a rock group.*
    c. *If De Morgan's Laws are a rock group, then the Rolling Stones are not a rock group.*
    d. *The Rolling Stones are not a rock group and De Morgan's Laws are not a rock group.*

27. Select the statement that is logically equivalent to: *A major dam on the upper Nile River must exist or the lower Nile will overflow its banks each year.*
    a. *If a major dam on the upper Nile River does exist, then the lower Nile will not overflow its banks each year.*
    b. *If no major dam on the upper Nile River exists, the lower Nile will overflow its banks each year.*
    c. *If the lower Nile overflows its banks each*

year, then a major dam on the upper Nile River does not exist.
    d. *A major dam on the upper Nile River exists and the lower Nile does not overflow its banks each year.*

28. Select the statement that is not logically equivalent to: *Angela takes physics or chemistry.*
    a. *If Angela does not take physics, then she takes chemistry.*
    b. *If Angela does not take chemistry, then she takes physics.*
    c. *It is false that Angela does not take chemistry and does not take physics.*
    d. *If Angela takes chemistry, then she does not take physics.*

29. Select the statement that is **not** logically equivalent: *If Pilar is in Soweto, then she is in South Africa.*
    a. *If Pilar is not in South Africa, then she is not in Soweto.*
    b. *Pilar is not in Soweto unless she is in South Africa.*
    c. *If Pilar is in South Africa, then she is in Soweto.*
    d. *Unless Pilar is in South Africa, she is not in Soweto.*

30. Select the statement that is logically equivalent to: *Janine plays tennis or basketball.*
    a. *If Janine plays tennis, then she does not play basketball.*
    b. *If Janine does not play tennis, then she plays basketball.*
    c. *If Janine plays basketball, then she does not play tennis.*
    d. *It is not true that Janine does not play tennis or does not play basketball.*

Valid Arguments Using Truth Tables

In this section arguments are determined to be valid or invalid using truth tables. At the end of this section you should be able to construct a truth table to decide whether an argument is valid or fallacious.

◊ **Definition**

A statement that is true in all cases is a **tautology**.

E
X
A
M
P
L
E

Consider the statement: $p \vee \sim p$. Let us construct a truth table for this compound statement.

Step 1

Since the statement is composed only of variations of simple statement p, there are only two cases for this table.

p can be true or false.

p
T
F

Step 2

Construct another column of values for $\sim p$. Complete the $\sim p$ column by negating the values in the p column.

p	~p
T	F
F	T

Step 3

Construct a column for $p \vee \sim p$. Complete this column by applying the disjunction to the values in the p column with those in the ~p column.

p	~p	p ∨ ~p
T	F	T
F	T	T

Sets and Logic

The truth table verifies that $p \vee \sim p$ is a tautology because the statement is true in all cases.

Let p represent: *You live in Florida.*
A tautology is:

  You live in Florida or you do not live in Florida. $(p \vee \sim p)$

This statement is true in all cases.

Many of the equivalences and negations that we previously discussed can be thought of as tautologies. For example, consider:

  $\sim(p \wedge q) \equiv \sim p \vee \sim q$

Both $\sim(p \wedge q) \rightarrow (\sim p \vee \sim q)$ and $(\sim p \vee \sim q) \rightarrow \sim(p \wedge q)$ are tautologies. If we show the truth table for $\sim(p \wedge q) \rightarrow (\sim p \vee \sim q)$, we have:

p	q	$p \wedge q$	$\sim(p \wedge q)$	$\sim p$	$\sim q$	$\sim p \vee \sim q$	$\sim(p \wedge q) \rightarrow (\sim p \vee \sim q)$
T	T	T	F	F	F	F	T
T	F	F	T	F	T	T	T
F	T	F	T	T	F	T	T
F	F	F	T	T	T	T	T

Since the statement in the last column is true in all cases, it is a tautology.

The arguments that we shall consider consist of two given premises and a conclusion. These statements can be arranged as shown below.

  Given Premises: Statement 1
         <u>Statement 2</u>
  Conclusion: $\therefore$ Statement 3

The argument is valid when (Statement 1 $\wedge$ Statement 2) $\rightarrow$ Statement 3 is a tautology. In other words, the validity of an argument can be determined by finding whether the conjunction of the premises implying the conclusion is a tautology.

Problem 1

  Show that the following argument is valid.
  Given Premises: $p \rightarrow q$
         <u>p </u>
  Conclusion: $\therefore q$

Solution

We must show that the conjunction of the premises $[(p \rightarrow q) \wedge p]$ implying the conclusion (q) is a tautology. The truth table below shows that $[(p \rightarrow q) \wedge p] \rightarrow q$ is a tautology.

p	q	$p \rightarrow q$	$(p \rightarrow q) \wedge p$	$[(p \rightarrow q) \wedge p] \rightarrow q$
T	T	T	T	T
T	F	F	F	T
F	T	T	F	T
F	F	T	F	T

Problem 2

Show that the following argument is valid.

Given Premises: $p \rightarrow q$

                            ~q

Conclusion: $\therefore$ ~p

Solution

We must show that the conjunction of the premises $[(p \rightarrow q) \wedge \sim q]$ implying the conclusion (~p) is a tautology. The truth table below shows that $[(p \rightarrow q) \wedge \sim q] \rightarrow \sim p$ is a tautology.

p	q	$p \rightarrow q$	~q	$(p \rightarrow q) \wedge \sim q$	~p	$[(p \rightarrow q) \wedge \sim q] \rightarrow \sim p$
T	T	T	F	F	F	T
T	F	F	T	F	F	T
F	T	T	F	F	T	T
F	F	T	T	T	T	T

Problem Set 10

Test the validity of the following arguments by a truth table.

1. $p \lor q$
    $\underline{\sim q}$
    $\therefore p$

2. $\sim p \rightarrow \sim q$
    $\underline{q}$
    $\therefore p$

3. $\sim p \rightarrow \sim q$
    $\underline{\sim q}$
    $\therefore \sim p$

4. $\sim p \rightarrow q$
    $\underline{p}$
    $\therefore \sim q$

5. $\sim p \rightarrow q$
    $\underline{\sim q}$
    $\therefore p$

6. $\sim p \lor q$
    $\underline{p}$
    $\therefore q$

Topic 11

Structure of Certain Valid and Invalid Arguments

The forms of some arguments occur frequently. In this section the forms of five valid and five invalid arguments are presented. At the end of this section you need to be able to recognize these frequently occurring arguments by their forms. You should be able to recognize these forms if an argument is presented in English and thereby label the argument valid or invalid.

There are five patterns that always form valid arguments regardless of the simple statements we substitute in the forms for the letters p, q and r. These five patterned arguments are listed on the next page.

Valid Form 1
An argument is **valid** (non-fallacious) if it appears in the form:

    premise $p \rightarrow q$

    premise $\underline{p \quad\quad}$

    conclusion $\therefore \ q$

This is the case because $[(p \rightarrow q) \wedge p] \rightarrow q$ is a tautology.

Valid Form 2
An argument is **valid** if it appears in the form:

    premise $p \rightarrow q$

    premise $\underline{\sim q \quad\quad}$

    conclusion $\therefore \ \sim p$

This is the case because $[(p \rightarrow q) \wedge \sim q] \rightarrow \sim p$ is a tautology.

Valid Form 3
An argument is **valid** if it appears in the form:

    premise $p \vee q$

    premise $\underline{\sim p \quad\quad}$

    conclusion $\therefore \ q$

This is the case because $[(p \vee q) \wedge \sim p] \rightarrow q$ is a tautology.

Valid Form 4
An argument is **valid** if it appears in the form:

    premise $p \vee q$

    premise $\underline{\sim q \quad\quad}$

    conclusion $\therefore \ p$

This is the case because $[(p \vee q) \wedge \sim q] \rightarrow p$ is a tautology.

Valid Form 5
An argument is **valid** if it appears in the form:

    premise $p \rightarrow q$

    premise $\underline{q \rightarrow r}$

    conclusion $\therefore \ p \rightarrow r$

                       $\therefore \sim r \rightarrow \sim p$

This is because $[(p \rightarrow q) \wedge (q \rightarrow r)] \rightarrow (p \rightarrow r)$ is a tautology. In addition, $[(p \rightarrow q) \wedge (q \rightarrow r)] \rightarrow (\sim r \rightarrow \sim p)$ is also a tautology.

Problem 1

Refer to the list of Valid Argument Forms and determine if the following argument fits one of these forms:

> If a land use plan is not put into operation, then the reef at Pennekamp State Park is in danger of extinction. In 1987 the reef at Pennekamp State Park was not in danger of extinction. Consequently, in 1987 a land use plan was put into operation.

Solution

Assign letters p and q to the simple statements.

Let p represent: A land use plan is not put into operation.

Let q represent: The reef at Pennekamp State Park is in danger of extinction.

The argument can now be translated symbolically.

$$p \rightarrow q$$
$$\frac{\sim q}{\therefore \sim p}$$

The argument is **valid** by the second of the valid argument forms. Notice the similarity of this form to the fact that an implication is equivalent to its contrapositive.

Problem 2

Is the following argument valid?

> Jack is studying or listening to music. Jack isn't studying.
> Thus, he is listening to music.

Solution

Since validity is determined by the form of an argument, assign letters to the simple statements.

Let p represent: Jack is studying.

Let q represent: Jack is listening to music.

Translate the argument symbolically.

$$p \vee q$$
$$\frac{\sim p}{\therefore q}$$

This argument is **valid** by the third of the valid argument forms. Notice that this form presents us with two possibilities (p or q) and then negates one of the possibilities (not p). This forces us to accept the truth of the second possibility (q).

Problem 3

Is the following argument valid?
    If one studies, one succeeds. If one succeeds, one finds creative work.
    Consequently, if one did not find creative work, then one did not study.

Solution

Let p represent: One studies.
Let q represent: One succeeds.
Let r represent: One finds creative work.

The argument takes on the following form:

$$p \rightarrow q$$
$$\underline{q \rightarrow r}$$
$$\therefore \sim r \rightarrow \sim p$$

This argument is **valid** by the last of the valid argument forms. Observe that if p implies q and q implies r, then p implies r (p → r). Since p → r forms a valid conclusion, its equivalent contrapositive (~r → ~p) must also form a valid conclusion.

There are five commonly misused arguments that are invalid. They follow.

Invalid Form 1 (The Fallacy of the Inverse)
An argument is **invalid** (fallacious) if it appears in the form:
    premise $p \rightarrow q$
    premise $\underline{\sim p}$
    conclusion $\therefore \sim q$
This is the case because [(p → q)∧ ~p] → ~q is not a tautology.

85

Invalid Form 2 (The Fallacy of the Converse)
An argument is **invalid** (fallacious) if it appears in the form:

premise	$p \rightarrow q$
premise	q
conclusion	$\therefore$ p

This is the case because $[(p \rightarrow q) \wedge q] \rightarrow p$ is not a tautology.

Invalid Form 3
An argument is **invalid** if it appears in the form:

premise	$p \vee q$
premise	p
conclusion	$\therefore$ $\sim q$

This is the case because $[(p \vee q) \wedge p] \rightarrow \sim q$ is not a tautology.

Invalid Form 4
An argument is **invalid** if it appears in the form:

premise	$p \vee q$
premise	q
conclusion	$\therefore$ $\sim p$

This is the case because $[(p \vee q) \wedge q] \rightarrow \sim p$ is not a tautology.

Invalid Form 5
An argument is invalid if it appears in the form:

premise	$p \rightarrow q$
premise	$q \rightarrow r$
conclusion	$\therefore r \rightarrow p$
	$\therefore \sim p \rightarrow \sim r$

This is the case because neither $[(p \rightarrow q) \wedge (q \rightarrow r)] \rightarrow (r \rightarrow p)$ nor $[(p \rightarrow q) \wedge (q \rightarrow r)] \rightarrow (\sim p \rightarrow \sim r)$ are tautologies.

Problem 4

Show that the following argument is invalid.
If a number is divisible by 14, then it is divisible by 7.
28 is divisible by 7. Consequently, 28 is divisible by 14.

Solution

Let p represent: A number is divisible by 14.
Let q represent: A number is divisible by 7.
The form of the argument is:

$$p \rightarrow q$$
$$\underline{q \qquad}$$
$$\therefore p$$

This is the invalid form called the fallacy of the converse and should remind
you that an implication is not equivalent to its converse. Observe that the
conclusion of the argument, 28 is divisible by 14, is true as an isolated statement, although the form of the argument is invalid. The conclusion does not
necessarily follow from the premises. This can be seen if we change the
argument's content, but retain the same form.

If a number is divisible by 14, it is divisible by 7.
21 is divisible by 7. Consequently, 21 is divisible by 14.

Problem 5

Show that the following argument is invalid.
Naomi is American or Israeli. She is American. Therefore, she is not Israeli.

Solution

Let p represent: Naomi is American.
Let q represent: Naomi is Israeli.
The form of the argument is:

$$p \vee q$$
$$\underline{p \qquad}$$
$$\therefore \sim q$$

This is the third of the invalid arguments appearing in the list of invalid
argument forms. Since we use "or" in the inclusive sense, Naomi can be both
American and Israeli. Just because she is American does not exclude the
possibility that Naomi is Israeli. More formally, we can show that this argument is invalid by showing that $[(p \vee q) \wedge p] \rightarrow \sim q$ is not a tautology.

Problem Set 11

1. Translate each argument listed below into its symbolic form. Then select the one argument in the list that is fallacious.
    a. Mathematics is boring or difficult. Mathematics certainly isn't boring. Consequently, mathematics must be difficult.
    b. If a number is divisible by 14, then it is divisible by 7. 28 is divisible by 14. Thus, 28 is divisible by 7.
    c. If one takes calculus, then one is intelligent. Rochelle is intelligent. Consequently, Rochelle is taking calculus.
    d. If one is Socrates, then one is human. If one is human, then one is mortal. Therefore, if one is Socrates, then one is mortal.

2. Translate each argument listed below into its symbolic form. Then select the one argument in the list that is fallacious.
    a. Mathematics is boring or difficult. Mathematics is difficult. Thus, mathematics is not boring.
    b. If a number is divisible by 14, then it is divisible by 7. 25 is not divisible by 7. As a result, 25 is not divisible by 14.
    c. If one takes calculus, then one is intelligent. Rochelle is taking calculus. Therefore, Rochelle is intelligent.
    d. If one is Socrates, then one is human. If one is human, then one is mortal. Therefore, if one is not mortal, then one is not Socrates.

3. All four of the following arguments have true conclusions when the conclusions are considered as isolated statements. However, not every argument in the list is valid.

Select the invalid argument.
    a. If a metrorail system is not in operation in Miami, there are enormous traffic delays. On March 1, 1964, a metrorail system was not in operation in Miami. Thus on March 1, 1964, enormous traffic delays occurred in Miami.
    b. If a metrorail system is not in operation in Miami, there are enormous traffic delays. On November 26, 1984, there was a metrorail system in operation in Miami. Therefore on November 26, 1984, there were no enormous traffic delays in Miami.
    c. If a number is divisible by 100, then it is divisible by 10. Since 300 is divisible by 100, we can conclude that 300 is divisible by 10.
    d. If a number is divisible by 100, then it is divisible by 10. 25 is not divisible by 10. Thus, 25 is not divisible by 100.

4. All of the following arguments have true conclusions, but not all of the arguments are valid. Which argument illustrates the fact that an argument may not be valid even though the conclusion is true?
    a. If a number is divisible by 40, then it is divisible by 20. 80 is divisible by 40. Thus, 80 is divisible by 20.
    b. If a number is divisible by 40, then it is divisible by 20. 75 is not divisible by 20. Therefore, 75 is not divisible by 40.
    c. All animals breathe and all dogs are animals. Consequently all dogs breathe. (Hint: When premises contain "all," "some," or "no," use set diagrams to determine validity.)

d. If a number is divisible by 40, then it is divisible by 20. 80 is divisible by 20. Thus, 80 is divisible by 40.

5. Which one of the following is fallacious?

a. Mathematics is applied or theoretical. Statistics for psychology is not a theoretical mathematics course. Thus, statistics for psychology is an applied mathematics course.

b. If you are playing the stereo, I can't hear you. I can hear you quite clearly. Therefore, you are not playing the stereo.

c. If the figure is a square, it's a quadrilateral. If it's a quadrilateral, it's a polygon. Thus, if the figure is a polygon, it's a square.

d. If it snows, at least one road remains open. It snowed on Monday. Thus, at least one road remained open on Monday.

6. Select the invalid argument.

a. If you are sexy, you have more fun. If you have more fun, you get into trouble. Therefore, if you do not get into trouble, you are not sexy.

b. If Englebert is an adolescent, he has pimples. Englebert is an adolescent. Therefore, Englebert has pimples.

c. If logic makes one sick, one is weird. Schmendrick is weird. Thus, logic makes Schmendrick sick.

d. One's throat is tense when one does not tell the truth. (If one does not tell the truth, then one's throat is tense.) At this moment Muamar is not suffering from a tense throat. Therefore, at this moment Muamar is telling the truth.

7. Use set diagrams when premises contain "all," "some," and "no," and forms of arguments when premises contain "if ... then" and "or" to select the one invalid argument in the following list.

a. All birds have feathers and all parakeets have feathers. Consequently, all parakeets are birds.

b. No people who assign work are lovable. All teachers assign work. Thus, no lovable people are teachers.

c. Oedipus didn't have a fatal flaw or he was banished. Oedipus had a fatal flaw. Therefore, Oedipus was banished.

d. If the function is differentiable, then it is continuous. This function is not continuous at point A. Thus, this function is not differentiable at point A.

8. Which argument listed below is invalid?

a. All insects have wings and no eagles have wings. Consequently, eagles are not insects.

b. Don is an artistic genius or he is afflicted with the psychopathology of schizophrenia. Don is certainly an artistic genius. Therefore, he is not afflicted with the psychopathology of schizophrenia.

c. All birds have feathers and all parakeets are birds. Consequently, all parakeets have feathers.

d. If one takes vitamins or exercises, one will be healthy. Juana is not healthy. Thus, Juana does not take vitamins and does not exercise.

9. Which one of the following is not valid?

   a. If the function is differentiable, then it is continuous. This function is differentiable at point A, so this function must be continuous at point A.

   b. If two lines are parallel, they have no point in common. These lines have a point in common, so these lines are not parallel.

   c. He's a scoundrel or a fool, and he's not a fool, so he must be a scoundrel.

   d. No mules have wings. I know this because all insects have wings and no mules are insects.

10. Which one of the following is not valid?

   a. If a person earns an A in calculus, then that person does not miss more than two classroom lectures. Jacques, a calculus student, missed five classroom lectures. Thus, Jacques did not earn an A in calculus.

   b. Maggie does not have a good time when she listens to sexist humor. At this moment Maggie is listening to a comedian whose material is sexist and racist throughout. Consequently, at this moment Maggie is not having a good time.

   c. A majority of teachers must vote in favor of a textbook or the book will not be adopted. Over 60% of the teachers did not vote in favor of *Tropic of Calculus*. Therefore, *Tropic of Calculus* was not adopted.

   d. If one is to answer the question correctly, then the first step is to find the length of the hypotenuse. Harry did not answer the question correctly. Therefore, Harry did not find the length of the hypotenuse.

Topic 12

Using Forms of Valid Arguments to Draw Logical Conclusions

In the introduction to this chapter we stated that one must be able to avoid arriving at conclusions hastily without considering all the evidence. One means of drawing conclusions that are warranted is through the use of the valid forms of arguments, as illustrated in the problems that follow. At the end of this section you should be able to use forms of valid arguments to deduce logical conclusions.

Problem 1

Draw a conclusion that will make the following argument valid.
If all people take exams honestly, then no supervision is needed.
Some supervision is needed.

Solution

Let p be: *All people take exams honestly.*
Let q be: *No supervision is needed.*
The form of the argument is:
$p \rightarrow q$ If all people take exams honestly, then no supervision is needed.
~q___ Some supervision is needed. (Recall that the negation of "no" is "some.")
∴~p

The conclusion ~p makes the argument valid. Since the negation of "all" is "some...not," we can conclude that:
Some people do not take exams honestly.

Problem 2

If one studies mathematics, then one will be logical. If one studies English, then one will have an excellent vocabulary. Judy studies mathematics and not English. Thus,

a.   Judy will be logical but not have an excellent vocabulary.
b.   Judy will be logical.
c.   Judy will not have an excellent vocabulary.
d.   None of the above is warranted.

Solution

Use letters to represent the simple statements.
Let p represent: *One studies mathematics.*
Let q represent: *One will be logical.*
Let r represent: *One studies English.*
Let s represent: *One will have an excellent vocabulary.*

We now arrange the premises to form two separate arguments.

$p \rightarrow q$ (If one studies mathematics, one will be logical.) $r \rightarrow s$ (If one studies English, one will have an excellent vocabulary.)

p (Judy studies mathematics.)   ~r (Judy does not study English.)

In the first argument a valid conclusion is q since

$$p \rightarrow q$$
$$\underline{p \quad\quad\quad}$$
$$\therefore q$$

is a valid form. Thus, Judy will be logical.

In the second argument ~s is not a valid conclusion since

$$r \rightarrow s$$
$$\underline{\sim r \quad\quad\quad}$$
$$\therefore \sim s$$

is not a valid form. We cannot validly conclude that Judy will not have an excellent vocabulary. The valid conclusion, then, corresponds to choice b. (Judy will be logical.)

Problem 3

We will go to the beach or we will go to the movies. We will not go to the movies. If it snows, we will not go to the beach. What can we logically (validly) deduce from these premises?

Solution

Use letters to represent the simple statements.
Let p represent: *We will go to the beach.*
Let q represent: *We will go to the movies.*
Let r represent: *It snows.*
By the first two premises, we have:

$p \lor q$ (We will go to the beach or the movies.)
~q~~   (We will not go to the movies.)

A valid conclusion is p, we will go to the beach.

By the last premise, we have $r \rightarrow$ ~p.   (If it snows, we will not go to the beach.)
We now combine this last premise with the valid conclusion p.
We now have:

$r \rightarrow$ ~p   (If it snows, we will not go to the beach.)
p _____   (We will go to the beach.)

A valid conclusion is ~r. We can deduce: It is not snowing.

Since we have two true conclusions, we can conclude:
We will go to the beach *and* it is not snowing.

Problem 4

Draw a conclusion that will make the following argument valid.
*If Sarah and Tim play, the team wins. The team lost on Tuesday
and Tim played.*

Solution

You may be able to immediately conclude that Sarah did not play. After all,
had she played, the team would have won and we are told that the team lost.
The conclusion (Sarah did not play) can also be shown to be valid using valid
forms.

Let p be: Sarah plays.
Let q be: Tim plays.
Let r be: The team wins.
We now translate from English into symbolic language.

$(p \land q) \to r$ (If Sarah and Tim play, the team wins.)

$\underline{\sim r }$ (The team lost on Tuesday.)

$\therefore \sim(p \land q)$ (It is not true that both Sarah and Tim played.)

Notice that the valid form that we
used could be thought of as:

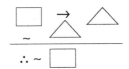

Our conclusion, ~(p ∧ q), can be rewritten by one of **De Morgan's Laws**. ~(p ∧ q)
is equivalent to ~p ∨ ~q (Sarah did not play or Tim did not play.) We still have not
incorporated the fact that Tim did play (q). Writing this underneath ~p ∨ ~q, we
obtain:

$$\sim p \lor \sim q$$
$$\underline{q}$$

Although it might not be obvious that this will lead to a valid conclusion, it will
become more evident if we think of ~p as ☐ and ~q as △ . The form of our
argument is:

The conclusion that we have boxed, namely ~p, forms a valid argument. The valid
conclusion (~p) translates as: *Sarah did not play.*

Problem Set 12

Draw a conclusion that will make each of the following arguments valid.

1. If all people obey rules, then no prisons are needed. Some prisons are needed.

2. If no people smoke cigarettes, then all people save money on health insurance. Some people do not save money on health insurance.

3. If one studies mathematics, then one will be logical. If one studies English, then one will have an excellent vocabulary. Joel is not logical. Joel does not study English.

4. If a person has a knowledge of music, then that person enjoys Mozart. If a person has a knowledge of theater, then that person enjoys Sondheim. Kathy enjoys Mozart and Kathy does not enjoy Sondheim.

5. If a person studies mathematics, then that person is logical. If a person studies English, then that person appreciates language. Angie studies English but not mathematics.

6. If it snows, we read or watch television. It snowed on Friday. We did not read on Friday.

7. It is not true that both Carmen and Marco study biology. Carmen does study biology.

8. If Susan studies and attends lecture, then she does well. Susan is not doing well and she is attending lecture.

9. If a student attends all lectures and does some homework problems, then that student passes the course. Fran failed the course and attended all lectures.

10. If it is Tuesday, then Javier has his philosophy course. When Javier has philosophy, he contemplates the meaning of existence.

11. If the medication is effective, then I will not miss class. If I do not miss class, then I will not fall behind.

12. Living in Florida is a necessary condition for living in Tampa. One lives in North America if one lives in Florida.

Draw two conclusions that will make each of the following arguments valid.

13. If a political system does not embody justice, then that system has no peace and that system must spend a great deal of money building jails. South Africa is a political system that does not embody justice.

14. If a person has good eye-hand coordination, then that person can hit and throw a ball. An outstanding baseball player has good eye-hand coordination.

15. If it rains or snows, then Pierre reads. Pierre did not read on Friday.

16. If a person studies mathematics, then that person is logical. If a person studies English, then that person appreciates language. Samir is not logical, but he did study English.

17. We will study or watch television. We will not study. If we pass the exam, we will not watch television.

Logic in Everyday Life

We have seen that valid forms of arguments and Euler circles are useful in arriving at conclusions that are warranted because the conclusions result in valid arguments. However, it is also possible to use more informal methods of reasoning to draw logical conclusions. Some of these methods are presented in the following problems. At the end of this section you should be able to use informal reasoning to deduce logical conclusions.

Problem 1

i.   *Any student who gets an F on a final exam does not pass the course.*
ii. *Receiving a grade of A, B, C, or D on a final exam is no guarantee of passing the course.*
iii. *On a final exam, 13 students scored A, 12 scored B, 20 scored C, 5 scored D, and 2 scored F.*

What can we conclude in this situation?
a.   Two or more students did not pass the course.
b.   Exactly two students did not pass the course.
c.   At most two students did not pass the course.
d.   None of the above can logically be concluded.

Solution

Since two students scored F, we know that by the first premise they did not pass the course. However, by the second premise, we are told that the other 50 students who scored A, B, C, or D on the final might not have passed the course. We can conclude that two or more students did not pass the course, option a.

Problem 2

Read the requirements and each applicant's qualifications for obtaining a $50,000 loan. Then identify which of the applicants would qualify for the loan.

To qualify for a loan of $50,000, an applicant must have a good credit rating and have an income of at least $35,000 if single or a combined income of more than $60,000 if married.

Evita Sanchez is single, earns $90,000, and has a bad credit rating.

Rudy Valentino is single, has a good credit rating, and works at two jobs. He makes $20,000 on one job and 50% of $20,000 on the second job.

Tom Mix is married, has a good credit rating, and earns $40,000. His wife earns $20,000.

a. Evita   b. Rudy   c. Tom   d. None of these

Solution

Evita Sanchez is not eligible for the loan because of her bad credit rating.

Rudy Valentino has good credit and earns $20,000 + (0.50)($20,000) = $20,000 + $10,000 = $30,000. Since he is single and does not have an income of at least $35,000, he does not qualify for the loan.

The Mix family brings in $60,000 a year. They do not qualify because they must earn more than $60,000.

None of these people is qualified for the loan, making the correct answer option d.

Problem 3

Marilyn, Bob, and Tony each have two different occupations which are also different from one another's. Their occupations are writer, architect, teacher, doctor, lawyer, and artist. Each character in the following premises is a distinct person.

1. The teacher and writer went skiing with Marilyn.
2. The doctor hired the artist to paint a landscape.
3. The doctor met with the teacher.
4. The artist is related to the architect.
5. Tony beat both Bob and the artist at tennis.
6. Bob lives next door to the writer.

Use the given statements to find each person's occupations.

Solution

Premise 5 tells us that Marilyn must be an artist.

Using premises 1, 4, and 2, we can conclude that Marilyn is not a teacher, writer, architect, or doctor. Thus, Marilyn is a lawyer.

Premise 6 tells us that Bob is not a writer. Therefore, he can be a teacher, architect, or doctor. From premise 3 we conclude that the doctor and the teacher are not the same person. This means that Bob must be an architect.

At this point, Bob is also either a teacher or a doctor, but not both. If Bob were a doctor, then Tony would be a teacher and a writer, which premise 1 indicates is not possible, since the teacher and writer are different people. Thus, Bob's other job is a teacher.

> Marilyn - artist and lawyer
> Bob - architect and teacher
> Tony - (the two remaining occupations) - doctor and writer

Problem Set 13

1. i. *Any student who gets lower than C on a final exam does not pass the course.*

   ii. *Receiving a grade of A, B, or C on a final exam is no guarantee of passing the course.*

   iii. *On a final exam, 5 students scored A, 5 scored B, 5 scored C, 5 scored D, and 5 scored F.*

   What can we logically conclude in this situation?

   a. Exactly 10 students did not pass the course.

   b. At most 10 students did not pass the course.

   c. 10 or more students did not pass the course.

   d. None of the above can logically be concluded.

2. In order to rent an apartment at Kendall Estates, one must pay the rent for the first and last month in advance, in addition to making a deposit for possible damages equal to 50% of the monthly rent. Kendall Estates charges $400 per month for a studio apartment and $550 per month for a one-bedroom apartment. Lena and Saul saved $1,350 to move into Kendall Estates. Which statement following can be correctly concluded?

   a. They did not save enough money to rent either apartment.

   b. They saved enough money to rent the studio and the one bedroom apartment.

   c. They saved enough money to rent the studio apartment and still have one additional month's rent. ·

   d. They saved enough money to rent the studio apartment and be precisely $50 short of paying an additional month's rent.

3. In order to get a loan, one must have a good credit rating and be single making at least $18,000 per year or be married with a combined salary of at least $35,000 per year.

   Tim is single and earns $90,000 per year. He has a bad credit rating.

   Ethel and Lee Fisher, a married couple, have a good credit rating. Ethel earns $20,000 per year and Lee earns $14,900 per year.

   Bob and Jane Hope, brother and sister (both unmarried), have good credit ratings. Jane earns $20,000 per year and Bob makes $17,000 per year.

   a. Tim is eligible for the loan.

   b. The Fishers are eligible for the loan.

   c. Bob is eligible for the loan.

   d. Jane is eligible for the loan.

4. (This logic problem dates back to eighth century writing.) A farmer needs to take his goat, wolf, and cabbage across a stream. His boat can hold him and one other passenger (the goat, wolf, or cabbage). If he takes the wolf with him, the goat will eat the cabbage. If he takes the cabbage, the wolf will eat the goat. Only when the farmer is present are the cabbage and goat safe from their respective predators. How does the farmer get everything across the stream?

5. As shown in the accompanying diagram, men (1), (2), and (3) are placed in a line, blindfolded, facing a wall. Three hats are then taken from a container of three tan hats and two black hats. The men are given that information, and the blindfolds are then removed. Each man, still in the same position, is asked to determine what color hat he is wearing. Man (3) responds, "I do not know what color hat I am wearing." Man (2), hearing the response and seeing the man and hat ahead of him, responds, "I do not know what color hat I am wearing." Man (1), seeing only the wall and hearing the two replies, says, "I know what color hat I am wearing." Which color is he wearing and how did he logically determine the color?

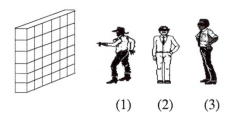

(1)   (2)   (3)

6. Observe the following series of letters. Then determine the logical way in which the missing letters have been removed.

A B D E F I J K L P Q R S T Y Z A B C D J K L M N O P

7. All but one of these three-digit numbers share a common feature. Which number does not logically belong in the list?

495   583   374   276   891
165   363   396

8. John, Jack, Joan, and Jane have occupations that consist of art critic, architect, acrobat, and aviator, but not necessarily in that order. Each person has one occupation and all people have different occupations. Joan has never heard of "perspective," and has no idea of who Pablo Picasso is. The aviator, who is happily married, earns more than his sister, the art critic. John is not married. Who can you conclude is the architect?

Chapter 1 Summary

1. Set Operations

a. The **complement** of set A (A') is the set of elements that are not in set A, but still in set U.

b. A **intersection** B (A ∩ B) is a set consisting of elements that are in both set A **and** set B.

c. A **union** B (A ∪ B) is a set consisting of elements in set A **or** set B or in both set A and set B.

Sets can be defined by listing their elements, describing their elements in words, or using set-builder notation. Visual relationships among sets are shown using Venn diagrams.

2. Basic Definitions of Logic

Negation	p	~p
	T	F
	F	T

		<u>Conjunction</u>	<u>Disjunction</u>	<u>Implication</u>	<u>Biconditional</u>
p	q	p ∧ q	p ∨ q	p → q	p ↔ q
T	T	T	T	T	T
T	F	F	T	F	F
F	T	F	T	T	F
F	F	F	F	T	T
		True only when both components are true.	True when at least one component is true.	False only with a true hypothesis and a false conclusion.	True when both components have the same truth value.

3. Equivalences and Nonequivalences

Equivalences for $p \rightarrow q$
a. $(p \rightarrow q) \equiv (\sim q \rightarrow \sim p)$, $\sim q \rightarrow \sim p$ is the contrapositive.
b. $(p \rightarrow q) \equiv (\sim p \lor q)$

Nonequivalences for $p \rightarrow q$
c. $(p \rightarrow q)$ is not equivalent to $(q \rightarrow p)$, the converse.
d. $(p \rightarrow q)$ is not equivalent to $(\sim p \rightarrow \sim q)$, the inverse.

Equivalences for $p \lor q$
e. $(p \lor q) \equiv (\sim p \rightarrow q)$
f. $(p \lor q) \equiv (\sim q \rightarrow p)$

Nonequivalences for $p \lor q$
g. $(p \lor q)$ is not equivalent to $(p \rightarrow \sim q)$.
h. $(p \lor q)$ is not equivalent to $(q \rightarrow \sim p)$.

Equivalences for $\sim(p \land q)$
i. $\sim(p \land q) \equiv (\sim p \lor \sim q)$
j. $\sim(p \land q) \equiv (p \rightarrow \sim q)$

Nonequivalences for $\sim(p \land q)$
k. $\sim(p \land q)$ is not equivalent to $(\sim p \land \sim q)$.
l. $\sim(p \land q)$ is not equivalent to $(p \land q)$.

Equivalences for Writing Negations
m. $\sim(p \land q) \equiv \sim p \lor \sim q$
n. $\sim(p \lor q) \equiv \sim p \land \sim q$
o. $\sim(p \rightarrow q) \equiv p \land \sim q$
p. $\sim(p \land q) \equiv p \rightarrow \sim q$

4. Negations For "All," "Some," and "No"

Statement	Negation
All. . .	Some. . . not
Some. . . not	All. . .
Some. . .	No. . .
No. . .	Some. . .

All . . .   No . . .

Negation

Some . . .   Some . . . not

5. English Equivalences

Statement	Equivalent(s)
All A are B.	There are no A that are not B.
Some A are not B.	Not all A are B.
Some A are B.	At least one A is a B.
No A are B.	All A are not B.
If p, then q	p implies q; p only if q; only if q, p; p is sufficient for q; q is necessary for p; not p unless q.
p if and only if q	p implies q and q implies p; p is equivalent to q; p is necessary and sufficient for q; q is necessary and sufficient for p.

6. Determining Whether or Not an Argument is Valid

a. If premises contain "if. . . then" or "or," use:

Valid Forms

$p \rightarrow q$ $p \rightarrow q$ $p \rightarrow q$ $p \vee q$ $p \vee q$
$\underline{p}$ $\underline{\sim q}$ $\underline{q \rightarrow r}$ $\underline{\sim p}$ $\underline{\sim q}$
$\therefore q$ $\therefore \sim p$ $\therefore p \rightarrow r$ $\therefore q$ $\therefore p$
                 $\therefore \sim r \rightarrow \sim p$

Invalid Forms

$p \rightarrow q$ $p \rightarrow q$ $p \vee q$ $p \vee q$
$\underline{q}$ $\underline{\sim p}$ $\underline{p}$ $\underline{q}$
$\therefore p$ $\therefore \sim q$ $\therefore \sim q$ $\therefore \sim p$

b. If premises contain "all," "some," or "no," use Euler circles:

    All A are B   Some A are B   No A are B

 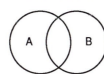 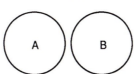

Sample Examination – Sets and Logic

1. Select the negation of: *The lawn must be fertilized monthly or it will not be green.*
    a. The lawn is not fertilized monthly or it is green.
    b. The lawn is not fertilized monthly and it is not green.
    c. The lawn is not fertilized monthly and it is green.
    d. If the lawn is not fertilized monthly, then it is green.

2. Select the negation of: *It is hot and it is not humid.*
    a. It is not hot and it is humid.
    b. It is not hot or it is humid.
    c. It is not hot and it is not humid.
    d. It is not hot or it is not humid.

3. Select the statement which is logically equivalent to: *It is not true that both the Rolling Stones and Pat Boone are rock groups.*
    a. The Rolling Stones are not a rock group and Pat Boone is not a rock group.
    b. The Rolling Stones are a rock group or Pat Boone is a rock group.
    c. If the Rolling Stones are not a rock group, then Pat Boone is not a rock group.
    d. If the Rolling Stones are a rock group, then Pat Boone is not a rock group.

4. Select the negation of: *Some people do not have good manners.*
    a. Some people have good manners.
    b. No people have good manners.
    c. All people have good manners.
    d. All people do not have good manners.

5. Select the negation of: *If one works hard, then one will be successful.*
    a. One does not work hard and one will not be successful.
    b. One works hard or one will not be successful.
    c. One works hard and one will not be successful.
    d. One works hard and one will be successful.

6. Select the statement that negates: *Terry plans to both do her homework and listen to the radio.*
    a. If Terry does not plan to do her homework, then she plans to listen to the radio.
    b. If Terry plans to do her homework, then she does not plan to listen to the radio.
    c. If Terry does not plan to do her homework, then she does not plan to listen to the radio.
    d. If Terry plans to do her homework, then she plans to listen to the radio.

7. Select the statement which is not logically equivalent to: *It is not true that both <u>Married with Children</u> and <u>Moby Dick</u> are television shows.*
    a. *Married with Children* is not a television show or *Moby Dick* is not a television show.
    b. If *Married with Children* is a television show, then *Moby Dick* is not a television show.
    c. It is not true that both *Moby Dick* and *Married with Children* are television shows.
    d. *Married with Children* is a television show and *Moby Dick* is a television show.

8. Select the statement which is logically equivalent to: *All politicians are corrupt.*
   a. There are no corrupt people who are politicians.
   b. There are no politicians who are not corrupt.
   c. There are some politicians who are not corrupt.
   d. There are no corrupt people who are not politicians.

9. Select the statement which is logically equivalent to: *If the play is <u>Macbeth</u>, Shakespeare is the author.*
   a. If Shakespeare is the author, the play is *Macbeth*.
   b. If Shakespeare is not the author, the play is not *Macbeth*.
   c. If the play is not *Macbeth*, Shakespeare is not the author.
   d. The play is *Macbeth* and Shakespeare is not the author.

10. Select the statement which is not logically equivalent to: *If Jones is in Boston, then he is in the East.*
    a. If Jones is not in the East, then he is not in Boston.
    b. Jones is not in Boston unless he is in the East.
    c. Jones is in the East when he is in Boston.
    d. If Jones is in the East, then he is in Boston.

11. Select the statement that is not logically equivalent to: *Anita is a chemist or owns a business.*
    a. If Anita is not a chemist, she owns a business.
    b. If Anita does not own a business, she is a chemist.
    c. If Anita is a chemist, she does not own a business.
    d. It is false that Anita is not a chemist and does not own a business.

12. Given that:
    i. *All biologists are scientists.*
    ii. *All chemists are scientists.*
    iii. *All scientists have college degrees.*
    iv. *Ray has a college degree.*
    Determine which of the following conclusions can be logically deduced.
    a. Some biologists are chemists.
    b. No biologists are chemists.
    c. Ray is either a biologist or a chemist.
    d. Some biologists do not have college degrees.
    e. People without college degrees are neither biologists nor chemists.

13. All of the following arguments have true conclusions, but one of the arguments is not valid. Select the argument that is not valid.
    a. Prolonged periods of cold will damage trees that are native to the Florida Keys. The gumbo limbo is a native Florida Keys' tree. Therefore, prolonged periods of cold will damage the gumbo limbo.
    b. All insects have wings and no mules have wings. Therefore, mules are not insects.
    c. All people who do well in solid geometry must sketch three-dimensional figures on two-dimensional surfaces. The ability to sketch three-dimensional figures on a two-dimensional surface necessitates good spatial relationships. Therefore, doing well in solid geometry necessitates good spatial relationships.
    d. Trees are plants. Palms are plants. Therefore, palms are trees.

14. Which one of the following is not valid?
    a. If I purchase season tickets to the football games, then I will not attend all lectures. If I do not attend all lectures, then I will not do well in school. Therefore, if I purchase season tickets to the football games, then I will not do well in school.
    b. If both the microphone and the air conditioning fail, the workshop will not be held. This Saturday the workshop was held although the air conditioning did fail. Therefore, this Saturday the microphone did not fail.
    c. No democracies are totalitarian. All dictatorships are totalitarian. Stalin's Russia was a dictatorship. Thus, Stalin's Russia was not a democracy.
    d. Miguel is blushing or he is sunburned. Miguel is definitely sunburned. Therefore, Miguel is not blushing.

15. Which one of the following is not valid?
    a. If one is a good baseball player, then one must have good eye-hand coordination. Todd does not have good eye-hand coordination. Therefore, Todd is not a good baseball player.
    b. If a parrot talks, it is intelligent. This parrot is intelligent. Therefore, this parrot talks.
    c. If one applies oneself, then one does not fall behind. Ana applies herself. Therefore, Ana does not fall behind.
    d. A majority of legislators must vote for a bill or that bill will not become law. A majority of legislators did not vote for legislation X. Therefore, legislation X did not become law.

16. Select the conclusion that will make the following argument valid. *If all people follow rules, then no criminal judges are needed. Some criminal judges are needed.*
    a. Some people follow rules.
    b. If no criminal judges are needed, then all people follow rules.
    c. No people follow rules.
    d. Some people do not follow rules.

17. Sets A, B, C, and U are related as shown in the set diagram. Which one of the following is true assuming none of the regions is empty?

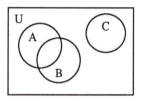

    a. Any element which is a member of set U is also a member of set A.
    b. Some elements of set A are also elements of set C.
    c. $A \cup B = \emptyset$
    d. Some elements belong to all three sets A, B, and U.

18. Select the statement that is the negation of: *If it rains, we do not go to the beach.*
    a. If it does not rain, then we go to the beach.
    b. It is raining and we do not go to the beach.
    c. If we go to the beach, then it is not raining.
    d. It rains and we go to the beach.

19. Two valid arguments are given below. Determine the symbolic form of the reasoning pattern used in both arguments.
    i.   *If you are playing the stereo softly, then I can hear you. I cannot hear you. Therefore, you are not playing the stereo softly.*
    ii. *Maggie has a good time if she plays a video game. Maggie is not having a good time. So, she is not playing a video game.*

    a. p → q   b. p → q   c. p → q   d. p → q
        ~p   q   ~q   q → r
        ∴ ~q   ∴ p   ∴ ~p   ∴ p → r

20. Select the symbolic form for each of the following arguments.
    i.   *If the Dolphins win or lose, then I will remain calm. The Dolphins win. Thus, I will remain calm.*
    ii. *If you read or watch television, you will fall asleep. You are reading. So, you will fall asleep.*

    a. (p ∧ q) → r   b. (p ∨ q) → r
        q   p
        ∴ r   ∴ r

    c. p → (q ∨ r)   d. (p ∧ q) → r
        p   p
        ∴ r   ∴ r

21. Select the symbolic form for each of the following arguments.
    i.   *If the sun shines, I go to the beach or go shopping. The sun is shining and I am not going to the beach. So, I am going shopping.*
    ii. *If I study, I get tired or frustrated. I am studying and not getting tired. Therefore, I am getting frustrated.*

    a. (r ∨ p) → q   b. r → (p ∨ q)
        r ∧ ~p   r ∧ ~p
        ∴ q   ∴ q

    c. r → (p ∨ q)   d. r → (p ∨ q)
        ~r ∧ ~p   r ∧ p
        ∴ q   ∴ q

22. Study the premises below. Select a logical conclusion if one is warranted. *No people who eat junk food as a steady diet are healthy. No substance abusers are healthy. Siham is healthy.*
    a. Some substance abusers eat junk food as a steady diet.
    b. All people who do not eat junk food as a steady diet are healthy.
    c. Siham is neither a substance abuser nor a person who eats junk food as a steady diet.
    d. None of the above is warranted.

23. Select the conclusion which will make the following argument valid. *If the Dolphins win the final game, then they are the best team in the country. If they are the best team in the country, then their supporters will be proud.*
    a. If their supporters are proud, then the Dolphins are the best team in the country.
    b. If their supporters are proud, then the Dolphins won the final game.
    c. If the Dolphins do not win the final game, then their supporters will not be proud.
    d. If their supporters are not proud, then the Dolphins did not win the final game.

24. Study the premises below. Select a conclusion that can be logically deduced if one is warranted. *All physicists are scientists. All biologists are scientists.*
    a. All physicists are biologists.
    b. Some physicists are biologists.
    c. No physicists are biologists.
    d. None of the above conclusions can be logically deduced.

25. Study the premises below. Select a conclusion if one is warranted. *All professional athletes are in good condition. Some teachers are professional athletes. Emile is a teacher.*
    a. All teachers who are professional athletes are in good condition and some teachers are in good condition.
    b. No person is a teacher, a professional athlete, and in good condition.
    c. Emile is in good condition.
    d. None of the above conclusions can be logically deduced.

26. Study the premises below. Select a logical conclusion if one is warranted.
    If both Mary and Thelma play, the team always wins. The team lost Saturday, but Thelma played Saturday.
    a. Mary played on Saturday.
    b. Mary did not play on Saturday.
    c. If Mary does not play or Thelma does not play, the team always loses.
    d. None of the above conclusions is warranted.

27. *I told Marilyn that if the river overflows, at least one of the three roads will remain open. I was wrong.*
    Select a logical conclusion if one is warranted.
    a. The river did not overflow and all three roads remained open.
    b. The river overflowed and all three roads remained open.
    c. The river overflowed and all three roads were closed.
    d. None of the above conclusions is warranted.

28. *If a person studies Latin, then that person has an excellent vocabulary. If a person studies mathematics, then that person thinks logically. Mark has an excellent vocabulary. Mark, however, did not study mathematics.*
    What can be validly deduced about Mark?
    i. *Mark studied Latin.*
    ii. *Mark does not think logically.*
    a. i only   b. ii only
    c. i and ii only
    d. None of the above statements can be validly deduced.

29. Select the rule of logical equivalence which directly (in one step) transforms statement (i) into statement (ii).
    i. *If roses are red, then violets are blue.*
    ii. *If violets are not blue, then roses are not red.*
    a. "If p, then q" is equivalent to "not p or q."
    b. "If p, then q" is equivalent to "if not q, then not p."
    c. "Not (p and q)" is equivalent to "not p or not q."
    d. "Not (not p)" is equivalent to "p."

30. Select the rule of logical equivalence which directly (in one step) transforms statement (i) into statement (ii).
    i. *If it is cold and snowing, then Bob is energetic.*
    ii. *If Bob is not energetic, then it is not cold or it is not snowing.*
    a. "If p or q, then r" is equivalent to "If not r, then not p and not q."
    b. "If p or q, then r" is equivalent to "If not r, then not p or not q."
    c. "If p and q, then r" is equivalent to "If not r, then not p and not q."
    d. "If p and q, then r" is equivalent to "If not r, then not p or not q."

31. Select the rule of logical equivalence illustrated by the following pair of equivalent statements:
    i. *If $|x| > 4$, then $x > 4$ or $x < -4$.*
    ii. *If $x \not> 4$ and $x \not< -4$, then $|x| \not> 4$.*
    a. "If p, then q or r" is equivalent to "if not q and not r, then not p."
    b. "If p, then q or r" is equivalent to "not p or q or r."
    c. The negation of "if p, then q or r" is equivalent to "p and not q and not r."
    d. None of the above

32. Any student who receives a grade of D or F on a final examination does not pass the course. On the other hand, a higher grade on the final examination is no guarantee of passing the course. This semester, final examination grades consisted of 2 As, 4 Bs, 8 Cs, 5 Ds, and 1 F. What can we logically conclude?
    a. Precisely 30% of the students did not pass the course.
    b. At most 70% of the students passed the course.

c. No more than 30% of the students failed the course.
d. None of the above conclusions is warranted.

33. To be eligible for admissions to a selective college, one must have a GPA of at least 3.85 and SAT scores of at least 650 or a GPA of at least 3.5 and SAT scores of at least 725. Isabel has a 3.9 GPA and an SAT score of 645. Eddie has a 3.52 GPA and an SAT score of 730. Mike has a 3.47 GPA and a perfect SAT score of 800. Who is eligible for admission?
    a. Isabel   b. Eddie
    c. Mike   d. None of these

34. Construct a truth table for $(p \vee \sim q) \rightarrow \sim p$ if the statements p and q occur in the following order:

p	q
T	T
T	F
F	T
F	F

Which of the following represents the final column of the truth values in the table?

a.	b.	c.	d.
F	T	F	T
F	F	F	T
T	T	F	F
T	T	T	F

35. The table at the right shows the numbers of cases for a truth table containing 1, 2, or 3 simple statements.

1 statement	2 statements	3 statements
p	p q	p q r
T	T T	T T T
F	T F	T T F
	F T	T F T
	F F	T F F
		F T T
		F T F
		F F T
		F F F

If a compound statement consists of 5 simple statements, how many cases would there be in the truth table?

   a.   15   b.   16   c.   32   d.   None of these

36. Select the rule of logical equivalence which directly (in one step) transforms statement (i) into statement (ii).
   i.   *It is not true that both George and Ira wrote music.*
   ii. *If George wrote music, then Ira did not write music.*

   a.   The negation of "p and q" is equivalent to "if p, then not q."
   b.   It is not true that both "p and q" is equivalent to "if not p, then q."
   c.   It is not true that both "p and q" is equivalent to "p and not q."
   d.   The correct equivalence rule is not given.

37. Select the statement which is logically equivalent to: *Joe grows mangos or oranges.*
   a.   If Joe grows mangos, he does not grow oranges.
   b.   If Joe grows oranges, he does not grow mangos.
   c.   If Joe does not grow mangos, he grows oranges.
   d.   Joe grows both mangos and oranges.

38. Why is the following argument valid?

$$\sim p \rightarrow r$$
$$\underline{\sim r}$$
$$\therefore \ p$$

   a.   Because $[(\sim p \rightarrow r) \vee \sim r] \rightarrow p$ is a tautology.
   b.   Because $[(\sim p \rightarrow r) \wedge \sim r] \rightarrow p$ is a tautology.
   c.   Because $[(\sim p \rightarrow r) \rightarrow \sim r] \wedge p$ is a tautology.
   d.   Because the form of every argument must be valid.

39. To move into an apartment at Euclid Estates, one must sign a one year lease, pay the first and last months' rent in advance, and pay a deposit according to the following schedule:

Apartment	Rent	Deposit
2-bedroom	$625 monthly	$500
1-bedroom	$500 monthly	$400

Harry and Leona have $1,760. What can we conclude in this situation?

a. They can rent the 1-bedroom, but not the 2-bedroom apartment.
b. They can rent the 2-bedroom apartment and have $20 left.
c. They can rent either apartment they choose.
d. They can rent the 1-bedroom apartment and have enough money left to purchase a $375 dishwasher.

40. If a person is a bigot, then that person suffers from a form of mental illness. If a person cheats on exams, then that person lacks basic ethics. Seth does not suffer from any form of mental illness. However, Seth does cheat on exams. What can be validly deduced about Seth?
    i. *Seth is not a bigot.*
    ii. *Seth lacks basic ethics.*

    a. i only
    b. ii only
    c. Both i and ii
    d. Neither i nor ii

41. If U = {0,1,2,...,9}, A = {1,3,4,8}, and B = {2,3,4,9}, then A' ∪ B is:

    a. set U
    b. set B
    c. {2,9}
    d. {0,2,3,4,5,6,7,9}

42. If U = {1,2,3,4,5}, A = {2,3,5}, and B = {1,4,5}, then (A ∩ B')' is:
    a. {1,2,3,5}
    b. {1,2,3}
    c. {1,2,3,4,5}
    d. {1,4,5}

43. Which of the following Venn diagrams represents the set (A ∪ B)'?

    a.

    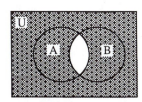

    b.

    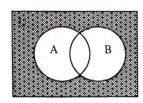

    c.

    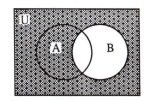

    d.

    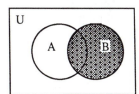

    e.

    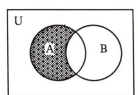

44. Sets A, B, C, and U are related as shown
    in the diagram. Which of the following
    statements is/are true assuming none of
    the regions is empty?

    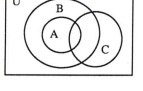

    i.   Any element of set U belongs to set C.
    ii.   An element of set A is also an element
          of set B.
    iii. Some elements of set B belong to set C.
    iv.   No element belongs to sets A, B, C, and U.

    a. i, ii and iii only   b. ii and iii only
    c. ii, iii and iv only   d. i and iv only

45. Sets A, B, C, D, and U are related as
    shown in the diagram. Which of the
    following statements is/are true assuming
    no regions are empty?

    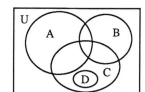

    i.   Some element belongs to all four
          sets A, B, C, and D.
    ii.   Some element of set C is also an
          element of set D.
    iii. Some element belongs to set A and set B, but not to set C.

    a. i only   b. ii only
    c. ii and iii only   d. i and iii only

Probability and Statistics

Many things in life have uncertainty associated with them. Regrettably, only taxes and death appear certain! Statements such as: "I will probably pass the math test," or "There is an 80% chance of rain today," or "The odds are 3 to 5 that the Dolphins will win the game," or "If I park in the faculty parking lot, I will most likely get a ticket," are typical instances in which the outcome is not certain. However, some confidence can be expressed that the prediction will eventually be verified.

All of us are required to make decisions based only on what is likely rather than that which is certain. In this chapter we will consider the theory of probability which enables us to study uncertainties mathematically.

The first important work in the area of probability was done by two mathematicians, Blaise Pascal and Pierre Fermat, in the seventeenth century. These men were really more interested in finding methods for winning at the gambling table than in the creation of a theory.

Probability theory plays a role in such games of chance as cards, dice, and roulette. The speculation involved in odds, expectations, and the chances of events occurring has always intrigued some people. For example, one can only speculate on the outcome of the toss of dice. It is not possible to control the outcome (if the dice are fair, that is). Probabilities have applications in everyday life also. Probabilities play a role in opinion polls, elections, quality control and genetics. Insurance companies use them to calculate life expectancy or the likelihood of automobile accidents.

Probability also plays a role in statistical studies. Because these studies use samples of the population, there is a degree of uncertainty associated with descriptions of the population.

Some people distrust statistics, believing they can be twisted to prove anything. To these people, statistics are mumbo-jumbo specifically designed to overwhelm and manipulate an unwary person. There are many abuses of statistics, but the blame should not rest with the statistical methods themselves. The problem lies with the individuals who use them. If there are indeed abuses, the reality is not that statistics lie, but that liars use statistics. It is important to detect these abuses of statistics and examine statistical results carefully before accepting them.

Of course, some people get carried away with the theory of probability. One man figured he could protect himself on a plane trip by taking a harmless bomb along with his baggage. He reasoned that the odds against any one person taking a bomb aboard were high, but the odds against two people doing it were astronomical. What do you think?

Topic 1

The Fundamental Counting Principle: Arrangements

The process of **counting** is an important part of the study of probability. In order for a probability to be calculated, it is necessary to count all the possible outcomes that can occur. In this section we will consider some ways of counting possible outcomes. At the end of this section you should be able to use the fundamental counting principle to determine the number of arrangements in a variety of situations without actually listing the arrangements.

Consider a women's track meet at Suntan University with the following four runners in the mile race: Maria, Aretha, Thelma, and Debbie. Points are to be awarded only to the women finishing first or second. In how many different ways can these four runners finish first or second? There is a need to count this number.

Observe that if Maria finishes first, then each of the other three runners could finish second. This observation might help us construct a **tree diagram** in which each of the ways that the runners can finish first or second is determined by reading along the branches of the diagram. The possible ways are shown below:

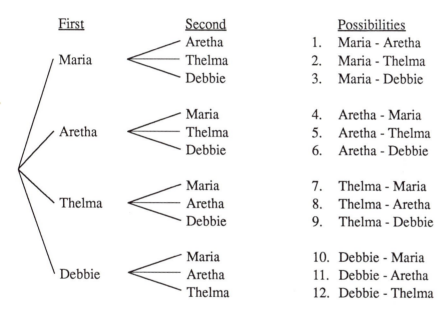

First	Second	Possibilities	
Maria	Aretha	1.	Maria - Aretha
	Thelma	2.	Maria - Thelma
	Debbie	3.	Maria - Debbie
Aretha	Maria	4.	Aretha - Maria
	Thelma	5.	Aretha - Thelma
	Debbie	6.	Aretha - Debbie
Thelma	Maria	7.	Thelma - Maria
	Aretha	8.	Thelma - Aretha
	Debbie	9.	Thelma - Debbie
Debbie	Maria	10.	Debbie - Maria
	Aretha	11.	Debbie - Aretha
	Thelma	12.	Debbie - Thelma

The tree diagram shows there are 12 possible ways (arrangements) for the runners to finish first and second in the race. Each of four runners could finish first and, for each of these possibilities, each of three runners could finish second.

Because constructing a tree diagram may be a tedious task, it is fortunate that there is a method of quickly and accurately counting the number of possibilities even in situations more complex than the example with the runners. This method is appropriately called **The Fundamental Counting Principle.**

> ## The Fundamental Counting Principle
>
> If a first task can be performed in m different ways, and a second task can be performed in n different ways, then the two tasks can be performed in that order in $m \cdot n$ different ways. If there are additional tasks, with a third task performed in p ways, a fourth task in q ways, etc., the principle can be extended as follows: $m \cdot n \cdot p \cdot q \cdot ...$

The following problems illustrate the use of **The Fundamental Counting Principle.**

Problem 1

In how many ways can first place and second place be taken in a race involving four runners?

Solution

Let m be the number of ways that the task of finishing first can be performed. Since the task of finishing first can be performed in 4 different ways, m = 4. The task of finishing second (n) can be performed in 3 different ways. Thus, n = 3. If one runner finished first, then 3 runners remain that could possibly finish second. **The Fundamental Counting Principle** says that the two numbers, 4 and 3, should be multiplied.

$$m \cdot n = 4 \cdot 3 = 12$$

There are 12 ways that the first place and second place can be taken in a race involving four runners. This result agrees with the number of possibilities obtained in the tree diagram.

Problem 2

How many arrangements of three letters can be formed from the letters of the word MATH if any letter may not be repeated? (Examples of arrangements of three letters are AMT, HMA, etc.)

Solution

This problem is an extension of **The Fundamental Counting Principle.** The task of filling the first position in this arrangement may be performed in any of four ways. This means that we can initially choose any one of the four letters — M, A, T, or H. Since we are not permitted to repeat the letters, the task of filling the second position may be performed in three ways. For example, if A had been chosen for the first position, we could now choose any one of the three remaining letters — M,T, or H for the second position. Finally, the task of filling the third position may be performed in two ways, choosing any one of the two remaining letters. To find the total number of arrangements of these letters that can be formed, we use **The Fundamental Counting Principle**.

$$4 \cdot 3 \cdot 2 = 24$$

Thus, 24 arrangements of three letters can be formed. AMT and HMA are two of these 24 arrangements.

Problem 3

A man has 2 different jackets, 5 different shirts and 3 different ties in his wardrobe. How many possible outfits can this man select to wear?

Solution

The task of selecting a jacket can be performed in two ways. The task of selecting a shirt can be performed in five different ways. The task of selecting a tie can be performed in three different ways. To find the total number of outfits this man could wear, we use **The Fundamental Counting Principle**:

$$2 \cdot 5 \cdot 3 = 30$$

Thus, the man can select 30 possible outfits.

Problem Set 1

Determine the solution of each of the following by using **The Fundamental Counting Principle.**

1. From a committee of 10 members, a chairperson, vice-chairperson and secretary are to be elected. Each person can fill only one position. In how many ways can it be done?

2. How many arrangements of 5 letters can be formed from the letters of the word LOGIC if no letter may be repeated?

3. How many arrangements of four letters may be formed using the vowels a, e, i, o, u if any letter may be repeated?

4. A person can order a new car with a choice of 6 possible colors, with or without air-conditioning, with or without automatic transmission, with or without power windows, and with or without a radio. In how many different ways can a new car be ordered in terms of these options?

5. At the Greasy Spoon Restaurant a person can order a dinner with or without salad, with or without beverage, with or without dessert, have the meat broiled rare, medium, or well done, and have the potato baked, mashed, or french fried. In how many different ways can a person order a dinner?

6. How many 7-digit telephone numbers can be formed using the decimal digits (0-9) if zero is not allowed as the first digit only, and any digit may be repeated?

7. Consider the digits 3, 6, 7, 8, 9.
   a. How many 4-digit numbers may be formed using these digits if the first digit must be 3, and any digit may be repeated?
   b. How many 3-digit numbers may be formed using these digits if the last digit must be 9, and any digit may be repeated?

8. How many student numbers can be issued at Ivy League University if each number consists of two letters of the alphabet followed by four decimal digits (0-9)? Any letter and any digit may not be repeated. (A calculator would be helpful.)

9. Consider the digits 1, 2, 3, 4, 5, 6.
   a. How many two-digit even numbers can be formed if any digit may be repeated?
   b. How many two-digit even numbers can be formed if any digit may not be repeated?

10. If a 3-digit number is formed from the digits 1, 2, 3, 4, how many arrangements give numbers that are greater than 300? No digit in an arrangement may be repeated.

11. In how many ways can 6 children be seated in 6 chairs in the front row of an auditorium?

12. In how many ways can the 5 players on a basketball team be introduced before the game?

13. There are 10 essay questions on a final examination. In how many different sequences could a student answer any three of these questions?

14. In how many ways can 4 old paintings be hung in each of 4 different places on the walls of a museum?

15. In how many ways can 5 people line up at a single stadium ticket window?

16. How many arrangements can be made using 3 of the letters of the word DOLPHIN if any letter is not repeated?

17. A team has 6 players but only 4 empty lockers in the gymnasium. In how many ways can the coach assign these lockers to the players assuming the lockers may not be used by more than one player?

18. Connie is holding 9 playing cards in her hand. If she randomly plays them one at a time, in how many ways can she play the first four cards?

Topic 2

The Fundamental Counting Principle: Combinations

This section presents a technique for finding the total number of selections of n objects taken r at a time. At the end of this section you should be able to determine the number of selections in these situations without actually listing the selections.

Let us recall again our four runners: Maria, Aretha, Thelma and Debbie. Suppose that only two of the runners are allowed to represent the college in the conference track meet. Listed below are all the possible pairs of two runners that could be selected.

1. Maria and Aretha
2. Maria and Thelma
3. Maria and Debbie
4. Aretha and Thelma
5. Aretha and Debbie
6. Thelma and Debbie

There are 6 possible groups of two that can be formed from our four runners. In other words, there are 6 subsets of size 2 that can be formed. The pair consisting of Maria and Aretha is the same pair as the one consisting of Aretha and Maria. In considering these pairs, the order in which the names appear is **not** important.

This discussion leads to the following definition.

◊ **Definition**

A **combination** is a group of n distinct objects taken r at a time, denoted by $\binom{n}{r}$, in which the order is not important.

A combination is also called a selection.

Alternate notations for a combination include $_nC_r$, C(n,r) and $C\,_r^{\,n}$.

We can now say that there are six combinations that can be formed by taking 4 runners 2 at a time.

Referring to our pair of runners in which 4 are being taken 2 at a time, n would represent 4 and r would represent 2. Thus, we could denote the combinations of 4 runners taken 2 at a time as $\binom{4}{2}$. Since there are 6 combinations that can be formed, $\binom{4}{2} = 6$.

Some situations involve a relatively small number of objects, making it possible to find the total number of combinations by making a list. However, if a situation involves a large number of objects, it is possible to use a formula containing factorials to find the total number of selections.

◊ **Definitions**

1. n! (read: n factorial) is the product of the integers from 1 to n.
   $$n! = n \cdot (n-1) \cdot (n-2) \cdot \ldots \cdot 3 \cdot 2 \cdot 1$$
2. 0! = 1

E X A M P L E S

a. $5! = 5 \cdot 4 \cdot 3 \cdot 2 \cdot 1 = 120$
b. $6! = 6 \cdot 5 \cdot 4 \cdot 3 \cdot 2 \cdot 1 = 720$

> The expression $\binom{n}{r}$ may be evaluated using the following formula.
> $$\binom{n}{r} = \frac{n!}{r!\,(n - r)!}$$

Problem 1

Evaluate $\binom{4}{2}$.

Solution

In the expression $\binom{4}{2}$, we know that n = 4, r = 2, and n − r = 4 − 2 = 2.

$$\binom{n}{r} = \frac{n!}{r!\,(n - r)!}$$

Thus, $\binom{4}{2} = \frac{4!}{2!\,(4 - 2)!} = \frac{4!}{2!\,2!} = \frac{4 \cdot 3 \cdot 2 \cdot 1}{2 \cdot 1 \cdot 2 \cdot 1} = \frac{\cancel{4} \cdot 3 \cdot \cancel{2} \cdot \cancel{1}}{\cancel{2} \cdot 1 \cdot \cancel{2} \cdot \cancel{1}} = 2 \cdot 3 = 6$$

Problem 2

Evaluate $\binom{5}{5}$.

Solution

Since n = 5 and r = 5, we obtain:

$$\binom{n}{r} = \frac{n!}{r!\,(n - r)!}$$

$$\binom{5}{5} = \frac{5!}{5!\,(5 - 5)!} = \frac{5!}{5!\,0!} = \frac{5 \cdot 4 \cdot 3 \cdot 2 \cdot 1}{5 \cdot 4 \cdot 3 \cdot 2 \cdot 1} = \frac{\cancel{5} \cdot \cancel{4} \cdot \cancel{3} \cdot \cancel{2} \cdot \cancel{1}}{\cancel{5} \cdot \cancel{4} \cdot \cancel{3} \cdot \cancel{2} \cdot \cancel{1}} = 1$$

This problem tells us that we can only obtain one combination (or selection) of a group of 5 objects if we take all 5 objects at a time.

We now see how the combination formula helps us to solve a problem.

Problem 3

Eight women try out for the basketball team. How many teams of 5 women could be formed by the coach?

Solution

Can you see that the order in the groups is not important? A team of 5 women can be tried out in any order. However, it would still be the same team. Thus, this problem deals with the combinations of 8 women taken 5 at a time. We may express this as $\binom{8}{5}$. In the expression $\binom{8}{5}$ we must recognize that n = 8, r = 5, and n − r = 8 − 5 = 3.

We can determine the answer using the formula: $\binom{n}{r} = \frac{n!}{r!\,(n\,-\,r)!}$

$$\binom{8}{5} = \frac{8!}{5!\,(8\,-\,5)!} = \frac{8!}{5!\,3!} = \frac{8 \cdot 7 \cdot 6 \cdot 5 \cdot 4 \cdot 3 \cdot 2 \cdot 1}{5 \cdot 4 \cdot 3 \cdot 2 \cdot 1 \cdot 3 \cdot 2 \cdot 1}$$

and $\frac{8 \cdot 7 \cdot 6 \cdot 5 \cdot 4 \cdot 3 \cdot 2 \cdot 1}{5 \cdot 4 \cdot 3 \cdot 2 \cdot 1 \cdot 3 \cdot 2 \cdot 1} = \frac{8 \cdot 7 \cdot \cancel{6} \cdot \cancel{5} \cdot \cancel{4} \cdot \cancel{3} \cdot \cancel{2} \cdot \cancel{1}}{\cancel{8} \cdot \cancel{4} \cdot \cancel{3} \cdot \cancel{2} \cdot \cancel{1} \cdot \cancel{3} \cdot \cancel{2} \cdot 1} = 8 \cdot 7 = 56$

The coach can form 56 possible teams of 5 women each.

In our next problem we will see that there are times in which combinations must be used along with **The Fundamental Counting Principle.**

Problem 4

A shipment of 7 fuses contains 5 good fuses and 2 defective fuses. If 3 fuses are selected at random from the shipment:

a. how many ways are there of selecting one defective fuse and two good fuses?

b. how many ways are there of selecting three good fuses?

Solution

a. Since order is not important, the number of ways of selecting 1 defective fuse is $\binom{2}{1}$ or 2. Corresponding to any one way of selecting one defective fuse, the number of ways of selecting two good fuses is $\binom{5}{2}$ or 10.

Using **The Fundamental Counting Principle** we obtain:

$$\binom{2}{1} \cdot \binom{5}{2} = 2 \cdot 10 = 20$$

Thus, the total number of ways of selecting one defective fuse and two good fuses is 20.

b. The number of ways of selecting 3 good fuses, $\binom{5}{3}$ or 10, and no defective fuses, $\binom{2}{0}$ or 1, is: $\binom{5}{3} \cdot \binom{2}{0}$ or $10 \cdot 1 = 10$.

The word permutation is used synonymously with arrangement. Recall that AB and BA are two different permutations (arrangements), but AB and BA represent the same combination or the same selection.

The major problem generally encountered in the study of permutations and combinations is the ability to distinguish between each in a given real-world situation. Remember that the question of **order** is important when considering a permutation; it is not important when considering a combination. It is often helpful to associate the word "arrangement" with a permutation and the words "group" and "selection" with a combination.

Problem Set 2

1. Would it be possible to evaluate an expression such as $\binom{3}{4}$? Why?

2. Evaluate each of the following:

    a. $\dfrac{6!}{4!\,2!}$ b. $\dfrac{8!}{5!\,3!}$ c. $\dfrac{10!}{4!\,6!}$

    d. $\dfrac{7!}{7!\,0!}$ e. $\dfrac{6!}{0!\,6!}$

3. Evaluate each of the following using the formula for combinations:

    a. $\binom{7}{2}$ b. $\binom{8}{3}$ c. $\binom{6}{6}$

    d. $\binom{7}{0}$ e. $\binom{5}{1}$

Probability and Statistics

The following six problems involve combinations. Evaluate each using the formula.

4. How many choices are there for one to select 4 magazines to read from a collection of 8 magazines?

5. A student located 8 books she needed at the library, but she can only check out three at a time. How many sets of three books can she possibly select?

6. Four out of seven cheerleaders must be selected to accompany the basketball team to the state tournament. How many groups of four could be picked?

7. A vending machine in the student center has 5 different sandwiches available. How many selections can a student make if he wishes to choose two different sandwiches for lunch?

8. There are 7 candidates running for 4 seats on a city council. How many different groups can be elected?

9. An office needs 5 typists, and 8 apply for the jobs. How many different groups of 5 typists can be hired?

10. The triangular array shown below is **Pascal's Triangle.** It may be used to find the number of combinations of n objects taken r at a time. Replace each of the combinations by its equivalent number to obtain an array of numbers. Then determine the numbers in the row where n = 4.

$n = 0$ $\binom{0}{0}$

$n = 1$ $\binom{1}{0}$ $\binom{1}{1}$

$n = 2$ $\binom{2}{0}$ $\binom{2}{1}$ $\binom{2}{2}$

$n = 3$ $\binom{3}{0}$ $\binom{3}{1}$ $\binom{3}{2}$ $\binom{3}{3}$

$n = 4$ ___   ___   ___   ___   ___

11. A committee of 8 people consists of 5 females and 3 males.
    a. How many sub-committees consisting of 4 people can be formed at random if each is to consist of 2 females and 2 males?
    b. How many sub-committees consisting of 4 people can be formed if each is to consist of 1 female and 3 males?

12. A carton contains 10 apples of which 3 are rotten.
    a. How many selections consisting of 5 apples each can be formed if each is to contain 3 good apples and 2 rotten apples?
    b. How many selections consisting of 5 apples each can be formed if each is to contain 5 good apples?

13. A basketball team has 7 good foul shooters and 4 poor foul shooters.
    a. How many teams of 5 players each can be formed at random if there are 4 good foul shooters and 1 poor foul shooter?
    b. How many teams of 5 players each can be formed at random if there is 1 good foul shooter and 4 poor foul shooters?

14. A bag contains 5 orange, 4 blue, and 2 white marbles.
    a. How many selections consisting of 6 marbles each can be formed if each is to consist of 3 orange, 2 blue, and 1 white marble?
    b. How many selections consisting of 4 marbles each can be formed if each is to consist of 3 blue and 1 white marble?

Topic 3

Random Experiments and Probability

This section presents the idea of random experiments. At the end of this section you need to be able to find the sample space for a random experiment, using this sample space to compute the probability of an event associated with the experiment. You should be able to find the probability of complementary events. You should be able to use your knowledge of arrangements and combinations (topics 1 and 2) to compute the probability of a particular arrangement or selection. Finally, you should also be able to translate probability statements to odds statements or odds statements to probability statements.

◊ Definitions

A **random experiment** is an act which yields an outcome that belongs to a known set of outcomes. The particular result that will be obtained is not known in advance of the act.

A random experiment's **sample space** is the set of all possible outcomes of the experiment.

An **event** (A) is a set of outcomes, but not necessarily all outcomes. An event is any subset of the sample space.

E
X
A
M
P
L
E
S

Each of these examples is a random experiment. The sample space will be designated by S.

a. Toss a single coin. The set of all possible outcomes is S = {H, T} where H stands for a head and T for a tail. An event for this experiment is {H}. This event, representing an outcome where the coin reads heads, is a subset of {H, T}.

b. A group contains 4 women and 3 men. Select one person from the group. The set of all possible outcomes is S = $\{W_1, W_2, W_3, W_4, M_1, M_2, M_3\}$, where W stands for woman and M for man. W_1, W_2 and W_3 represent three particular women. An event for this random experiment is selecting a man, represented by $\{M_1, M_2, M_3\}$. Again, $\{M_1, M_2, M_3\}$, having three possible outcomes, is a subset of the sample space which has seven possible outcomes.

◊ **Definition**

The **probability** of an event A, denoted by P(A), may be expressed as the ratio of the number of elements in event A to the total number of elements in the sample space S of the experiment.

$$P(A) = \frac{\text{number of elements in A}}{\text{number of elements in S}}$$

The probability of an event is expressed as a fraction in which the numerator is the number of elements in the event, and the denominator is the number of elements in the sample space.

E
X
A
M
P
L
E
S

a. Consider, again, the coin toss with S = {H, T}. Let us find the probability that the outcome will be heads. The event is the set A = {H}. Set A has 1 element and the sample space has 2 elements. Therefore,

$$P \text{ (heads)} = P(A) = \frac{\text{number of elements in A}}{\text{number of elements in S}} = \frac{1}{2}$$

b. Again, consider the group of 4 women and 3 men. If we select one person from the group, let us find the probability that a man is selected. The event is the set A = $\{M_1, M_2, M_3\}$ containing 3 elements. The sample space is S = $\{W_1, W_2, W_3, W_4, M_1, M_2, M_3\}$ with 7 elements. Therefore,

$$P \text{ (selecting a man)} = P(A) = \frac{\text{number of elements in A}}{\text{number of elements in S}} = \frac{3}{7}$$

Problem 1

Four slips numbered 3, 6, 9, and 12 are in a box. A random experiment consists of selecting two slips from the box. After the first slip is selected, it is not replaced in the box. A second slip is then selected. (We say, more informally, that the two slips are selected without replacement.)

a. What is the sample space for this experiment?

Solution

We must list all possible outcomes. Thus,

$$S = \left\{ \begin{array}{l} (3,6), \ (3,9), \ (3,12), \ (6,3), \ (6,9), \ (6,12), \\ (9,3), \ (9,6), \ (9,12), \ (12,3), \ (12,6), \ (12,9) \end{array} \right\}.$$

Observe that (3,3), (6,6), (9,9), and (12,12) are not elements of S since we cannot select the same slip twice. The sample space has 12 outcomes.

b. What is the probability that the sum of the two numbers selected is odd?

Solution

The event
$$A = \{(3,6), (3,12), (6,3), (6,9), (9,6), (9,12), (12,3), (12,9)\}$$
because these elements all have an odd sum. There are 8 elements in A.

$$\text{Therefore, P(A)} = \frac{\text{number of elements in A}}{\text{number of elements in S}} = \frac{8}{12} = \frac{2}{3}$$

c.   What is the probability that the sum of the two numbers selected is greater than 8?

Solution

All the possible outcomes have a sum greater than 8, and so A = S.

$$\text{Thus, P(A)} = \frac{\text{number of elements in A}}{\text{number of elements in S}} = \frac{12}{12} = 1$$

d.   What is the probability that the sum of the two numbers selected is greater than 21?

Solution

None of the possible outcomes has a sum greater than 21, and so A = Ø.

$$\text{Thus, P(A)} = \frac{\text{number of elements in A}}{\text{number of elements in S}} = \frac{0}{12} = 0$$

The preceding sample problem illustrates some important ideas about probability.

The probability of an event P(A):
1.   is always greater than or equal to zero and less than or equal to 1.
     Symbolically, $0 \leq P(A) \leq 1$.
2.   is zero if the event cannot occur. $P(\emptyset) = 0$.
3.   is one if the event is certain to occur. If A = S, P(A) = 1.

Another important idea related to probability deals with the probability that event A will not occur.

$$P(A \text{ will not occur}) = 1 - P(A \text{ will occur})$$
$$\text{Equivalently, } P(A') = 1 - P(A)$$

a. If the probability of selecting a man is $\frac{3}{7}$, the probability of not selecting a man is: $1 - \frac{3}{7} = \frac{7}{7} - \frac{3}{7} = \frac{4}{7}$.

b. If the probability of rain is $\frac{4}{11}$, the probability that it will not rain is:
$1 - \frac{4}{11} = \frac{11}{11} - \frac{4}{11} = \frac{7}{11}$

In probability theory, events A and A' are called complementary events. Since an event must either occur or not occur, the sum of the probability that the event will occur and the probability the event will not occur is 1. Thus, $P(A) + P(A') = 1$. Solving for $P(A')$, we obtain $P(A') = 1 - P(A)$, precisely the formula used in the preceding examples.

The idea of complementary events can be related to notions in set theory. In the Venn diagram on the right, the sample space S serves as the universal set. Event A and event A', the complementary event, are represented. Observe that $A \cup A' = S$ and $A \cap A' = \emptyset$.

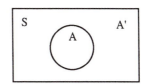

Problem 2

Two common sources of entertainment for Americans are movies and live theater. Sixty percent of Americans go to the movies but not live theater, while 15% go to both. What is the probability that a randomly selected American does not go to the movies?

Solution

The Venn diagram on the right shows 60% of Americans attending movies but not live theater and 15% attending both. Since
$P(A') = 1 - P(A)$,

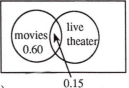

$$P(\text{not going to movies}) = 1 - P(\text{going to movies})$$
$$= 1 - (0.60 + 0.15)$$
$$= 1 - 0.75$$
$$= 0.25$$

The probability that a randomly selected American does not go to the movies is 0.25 (or equivalently 25% or $\frac{1}{4}$).

The next problems illustrate how **The Fundamental Counting Principle** and permutations can be used to determine probabilities.

Problem 3

Consider the digits 3, 4, 5, and 8. If a three digit number is formed, what is the probability that the number is less than 500? Assume that no digit may be used more than once.

Solution

Our probability fraction is:

$$\frac{\text{The number of arrangements giving numbers less than 500}}{\text{The total number of arrangements using three digits}}$$

To obtain the numerator of the probability fraction, we must realize that to get a number less than 500, the first digit must be either 3 or 4. Thus, there are two possible ways to fill the first position. Once 3 or 4 is selected, and since the digits may not be repeated, there are three numbers remaining to choose from for the second position and three ways to fill the second position. Once the first two digits are used, there are two more digits to choose from for the third position or two possible ways to fill the third position. Using **The Fundamental Counting Principle**, the total number of arrangements giving numbers less than 500 is: 2 • 3 • 2 or 12. This number is the numerator of the probability fraction.

To obtain the denominator of the probability fraction, it is necessary to find the total number of arrangements (permutations) using the given digits. The first position can be filled in four ways, the second in three ways, the third in two ways. By **The Fundamental Counting Principle**, the total number of arrangements using three digits is 4 • 3 • 2 or 24. Thus, 24 is the denominator of the probability fraction. The probability that the number selected is less than 500 is $\frac{12}{24}$ or 0.5.

Problem 4

Consider all arrangements that could be made of the four letters B, A, C, K if no letter can be repeated. BACK, ACKB are examples. What is the probability that an arrangement selected at random will begin with the letter A?

Solution

$$P(\text{arrangement begins with A}) = \frac{\text{number of arrangements with A first}}{\text{number of arrangements of 4 letters}}$$

Number of arrangements with A first:

$$1 \text{ way(A)} \cdot 3 \text{ ways} \cdot 2 \text{ ways} \cdot 1 \text{ way} = 1 \cdot 3 \cdot 2 \cdot 1 = 6$$

Number of arrangements with 4 letters:

$$4 \text{ ways} \cdot 3 \text{ ways} \cdot 2 \text{ ways} \cdot 1 \text{ way} = 4 \cdot 3 \cdot 2 \cdot 1 = 24$$

Hence the probability is $\frac{6}{24} = \frac{1}{4}$.

There are times when combinations must be used along with **The Fundamental Counting Principle** to determine probabilities.

Problem 5

A committee contains 7 people of whom 4 are women. Three people are randomly selected to write the committee report. Find the probability that exactly two of the three people selected are women.

Solution

The phrase "exactly two of the three people selected are women" implies two women and one man. The number of ways of selecting two women is $\binom{4}{2}$ because there are four women on the committee. The order is not important. Corresponding to each way of selecting two women there are $\binom{3}{1}$ ways of selecting a man. **The Fundamental Counting Principle** states that the total number of ways of selecting two women and one man is

$$\binom{4}{2} \cdot \binom{3}{1} = 6 \cdot 3 = 18.$$

The total number of ways of selecting three people from seven is $\binom{7}{3}$ or 35.

The probability fraction is: $\dfrac{\text{the number of ways of selecting two women and one man}}{\text{the total number of ways of selecting three people from seven people}}$

The probability that exactly two of the three people are women is:

$$\frac{\binom{4}{2} \cdot \binom{3}{1}}{\binom{7}{3}} = \frac{6 \cdot 3}{35} = \frac{18}{35}$$

Problem 6

An urn contains 8 balls. Five are black and three are white. Three balls are randomly selected from the urn. What is the probability that they are all black?

Solution

The order in which the balls are selected is not important. If three black balls are selected out of 5, $\binom{5}{3}$, and none of the white balls, $\binom{3}{0}$, the **Fundamental Counting Principle** gives $\binom{5}{3} \cdot \binom{3}{0} = 10 \cdot 1 = 10$

The total number of ways of selecting three balls out of eight is $\binom{8}{3}$ or 56.

The probability fraction is: $\dfrac{\text{the number of selecting 3 black balls out of 5}}{\text{the total number of ways of selecting 3 balls out of 8}}$

The probability that all 3 balls selected are black is:

$$\frac{\binom{5}{3} \cdot \binom{3}{0}}{\binom{8}{3}} = \frac{10 \cdot 1}{56} = \frac{10}{56} = \frac{5}{28}$$

The probability of an event occurring is different from the odds in favor of the event, but there is a direct relationship between them.

◊ **Definition**

The **odds in favor of an event** is the ratio:

$$\frac{\text{the probability the event will occur}}{\text{the probability the event will not occur}} = \frac{P(A)}{P(A')}$$

Problem 7

A department store is giving a free gift to any customer whose receipt has a star on it. The department store has printed a star on every tenth receipt. What are the odds in favor of a customer getting a free gift?

Solution

If A is the event of getting a gift, then $P(A) = \frac{1}{10}$ because a star is on every tenth receipt.

The probability of not getting a gift, $P(A')$, is $1 - \frac{1}{10}$ or $\frac{9}{10}$. Thus the odds in favor of a gift are:

$$\frac{P(A)}{P(A')} = \frac{\frac{1}{10}}{\frac{9}{10}} = \frac{1}{10} \cdot \frac{10}{9} = \frac{1}{9}$$

The odds in favor of a free gift are 1 to 9, written as $1 : 9$.

Two additional ideas are related to the odds of an event.

1. If the odds in favor of A are a to b, the **odds against A** are b to a.
2. If the odds in favor of A are a to b, the probability that A will occur is $\frac{a}{a + b}$.

E
X
A
M
P
L
E
S

a. If the odds in favor of a free gift are 1 to 9 (1:9), the odds against a free gift are 9 to 1 (9:1).

b. If the odds in favor of a free gift are 1 to 9, the probability of getting a free gift is $\frac{a}{a + b} = \frac{1}{1 + 9} = \frac{1}{10}$.

c. If the odds in favor of a horse's winning a race are 2 to 3, the probability that the horse will win the race is $\frac{a}{a + b} = \frac{2}{2 + 3} = \frac{2}{5}$.

Problem Set 3

1. A group consists of 10 men and 5 women. If one person is selected from the group, find the probability that:
    a. a man is selected.
    b. a woman is selected.

2. A group consists of 30 Democrats, 40 Republicans, and 20 Independents. If one person is selected from the group, find the probability that:
    a. a Democrat is selected.
    b. an Independent is selected.
    c. an Independent is not selected.

3. A bag contains 3 black balls and 6 red balls. One ball is drawn at random. What is the probability that the ball selected is not black?

4. A spinner for a child's game may point to any of seven numbers equally. The numbers are 1,2,3,4,5,6, and 7. Thus S = {1,2,3,4,5,6,7}.
   a. What is the probability that the spinner will point to an odd number?
   b. What is the probability that the spinner will point to a number less than 6?

5. Twenty numbered slips of paper are placed in a bowl. The slips are numbered from 1 to 20.
   a. What is the probability of drawing a number that is divisible by 5?
   b. What is the probability of drawing a number that is less than 9?
   c. What is the probability of drawing a number that is less than 21?
   d. What is the probability of drawing a number that is greater than 21?

6. A fair coin is tossed two times in succession. The sample space S associated with this experiment is S = {HH, HT, TH, TT}. Since there are 4 possible outcomes in the sample space, the probability of each outcome is $\frac{1}{4}$.
   a. What is the sum of the probabilities associated with each outcome in the sample space?
   b. What is the probability of obtaining two Heads?
   c. What is the probability of obtaining a Head and a Tail?
   d. What is the probability of obtaining a Head on the second toss?
   e. What is the probability of obtaining at least one Head?

7. A fair coin is tossed three times in succession. The sample space S associated with this experiment is: S = {HHH, HHT, HTH, HTT, THH, THT, TTH, TTT}. Since there are 8 possible outcomes in the sample space, the probability of each outcome is $\frac{1}{8}$.
   a. What is the sum of the probabilities in the sample space?
   b. What is the probability of obtaining all Heads?
   c. What is the probability of obtaining exactly one Tail?
   d. What is the probability of obtaining at least two Heads?

8. A spinner for a child's game may point to any of three numbers equally. The numbers are 1,2, and 3. A random experiment consists of spinning the spinner twice.
   a. What is the sample space associated with this experiment?
   b. What is the probability that the spinner will point to two numbers whose sum is greater than or equal to 5?
   c. What is the probability that the spinner will point to two numbers whose sum is even?
   d. What is the probability that the spinner will first point to an odd number and then an even number?

9. Three slips of paper numbered 1,2, and 3 are in a box. A slip of paper is drawn and not put back into the box. A second slip of paper is then selected.
   a. What is the sample space associated with this experiment?
   b. What is the probability that the sum of the two selected numbers is divisible by 2?

10. Box I contains slips with the numbers 1,2,3, and 4. Box II contains slips with the numbers 1,2,3, and 4. A random experiment consists of selecting a slip from each box, first from box I and then from box II. Find the probability that the sum of the two selected numbers is greater than or equal to 6.

11. The probability that it will rain is $\frac{3}{7}$.
    a. What is the probability that it will not rain?
    b. What are the odds in favor of rain?
    c. What are the odds against rain?

12. A supermarket awards a prize to every customer who receives a receipt with a star printed on it. A star is printed on every fifth receipt. What are the odds in favor of winning a prize?

13. The odds in favor of winning a prize are 1 to 10,000. What is the probability of winning the prize?

14. The odds against Rhoda winning the election are 4:7. What is the probability that Rhoda will win the election?

15. What is the probability of rolling a sum of 13 by tossing a single fair die two times in succession?

16. A bag contains 3 white balls and 3 black balls. If one ball is drawn from the bag, what is the probability that it is black or white?

17. The probability of obtaining all Tails if a fair coin is tossed three times in succession is $\frac{1}{8}$. What is the probability of not obtaining all Tails?

18. If the probability that it will rain on a given day is 0.25, what is the probability that it will not rain?

19. What is the probability that the next person you meet was not born on a Friday?

20. A fair die is tossed. What is the probability that the number obtained is not 7?

21. A bag contains 4 green marbles, 3 red marbles, and 5 blue marbles. If one marble is drawn from the bag:
    a. What is the probability that it is not green?
    b. What is the probability that it is purple?
    c. What is the probability that it is not purple?

22. Two popular kinds of television programs for American adults are comedies and dramas. Forty percent of American adults watch comedies but not dramas, while 15% watch both. What is the probability that a randomly selected American adult who watches television does not watch comedies?

23. Consider the digits 2, 5, 6, 7, and 8. No digit is to be used more than once.
    a. If a three digit number is formed, what is the probability that the number is less than 800?
    b. If a three digit number is formed, what is the probability that the number is odd? (Hint: The number must end with 5 or 7.)
    c. If a three digit number is formed, what is the probability that it begins with 5?
    d. If a four digit number is formed, what is the probability that the number is even?

24. Using the digits 2, 5, 8, and 9 and the digits may be repeated, what is the probability of forming a three digit even number greater than 900?

25. Consider the letters S, T, A, and R. If a four letter arrangement is made repeating any letter, what is the probability that it will begin with A and end with S?

26. Martha, Lee, Marilyn, Paul, and Ann have all been invited to a dinner party. If they arrive randomly and at different times, what is the probability that:
    a. Martha will arrive second?
    b. Marilyn will arrive first and Lee last?
    c. they will arrive in the following order: Paul, Martha, Marilyn, Lee, and Ann?

27. A box contains 6 beach balls consisting of 2 orange balls and 4 blue balls. If 4 balls are drawn at random from the box, find the probability that:
    a. one is orange and 3 are blue.
    b. all four are blue.
    c. 2 are orange and 2 are blue.

28. If 3 students are selected at random from a class of 5 men and 7 women, find the probability that:
    a. all 3 are men.
    b. all 3 are women.
    c. there is 1 man and 2 women.

29. A committee of 5 people is selected at random from a legislative delegation of 8 Democrats, 5 Republicans, and 2 Independents. Find the probability that the committee consists of:
    a. 3 Democrats and 2 Republicans.
    b. 1 Democrat, 3 Republicans, and 1 Independent.
    c. 5 Republicans.
    d. 2 Democrats, 1 Republican, and 2 Independents.

Topic 4

The Addition Rules for Probability

Many probability situations involve outcomes which allow for one event or another event. This situation frequently uses the connective "or" between the events. At the end of this section you should be able to compute probabilities associated with this situation.

Consider the Venn diagram shown in which the numbers represent the number of elements contained in each region.

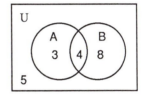

We know that the number of elements in A ∪ B, denoted by n(A ∪ B), is 3 + 4 + 8 or 15. The number of elements in set A, n(A), is 3 + 4 or 7. The number of elements in set B, n(B), is 4 + 8 or 12. Is it true that n(A ∪ B) = n(A) + n(B)? No. We can verify this by:

$$n(A \cup B) = n(A) + n(B)$$
$$15 \quad \neq \quad 7 + 12$$

The reason for this inequality is that the number of elements in **both** set A and set B (4) was counted **twice** in computing n(A) + n(B). We should have counted the 4 elements only **once**. Thus, we must subtract one of the quantities that we originally added twice. Note that this quantity lies within A ∩ B.

$$n(A \cup B) = n(A) + n(B) - n(A \cap B)$$
$$15 \quad = \quad 7 \ + \ 12 \ - \quad 4$$
$$15 \quad = \ 15$$

This relationship in set theory will have a corresponding application in probability theory and we refer to it as the:

> **General Addition Rule for Probability**
> If A and B are any two events for an experiment, then
> $$P(A \cup B) = P(A) + P(B) - P(A \cap B)$$

If A and B are two events in a sample space, the union of A and B, (A $\cup$ B), is the event composed of all the outcomes in event A **or** event B. It will be helpful to interpret P(A $\cup$ B) as P(A or B). The intersection of A and B, (A $\cap$ B), is the event composed of all the outcomes which are in **both** A and B. It will be helpful to interpret:

$$P(A \cap B) \text{ as } P(A \text{ and } B \text{ occur simultaneously}).$$

The General Addition Rule is used to find the probability of two events connected by the word "or." Thus, the rule is often restated in any of the following ways:
1. **P(A or B) = P(A) + P(B) − P(A and B occur simultaneously)**
2. **P(A or B) = P(A) + P(B) − P(A and B)**
3. **P(A or B) = P(A) + P(B) − P(A $\cap$ B)** For the sake of consistency, we will use this form in our solved problems.

Problem 1

What is the probability of rolling a 1 **or** a 5 on one roll of a fair die?

Solution

Let A to be the event of rolling a 1.
$$\text{Then, } P(A) = \tfrac{1}{6}$$

Let B to be the event of rolling a 5.
$$\text{Then, } P(B) = \tfrac{1}{6}$$

Notice that event A and event B are **mutually exclusive events.** Two events are said to be mutually exclusive if the occurrence of one event excludes the occurrence of the other event. Mutually exclusive events cannot occur at the same time. It is not possible to roll a 1 and a 5 on the same toss. Since it is impossible for event A and event B to occur at the same time, the probability of this happening is 0. In other words,

$$P(A \cap B) = P(A \text{ and } B \text{ occur simultaneously}) = 0.$$
$$P(A \text{ or } B) = P(A) + P(B) - P(A \cap B)$$
$$= \tfrac{1}{6} + \tfrac{1}{6} - 0$$
$$= \tfrac{2}{6} \text{ or } \tfrac{1}{3}$$

There are two numbers on the die that are involved in this problem, namely 1 and 5. The probability of rolling 1 or 5 is $\tfrac{2}{6}$ or $\tfrac{1}{3}$.

Problem 2

A committee consists of 5 Democrats, 4 Republicans, and 2 Independents. If one person is selected at random, what is the probability the person is a Democrat **or** a Republican?

Solution

If A is the event the person selected is a Democrat, then $P(A) = \frac{5}{11}$.

If B is the event the person selected is a Republican, then $P(B) = \frac{4}{11}$.

The events are mutually exclusive. One cannot be both a Democrat and Republican. Consequently,

$$P(A \cap B) = P(A \text{ and } B \text{ occur simultaneously}) = 0.$$

and

$$P(A \text{ or } B) = P(A) + P(B) - P(A \cap B)$$

$$= \frac{5}{11} + \frac{4}{11} - 0$$

$$= \frac{9}{11}$$

Thus, the probability that the person is a Democrat or a Republican is $\frac{9}{11}$.

The two preceding problems give rise to the:

> **Special Addition Rule for Probability:**
> If A and B are two mutually exclusive events, then
> $$P(A \cup B) = P(A) + P(B)$$

An equivalent form of the Special Addition Rule is:

$$P(A \text{ or } B) = P(A) + P(B)$$

Let us now consider the addition rule as it relates to events that are not mutually exclusive.

Problem 3

What is the probability of rolling a 5 **or** a number greater than 4 on one roll of a fair die?

Solution

Let us consider A to be the event of rolling a 5.

Therefore, $P(A) = \frac{1}{6}$.

Let us consider B to be the event of rolling a number greater than 4 (5 or 6).

Hence $P(B) = \frac{2}{6}$.

Observe here that event A and event B are **not** mutually exclusive events. They could both occur simultaneously. Certainly a 5 on the die is both an outcome in event A and event B. Since the probability of obtaining a 5 is $\frac{1}{6}$ we say that

$$P(A \cap B) = P \text{ (A and B occur simultaneously)} = \frac{1}{6}.$$

To compute the probability we have:

$$
\begin{aligned}
P(A \text{ or } B) &= P(A) + P(B) - P(A \cap B) \\
&= \frac{1}{6} + \frac{2}{6} - \frac{1}{6} \\
&= \frac{2}{6} \text{ or } \frac{1}{3}
\end{aligned}
$$

Problem 4

The probability that Doug will read a book on a Saturday night is 0.6, and the probability that he will listen to records is 0.4, and the probability that he will do both is 0.3. What is the probability that Doug will read a book **or** listen to records?

Solution

These events are **not** mutually exclusive. They could occur simultaneously.

If P(A) is the probability that Doug will read a book,

then $P(A) = 0.6$.

If P(B) is the probability that Doug will listen to records,

then $P(B) = 0.4$.

$P(A \cap B)$ is the probability that Doug will simultaneously read a book and listen to records.

$$P(A \cap B) = 0.3$$
$$P(A \text{ or } B) = P(A) + P(B) - P(A \cap B)$$
$$= 0.6 + 0.4 - 0.3$$
$$= 0.7$$

Thus, the probability that Doug will read a book or listen to records is 0.7.

A table describing the relative frequency of occurrence of all possible outcomes often forms the basis of solving real-world problems involving probability. The table below is based on the fact that between 1970 and 1977 approximately 12,000 people were killed on scheduled and non-scheduled airline flights. The table below provides the "when and how" of these air deaths. (Assume all events are mutually exclusive.)

When and How	Percent of All Air Deaths
During Take-Off and Climb	20
en Route	14
During Approach	31
During Landing	19
As a Result of Terrorism	7
As a Result of Collisions	9

Problem 5

What is the probability that an air death occurs during landing?

Solution

This information is provided directly by the table. We see that 19% of the air deaths occur during landing $\left(\frac{19}{100}\right)$, so the probability can be expressed as 0.19.

Problem 6

What is the probability that an air death occurs as a result of terrorism or collisions?

Solution

Since the events in the table are mutually exclusive, if A is the event "terrorism," and B is the event "collisions,"

$$P(A \text{ or } B) = P(A) + P(B)$$
$$= 0.07 + 0.09$$
$$= 0.16$$

The probability that an air death occurs as a result of terrorism or collision is 0.16.

Problem 7

What is the probability that an air death is neither the result of terrorism nor collisions?

Solution

The outcome "neither terrorism nor collisions" is the complement of "terrorism or collisions." If C is the event "terrorism or collisions,"

$$P(\text{neither terrorism nor collisions}) = P(C')$$
$$= 1 - P(C)$$
$$= 1 - 0.16 \text{ (from Problem 6)}$$
$$= 0.84$$

The probability that an air death is neither the result of terrorism nor collisions is 0.84.

Problem 8

How many of the next 400 air deaths would one expect to take place en route or during approach?

Solution

Since the events are mutually exclusive, the probability of an air death en route or during approach is $0.14 + 0.31 = 0.45$. We would expect 45% of the next 400 air deaths or $(0.45)(400) = 180$ deaths to take place en route or during approach.

Problem 9

If it is known that an air death was not a result of terrorism or collisions, find the probability that it took place during landing.

Solution

One way to approach this problem is to first exclude the last two rows from the given table. Thus,

$$P(\text{landing}) = \frac{\text{percent of deaths during landing}}{\text{percent of deaths in all categories excluding terrorism and collisions}}$$

$$= \frac{19}{20 + 14 + 31 + 19} = \frac{19}{84}$$

Problem Set 4

1. A box contains 3 green marbles, 2 red marbles, and 5 white marbles. If a marble is drawn at random from the box, find the probability that:
    a. the marble is green or red.
    b. the marble is white or red.
    c. the marble is neither white nor red.

2. A fair die is rolled. What is the probability that the number obtained:
    a. will be an even number or a number greater than 2?
    b. will be an odd number or a number greater than 1?

3. Twenty numbered slips of paper are placed in a box. The slips are numbered from 1 to 20. What is the probability of drawing a number that is odd or exactly divisible by 5?

4. Suppose one letter of the English alphabet is selected at random. Find the probability that the letter selected:
    a. is a vowel.   b. precedes the letter m.
    c. precedes the letter m or is a vowel.

5. The probability that a tourist will visit Key West is 0.6. The probability that he/she will visit St. Augustine is 0.4, and the probability that he/she will visit both Key West and St. Augustine is 0.3. What is the probability that the tourist will visit Key West or St. Augustine?

6. At an international meeting, 30 percent of the delegates speak English, 40 percent of the delegates speak Spanish, and 20 percent speak both English and Spanish. If a delegate is randomly selected, what is the probability that the delegate speaks English or Spanish?

7. In a civic club, the probabilities that a person selected will have the following characteristics are: a politician: 0.75, corrupt: 0.15, a politician and corrupt: 0.10. Find the probability that the person:
    a. is a politician or corrupt.
    b. is neither a politician nor corrupt.

Use the table on page 143 to answer these questions.

8. What is the probability that an air death occurs during approach?

9. What is the probability that an air death occurs en route or during landing?

10. What is the probability that an air death occurs neither en route nor during landing?

11. How many of the next 400 air deaths would one expect to occur during take-off and climb or en route?

12. How many of the next 400 air deaths would one expect to occur neither en route nor during landing?

13. If it is known that an air death did not occur during approach or landing, find the probability that it took place en route.

14. If it is known that an air death did not occur en route, during approach, during landing, as a result of terrorism, or as a result of collisions, find the probability that it took place during take-off and climb.

The following is a description of students at a college by gender and student classification.

	Freshman	Sophomore	Junior	Senior
Male	13%	10%	29%	8%
Female	15%	8%	7%	10%

Use this table to answer problems 15 through 22.

15. Find the probability that a randomly selected college student is female.

16. Find the probability that a randomly selected college student is a freshman.

17. Find the probability that a randomly selected college student is a junior or a senior.

18. Find the probability that a randomly selected college student is a sophomore if it is known that the student is female.

19. Find the probability that a randomly selected college student is a freshman or a sophomore if it is known that the student is male.

20. Find the probability that a randomly selected college student is neither a freshman nor a junior if it is known that the student is not female.

21. If it is known that a student is not a junior or a senior, find the probability of randomly selecting a sophomore.

22. If it is known that a student is not a freshman or a sophomore, find the probability of randomly selecting a junior or a senior.

Topic 5

The Multiplication Rules for Probablity

Many probability situations involve two events occurring together or events occurring in succession. This situation frequently uses the connective "and" and "followed by" between the events. At the end of this section you need to be able to compute probabilities associated with these situations.

◊ **Definition**

Two events are said to be **independent** if the occurrence of one event does not affect the probability of the occurrence of the other event.

1. If a fair coin is tossed two times in succession, the outcome of the first toss does not affect the probability of the outcome of the second toss. These two events are independent events.

2. If a fair die is rolled two times in succession, the outcome of the first roll does not affect the probability of the outcome of the second roll. These two events are considered independent events.

3. If two cards are drawn in succession from a deck of 52 playing cards with the first card not replaced before the second card is drawn, the occurrence of the first draw affects the probability of the occurrence of the second draw. These two events are not independent events.

The notion of independent events gives rise to the:

> **General Multiplication Rule for Probability:**
> If A and B are any two events, the probability of A occurring followed by B occurring equals the probability of A occurring, P(A), multiplied by the probability of B occurring given that A has already occurred, denoted P(B|A).
> P(A followed by B) = P(A) • P(B given that A has occurred)
> = P(A) • P(B|A).

If two events A and B are independent events, then P(B|A) = P(B). This fact gives rise to:

> **Special Multiplication Rule for Probability:**
> If A and B are independent events, then
> **P(A followed by B) = P(A) • P(B)**

The Special Multiplication Rule can be extended to include three or more independent events. If A, B, and C are independent events, then

P(A followed by B followed by C) = P(A) • P(B) • P(C)

The multiplication rules are used to find the probability of events connected by "and." Thus, the General Multiplication Rule is often restated in one of the following ways:

1. **P(A and then B) = P(A) • P(B|A)**
2. **P(A and B) = P(A) • P(B|A)**
3. **P(A ∩ B) = P(A) • P(B|A)**

In our solved problems, the relationships that will be most helpful to us are those that appear originally in the statements of the General and Special Multiplication Rules.

Problem 1

If a fair coin is tossed two times in succession, what is the probability of obtaining a Tail on the first toss **and** a Head on the second toss?

Solution

If A is the event of obtaining a Tail on the first toss, then $P(A) = \frac{1}{2}$. If B is the event of obtaining a Head on the second toss, then $P(B) = \frac{1}{2}$. Notice that the probability of event B is identical to the probability of event A although event A has already occurred. The occurrence of the first toss did not affect the probability of the occurrence of the second toss. Thus, events A and B are **independent events.** We obtain:

$$
\begin{aligned}
P(A \text{ followed by } B) \quad &= \quad P(A) \cdot P(B) \\
&= \quad \frac{1}{2} \cdot \frac{1}{2} \\
&= \quad \frac{1}{4}
\end{aligned}
$$

Therefore, the probability of obtaining a Tail and then a Head is $\frac{1}{4}$. Recall again the set representing the sample space when one coin is tossed two times: {HH, HT, TH, TT}. Notice that the probability of obtaining a Tail on the first toss and a Head on the second toss (TH) is indeed $\frac{1}{4}$. This agrees with the result obtained by using the multiplication rule.

Problem 2

A group contains 3 Democrats, 2 Republicans, and 5 Independents. Two people are drawn at random without replacement.

a.   Find the probability that the first person chosen is a Democrat and the second person chosen is a Republican.

Solution

If A is the event of choosing a Democrat on the first pick, then $P(A) = \frac{3}{10}$.

The group now contains 2 Democrats, 2 Republicans, and 5 Independents. If $P(B|A)$ is the probability of choosing a Republican on the second pick given that the first person chosen was a Democrat, then $P(B|A) = \frac{2}{9}$ because there are 2 Republicans and only 9 people in the group.

Thus, $P(A \text{ followed by } B) = P(A) \cdot P(B|A) = \frac{3}{10} \cdot \frac{2}{9} = \frac{1}{15}$

b.   Find the probability that both persons chosen are Independents.

Solution

We must find the probability of selecting an Independent followed by an Independent. If A is the event of choosing an Independent on the first pick, $P(A) = \frac{5}{10}$. The group now contains 3 Democrats, 2 Republicans, and only 4 Independents. If $P(B|A)$ is the probability of choosing an Independent on the second pick given that the first person chosen was an Independent, then $P(B|A) = \frac{4}{9}$.

Thus, $P(A \text{ followed by } B) = P(A) \cdot P(B|A) = \frac{5}{10} \cdot \frac{4}{9} = \frac{2}{9}$

c.   Find the probability that neither person chosen is a Democrat.

Solution

We must find the probability of a non-Democrat followed by a non-Democrat. If A is the event of selecting a non-Democrat on the first choice, $P(A) = \frac{7}{10}$ since there are 7 non-Democrats and 10 people. The events in this problem are dependent. The probability of the second event, $P(B|A)$, represents the probability of selecting a non-Democrat second given that we have already chosen a non-Democrat first. When we choose a second person, the group consists of 6 non-Democrats and 9 people, so $P(B|A) = \frac{6}{9}$.

Thus, $P(A \text{ followed by } B) = P(A) \cdot P(B|A) = \frac{7}{10} \cdot \frac{6}{9} = \frac{7}{15}$

Problem 3

Twenty percent of the basketballs manufactured by a company are defective. If two balls are randomly selected with replacement, find the probability that at least one ball is defective.

Solution

Let D represent the event of selecting a defective ball and D' not selecting a defective ball. We are given that
$$P(D) = 20\% = \frac{1}{5}.$$
$$\text{Thus } P(D') = 1 - P(D) = 1 - \frac{1}{5} = \frac{4}{5}.$$
(The probability of selecting a good ball, one that is not defective, is $\frac{4}{5}$.) Now we must analyze the English expression "at least one ball is defective." This means that one or possibly both balls selected are defective. The only way that this would not happen is if we were to select two good balls in a row. These events are complements and we can write:

$$P(\text{at least one is defective}) = 1 - P(\text{both are good})$$

If both balls selected are good, we have:

$$P(D' \text{ followed by } D') = P(D') \cdot P(D')$$
$$= \frac{4}{5} \cdot \frac{4}{5} = \frac{16}{25}$$

Thus, $P(\text{at least one is defective}) = 1 - P(\text{both are good})$
$$= 1 - \frac{16}{25} = \frac{9}{25}$$

The probability that at least one ball is defective is $\frac{9}{25}$.

Problem 4

A group consists of 10 women and 10 men. If two people are randomly selected without replacement, find the probability of selecting two women or two men.

Solution

We must first find the probability of two women, or a woman followed by a woman. If A is the event of selecting a woman on the first choice, P(A) is $\frac{10}{20} = \frac{1}{2}$, since there are 10 women and 20 people. The probability of the second event, P(B|A), represents the probability of selecting a woman second given that we have already selected a woman. $P(B|A) = \frac{9}{19}$, since there are now only 9 women left and 19 people in the group. Thus,

$$
\begin{aligned}
\text{P(A followed by B)} \quad &= \text{P(two women)} \\
&= \text{P(A)} \cdot \text{P(B|A)} \\
&= \frac{1}{2} \cdot \frac{9}{19} \\
&= \frac{9}{38}
\end{aligned}
$$

In the same way, the probability of selecting two men is also $\frac{9}{38}$.

Using the addition rule of probability:

P(Two Women or Two Men)

$$
\begin{aligned}
&= \text{P(Two Women)} + \text{P(Two Men)} - \text{P(Two Women} \cap \text{Two Men)} \\
&= \text{P(Two Women)} + \text{P(Two Men)} - \text{P(\o)} \\
&= \frac{9}{38} + \frac{9}{38} - 0 = \frac{18}{38} = \frac{9}{19}
\end{aligned}
$$

The probability of selecting two women or two men is $\frac{9}{19}$. (Observe that selecting two women excludes selecting two men and vice-versa. Since these events are mutually exclusive, we subtracted 0, the probability of them both happening together.)

Problem Set 5

1. A dial can land on any of eight numbers, 1 through 8. If the dial is spun and then a coin is tossed, what is the probability that the dial will point to a number greater than 3 and the coin will land on heads?

2. A group contains 5 men and 7 women. If two people are selected at random without replacement, find the probability that:
   a. the first is a woman and the second is a man.
   b. both are men.
   c. both are women.

3. A group consists of 7 Democrats, 2 Republicans, and 1 Independent. If two people are chosen at random (without replacement), find the probability that:
   a. both are Democrats.
   b. neither is a Democrat.

4. The probability of having cavity problems is $\frac{2}{3}$. The probability of having stomach problems is $\frac{3}{8}$. If these events are independent but not mutually exclusive:
   a. What is the probability of having both cavity and stomach problems simultaneously?
   b. What is the probability of having cavity or stomach problems?

5. A fair die is rolled three times in succession. Find the probability that:
   a. an odd number is tossed on the first toss.
   b. a 1 is tossed on the first two tosses.
   c. a 1 is tossed on the first toss and not tossed on the second toss or the third toss.

6. The probability that x will be alive in 30 years is 0.8, and the probability that y will be alive in 30 years is 0.6. What is the probability that they will both be alive in 30 years? Assume independence of x and y.

7. On a given day the probability that it will rain in Miami is 0.7 and the probability that it will rain in Jacksonville is 0.4. Assuming independence, find the probability that:
   a. it will rain in both cities.
   b. it will rain in neither city.
   c. it will rain only in Miami.

8. The probability of a husband voting in an election is 0.3 and the probability of a wife voting is 0.5. What is the probability of their both not voting? Assume independence of the husband and wife.

9. A box contains 3 red balls, 2 white balls, and 5 blue balls. Two balls are drawn in succession from the box without replacement. What is the probability that neither ball is red?

10. 10% of the pens manufactured by a company are defective. Suppose that two pens are randomly selected with replacement.
    a. Find the probability that both of them are defective.
    b. Find the probability that at least one pen is defective.

11. A box contains 10 tennis balls, of which 2 are defective. If two balls are randomly selected without replacement:
    a. Find the probability that both of them are defective.
    b. Find the probability that at least one ball is defective.

12. A group contains 5 women and 5 men. If 2 people are randomly selected without replacement, find the probability that they are both women or both men.

The Statistical Research Method

In this section we consider the general steps involved in statistical research. At the end of the section you should be able to identify an appropriate sampling technique for obtaining an unbiased sample in a given situation. You should be able to interpret data presented non-graphically, understanding concepts of cumulative frequency and percentile rank. Finally, you should be able to infer relations from studying statistical data that appears both graphically and non-graphically.

The spirit of the researcher can be found in many of us. Most people have ideas (hypotheses) about reality which can be tested by doing systematic research. The first step in research is to reduce our problem to a testable hypothesis, usually stated as a negation, and called a null hypothesis. The table below shows some common forms of null hypotheses with specific examples.

NULL HYPOTHESIS	EXAMPLE
There is no difference between two populations with respect to a given characteristic.	Political liberals and political conservatives do not differ with respect to permissive child-rearing methods.
There are no differences among three or more populations with respect to a given characteristic.	The upper, middle, and lower classes do not differ with respect to IQ.
There is no degree of association between variable x and variable y.	There is no degree of association between years of school completed and score on a test measuring prejudice.

These examples mention groups that the researcher is interested in — political liberals, conservatives, the upper class, people who have completed 16 years of school, and so on. The entire group whose properties are to be analyzed is known as the population or universe. Since the researcher operates with limited time, energy, and economic resources, the researcher studies only a sample or a subset of the population, a smaller number of individuals taken from the population. Through the sampling process, the researcher seeks to generalize from the sample to the entire population from which the sample was taken. Consequently, it is extremely important that the sample be representative of the population in that the sample has the same distribution of characteristics as the population.

◊ **Definition**

A **random sample** is a sample obtained in such a way that every element in the population has an equal chance to be selected for the sample.

Problem 1

The city council of a large city needs to know whether the people of the city will support the construction of a new fine arts center. The council decides to survey a random sample of the city's residents. Which procedure listed below is most appropriate for obtaining an unbiased sample?

a. Survey a random sample of all the professional actors living in the city.
b. Survey 50,000 individuals who are randomly selected from a list of all residents for the entire state in which the city is located.
c. Survey every third person who walks into City Hall on three randomly selected days.
d. Survey all the city residents who live in 25 randomly selected neighborhoods within the city.

Solution

a. The professional actors living in the city would most likely support a fine arts center. The actors are not representative of the city's people. Each person living in the city does not have an equal chance of being selected by this process.

      b.   The problem with this option is that the sample is not being drawn from the target population. By surveying people from the state, the researcher is selecting from a population outside the target population.

      c.   This, too, is not appropriate for an unbiased sample. Each of the city's residents does not have a chance of being selected by surveying people who enter City Hall.

      d.   This is the most appropriate procedure, often called cluster sampling. This method, excellent for large populations, divides the population into a number of subpopulations, called clusters. Some of the clusters are randomly selected, with sampling carried out only in these clusters.

If a sample is not representative of the population being described, distortion is inevitable. To avoid sampling error, the sample must be relatively large, representative and random. We certainly could not predict the outcome of an election by sampling only ten people. At times, however, even a massive sample can result in distortion.

EXAMPLE

In 1936, the *Literary Digest* mailed out millions of ballots to voters throughout the country. The results poured in, and the *Literary Digest* predicted a landslide victory for Republican Alf Landon over Democrat Franklin Roosevelt.

The *Literary Digest* was wrong in their prediction because the mailing lists the editors used were from directories of automobile owners and telephone subscribers. People prosperous enough to own cars in the heart of the Depression tended to be somewhat more Republican than those who did not, so although the sample was massive, it was biased toward the affluent, and in 1936 many Americans voted along economic lines. (A victim of both the Depression and the 1936 fiasco, the *Literary Digest* folded in 1937.)

Once a testable hypothesis and sampling technique have been developed, the researcher uses an appropriate set of instruments to collect data from the sample. The data can be presented non-graphically or through the use of line, bar, and circle graphs.

Data collected from a random sample can be presented by using an **ungrouped frequency distribution**. Such a distribution consists of two columns of numbers. The possible data values are listed in one column (generally from the smallest to the largest). The adjacent column is labeled "frequency" or "f" and indicates the number of times each value occurs.

Problem 2

Consider the following random sample in which the data items are:

4, 3, 7, 5, 5, 1, 2, 2, 6, 4, 3, 1, 2, 7, 6, 6, 5, 4, 3, 5, 4, 4, 3

Construct an ungrouped frequency distribution.

Solution

Two columns are formed. One lists all possible data values (from smallest to largest). The other indicates the number of times the value occurs in the sample.

data value	f	
1	2	(The value 1 occurs twice.)
2	3	(The value 2 occurs 3 times.)
3	4	
4	5	
5	4	
6	3	
7	2	

An ungrouped frequency distribution can be cumbersome when there is a large number of items in the data. A more compact form for presenting data is through the use of a grouped frequency distribution, tallying the scores into intervals.

E
X
A
M
P
L
E

The accompanying grouped frequency distribution, with intervals arranged from largest to smallest, shows the final examination grades for 71 students. Notice that by grouping scores, each test score has lost its individual identity.

Grouped Frequency Distribution of Final Grades for 71 Students

Class Interval	f
95 - 99	3
90 - 94	2
85 - 89	4
80 - 84	7
75 - 79	12
70 - 74	17
65 - 69	12
60 - 64	5
55 - 59	5
50 - 54	4
	Total 71

◊ **Definition**

In a frequency distribution, the **cumulative frequency**, denoted by c.f., associated with any given class, is the sum of the frequency in that class and the frequencies in all the classes that appear below the given class in the distribution.

E
X
A
M
P
L
E

A c. f. (cumulative frequency) column is added to the grouped frequency distribution of the preceding example.

Class Interval	f	c.f. (cumulative frequency)	
95 - 99	3	71	(68 + 3)
90 - 94	2	68	(66 + 2)
85 - 89	4	66	(62 + 4)
80 - 84	7	62	(55 + 7)
75 - 79	12	55	(43 + 12)
70 - 74	17	43	(26 + 17)
65 - 69	12	26	(14 + 12)
60 - 64	5	14	(9 + 5)
55 - 59	5	9	(4 + 5)
50 - 54	4	4	
Total	71		

Researchers often talk about the percentile rank of a score.

◊ **Definition**

The **percentile rank** of a score is a single number which indicates the percent of cases in a distribution which fall below any given score.

Problem 3

The table below indicates scores on a 400-point exam and their corresponding percentile ranks.

Score	Percentile Rank
380	99
350	87
320	72
290	49
260	26
230	8
200	1

What percentage of examinees scored between 230 and 290?

Solution

The 49 to the right of 290 indicates that 49% of the scores fall below 290.
The 8 to the right of 230 indicates that 8% of the scores fall below 230. Thus, the percentage of scores between 230 and 290 is 49% – 8% or 41%.

Problem 4

The table below shows the distribution of income levels in a community that appears to have a very small middle class.

Income Level	Percent of People
$0 - 9,999	7
10,000 - 14,999	24
15,000 - 19,999	3
20,000 - 24,999	2
25,000 - 34,999	7
35,000 - 49,999	1
50,000 - 79,999	25
80,000 - 119,999	11
120,000 and over	20

a. What percentage of people have incomes of at least $35,000?
b. Identify the amount below which 36% of the people in the community have lower incomes.

Solution

a. We must find the percentage of people whose incomes are $35,000 or more. If we focus on the last four classes, this percentage is 1% + 25% + 11% + 20%. The sum indicates that 57% of the people have incomes of at least $35,000.

b. To identify the amount below which 36% of the people in the community have lower incomes, we begin by adding the percents in the right column, starting with 7%, until we reach 36%.

$$7\% + 24\% + 3\% + 2\% = 36\%$$

We see that 36% of the people fall below the class $25,000 - 34,999. The lower class limit in this class is $25,000. Thus, $25,000 is the amount below which 36% of the people in the community have lower incomes.

Statistical research can be misinterpreted through distortion due to drawing incorrect conclusions when examining data.

E
X
A
M
P
L
E

The number of salespersons and yearly sales revenue are given below.

Year	Number of Salespersons	Yearly Sales (in $100,000)
1986	45	3.70
1987	53	4.25
1988	57	5.36
1989	61	6.42
1990	70	7.30

We cannot conclude that increasing the number of salespersons caused increased sales, since increased yearly sales may be due to a number of other factors. Nor can we conclude that increased sales caused the company to expand its sales force. There certainly does seem to be a positive association between the number of salespersons and yearly sales—that is, as one increases the other increases, but this does not indicate a causal relationship in either direction. The number of salespersons might, however, provide executives of the company some useful information in terms of predicting yearly sales.

The final step in research involves the analysis of data using statistics. Statistics may be defined as a set of techniques for the reduction of quantitative data (that is, a series of numbers) to a small number of more convenient and easily communicated descriptive terms. Some of these descriptive terms, called statistics of central tendency and variability, will be discussed in the sections that follow.

Statistics are also used to make decisions about accepting or rejecting the null hypothesis. By chance alone the researcher can always expect some difference between a random sample and the population from which it is drawn. Known as sampling error, this difference results regardless of how well the sampling plan has been designed and carried out. It is at this point that ideas about probability enter the research method. Through an understanding of the normal distribution (discussed in topic 9), the researcher can establish degrees of confidence to determine if sample differences reflect true population differences and not just sampling error. The researcher always risks the error of rejecting the null hypothesis when it should be accepted, or accepting the null hypothesis when it should be rejected. Because of sampling error, the risk of deciding what to do with the null hypothesis, through statistical decision making, means that there is no certainty of not making an error. This is a risk of statistical decision making that the researcher must be willing to take.

Problem Set 6

1. A group of hotel owners in a large city are interested in doing an attitudinal questionnaire regarding opinions about legalized casino gambling. The owners decide to conduct a survey among citizens of the city to discover their opinions about casino gambling. Which of the following would be most appropriate for selecting an unbiased sample?
   a. randomly surveying people who live in oceanfront condominiums in the city
   b. surveying the first two hundred people whose names appear in the city telephone directory
   c. randomly selecting geographic clusters of the city and then randomly surveying people within the selected clusters
   d. randomly surveying people at six of the largest nightclubs in the city

2. The government of a large city needs to determine if the city's residents will support the construction of a new jail. The government decides to conduct a survey of a sample of the city's residents. Which one of the following procedures would be most appropriate for obtaining an unbiased sample of the city's residents?
   a. Survey a random sample of the employees and inmates at the old jail.
   b. Survey every fifth person who walks into City Hall on a given day.
   c. Survey a random sample of persons within each geographic region of the city.
   d. Survey the first 200 people listed in the city's telephone directory.

Probability and Statistics

3. Find the cumulative frequency associated with each class in this distribution.

class	f
170 - 189	7
150 - 169	12
130 - 149	16
110 - 129	25
90 - 109	19
70 - 89	13
50 - 69	8

4. Use the table in problem 3 to answer these questions.
   a. What percentage of examinees scored between 260 and 320?
   b. What percentage of examinees scored at least 350?

5. Use the table in Problem 4, pg. 159, to answer these questions.
   a. What percentage of people have incomes of at least $25,000?
   b. What percentage of people have incomes of at most $14,999?
   c. Identify the amount below which 44% of the people in the community have lower incomes.
   d. Identify the amount above which 31% of the people in the community have higher incomes.

6. The graph below shows the amount of sales generated by an advertising agency from 1983 through 1991.

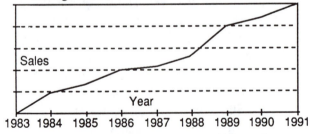

Which one of the following is true according to the graph?
   a. From 1983 through 1991 sales increased by millions of dollars.
   b. Sales began to stabilize from 1988 onward.
   c. There is no trend in sales over time.
   d. Sales steadily increased over time.

7. The following plot depicts the number of seals sighted and the average temperature on Limantour Beach of the Point Reyes peninsula (Point Reyes, California) for 10 days.

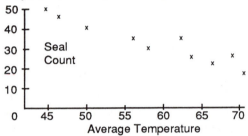

Which one of the following is true according to the graph?
   a. There is no association between seal count and the average temperature.
   b. Increased average temperature caused the decrease in seal count.
   c. The seal count began to stabilize as the temperature rose above 55 degrees.
   d. When the average temperature was 50 degrees, approximately 42 seals were sighted.

8. Use the bar graph below showing crimes in a community:
   a. Approximately how many crimes were committed in 1974?
   b. Between which two consecutive years occurred the greatest increase in crimes?

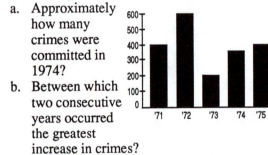

   c. Which two years had comparable numbers of crimes?
   d. About how many more crimes were committed in 1972 than 1973?

9. Which one of the following is false according to the bar graph?

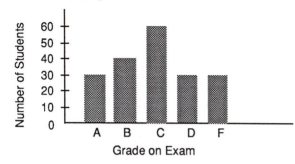

Grade on Exam

a. More students earned Bs than Fs on the exam.
b. The number of students earning the grade of C was double the number earning the grade of F.
c. 200 students took the exam.
d. If D is considered to be the lowest passing grade, then around 16% of the students who took the exam failed it.

10. In the circle graph shown, how much more money for every $10,000 is spent on education than on utilities?

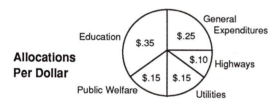

Allocations Per Dollar

11. Use the circle graph below to select the false statement.

How John Spent His $1000 Paycheck Each Month

a. John spends $3,600 per year on mortgage payments.
b. John spends $200 per month on his car.
c. John spends the same amount on utilities as on clothing.
d. John's medical expenses are $800 per year.

12. The line graph below shows the number of shares of a certain stock sold from June to December.

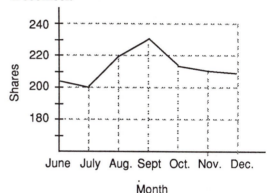

Month

a. What is the percent increase from July to September? (Hint: The fraction for percent increase is the amount of increase divided by the original amount.)
b. What is the percent decrease from September to December? (Hint: The fraction for percent decrease is the amount of decrease divided by the original amount.) Round your answer to the nearest tenth of a percent.

13. The circle graph below shows the amount of money contributed to five charitable organizations. What percent of total money is contributed to organizations 2, 4, and 5 combined?
a. 75%
b. 37.5%
c. 30%
d. 15%

$10 mil
$20 mil
5
4
1
3
$25 mil
$100 mil
2
$45 mil

Topic 7

Descriptive Statistics Of Central Tendency

One of the important tasks of the statistician is to describe a set of data quantitatively. Values called statistics of central tendency indicate where the data tend to cluster. At the end of this section you need to be able to compute these values. You should also know the relative positions of these values in a variety of distributions.

Descriptive statistics condense large amounts of data to a smaller amount of descriptive numbers. Central tendency statistics answer the question: On the whole (on the average), how did the sample do? The three measures of central tendency are defined below.

◊ Definitions

Central Tendency Statistics

1. The **mode** — The mode is the most frequent score or scores. If there is no value that occurs most often, the set of data has no mode.

2. The **median** ($\bar{x}$) — The median for a set of data, arranged in order of size, is the score in the middle (when there is an odd number of scores) or the average of the two scores in the middle (when there is an even number of scores).

3. The **mean** ($\bar{x}$) — The mean is the arithmetic average of all the scores found by finding their sum and dividing by the number of scores. The formula below for finding the mean uses the symbols Σx which indicates the sum of all the scores and n which stands for the number of scores.

$$\bar{x} = \frac{\Sigma x}{n}$$

Problem 1

In each set of data, find the mean, median and mode.
a.   {91, 93, 95, 95, 97, 99}

Solution

Mean: $\dfrac{\text{Sum of all scores}}{\text{Number of scores}} = \dfrac{91 + 93 + 95 + 95 + 97 + 99}{6} = \dfrac{570}{6} = 95$

Median: The scores are in order of size. Since there are six scores (an even number of scores), the median is the average of the two middle scores, 95 and 95. The median is $\dfrac{190}{2}$ or 95.

Mode: The most frequent score is 95.

In this distribution of scores, the mean, median and mode have identical values. The distribution begins to suggest the case where most of the scores are clustered at the center (at the mean), with scores increasing and decreasing from the mean in an identical fashion.

The bell-shaped graph suggested by this situation is shown at the right. We will discuss distributions with bell-shaped curves in Topic 9.

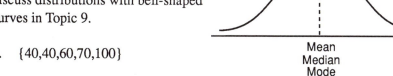

Mean
Median
Mode

b.   {40, 40, 60, 70, 100}

Solution

Mean: $\dfrac{\Sigma x}{n} = \dfrac{40 + 40 + 60 + 70 + 100}{5} = \dfrac{310}{5} = 62$

Median: The scores are in order of size. Since there are five scores (an odd number of scores), the median is the score in the middle. The median is 60.

Mode: The most frequent score is 40.

This distribution begins to suggest the case of many low scores and just a few extreme high scores. The mean is pulled in the direction of the rare scores, in this situation the extreme score of 100. The mean of a distribution is affected by rare extreme values in the data and is pulled in the direction of the extreme values.

The graph suggested by this situation of many low scores and a few high scores is shown at the right. Notice that the mode lies to the left of the median since it is the value that occurs most often.

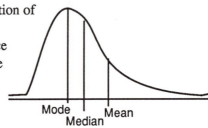

Mode
Median
Mean

c.   {30,70,90,100,100,100}

Solution

Mean: $\dfrac{\Sigma x}{n} = \dfrac{30 + 70 + 90 + 100 + 100 + 100}{6} = \dfrac{490}{6} = 81\frac{2}{3}$

Median: The scores are in order of size. Since there are six scores (an even number of scores), the median is the average of the two middle scores, 90 and 100. The median is $\dfrac{190}{2}$ or 95.

Mode: The most frequent score is 100.

This distribution begins to suggest the case of many high scores (90,100,100,100) and a few extreme low scores. The mean is, once again, pulled in the direction of the extreme score (the 30) and is now smaller than the median and the mode.

The graph suggested by this situation of many high scores and a few low scores is shown at the right. The mean lies to the left of the median because the mean is affected by extreme data values. The mode lies to the right of the median since the mode is the value that occurs most often and the very high scores occur most frequently.

Mean
Median
Mode

d.   {7.2, 2.3, 3.9, 1.1}

Solution

Mean: $\dfrac{\Sigma x}{n} = \dfrac{7.2 + 2.3 + 3.9 + 1.1}{4} = \dfrac{14.5}{4} = 3.625$

Median: First arrange the scores in order of size. 1.1, 2.3, 3.9, 7.2.
With four (even) scores, the median is the average of the two
middle scores. The median is $\dfrac{2.3 + 3.9}{2} = \dfrac{6.2}{2} = 3.1$

Mode: Since each score occurs once, there is no mode.

Problem 2

In the set $\{3,5,8,12\}$, x is a central tendency statistic and $x = 7$.
Find x in the set $\{1.1, 2.3, 3.8, 7.2, 8.1\}$.

Solution

We must determine if x represents mode, median, or mean. Since the set
$\{3,5,8,12\}$ has no mode and $x = 7$, x is not the mode. The median of the set
$\{3,5,8,12\}$ is $\dfrac{5 + 8}{2}$ or 6.5. Since $x = 7$, x is not the median.

The mean of the set $\{3,5,8,12\}$ is $\dfrac{3 + 5 + 8 + 12}{4} = \dfrac{28}{4} = 7.$

Since $x = 7$, x is the mean. Thus, finding x for the set
$\{1.1, 2.3, 3.8, 7.2, 8.1\}$
is equivalent to finding the mean of the data in the set.

$$x = \dfrac{1.1 + 2.3 + 3.8 + 7.2 + 8.1}{5} = \dfrac{22.5}{5} = 4.5$$

The fact that a single extreme value can greatly affect the mean can result in giving
the extreme value too much influence. For example, the ages of five people are 3, 4,
5, 6 and 27. The mean age is $\dfrac{45}{5}$ or 9 years. However, to say that the average age is
9 years misrepresents the situation since 4 of the 5 people are younger than 9 years.
In this case, the mean is not really the most typical number of the data it is supposed
to describe.

Probability and Statistics

Like the mean, one and only one median can be determined for a set of data. Like the mean, the median may or may not be one of the data items. Unlike the mean, the median is not dependent upon every item in the data. The median is not affected by an extreme value. Rather, the median is affected by the position of each data item but not the value of each item. For the set of data {2,4,5,6,8}, $\bar{x} = 5$. For the set of data {2,4,5,6,20}, $\bar{x} = 5$.

In certain instances, the median better describes the most typical value than the mean. To illustrate, the mean of the set {3,4,5,6,27} is 9, which is greater than four of the five data items. The median is 5 and better describes the most typical value.

Keeping in mind that the mean is pulled in the direction of extreme scores and that the mode is the most frequent score, it is possible to determine the relative positions of mean, median, and mode in a variety of distributions even if we cannot determine the specific value for each of these statistics.

E X A M P L E In a mathematics class, half the students scored 85 on an achievement test. Most of the remaining students scored 75 except for a few who scored 20. In this distribution of relatively high scores, we can certainly conclude that the mode is 85, since it is the score that occurs most frequently. Since the mean is pulled in the direction of the extreme scores, we see that the mean will be lowered by the few scores of 20. Consequently, the mode is greater than the mean. Depending on the number of scores, the median will either be 85 or the average of 85 and 75, although it will certainly have a greater value than the mean which, again, is pulled downward by the few 20s.

E X A M P L E On a statistics test, over half the students scored 75. Most of the remaining students scored 50. A few scored 100. In this distribution, we can immediately conclude that the mode is 75, since it is the score that occurs most frequently. The median is also 75 because if any score occurs more than half the time, it must be the score in the middle when data are arranged in order. Thus, the mode and the median have the same value. Every score of 50 and every score of 100 will keep the mean balanced at 75, but since there are more 50s than 100s, the mean will be pulled below 75. Thus, the mean is less than both the mode and the median.

In order to compute the mean from a frequency distribution, we can use the formula

$$\bar{x} = \frac{\Sigma xf}{n} \quad \text{in which}$$

x   refers to the score.

f   refers to the frequency of each score.

xf   refers to the product of each score and its frequency of occurrence.

Σxf refers to the sum of the xf's.

n   refers to the total frequency of the entire distribution.

Problem 3

Find the mean of the frequency distribution shown below.

x	f
1	1
2	3
3	4
4	4
5	6
6	5
7	3
8	2

Solution

A third column, showing the product of each score and its frequency of occurrence (xf), is now added to the table. The sum of xf's (Σxf) appears at the bottom of this column. Thus,

$$\bar{x} = \frac{\Sigma xf}{n} = \frac{132}{28} = 4.71$$

x	f	xf
1	1	1
2	3	6
3	4	12
4	4	16
5	6	30
6	5	30
7	3	21
8	2	16
	n=28	Σxf=132

169

Problem 4

The table below shows the distribution of the ideal number of children based on a Gallup poll conducted in the spring of 1976 in America, Australia, and Japan. (The poll question asked: "If a young married couple could have as many or as few children as they wanted during their lifetime, what number would you, yourself, suggest?")

Proportion of Respondents

Ideal Number of Children	USA	Australia	Japan
0	.06	.02	.00
1	.05	.06	.00
2	.52	.38	.41
3	.19	.25	.44
4	.18	.29	.15

a. Determine the median ideal number of children in the USA.
b. Determine the modal ideal number of children in Japan.
c. Determine the mean ideal number of children in Australia.

Solution

The problem becomes somewhat easier if we change the proportions to percents, and then drop the percent signs, thinking of the number of times that each score occurs out of a total of 100 cases. We obtain the following distribution:

Number of Respondents

Ideal Number of Children	USA f	Australia f	Japan f
0	6	2	0
1	5	6	0
2	52	38	41
3	19	25	44
4	18	29	15
	n = 100	n = 100	n = 100

a.   The median ideal number of children in the USA is the score in $\frac{n+1}{2}$ position. Since $\frac{n+1}{2} = \frac{100+1}{2} = 50.5$, we want the average of the scores in 50th and 51st positions. The USA column indicates that the score 2 falls in positions 12 through 63 inclusively, meaning that it certainly is the average of scores in positions 50 and 51. The median ideal number of children in the USA is 2.

b.   The modal ideal number of children in Japan corresponds to the score with the greatest frequency. Focusing on the last column, we see that the greatest frequency is 44, corresponding to a score of 3. The modal ideal number of children in Japan is 3.

c.   Using the same approach as problem 3, we can compute the mean for the Australia column using the formula $\overline{x} = \frac{\Sigma xf}{n}$.

x	f (Australia)	x f
0	2	0
1	6	6
2	38	76
3	25	75
4	29	<u>116</u>
		$\Sigma xf = 273$

$$\overline{x} = \frac{\Sigma xf}{n} = \frac{273}{100} = 2.73$$

The mean ideal number of children in Australia is 2.73.

Problem Set 7

1.   Find the mode, median, and mean: 9,7,4,9,5

2.   Find the mode, median, and mean:
1,3,5,10,8,5,6,8

3.   Use the graph at the right indicating enrollment in Orange High School for grades 7 through 12 for the following:
   a.   Find the mean number of pupils in grades 7 through 12.
   b.   Find the median number of pupils in grades 7 through 12.
   c.   Find the modal number of pupils in grades 7 through 12.

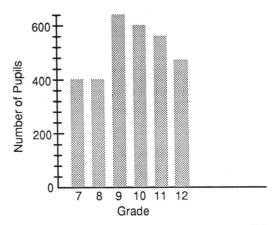

171

Probability and Statistics

4. Three sets of data are shown below. In each case, the value of x represents the same type of measure of central tendency. What is the value of x for the following list of numbers?
{5,5,10,12}

8	3	2
9	5	2
9	5	3
10	7	9
x = 9	x = 5	x = 4

a. 5   b. 7.5   c. 8   d. 10

5. For the following groups of numbers, the value x represents the same type of measure of central tendency.

5,2,6,1,7   x = 5
4,2,9,8,3,10   x = 6
5,7,9,11,12   x = 9

Find x for the group 5,10,6,5,5.

a. 5   b. 5.5   c. 6   d. 6.5

6. The graph below shows the temperature at five locations at noon on Dec. 25, 1970.

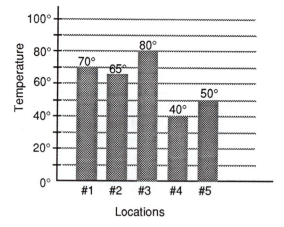

Which one of the following statements is true according to the graph?

a. The mean temperature for the five locations is 61°, and the median temperature for the five locations is 80°.

b. The mean temperature for the five locations is 60°, and the median temperature for the five locations is 65°.

c. The mean and the median temperatures for the five locations differ by 4°.

d. Location #4 had only $\frac{1}{3}$ the temperature as location #3 at noon on Dec. 25, 1970.

7. The graph shown below depicts the distribution of scores for a final examination in mathematics. Select the statement that is true about the distribution of scores.

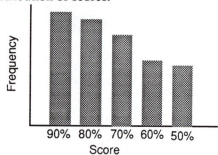

a. The median is greater than the mode.
b. The mean is less than the mode.
c. The median and the mode have identical values.
d. The mean and the mode have identical values.

8. This past year 400 waterfront homes were sold in the Upper Keys. Precisely 300 homes sold for $150,000. Some homes sold in the $150,000 to $250,000 range, and some sold in the $250,000 to $1,000,000 range. Six of the houses sold for more than $1,000,000. Which of the following is true about the distribution for the prices of the homes?

a. The mean, median, and mode have identical values.
b. The mean is less than the median.
c. The mean is greater than the median.
d. The mode is greater than the mean.

9. In a class of 100 students, 60 students scored 55% on an examination. The remaining students scored between 90% and 95%. Select the statement that is true about the distribution of scores.
   a. The mode is greater than the mean.
   b. The mode and the median have the same value.
   c. The mode is greater than the median.
   d. The median is greater than the mean.

10. The graph below shows a distribution of years of education for people in a particular community. Select the statement that is true about the distribution of years of education.

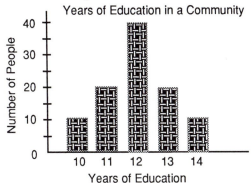

   a. The mode is greater than the median.
   b. The mean is less than the mode.
   c. The mean, median, and mode are equal.
   d. The mode is less than the median.

11. For the following sets of numbers, the value x represents the same type of measure of central tendency.
   {4, 4, 4, 4, 4}   x = 4
   {2, 3, 3, 5, 8}   x = 3
   {5, 6, 8, 9}   x = 7
   What is the value of x for:
   {0.01, 0.01, 0.1, 0.4}?
   a. 0.01   b. 0.105   c. 0.55   d. 0.055

12. The scores of attitudes toward minorities for 31 students were arranged in the accompanying frequency distribution. Higher scores indicate more favorable attitudes. Find the mode, median, and mean for these scores.

Attitude Score	f
1	2
2	4
3	5
4	7
5	6
6	4
7	3

$$n = 31$$

13. Use the table in Problem 4, pg. 170 to answer these questions.
   a. Determine the median ideal number of children in Australia and Japan.
   b. Determine the modal ideal number of children in the USA and Australia.
   c. Determine the mean ideal number of children in the USA and Japan.

14. A student's parents promise to purchase a motorcycle for her if she has an A average. Her examination grades are 97%, 97%, 41%, 5% and 13%. The student tells her parents that her average is an A. How is this student lying with statistics?

Descriptive Statistics Of Variability

This section presents two ways of describing the variability of a set of data. At the end of the section you need to be able to compute the range and standard deviation for a set of data.

Measures of variability answer the question:
What was the spread of scores for the sample?

Two measures of variability are considered here:
1. The range is the numerical difference between the highest and lowest score.
2. The standard deviation (denoted by s). Informally speaking, this statistic gives the average of the deviations of all raw scores from the mean. The formula for finding standard deviation is:

$$s = \sqrt{\frac{\Sigma(x - \bar{x})^2}{n}}$$

In words the formula states:

a. Subtract the mean from each score. $(x - \bar{x})$

b. Square each difference. $(x - \bar{x})^2$

c. Add all the squared differences. $\Sigma(x - \bar{x})^2$

d. Divide by the number of scores, n. $\dfrac{\Sigma(x - \bar{x})^2}{n}$

e. Take the square root of the quotient. $s = \sqrt{\dfrac{\Sigma(x - \bar{x})^2}{n}}$

Problem 1

Using the following list of raw data: 5,5,6,8,9,9,10,10,10
Find the mean, range, and standard deviation.

Solution

$$\text{Mean} = \frac{5 + 5 + 6 + 8 + 9 + 9 + 10 + 10 + 10}{9} = \frac{72}{9} = 8$$

Range = highest score – lowest score = 10 – 5 = 5

Making a table like the one below is helpful in computing the standard deviation.

Score	Score – Mean	(Score – Mean)^2
x	x – 8	(x – 8)^2
5	-3	9
5	-3	9
6	-2	4
8	0	0
9	1	1
9	1	1
10	2	4
10	2	4
10	2	4
		$\Sigma(x - \bar{x})^2 = 36$

$$s = \sqrt{\frac{\Sigma(x - \bar{x})^2}{n}} = \sqrt{\frac{36}{9}} = \sqrt{4} = 2$$

Informally speaking, we can say that on the average the scores deviate 2 units from the mean.

Problem Set 8

1. Find the mean, range and standard deviation of: 10,11,13,14, and 17.

2. Find the mean, range, and standard deviation of: 8,10,12, 16, and 19.

3. Compute the standard deviation of the following set of data: {4,7,10,8,6,7}

4. Compute the standard deviation of the following set of data: {5,8,11,4,6,2,4,8}

5. Given the data: 7, 7, 7, 7. Without actually computing the standard deviation, which of the following best approximates the standard deviation?

    a. 7   b. 0   c. 28

    d. cannot be determined without actual computation

6. Given the data: 7, 9, 10, 11, 13. Without actually computing the standard deviation, which of the following best approximates the standard deviation?

   a. 10   b. 6   c. 2   d. 20

7. Two classes have means of 70%. Group 1 has a standard deviation of 5%. Group 2 has a standard deviation of 15%. Which group would be easier to teach?

Topic 9

The Normal Distribution

In research many distributions of data have similar bell-shaped curves. At the end of this section you need to know the characteristics of these distributions. You should also be able to solve problems based upon these bell-shaped graphs.

In Topic 7 we observed that graphs of data can assume a variety of shapes. Of particular interest to us is the situation where most of the scores are clustered at the center (representing mean, median and mode), with scores increasing and decreasing from the mean in a symmetric fashion.

Such a distribution of data is called a **normal distribution** and the continuous curve, shown at the right, is called a **normal curve**. We consider that the total area under the normal curve represents 100% of the data in the distribution. Stated another way, we say that the total area under the curve is equal to 1.

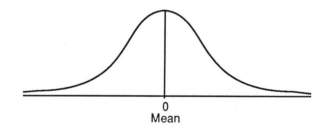

The normal distribution plays an important role in many situations where data are collected. Indeed, much of what comprises the formal study of elementary statistics involves the normal distribution. This is because measurements of data collected in nature often follow distributions that are approximately normal. The heights and weights of large populations of human beings are examples of distributions that are approximately normal. In these distributions, the data items tend to cluster around the mean and become more spread out as they differ from the mean. Theoretically, the normal curve represents a complicated mathematical formula rather than an actual set of data.

Values called **z scores** or **standard scores** are assigned to points on the horizontal axis, as shown. Each z score represents the distance from the mean in standard deviation units. Any item in the data can be converted to its matching z score by the use of the following conversion formula:

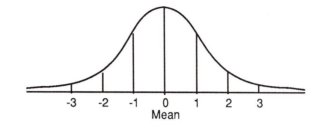

$$z = \frac{\text{(data item's value)} - \text{mean}}{\text{standard deviation}}$$

Since the researcher must distinguish between characteristics of the sample studied and the population to which we generalize, two different symbols are used to represent the mean and the standard deviation.

Symbols for the Mean and Standard Deviation	
Sample	Population
Mean: x̄	μ ("mu")
Standard Deviation: s	σ ("sigma")

Consequently, differences between x̄ and μ, as well as s and σ, are related to sampling error. Because the normal distribution is a theoretical distribution based upon an entire population, the letters μ and σ are used to symbolically describe a z score.

$$z = \frac{x - \mu}{\sigma}$$

Problem 1

Consider the following data on two tests with normal distributions:

	Your Score	Mean for Test	Standard Deviation for Test
Arithmetic Test	70	60	20
Vocabulary Test	66	60	2

a. Convert your scores to z scores.

Solution

Arithmetic z score = $\frac{x - \mu}{\sigma} = \frac{70 - 60}{20} = \frac{10}{20} = 0.5$

(The arithmetic score is half a standard deviation above the mean.)

Vocabulary z score = $\frac{x - \mu}{\sigma} = \frac{66 - 60}{2} = \frac{6}{2} = 3$

(The vocabulary score is 3 standard deviations above the mean.)

b.   Indicate where your scores fall on the horizontal axis of the normal curve.

Solution

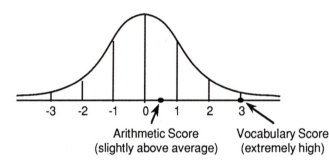

Arithmetic Score
(slightly above average)

Vocabulary Score
(extremely high)

The graph at the right is, again, the normal curve. By looking at its shape, we can get an idea of the important properties of the normal distribution.

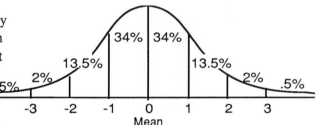

1.   The normal curve represents a mathematical equation rather than an actual set of data, but many sets of data conform to this theoretical notion.

2.   Most of the scores in the normal curve are clustered about the mean. As the deviation from the mean increases, there are fewer and fewer scores.

3. The normal curve is symmetric about the mean. If the graph of the curve were folded along the mean (its highest point), two congruent halves would be created. 50% of the scores are above the mean and 50% are below the mean. Observe that :
    34% + 13.5% + 2% + 0.5% = 50%.

4. The peak point of the normal curve corresponds with the mean, the median, and the mode of its distribution. In other words, the mean, median and mode have identical values. Expressed as a z score, this value is 0.

5. The horizontal axis is generally labeled with z scores, 0 at the mean, positive z scores to the right of the mean and negative z scores to the left.

6. The tails of the curve that approach but never touch the horizontal axis are very close to it at z scores of 3 and -3.

7. The area between the mean and 1 standard deviation above the mean is approximately 34% of the total area under the curve. Thus, the probability of randomly selecting a data item between the mean and z = 1 is approximately 0.34.

8. The area between 1 and 2 standard deviations above the mean is approximately 13.5% of the total area under the curve. The probability of randomly selecting a data item between z = 1 and z = 2 is approximately 0.135. By symmetry, the area between z = -1 and z = -2 is also approximately 13.5% of the total area under the curve.

9. The area between 2 and 3 standard deviations above the mean is approximately 2% of the total area under the curve. Approximately 0.5% of the data fall more than 3 standard deviations above the mean. Actually, some data fall further than 4 standard deviations above the mean, although the probability of randomly selecting a data item greater than z = 3 is only 0.005 (or $\frac{5}{1000}$).

Problem 2

Suppose the height of college students is normally distributed with a mean of 70.2 inches and a standard deviation of 5.3 inches. What percent of the students have a height of less than 59.6 inches?

Solution

Step 1
Draw a normal curve in which the mean of 70.2 corresponds to the z value of 0 on the standard normal curve and represent 59.6 on the horizontal axis.

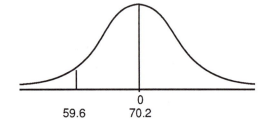

Step 2
Shade the portion of the area under the curve that represents the percent of the students having a height of less than 59.6 inches.

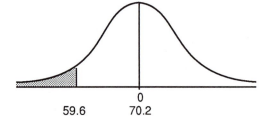

Step 3
Convert 59.6 to a z value.

$$z = \frac{x - \mu}{\sigma} = \frac{59.6 - 70.2}{5.3} = \frac{-10.6}{5.3} = -2$$

Thus, the value 59.6 lies 2 standard deviations below the mean.

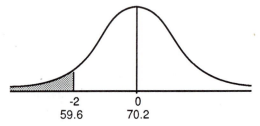

Step 4
Recall that the area between the mean and 2 standard deviations below the mean is approximately 47.5% (34% + 13.5%). Thus, the shaded area represents 50% − 47.5% or 2.5%. Approximately 2.5% of the students have a height of less than 59.6 inches.

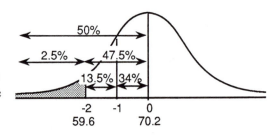

We know that integral z values such as -3, -2, -1, 0, 1, 2 and 3 define particular areas under the normal curve between these values and the mean. If the conversion formula for z yields a non-integral value such as 1.25, then a special table is required to find area. Such a table, called the Z Table, appears below. The z scores in this table begin at 0 and include increments of $\frac{1}{4}$.

Z Table

Standard deviations above mean	Area between mean and indicated standard deviation above mean
0.00	0.000
0.25	0.099
0.50	0.192
0.75	0.273
1.00	0.341
1.25	0.394
1.50	0.433
1.75	0.460
2.00	0.477
2.25	0.488
2.50	0.494
2.75	0.497
3.00	0.499

For example, this table tells us that the percent of area under the normal curve between z = 0 and z = 1.25 is 0.394 = 39.4%, as shown in the graph at the right. Observe that the left column of the table involves a z score. The right column gives the percent of area between z = 0 and the z value in the left column.

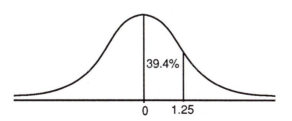

39.4%

0   1.25

Problems involving the normal curve can be solved using the Z Table and the following procedure:

> **Procedure For Solving Problems Based Upon The Normal Distribution**
>
> 1. Convert all data items to z scores using $z = \frac{x - \mu}{\sigma}$.
>
> 2. Make a sketch of the normal curve. Along the horizontal axis show the mean $(z = 0)$ and all z scores obtained in Step 1. Shade the region whose area is desired.
>
> 3. Use the Z table to fill in the appropriate percents under the curve, and answer the question.

Problem 3

The mean weight of newborn babies is 7 pounds and the standard deviation is 0.8 pounds. The characteristic of weight of newborn infants is normally distributed.

a. What percent of newborn babies weigh more than 8 pounds?

Solution

Step 1
Convert 8 to a z value.
$$z = \frac{x - \mu}{\sigma} = \frac{8 - 7}{.8} = \frac{1}{.8} = 1.25$$

Step 2
Make a sketch. The shaded region represents the percent of babies weighing more than 8 pounds.

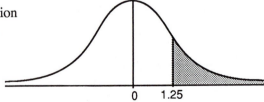

Step 3

Use the Z Table. As shown at the right, the table indicates that 39.4% of the infants weigh between the mean (7 pounds; z = 0) and z = 1.25 (where 1.25 represents 8 pounds). The total area

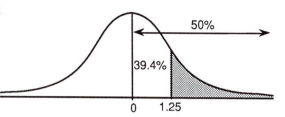

above the mean is 50%. Thus the area of the shaded region is 50% – 39.4% = 10.6%. Approximately 10.6% of the infants weigh more than 8 pounds.

b. What percent of newborn babies weigh between 6 and 8 pounds?

Solution

Step 1

Convert 6 and 8 to z values.

$$z = \frac{x - \mu}{\sigma} = \frac{6 - 7}{.8} = \frac{-1}{.8} = -1.25$$

From part a, z(8) = 1.25.

Step 2

Make a sketch. The shaded region represents the percent of babies weighing between 6 and 8 pounds.

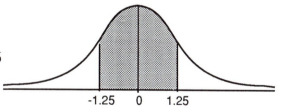

Step 3

Use the Z Table. As shown at the right, the table indicates that 39.4% of the infants weigh between z = 0 and z = 1.25. By symmetry, the area between the mean and

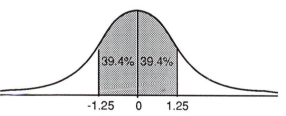

1.25 is the same as the area between the mean and -1.25, also 39.4%. The sketch indicates that the desired area can be obtained by adding these percents.

$$39.4\% + 39.4\% = 78.8\%.$$

Approximately 78.8% of the infants weigh between 6 and 8 pounds. Said in another way, the probability of randomly selecting a newborn baby weighing between 6 and 8 pounds is 0.788 (or 0.79, rounded to the nearest hundredth).

c.   What percent of newborn babies weigh between 8 and 9 pounds?

Solution

Step 1
Convert 8 and 9 to z values.
From part a, z(8) = 1.25
$$z = \frac{x - \mu}{\sigma} = \frac{9 - 7}{.8} = \frac{2}{.8} = 2.5$$

Step 2
Make a sketch. The shaded region represents the percent of babies weighing between 8 and 9 pounds.

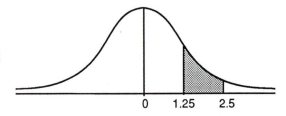

Step 3
Use the Z Table. As shown at the right, the table indicates that 39.4% of the area falls between z = 0 and z = 1.25. Furthermore, 49.4% of the area falls between z = 0 and z = 2.5. The sketch indicates that the desired area can be obtained by subtracting these percents.

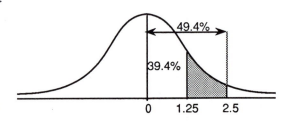

49.4% − 39.4% = 10%.

Approximately 10% of the infants weigh between 8 and 9 pounds. Thus, the probability of randomly selecting a newborn baby weighing between 8 and 9 pounds is 0.1 (or $\frac{1}{10}$).

Problem Set 9

1. Label each statement below as true or false for a set of scores that is normally distributed.
   a. The probability of selecting a score between the mean and 1 standard deviation above the mean is approximately 0.34.
   b. 68% of the scores are between the mean and the median.
   c. The percentage of scores above any score is equal to the percentage of scores below that score.
   d. The mean and the median have the same value.
   e. 50% of the scores fall at or above the mean.
   f. The normal curve is symmetric.
   g. The percent of scores between one and two standard deviations equals the percent of scores between two and three standard deviations.
   h. The percent of scores between +1 and +2 standard deviations equals the percent of scores between -1 and -2 standard deviations.
   i. All but 5% of the scores fall within two standard deviations of the mean score.
   j. All of the scores must fall within four standard deviations of the mean.

Use the approximate percents under the normal curve for integral values of z (that is, 34%, 13.5%, 2% and 0.5%) to answer questions 2 and 3.

2. In a large city the graduating scholastic averages of high school students are normally distributed with a mean of 78 and a standard deviation of 6. Find:
   a. the percent of students who have averages of more than 72.
   b. the probability that a student has an average of more than 72.
   c. the percent of students who have averages of less than 72.
   d. the probability that a student has an average of less than 72.
   e. the percent of students who have averages between 84 and 90.
   f. the probability that a student has an average between 84 and 90.
   g. the percent of students who have averages between 72 and 84.
   h. the probability that a student has an average between 72 and 84.

3. The mean weight of 1,000 male students at a certain college is 160 pounds, and the standard deviation is 12.5 pounds. Assume that the weights are normally distributed.
   a. How many students weigh between 147.5 pounds and 172.5 pounds?
   b. How many students weigh less than 147.5 pounds?

Probability and Statistics

Use the Z Table to answer questions 4-6.

Standard deviations above mean	Area between mean and indicated standard deviation above mean
0.00	0.000
0.25	0.099
0.50	0.192
0.75	0.273
1.00	0.341
1.25	0.394
1.50	0.433
1.75	0.460
2.00	0.477
2.25	0.488
2.50	0.494
2.75	0.497
3.00	0.499

4. The IQs of individuals in a population are approximately normally distributed with a mean of 100 and a standard deviation of 10.
   a. What percent of individuals have IQs greater than 125?
   b. What percent of individuals have IQs between 105 and 115?
   c. Find the probability of randomly selecting an individual with an IQ between 80 and 105.
   d. If 100,000 individuals are randomly sampled from the population, approximately how many will have IQs between 80 and 105?
   e. What percent of individuals have IQs less than 105?

5. The mean weight of 100 women is 115 with a standard deviation of 10. If the weights are normally distributed, find:
   a. the percent of women who weigh more than 130 pounds.
   b. the number of women who weigh less than 117.5 pounds.
   c. the number of women who weigh between 110 and 130 pounds.
   d. the percent of women who weigh between 90 and 127.5 pounds.

6. The mean age of 1,000 people living in a retirement community is 68 years with a standard deviation of 4 years. Assume that the ages are normally distributed. Find:
   a. the number of people with ages between 66 and 74 years.
   b. the percent of people whose ages exceed 70 years.
   c. the number of people whose ages are between 62 and 66 years.

7. Study the three examples below, in which each data item for a normal distribution is converted to the z score at the right.

Data Item	Standard z Score
102	-1
108	0
120	2

What is the z score for a data item of 123?

Chapter 2 Summary

1. The Fundamental Counting Principle

If task 1 can be performed in m ways, task 2 in n ways, task 3 in p ways, task 4 in q ways, etc., then all tasks can be performed in m • n • p • q ... ways.

2. Permutations

The number of permutations (arrangements) of n distinct objects taken r at a time can be computed by the Fundamental Counting Principle. Order is important in permutation situations.

3. Combinations

The number of combinations (selections) of n distinct objects taken r at a time, denoted by $\binom{n}{r}$, is $\frac{n!}{r!\,(n - r)!}$. Order is not important in combination situations.

4. Sample Space

The set of all possible outcomes in an experiment is called the sample space, denoted by S. An event, A, is a subset of the sample space.

5. Probability

a. $P(A) = \dfrac{\text{the number of outcomes in A}}{\text{the number of outcomes in the sample space}}$

b. If A cannot occur, $P(A) = 0$.

c. If A is certain to occur, $P(A) = 1$

d. $0 \leq P(A) \leq 1$

e. $P(A') =$ the probability that A will not occur $= 1 - P(A)$

f. $P(A \text{ or } B) = P(A) + P(B) - P(A \text{ and } B \text{ occur simultaneously})$
    Equivalently: $P(A \text{ or } B) = P(A) + P(B) - P(A \cap B)$

g. If A and B are mutually exclusive, $P(A \cap B) = 0$.
    Thus, $P(A \text{ or } B) = P(A) + P(B)$.

    h.   If A and B are independent events (the occurrence of A does not affect the occurrence of B), then: P(A followed by B) = P(A) • P(B).

    i.   If A and B are dependent events (the occurrence of A affects the occurrence of B), then:

$$P(A \text{ followed by } B) = P(A) \cdot P(B \text{ given that A has occurred}).$$

Equivalently: P(A followed by B) = P(A) • P(B|A)

    j.   The probability of a permutation (arrangement) is

$$\frac{\text{the number of ways of forming the permutation}}{\text{the total number of arrangements}}$$

The numerator and denominator are computed using the Fundamental Counting Principle (see item 1).

    k.   The probability of a selection (combination) is

$$\frac{\text{the number of ways of making that selection}}{\text{the total number of selections}}$$

The numerator and denominator of the probability fraction are computed using the combination formula (see item 3). The numerator may also require use of The Fundamental Counting Principle (see item 1).

6. Odds

    a.   The odds in favor of A = $\dfrac{P(A)}{P(A')}$

    b.   If the odds in favor of A are a : b (a to b), then the odds against A are b : a and $P(A) = \dfrac{a}{a+b}$.

7. Samples

    a.   Samples should be representative of the population from which they are drawn.

    b.   Random samples are obtained in such a way that each member of the population has an equal chance of being selected.

8. Statistics of Central Tendency

    a.   **The Mean:** $= \dfrac{\text{the sum of the scores}}{\text{the number of scores}}$

b.   **The Median:** The middle item or the mean of the the two items nearest the middle when the data are arranged in order of size.

c.   **The Mode:**
The value(s) occurring most often in a set of data.

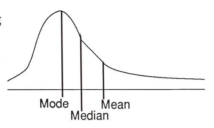 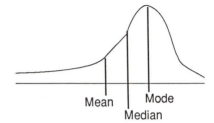

d.   The mean is pulled in the direction of the extreme scores.

e.   Computing the mean:
Ungrouped data: $\bar{x} = \frac{\Sigma x}{n}$

Frequency distribution: $\bar{x} = \frac{\Sigma xf}{n}$

9. The Standard Deviation

a.   Informally speaking, the standard deviation describes the average of the distances that the data items deviate from the mean.

b. $s = \sqrt{\dfrac{\Sigma(x - \bar{x})^2}{n}}$

10. The Normal Curve

a.   Properties of the Normal Curve

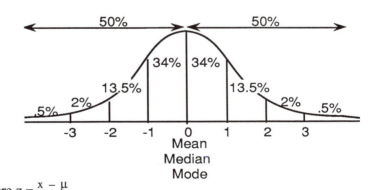

1.   The mean, median and mode have the same value.

2.   The curve is symmetric with respect to the mean.

3.   The horizontal axis is expressed in z values, standard scores or standard deviation units, where $z = \frac{x - \mu}{\sigma}$.

b.   To solve a problem involving the normal curve:
Make a sketch and shade the desired region. Change all scores to z values. Use the z table or, if z is an integer, the percents that appear under the normal curve in item 10a above.

Sample Examination – Probability and Statistics

1. Two-digit numbers larger than 88 are written on separate slips of paper and placed in a hat. If the number on the slip selected is odd, which set represents an appropriate sample space associated with this experiment?
   a. {90, 92, 94, 96, 98}
   b. {89, 90, 91, 92, 93, 94, 95, 96, 97, 98}
   c. {x | 88 < x ≤ 99}
   d. {91, 93, 95, 97, 99}
   e. none of the above

2. A bowl contains three red balls (R_1, R_2, R_3). If two balls are drawn in succession without replacement, which set is an appropriate sample space for this experiment?
   a. {R_1,R_2,R_3}
   b. {(R_1,R_2), (R_1,R_3), (R_2,R_1), (R_3,R_1)}
   c. {(R_1,R_2), (R_1,R_3), (R_2,R_3), (R_2,R_1), (R_3,R_1), (R_3,R_2)}
   d. {(R_1,R_2), (R_1,R_3), (R_2,R_1), (R_2,R_3), (R_3,R_1)}
   e. none of the above

3. A bag contains 2 green balls, 3 red balls, and 4 white balls. One ball is chosen at random from the bag. What is the probability that the ball is white?
   a. $\frac{4}{9}$ b. $\frac{4}{5}$ c. $\frac{7}{9}$
   d. $\frac{2}{9}$ e. none of these

4. If a fair coin is tossed 5 times in succession, the probability that all tosses are Heads is $\frac{1}{32}$. What is the probability that not all tosses are Heads?
   a. 32   b. $\frac{1}{2}$ c. $\frac{31}{32}$
   d. $\frac{15}{16}$ e. none of these

5. What is the probability of obtaining a Head or a Tail if a fair coin is tossed one time?
   a. 0   b. 1   c. 0.5
   d. 0.25   e. none of these

6. Five slips of paper numbered from 1 to 5 are placed in a hat. If one slip is drawn at random, what is the probability that the number is even or greater than 3?
   a. $\frac{2}{5}$ b. $\frac{4}{5}$ c. $\frac{3}{5}$
   d. $\frac{4}{25}$ e. none of these

7. A student is selected at random from a group of 100 students in which 6 take math, 10 take English and 4 take both. What is the probability that the selected student takes math or English?
   a. 0.16   b. 0.12   c. 0.60
   d. 0.20   e. none of these

8. The probability that Mary has a dog is 0.5. The probability that a dog has fleas is 0.8. What is the probability that Mary has a dog with fleas?
   a. 1   b. 0.6   c. 0.4
   d. 0.2   e. none of these

9. A box contains 5 white balls, 4 green balls, and 3 blue balls. Two balls are drawn in succession without replacement. What is the probability that the first ball is green and the second ball is blue?
   a. $\frac{1}{11}$ b. $\frac{1}{9}$ c. $\frac{14}{33}$
   d. $\frac{2}{3}$ e. none of these

10. If two balls are drawn in succession without replacement from a bag containing 3 red balls and 4 yellow balls, what is the probability that neither ball is yellow?
    a. $\frac{6}{49}$ b. $\frac{2}{7}$ c. $\frac{1}{7}$
    d. $\frac{16}{49}$ e. none of these

11. How many 3 digit numbers may be formed using the digits 4, 6, 8, and 9 if no digit may be repeated?
    a. 12   b. 24   c. 48
    d. 64   e. none of these

12. In how many different ways can five students sit in five chairs arranged in a row?
    a. 24   b. 1   c. 60
    d. 5   e. 120

13. How many selections of 4 gifts may be chosen from a collection of 6 different gifts?
    a. 30   b. 60   c. 15
    d. 120   e. none of these

14. A box contains 3 red balls and 5 yellow balls. If one ball is drawn at random, what are the odds in favor of obtaining a red ball?
    a. 3 to 8   b. 3 to 5   c. 5 to 3
    d. 5 to 8   e. none of these

15. Six slips of paper numbered from 1 to 6 are placed in a container. One slip is selected at random. What are the odds against obtaining a number greater than 5?
    a. 1 : 6   b. 6 : 1   c. 1 : 3
    d. 5 : 1   e. none of these

16. The odds against a candidate's election are 2 to 1. With these odds, what is the probability that the candidate will be elected?
    a. $\frac{2}{3}$ b. $\frac{1}{3}$ c. $\frac{3}{2}$
    d. $\frac{3}{1}$ e. none of these

17. Two people are chosen from a group of six Europeans and six Africans. What is the probability that the two people selected are either both Europeans or both Africans if the random selection is done without replacement?
    a. $\frac{5}{11}$ b. $\frac{5}{22}$ c. $\frac{1}{2}$
    d. $\frac{2}{6}+\frac{2}{6}$ e. none of these

18. The three letters A, B, and C form three two-member combinations: (A,B), (A,C), (B,C). In considering these pairs, the order in which the letters appear is not important. Consequently, four letters A, B, C, and D form six two-member combinations: (A,B), (A,C), (A,D), (B,C), (B,D), (C,D). Similarly, five letters A, B, C, D, and E form ten two-member combinations: (A,B), (A,C), (A,D), (A,E), (B,C), (B,D), (B,E), (C,D), (C,E), (D,E). How many two-member combinations can be formed using the six letters A, B, C, D, E, and F?
    a. 18   b. 15   c. 21
    d. 12   e. none of these

19. A box contains three slips of paper numbered 1, 2, and 4. Two slips are drawn without replacement. What is the probability that the sum of the two numbers selected is odd?
    a. $\frac{1}{3}$ b. $\frac{1}{2}$ c. $\frac{2}{3}$
    d. $\frac{5}{6}$ e. none of these

20. A tourist wishes to visit Miami, Ft. Lauderdale, and Palm Beach in a random order. What is the probability that the tourist will visit Palm Beach first, Ft. Lauderdale second, and Miami third?
    a. $\frac{1}{3}$ b. $\frac{1}{6}$ c. $\frac{1}{9}$
    d. $\frac{1}{27}$ e. none of these

21. Box A contains two cards numbered 2 and 4. Box B contains three cards numbered 1, 3, and 5. An experiment consists of selecting a card from each box, first from box A and then from box B. The sample space is:
    S = {(2,1), (2,3), (2,5), (4,1) (4,3), (4,5)}
    What is the probability of selecting one element from this set whose sum is divisible by 3 or greater than 6?
    a. $\frac{1}{3}$ b. $\frac{2}{3}$ c. $\frac{1}{6}$
    d. $\frac{5}{6}$ e. none of these

22. A door prize at a dance is awarded to people who obtain a receipt stamped with the letter P. The management has stamped every 15th receipt with a P. Under these conditions, what are the odds against winning a door prize?
   a. 1:15   b. 15:1   c. 1:14
   d. 14:1   e. none of these

23. A box contains 6 orange marbles and 2 blue marbles. If 3 marbles are drawn at random from the box, find the probability that 2 are orange and 1 is blue.
   a. 30   b. $\frac{15}{56}$ c. $\frac{15}{28}$
   d. $\frac{5}{14}$ e. none of these

24. How many four digit odd numbers can be formed using the digits 1, 2, 4, 5, and 6 if no digit can be repeated?
   a. 12   b. 30   c. 48
   d. 120   e. none of these

25. The well-balanced spinner shown at right is spun twice. What is the probability that the pointer will stop at red on the first spin and then on green on the second spin?

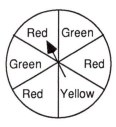

   a. $\frac{1}{2} \cdot \frac{1}{3}$ b. $\frac{1}{2} \cdot \frac{2}{5}$ c. $\frac{1}{6} \cdot \frac{1}{6}$
   d. $\frac{1}{2} + \frac{2}{5}$ e. none of these

26. Consider all four-letter arrangements using the letters A, B, C, and D. Letters are not to be repeated. If all such arrangements are written on a card with one arrangement per card and these cards are placed into a box, what is the probability of randomly selecting an arrangement with A first and D last?
   a. $\frac{1}{6}$ b. $\frac{1}{8}$ c. $\frac{1}{12}$
   d. $\frac{1}{24}$ e. none of these

27. How many ways can 10 people be awarded first, second, and third prize in an art contest, assuming no person can win more than one prize?
   a. 120   b. 720   c. 1000
   d. 10!   e. none of these

28. On a two question multiple choice test, each question has four possible answers, one of which is correct. If you must guess at both questions, what is the probability that you will answer both questions correctly?
   a. $\frac{1}{2}$ b. $\frac{1}{4}$ c. $\frac{1}{8}$
   d. $\frac{1}{16}$ e. none of these

29. One group contains four men and two women. A second group contains three men and five women. Suppose that a person is selected from each group, first from group one and then from group two. What is the probability that both selections are men **or** both selections are women?
   a. $\frac{11}{24}$ b. $\frac{13}{24}$ c. $\frac{11}{21}$
   d. $\frac{13}{21}$ e. none of these

30. Two common sources for receiving the news are magazines and television. Forty percent of American adults get the news from television but not magazines, while 25% receive the news from both television and magazines. What is the probability that a randomly selected adult does not receive the news from television?
   a. 0.85   b. 0.65   c. 0.35
   d. 0.15   e. none of these

The table below shows the distribution of the cause of fires in a particular state.

Cause	Percent of All Fires
Electrical System	8
Heating System	6
Smoking	20
Cooking	37
Appliances	19
Other	10

Use the table to answer problems 31-33.

31. How many of the next 600 fires would one expect to be caused by heating systems or smoking?
   a. 26   b. 154   c. 156
   d. 444   e. none of these

32. What is the probability that a fire is caused by neither cooking nor appliances?
   a. 0.56   b. 0.44   c. 0.34
   d. 0.10   e. none of these

33. If it is known that a fire has not been caused by the electrical or heating systems, find the probability that it was caused by smoking.
   a. $\frac{10}{43}$ b. $\frac{33}{43}$ c. $\frac{1}{5}$
   d. $\frac{7}{10}$ e. none of these

34. A condominium community contains apartments in five different models, each offered in three different color schemes, either with or without a screened porch. How many buying options are available?
   a. 3   b. 10   c. 15
   d. 30   e. none of these

35. Six men and four women are competing to become members of a tennis team that will consist of three men and three women. How many different teams can be selected?
   a. 80   b. 24   c. 10
   d. 9   e. none of these

36. A particular automobile model can be purchased with or without the following options: radial tires, air conditioning, stereo, cruise control. How many different arrangements of these options are available?
   a. 16   b. 8   c. 4
   d. 1   e. none of these

37. Ten percent of the pens that are made by a ballpoint pen manufacturer leak. If two pens are randomly selected with replacement, find the probability that at least one of them leaks.
   a. $\frac{1}{5}$ b. $\frac{1}{10}$ c. $\frac{19}{100}$
   d. $\frac{81}{100}$ e. none of these

38. A box contains eight pens, of which two are defective. If two pens are randomly selected without replacement, find the probability that at least one pen is defective.
   a. $\frac{1}{4}$ b. $\frac{1}{28}$ c. $\frac{13}{28}$
   d. $\frac{15}{28}$ e. none of these

39. A recent survey indicated that ten percent of high school students participate in collegiate theater. Of these, two percent become professional actors. What is the probability that a randomly selected high school student will both participate in collegiate theater and become a professional actor?
   a. 0.002   b. 0.003   c. 0.02
   d. 0.03   e. none of these

40. If Earl is one of 20 students registered for college algebra, and two people are randomly selected to attend a convention, what is the probability that Earl will be one of the selected people?
   a. $\frac{1}{10}$ b. $\frac{1}{20}$ c. $\frac{1}{40}$
   d. $\frac{1}{400}$ e. none of these

41. Find the mean of the data:
    {7, 4, 8, 9, 5, 3, 6, 10, 7, 11}

    a. 5　　b. 6　　c. 7　　d. 8

42. Find the median of the data:
    {7, 5, 9, 4, 3, 10, 8, 6, 2}
    a. 3　　b. 6　　c. 6.5　　d. 7

43. Find the median of the data:
    {7, 3, 9, 7, 3, 8, 6, 4}
    a. 6　　b. 7　　c. 8　　d. 6.5

44. Find the mode of the data:
    {3, 6, 9, 5, 3, 6, 5, 3, 8}
    a. 3　　b. 5　　c. 6　　d. 3 and 5

45. Three sets of data are shown at the right. The x-numbers are the same measure of central tendency.

5	4	5
2	2	7
6	9	9
1	8	11
7	3	12
	10	

    x = 5　　x = 6　　x = 9

    Find the value of x for the set of data shown at the right.

    5
    10
    6
    5

    x = __

    a. 5　　b. 5.5　　c. 6　　d. 6.5

46. To be eligible for the math club, a student must have a mean grade on three qualifying exams of at least 88% and a median grade of at least 90%. Mary has grades of 87%, 87% and 100%. Bob has grades of 80%, 95% and 100%. Susan has grades of 100%, 75% and 100%. Which student(s) is/are eligible for the math club?
    a. Bob and Mary　　b. Mary and Susan
    c. Bob and Susan　　d. Bob only

47. The city council of a large city needs to know if its residents will support the building of three new schools. The council decides to conduct a survey of a sample of the city's residents. Which procedure would be most appropriate for obtaining an unbiased sample of the city's residents?
    a. Survey a random sample of teachers who live in the city.
    b. Survey 100 individuals who are randomly selected from a list of all people living in the state in which the city in question is located.
    c. Survey a random sample of persons within each neighborhood of the city.
    d. Survey every tenth person who enters City Hall on a randomly selected day.

48. The bar graph below shows the market value of a home for each of five years. Which one of the following is true according to the graph?

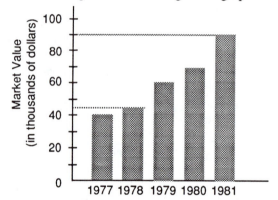

    a. The percent increase in value from 1977 to 1979 is $33\frac{1}{3}\%$.
    b. The value of the home in 1981 was $9,000.
    c. The mean value of the home for the five years exceeds the median value by $1,000.
    d. The mean value of the home for the five years is $60,000.

49. The graph below represents the monthly temperature for 6 months of the year. The readings for March and June fall exactly midway between the horizontal lines. Which one of the following is true according to the graph?

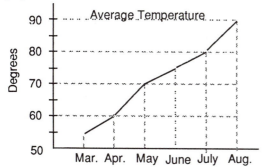

a. The percent increase in temperature from April to August is $33\frac{1}{3}\%$.

b. The mean and median temperatures for the six months differ by less than one degree.

c. The modal temperature for the six months is 90 degrees.

d. The value of the mean temperature for the six months is exactly 71 degrees.

50. The circle graph below shows money contributed to five charities (numbered from 1 to 5). What percent of the money is contributed to charities 1 and 2 combined?

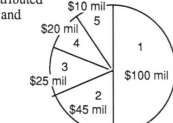

a. 145%
b. 95%
c. 72.5%
d. 70.5%

51. Which of the following statements is true for a set of scores that is normally distributed?

a. The percent of scores between the mean and one standard deviation equals the percent of scores between one and two standard deviations.

b. The percent of scores above any score is equal to the percent of scores below that score.

c. All of the scores must fall within four standard deviations of the mean.

d. The mean, median and mode have the same value.

52. Study the three examples below in which each score for a normal distribution is converted to the z value at the right.

score	standard z value
100	-1
105	0
115	2

What is the z value for a score of 117?
a. 2.25   b. 2.4   c. 2.5   d. 3

53. Use the table shown below to answer the question.

Standard deviations above mean	Proportion of area between mean and indicated standard deviation above mean
0.00	.000
0.25	.099
0.50	.192
0.75	.273
1.00	.341
1.25	.394
1.50	.433
1.75	.460
2.00	.477
2.25	.488
2.50	.494
2.75	.497
3.00	.499

One hundred high school students took an aptitude test which has a mean of 50 and a standard deviation of 10. If their scores are normally distributed, approximately what proportion of the students scored between 55 and 65?

a. 0.9   b. 0.24   c. 0.43   d. 0.63

54. On a recent examination over half the students had a score of 85%. Of the remaining students, most scored between 60% and 80% with the exception of 5% of the group that scored below 20%. Which one of the following is true about the distribution of scores in this situation?
    a. The mode and the mean have the same value.
    b. The mode and the median have the same value.
    c. The mean is greater than the mode.
    d. At least one student scored 10%.

55. The graph below represents the distribution of ages of students at a day camp. Select the statement that is true about the distribution of ages.

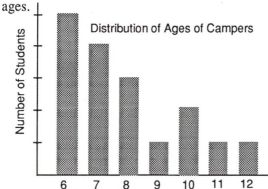

    a. The mode is equal to the median.
    b. The mode is equal to the mean.
    c. The mode is greater than the mean.
    d. The mode is less than the median.

56. In a class of 100 students, 45 students scored 80% on an examination. Of the remaining 55 students, 20 scored between 60% and 70%, and 35 scored under 50%. Select the statement that is true about this distribution of scores.
    a. The mode is greater than the mean.
    b. The mode and the median have the same value.
    c. The mean, median, and mode have the same value.
    d. The exact value for all three statistics of central tendency is unknown.

57. In a set of scores that is normally distributed, 140 has a z-score of 0 and 132 has a z-score of -1. What score has a z-score of 1.25?

    a. 150   b. 152   c. 152.25   d. 152.5

58. Compute the standard deviation for the following set of data: {8, 10, 12, 16, 19}

    a. 4   b. 13   c. 16
    d. None of these

59. The table below indicates scores on a 400-point exam and their corresponding percentile ranks.

Score	Percentile Rank
380	99
350	87
320	72
290	49
260	26
230	8
200	1

    What percentage of examinees scored between 230 and 290?
    a. 41%   b. 49%   c. 72%   d. 98%

The table below shows the distribution of income levels in a community. Refer to this table to answer problems 60 and 61.

Income Level	Percent of People
$0-4,999	7
5,000-9,999	9
10,000-14,999	12
15,000-19,999	18
20,000-24,999	24
25,000-29,999	20
30,000-34,999	7
35,000-39,999	2
40,000 and over	1

60. What percentage of people have incomes of at least $25,000?
    a. 10%   b. 30%   c. 54%   d. 70%

61. Identify the income level which has 28% of the people in the community with lower incomes.
    a. $10,000   b. $14,999
    c. $15,000   d. $19,999

The table below shows the distribution of the number of children in families of a community. Refer to this table to answer problems 62 and 63.

Number of Children	Proportion of Families
0	.45
1	.25
2	.20
3	.05
4	.04
5	.01

62. What is the median number of children per family?
    a. 0   b. 0.5   c. 1   d. 1.5

63. What is the mean number of children per family?
    a. 1   b. 1.01   c. 1.03   d. 1.5

64. The table below indicates the fastest running times (for 26.5 miles) from 1980 through 1989.

Year	Fastest Running Time (in minutes)
1980	155
1981	148
1982	140
1983	134
1984	130
1985	127
1986	126
1987	126
1988	126
1989	126

Which one of the following is true?
a. The fastest running times began to stabilize in 1985.
b. There is no trend in running times for the years shown in the table.
c. With each year in the 1980s, running time steadily decreased.
d. By the mid-1980s, running times only slightly decreased or stabilized.

65. The graph below depicts the number of whales sighted (o) and the number of seals sighted (x) at Point Reyes National Seashore in California.

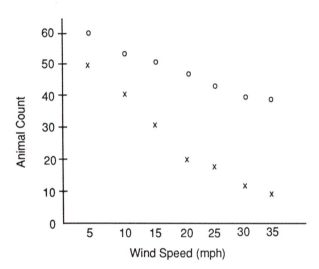

Which one of the following is true?
a. Increased wind speed was directly responsible for the decrease in the number of whales and seals that were sighted.
b. There is an association between wind speed and animal count only for the seals.
c. Approximately 45 seals were sighted when the wind speed was 15 mph.
d. Fewer whales and seals tend to be sighted as the wind speed increases; a stronger relationship exists for the seals than for the whales.

Chapter 3

Informal Geometry

The principles of geometry presented in this chapter are basically those originally established by the Greek mathematician, Euclid, more than 2,000 years ago. These principles comprise what has come to be called Euclidean geometry. This formal geometry is approached in a logical manner. Specific statements (theorems) are proved by reasoning while other statements (axioms or postulates) are accepted without proof.

Much of Euclid's work was based on the parallel postulate that states through a given external point there is only one line that is parallel to a given line. We shall use this postulate to show that the sum of the measures of the three interior angles of a triangle is 180 degrees. However, it was discovered in the nineteenth century that there is a kind of geometry, called hyperbolic geometry, in which Euclid's parallel postulate does not apply. Hyperbolic geometry, useful to Einstein in supplying the mathematics behind relativity theory, sets up a logical structure in which the shortest paths between points are curved lines and triangles no longer contain an angle sum of 180 degrees.

Euclidean geometry is, however, an excellent approximation of physical space. The study of Euclidean geometry should enhance your ability to reason logically based upon a geometric figure. One word of caution. Since this chapter often considers Euclidean ideas within an algebraic context, you might find it useful to review the solution of first degree equations and proportions, discussed under Topics 4 and 7 in Chapter 4.

Lines and Line Segments

Formal geometry emphasizes proving statements, called theorems, using other statements (axioms or postulates) that are accepted without proof. By contrast, the approach of informal geometry is based on observation and intuition. This section contains the basic language and notations for informal geometry. Measurement of line segments is discussed. At the end of this section you should be able to round a linear measurement, convert from one unit of linear measure to another, and solve problems that deal with measurement of line segments.

Point is a basic idea of informal geometry. A point may be thought of as a precise location or some fixed position. A point has no size or dimension. It is invisible. However, a point can be represented on paper by drawing a dot. The representation for a point shown at the right and labeled A can be seen, but the point itself has no size. Points are frequently denoted by capital letters, and the representation above could be referred to as point A.

The notion of **line** is another basic term which depends upon the intuitive ideas of line. The figure at the right is a representation of a line, and the small letter m indicates it could be referred to as line m. The arrowheads indicate that the line continues even though the drawing stops. In general, the word line means straight line and should be interpreted that way unless specifically directed otherwise. Since the two distinct points A and B determine line m, the straight line is symbolized as $\overleftrightarrow{AB}$ and read as **line AB**. Thus, a line may be named by any two of its points. Notice that $\overleftrightarrow{AB}$ is the same line as $\overleftrightarrow{BA}$.

◊ Definition

A **line segment** is a portion of a line that consists of
two endpoints and all the points between them.

A line segment can be represented by a figure that looks like this:

A   B

◊ Definitions/Notations

Line segment AB is represented by $\overline{AB}$. The symbol AB
refers to the distance between A and B, or the **measure**
of $\overline{AB}$. The number AB is called the length of segment
$\overline{AB}$. If two line segments have the same length
(AB = CD), they are said to be **congruent**, denoted by
$\overline{AB} \cong \overline{CD}$ ($\overline{AB}$ is congruent to $\overline{CD}$). Thus $\overline{AB} \cong \overline{CD}$ means
that AB = CD.

Problem 1

Use the figure at the right.
If AB = 9 centimeters, find
the length of $\overline{DB}$.

Solution

We must first find x.

$$x + 2x + 3x \ = \ 9$$
$$6x \ = \ 9$$
$$x \ = \ \frac{3}{2}$$

Thus 3x (the length of $\overline{DB}$) is $\frac{9}{2}$ or $4\frac{1}{2}$ cm. We write DB = $4\frac{1}{2}$ cm.

Informal Geometry

Observe that although we cannot measure a line because it extends infinitely in both directions, we can measure line segments. In the example above, the linear measurement $4\frac{1}{2}$ centimeters consists of two parts: a numerical expression and a unit of measure (centimeters).

Linear units for measuring line segments are summarized in the following table.

Table of Linear Measure

English System

$$12 \text{ inches (in)} = 1 \text{ foot (ft)}$$
$$3 \text{ ft} = 1 \text{ yard (yd)}$$
$$36 \text{ in} = 1 \text{ yd}$$
$$5,280 \text{ ft} = 1 \text{ mile}$$

Metric System

The basic unit is the meter (m).
    (1 meter is slightly larger than a yard and is approximately 39.37 inches.)

1 millimeter (mm) = $\frac{1}{1000}$ of a meter (1 mm = 0.001 m and 1 m = 1000 mm)

1 centimeter (cm) = $\frac{1}{100}$ of a meter (1 cm = 0.01 m and 1 m = 100 cm)

1 decimeter (dm) = $\frac{1}{10}$ of a meter (1 dm = 0.1 m and 1 m = 10 dm)

1 dekameter (dam) = 10 meters (1 dam = 10 m and 1 m = 0.1 dam)

1 hectometer (hm) = 100 meters (1 hm = 100 m and 1 m = 0.01 hm)

1 kilometer (km) = 1000 meters (1 km = 1000 m and 1 m = 0.001 km)

    (1 kilometer is approximately $\frac{3}{5}$ miles.)

E X A M P L E S

1. $7.2 \text{ m} = 7.2(1000 \text{ mm}) = 7,200 \text{ mm}$

2. $7.2 \text{ m} = 7.2(100 \text{ cm}) = 720 \text{ cm}$

3. $7.2 \text{ m} = 7.2(10 \text{ dm}) = 72 \text{ dm}$

4. $7.2 \text{ m} = 7.2(0.001 \text{ km}) = 0.0072 \text{ km}$

Problem 2

Packages are wrapped with tape that costs 40 cents per meter. If each package requires 25 centimeters of tape, find the cost of wrapping 500 packages.

Solution

$$25 \text{ cm} \times 500 \text{ packages} = 12{,}500 \text{ cm}$$
$$= (12{,}500)(0.01 \text{ m})$$
$$= 125 \text{ meters}$$

The cost is $(125)(0.4) = \$50$

The distance around a geometric figure is its **perimeter**. The perimeter is the sum of the lengths of the line segments that make up the figure and is consequently stated in linear units.

E
X
A
M
P
L
E

The perimeter of the accompanying triangle is:

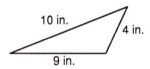

10 in. 4 in. 9 in.

$10 + 9 + 4$ or 23 inches

Problem 3

The length of a rectangle is five more than three times its width. If the perimeter of the rectangle is 42 centimeters, find the length and width.

Solution

Let x = width. Then "5 more than 3 times the width" is 3x + 5. Thus, 3x + 5 = length. (Line segments lying opposite one another in a rectangle have equal measures.)

The rectangle is pictured at the right. Since its perimeter is 42 centimeters, the following equation may be written and solved.

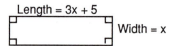

$$(3x + 5) + x + (3x + 5) + x = 42$$
$$8x + 10 = 42$$
$$8x = 32$$
$$x = 4$$

The width (x) is 4 cm.
The length (3x + 5) is 3 • 4 + 5 or 12 + 5 or 17 cm.

Linear measurements are frequently rounded to a given unit of measure. If a measurement is less than half of the unit, we simply round it to the next smaller unit. If a measurement is one half or more of the unit, we round it to the next larger unit. Thus, a measurement of $21\frac{1}{3}$ yd (unit of measure: one yard) would be rounded to 21 yd because $\frac{1}{3}$ is less than half of the unit. Similarly, a measurement of 21.6 centimeters (unit of measure: one centimeter) would be rounded to 22 centimeters because 0.6 is more than half of the unit.

E X A M P L E S

a. To round 6.635 centimeters to the nearest hundredth centimeter, look first at the hundredths digit, which is 3, and then look at the first digit to the right. If that digit is 0, 1, 2, 3, or 4, leave the hundredths digit unchanged. If the digit is 5, 6, 7, 8, or 9, increase the hundredths digit by 1. Since the digit to the right of the hundredths digit is 5, 6.635 rounded to the nearest hundredth is 6.64 centimeters.

b. 6.635 centimeters, rounded to the nearest tenth, is 6.6 centimeters because the digit to the right of the tenth digit is 3 (less than 5) and so the tenth digit, 6, is left unchanged.

c. 9 yd 2 ft, rounded to the nearest yard, is 10 yd because 2 feet is more than half a yard (3 ft = 1 yd).

d. 13 ft 5 in, rounded to the nearest foot, is 13 ft because 5 inches is less than half a foot (12 in = 1 ft).

e. The measure of line segment $\overline{AB}$, shown at the right, can be rounded to the nearest inch. The answer is either 1 inch or 2 inches. Since B is more than midway between 1 and 2, the answer is 2 inches.

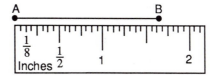

f. AB can be rounded to the nearest half inch. The answer is either $1\frac{1}{2}$ inches or 2 inches. Since B is less than midway between $1\frac{1}{2}$ and 2, the answer is $1\frac{1}{2}$ inches.

g. AB can be rounded to the nearest $\frac{1}{4}$ inch. The answer is either $1\frac{2}{4}$ inches $(1\frac{1}{2}$ in) or $1\frac{3}{4}$ inches. Since B is exactly midway between $1\frac{2}{4}$ and $1\frac{3}{4}$, the answer is $1\frac{3}{4}$ inches.

Problem Set 1

1. If AD = 35 inches, find AB.

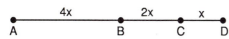

2. Convert:
    a. 3.7 m = _____ mm
    b. 5.2 m = _____ cm
    c. 9.1 m = _____ dm
    d. 4.8 m = _____ km

3. What is the perimeter, in kilometers, of a four-sided figure having sides measuring 720 meters, 300 meters, 450 meters and 200 meters?

4. Pipe, having a diameter of 6 mm, is to be placed along a path measuring 10 km. If pipe costs 20 cents per meter, find the total expense (in dollars) of laying the pipe.

5. What is the perimeter, in feet, of a four-sided figure whose sides measure 10.7 yards each?

6. A rectangular field is 70 feet long and 30 feet wide. If fencing costs $2.00 per yard, how much will it cost to enclose the field?

7. The length of a rectangle is twice the width. If the perimeter is 60 feet, find the dimensions of the rectangle.

8. The length of a rectangle is three more than two times the width. If the perimeter is 30 inches, find the dimensions of the rectangle.

9. Round each of the following.
   a. 9 yd 1 ft (to the nearest yard)
   b. 4 yd 2 ft (to the nearest yard)
   c. 3 ft 7 in (to the nearest foot)
   d. $3\frac{2}{3}$ yd (to the nearest yard)
   e. 6.5 in (to the nearest inch)
   f. 37.5 cm (to the nearest centimeter)
   g. 5.6874 km (to the nearest kilometer)
   h. 2,500.5 km (to the nearest kilometer)
   i. 2.735 km (to the nearest tenth of a kilometer)
   j. 24.2739 cm (to the nearest hundredth of a centimeter)
   k. 62.3019 m (to the nearest thousandth of a meter)
   l. 5,475 ft (to the nearest hundred feet)

11. Round the reading on the gram scale shown below to the nearest:
    a. 5 grams
    b. 10 grams
    c. whole gram

12. You should be aware of the relationships listed below.
    4 quarts (qt) = 1 gallon (g)
    2 pints (p) = 1 quart
    16 ounces (oz) = 1 pound (lb)
    60 seconds (sec) = 1 minute (min)
    Use these relationships to round:
    a. 7 lb 6 oz to the nearest lb
    b. 13 lb 9 oz to the nearest lb
    c. 5 gallons 3 quarts to the nearest gallon
    d. 17 gallons 1 quart to the nearest gallon
    e. 17 quarts to the nearest gallon
    f. 200 seconds to the nearest minute

10. Use the ruler shown below. Find the measure of:
    a. $\overline{AB}$ to the nearest inch
    b. $\overline{AB}$ to the nearest $\frac{1}{2}$ inch
    c. $\overline{AB}$ to the nearest $\frac{1}{4}$ inch
    d. $\overline{AB}$ to the nearest $\frac{1}{8}$ inch
    e. $\overline{AC}$ to the nearest inch
    f. $\overline{AC}$ to the nearest $\frac{1}{2}$ inch
    g. $\overline{AC}$ to the nearest $\frac{1}{4}$ inch
    h. $\overline{AC}$ to the nearest $\frac{1}{8}$ inch

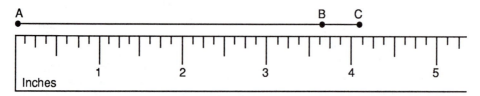

Angles

This section deals with angles. At the end of this section you need to know what is meant by an angle, be able to correctly name a given angle and be able to define and recognize acute angles, right angles, obtuse angles, straight angles, perpendicular lines, complementary angles, supplementary angles, adjacent angles and vertical angles. You should be able to find the complement or the supplement of a given angle. Finally, you should be aware that vertical angles are congruent.

The definition of an angle is based upon the concept of a ray, which in turn is based upon the idea of a half-line. We know that point C on line m at the right separates the line into half-lines. Point C, the separation point, is not a part of either half-line, yet is called the endpoint of either half-line. The symbol for the half-line to the right of point C is $\overset{\circ}{CB}$ (read half-line CB), and the symbol for the half-line to the left of point C is $\overset{\circ}{CB}$. Notice that the notation (o) over the C indicates that point C is not contained in either half-line. Notice also that $\overset{\circ}{CB}$ does not represent the same set of points on line m as $\overset{\circ}{BC}$.

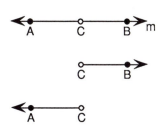

◊ **Definition**

A **ray** is the union of a half-line and its endpoint.

In the figure at the right, the ray whose endpoint is C and extends to the right is read ray CB and is denoted by $\overrightarrow{CB}$. The ray whose endpoint is C and extends to the left is read ray CA and is denoted by $\overrightarrow{CA}$. The first letter in the symbol indicates the endpoint and the second letter indicates any point on the ray. Notice that $\overrightarrow{CB}$ and $\overrightarrow{CA}$ name different sets of points as do $\overrightarrow{CB}$ and $\overrightarrow{BC}$.

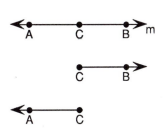

Note

A ray has an endpoint and proceeds indefinitely along the line in one direction. Any point on a line may be an endpont and there are two different rays emanating in either direction from that endpoint.

◊ **Definition**

A **plane angle** is the set of points formed by the union of two rays that have a common endpoint. The common endpoint is called the **vertex** of the angle.

E
X
A
M
P
L
E

The angle at the right is **angle PDQ** (denoted ∠PDQ) or **angle QDP** (denoted ∠QDP) or simply ∠D. The letter representing the vertex of the angle is the middle letter when three letters name the angle. Each ray is a side of the angle.

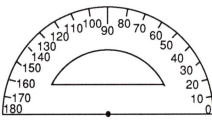

The measurement of an angle indicates the number of unit angles it contains. The basic unit angle for measuring any given angle is a small angle with measure one degree, 1°.

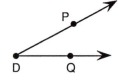

A degree is $\frac{1}{360}$ of a complete revolution. An instrument for measuring angles is a **protractor**. It contains many unit angles (degrees) placed side-by-side so that measuring can be done easily. Observe that the protractor at the right contains 180 degrees, 180°.

E
X
A
M
P
L
E

In the figure at the right ∠ABC has been superimposed upon a protractor.

We see that the measure of this angle is 30 degrees, 30°. We write:

$$m\angle ABC = 30°$$

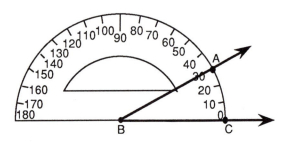

===
◊ **Definition/Notation**

Two angles that have the same measure are said to be
congruent. The symbol for congruence is ≅
m∠A = m∠B is equivalent to ∠A ≅ ∠B.
===

One way of classifying angles is by size as determined by their degree measures.

Acute   **Right**   **Obtuse**   **Straight**
Less than 90°   Exactly 90°   More than 90°, but   Exactly 180°
                                      less than 180°

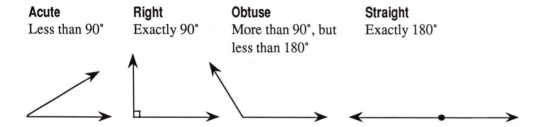

Observe the small square shown at the vertex of all right angles.

E
X   Using the protractor at the
A   right, we can find the meas-
M   ure of each angle and then
P   classify the angle by its size.
L
E
S

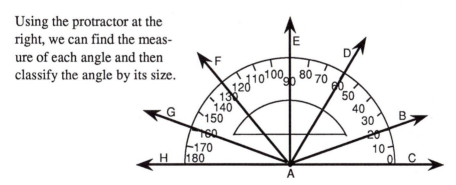

   a.   m∠EAD   =   30°;   acute

   b.   m ∠HAE   =   90°;   right

   c.   m ∠FAC   =   130°;   obtuse

   d.   m ∠HAC   =   180°;   straight

Informal Geometry

Another way of classifying angles is by pairs which have a special relationship.

Complementary Angles:
Two angles whose measures have a sum of 90°.

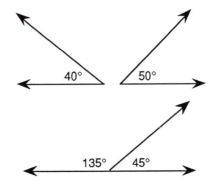

Supplementary Angles:
Two angles whose measures have a sum of 180°.

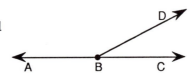

Adjacent Angles:
Two angles sharing a common vertex and a common ray (side) between them.
∠ABD and ∠DBC are adjacent angles.

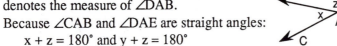

Vertical Angles:
Two angles whose rays share only common endpoints of the same lines. In the figure, ∠CAD and ∠EAB is one pair of vertical angles. ∠DAB and ∠CAE are also vertical angles.

Let us again consider the measure of vertical angles ∠CAD and ∠EAD, denoted by x and y, as shown in the accompanying diagram. Furthermore, z denotes the measure of ∠DAB.

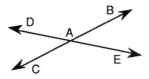

Because ∠CAB and ∠DAE are straight angles:

$x + z = 180°$ and $y + z = 180°$

This means that:

$x + z = y + z$

Subtracting z from both sides of the equation, we obtain:

$x = y$

In a similar way we can prove that the other pair of vertical angles have the same measure.

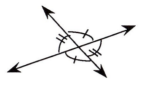

Vertical angles
are congruent
(equal in measure).

◊ Definition/Notation

Two lines or line seg-
ments that intersect to
form right angles are
perpendicular, denoted by
⊥. We can write
$\overleftrightarrow{AB} \perp \overleftrightarrow{CD}$ (in the case of
lines) or $\overline{AB} \perp \overline{CD}$ (in the
case of line segments).

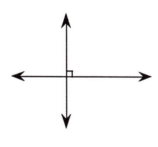

Problem 1

a.   Find the complement of an angle measuring 70°.

Solution

Complementary angles have a sum of 90°. The complement of an angle can
be found by subtracting the measure of the angle from 90°.
Since 90° – 70° = 20°, the desired angle measures 20°.

b.   Find the supplement of an angle measuring 150°.

Solution

Supplementary angles have a sum of 180°. The supplement of an angle can be
found by subtracting the measure of the angle from 180°.
Since 180° – 150° = 30°, the desired angle measures 30°.

Problem 2

Use the figure at the right for
parts a, b, and c.

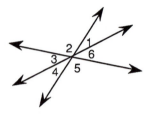

a.   Which angle(s) is/are adjacent to ∠1?

Solution

Adjacent angles share a common vertex and a common side between them.
∠1 and ∠6 are adjacent. ∠1 and ∠2 are also adjacent.

b.   Which angle is vertical to ∠1?

Solution

∠4 is vertical to ∠1 since its rays are obtained by extending the sides of
∠1 through the vertex.

c.   Which angles in the sketch are congruent?

Solution

Vertical angles are congruent. Therefore, m∠1 = m∠4, m∠2 = m∠5, and
m∠3 = m∠6.

Problem 3

a.   Use the figure at the right and find
the measure of the two acute angles.

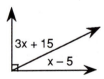

3x + 15

x − 5

Solution

From the sketch we can see that the angles are complementary. This provides the basis for writing the equation:

$$(x - 5) + (3x + 15) = 90$$
$$4x + 10 = 90$$
$$4x = 80$$
$$x = 20$$

The angle measures are:

$$x - 5 = 20 - 5 = 15° \text{ and}$$
$$3x + 15 = 3(20) + 15 = 75°.$$

b. Use the figure at the right. Find the measures of the acute and obtuse angles.

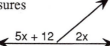

Solution

The sketch shows that the angles are supplementary and this provides the basis for writing the equation:

$$(5x + 12) + 2x = 180$$
$$12 + 7x = 180$$
$$7x = 168$$
$$x = 24$$

The angle measures are:

$$5x + 12 = 5(24) + 12 = 132° \text{ and}$$
$$2x = 2(24) = 48°.$$

Problem Set 2

1. Name this angle in four ways.

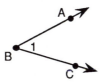

2. Classify each angle shown below by its size.

a.   b.   c.   d.

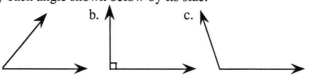

213

3. Find the complement of an angle measuring 78°.

4. Find the supplement of an angle measuring 78°.

5. Use the sketch shown below to answer a, b, and c.

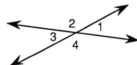

   a. Which angles are adjacent to ∠1?
   b. Which angle is congruent to ∠1?
   c. Which angles are supplementary to ∠4?

6. Find x and then find the measures of the two angles.

   2x + 50
   4x + 10

7. Find x and then find the measures of the two angles.

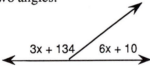

   3x + 134   6x + 10

8. Find x in degrees.

   x
   25°

9. Find x in degrees.

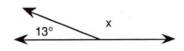

   13°   x

Use the protractor pictured below to find the measures of the following angles and then indicate if the angle is acute, right, obtuse, or straight.

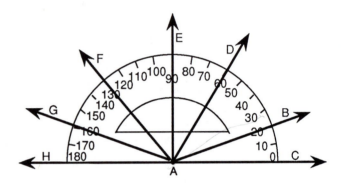

10. ∠DAB

11. ∠BAF

12. ∠CAH

13. ∠EAC

14. In the figure at the right, $\overline{CD} \perp \overline{AD}$. If m∠BDC = 35°, find m∠ADB.

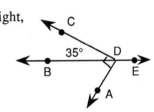

   C
   35°   D
   B   E
        A

Topic 3

Parallel Lines

In many situations two parallel lines are intersected by a third line. In this section names and properties of the angles created by this situation are presented. At the end of this section you should be able to use this information to solve related problems. You should be able to use given congruent angles and supplementary angles to determine that two lines are parallel. You must also know the important angle relationships for any triangle.

◊ Definition

Lines in the same plane that do not intersect are called **parallel lines**.

Line m_1 is parallel to line m_2 in plane P since they do not intersect at any point no matter how far the lines are extended. Only one plane may contain these parallel lines.

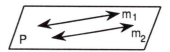

Lines that do not lie in the same plane are not considered parallel even though they never intersect. This situation is illustrated by lines m_1 and m_2 in the figure at the right.

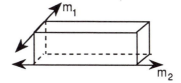

Suppose we know that lines m_1 and m_2, shown at the right, are parallel. These lines are intersected by a third line, m_3, called a **transversal**. Eight angles are formed.

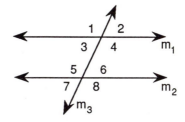

Informal Geometry

In the following figures, $\angle 5$ and $\angle 4$ are **alternate interior angles**.

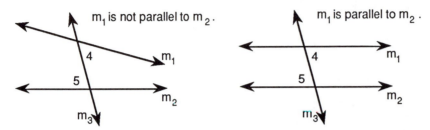

Observe that the lines cut by the transversal may or may not be parallel. The **alternate interior angles** are pairs of angles whose interiors lie between m_1 and m_2, but on opposite sides of the transversal. It appears that these angles are congruent when m_1 and m_2 are parallel. Furthermore, focusing on the figure at the left, if we were to move m_1 so that $m\angle 4 = m\angle 5$, m_1 would be parallel to m_2. These observations lead to the following result.

> Given two lines cut by a transversal. If the lines are parallel, then an alternate interior angle pair is congruent. Conversely, if an alternate interior angle pair is congruent, then the lines are parallel.

Armed with this result, we can establish other congruent angle pairs in the parallel line situation. In the accompanying diagram, m_1 and m_2 are parallel. The congruent alternate angle pairs are designated by one demarkation ($\angle 5 \cong \angle 4$) and two demarkations ($\angle 3 \cong \angle 6$).

Now let us add to the diagram the fact that vertical angles are congruent. Using similar demarkations to denote congruent angles, we obtain the figure on the right.

In the preceding figure, $\angle 1$ and $\angle 8$ are said to be **alternate exterior angles**. These angles lie outside the parallel lines but on opposite sides of the transversal. Another pair of alternate exterior angles is $\angle 2$ and $\angle 7$. The figure indicates that **when two lines are parallel, alternate exterior angles have the same measure.** Thus, $\angle 1 \cong \angle 8$ and $\angle 2 \cong \angle 7$. Two lines are parallel if and only if each pair of alternate exterior angles is congruent.

216

Corresponding angles are two non-adjacent angles whose interiors lie on the same side of the transversal such that one angle lies between the parallel lines and the other lies outside the parallel lines. In the preceeding figure, four pairs of corresponding angles are $\angle 1$ and $\angle 5$, $\angle 2$ and $\angle 6$, $\angle 3$ and $\angle 7$, and $\angle 4$ and $\angle 8$.

Notice that the figure indicates that **when two lines are parallel, corresponding angles have the same measure.** Thus $\angle 1 \cong \angle 5$, $\angle 2 \cong \angle 6$, $\angle 3 \cong \angle 7$, and $\angle 4 \cong \angle 8$. Two lines are parallel if and only if each pair of corresponding angles is congruent.

Notice, in the preceding figure, that $\angle 3$ and $\angle 5$ is a pair of **interior angles on the same side of the transversal** whose interiors lie between the parallel lines. Another pair of angles is $\angle 4$ and $\angle 6$. From the figure, we see that $m\angle 4 + m\angle 2 = 180°$. Since $m\angle 2 = m\angle 6$, this means that $m\angle 4 + m\angle 6 = 180°$. This shows that, **when two lines are parallel, interior angles on the same side of the transversal are supplementary**. In a similar way we can show that, **when two lines are parallel, exterior angles on the same side of the transversal are supplementary.** ($m\angle 1 + m\angle 7 = 180°$ and $m\angle 2 + m\angle 8 = 180°$)

We summarize these results as follows:

> ### Principle for Parallel Lines
>
> If two parallel lines are intersected by a transversal, each angle pair that is formed is congruent or supplementary.

Problem 1

Find the measure of all the angles in the accompanying figure if m_1 is parallel to m_2.

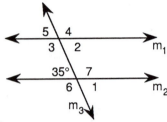

Solution

$m\angle 1 = 35°$ since vertical angles are congruent.
$m\angle 6 = 180 - 35 = 145°$ since $\angle 1$ and $\angle 6$ are supplementary.
$m\angle 7 = 180 - 35 = 145°$ (or $\angle 7 \cong \angle 6$ since these are vertical angles)
$m\angle 3 = 145°$ because $\angle 3 \cong \angle 7$.

These are alternate interior angles (on opposite sides of the transversal and within the parallel lines).

$m\angle 2 = 180 - 145 = 35°$
$m\angle 4 = 145°$ because $\angle 4 \cong \angle 7$.

These are corresponding angles (above the parallel lines and to the right of the transversal).

(Or $\angle 4 \cong \angle 3$ since these are vertical angles)

$m\angle 5 = 180 - 145 = 35°$ since $\angle 5$ and $\angle 4$ are supplementary.

Notice that if the size of one angle is known when a transversal intersects parallel lines, then all other seven angles can be found. Three of the other angles will have equal measure as vertical, corresponding, alternate interior or alternate exterior angles. The other four angles will be supplementary.

Problem 2

In the accompanying figure, m_1 is parallel to m_2. Find x, and then find the measure of the angles.

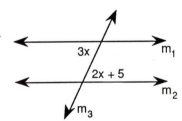

Solution

Since the lines are parallel, the alternate interior angles are equal in measure. Thus, we solve the following equation.

$$3x = 2x + 5$$
$$x = 5 \ (5°)$$

The angles measure $3x = 3(5) = 15°$ and $2x + 5 = 2(5) + 5 = 10 + 5 = 15°$.

Problem 3

Which statement listed below is true
for the line diagram shown at the right?
All lines lie in the same plane.

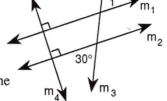

a.   Although m_1 and m_2 appear to be parallel,
     not enough information is given to determine
     with certainty that they are parallel.
b. $\angle 1$ is supplementary to the angle measuring 30°.
c.   Lines m_3 and m_4 will intersect somewhere in the plane.
d.   Lines m_1 and m_4 form the only pair of perpendicular lines.

Solution

a is false. The diagram shows two 90° angles in the same corresponding
position. With m_4 as a transversal, if the corresponding angles are congruent,
then lines m_1 and m_2 must be parallel.

b is false. Because m_1 and m_2 are parallel, we consider m_3 as a transversal.
If the lines are parallel, alternate exterior angles are congruent. Thus,
$m\angle 1 = 30°$. The angles are not supplementary.

c is true. A line extends indefinitely in both directions. Since m_3 and m_4 are
not parallel, they do intersect.

d is false. Lines m_2 and m_4 also form a right angle and are consequently
perpendicular.

> **Notation for Parallel Lines**
>
> $\overleftrightarrow{AB} \parallel \overleftrightarrow{CD}$ means line AB is parallel to line CD.

Informal Geometry

Properties involving parallel lines can be used to prove important angle relationships for triangles. In the accompanying diagram, △ABC (triangle ABC) has its three interior angles denoted by 1, 2, and 3. Through B we have drawn line L parallel to $\overline{AC}$. Since L is a straight line:

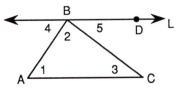

$$m\angle 4 + m\angle 2 + m\angle 5 = 180° \quad \text{(i)}$$

Since parallel lines imply congruent alternate interior angles, we see that:

$$m\angle 1 = m\angle 4 \text{ and } m\angle 3 = m\angle 5$$

Substituting m∠1 for m∠4 and m∠3 for m∠5 into statement (i) we obtain:

$$m\angle 1 + m\angle 2 + m\angle 3 = 180°$$

This can be stated by the following familiar result.

> In any triangle, the sum of the measures of the three interior angles is 180°.

In the accompanying figure, ∠6 is called an **exterior angle** of △ABC. The exterior angle is the angle formed between the extension of one side of the triangle and one of the triangle's original sides. Exterior ∠6 is supplementary to interior ∠3. In terms of ∠6, the other two angles of the triangle (∠1 and ∠2) are called the **remote interior angles**.

We previously proved that:

$$m\angle 1 + m\angle 2 + m\angle 3 = 180°$$

Since ∠3 and ∠6 are supplementary:

$$m\angle 3 + m\angle 6 = 180°$$

This means that:

$$m\angle 3 + m\angle 6 = m\angle 1 + m\angle 2 + m\angle 3$$

Subtracting m∠3 from both sides of the equation, we obtain:

$$m\angle 6 = m\angle 1 + m\angle 2$$

This can be stated in the following way.

> In any triangle, the measure of an exterior angle is the sum of the measures of the two remote interior angles.

Problem 4

Find x (in degrees), and then find the measures of the three angles in the accompanying figure.

Solution

The sum of the measures of the angles is 180°. Thus, we solve the following equation.

$$x + 4x + 5x = 180$$
$$10x = 180$$
$$x = 18 \quad (18°)$$

The angles measure $x = 18°$; $4x = 4(18) = 72°$; and $5x = 5(18) = 90°$.

Problem 5

Find the measure of all missing angles in the figure at right.

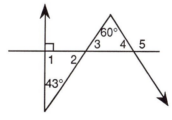

Solution

m∠1 = 90° since it is supplementary to the right angle.
m∠2 can be found using the idea that the sum of the measures of the angles of a triangle is 180°.
m∠1 + 43° = 90 + 43 = 133° and m∠2 = 180 − 133 = 47°.
m∠3 can be found using the idea that vertical angles are congruent.
∠3 ≅ ∠2. Thus, m∠3 = 47°.
To find m∠4, we can add m∠3 + 60° and then subtract from 180°.
m∠3 + 60° = 47 + 60 = 107° and m∠4 = 180 − 107 = 73°.
∠5 is supplementary to ∠4.
Thus, m∠5 = 180 − m∠4 = 180 − 73 = 107°.

Problem 6

In the accompanying figure, m_1 is parallel to m_2. Find $m\angle 1$.

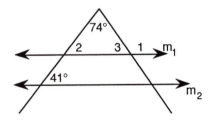

Solution

We can immediately find $m\angle 2$: $m\angle 2 = 41°$ since, when lines are parallel, the corresponding angles are congruent.

Since a triangle has an angle sum of 180°, we can find $m\angle 3$ by adding $m\angle 2$ to 74°($41° + 74° = 115°$) and subtracting this result from 180°. Thus, $m\angle 3 = 180 - 115 = 65°$. $\angle 1$ is supplementary to $\angle 3$. Thus, $m\angle 1 = 180 - 65 = 115°$.

Problem 7

Find the measure of $\angle 1$ in the figure at the right.

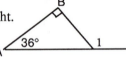

Solution

Since $\angle 1$ is an exterior angle,
$$m\angle 1 = m\angle A + m\angle B$$
$$= 36 + 90$$
$$= 126 \quad \text{Thus, } m\angle 1 = 126°.$$

Problem Set 3

Consider the accompanying figure in which m_1 is parallel to m_2 and m_3 is a transversal:

1. Name the angles that have the same measure as $\angle 3$.

2. Name the angles that are supplementary to $\angle 5$.

3. Name the angles that have the same measure as $\angle 2$.

4. Name the angles that are supplementary to $\angle 7$.

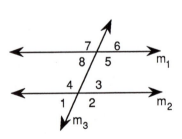

Chapter 3

5. If m_1 is parallel to m_2, find the measure of the remaining angles.

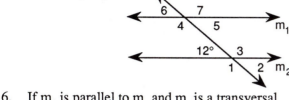

6. If m_1 is parallel to m_2 and m_3 is a transversal, find m∠x.

7. If m_1 is parallel to m_2 find m∠x.

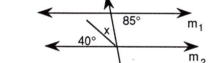

8. Find the value of x, and then find the measure of the angles if m_1 and m_2 are parallel lines.

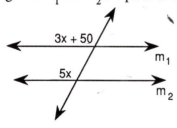

9. The diagram below shows four lines in the same plane. Line m_1 is parallel to m_2. Which of the following is true?

a. ∠A ≅ ∠B

b. ∠D ≅ ∠E

c. m∠C ≠ m∠D

d. Lines m_3 and m_4 do not intersect.

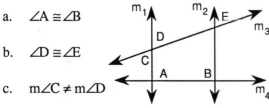

10. The diagram shows four lines in the same plane. Which one statement is true based upon this diagram?

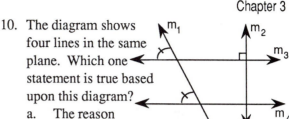

a. The reason that lines m_3 and m_4 are parallel is because the two congruent angles marked with one stroke are alternate interior angles.

b. Although m_4 and m_2 appear to be perpendicular, not enough information is given to determine with certainty that they are indeed perpendicular.

c. Lines m_1 and m_2 will intersect somewhere in the plane.

d. The quadrilateral formed by the intersecting lines has opposite sides parallel.

11. The diagram shows three lines in the same plane. Lines m_1 and m_2 are parallel. Which of the following is/are true?

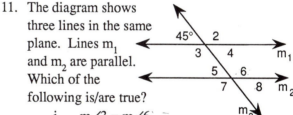

i. m∠3 = m∠6
ii. m∠8 = 45°
iii. m∠5 = m∠6

a. i only
b. ii only
c. iii only
d. i and ii only

12. The diagram shows four lines in the same plane. Lines m_1 and m_2 are parallel. Find the measure of each angle in the diagram.

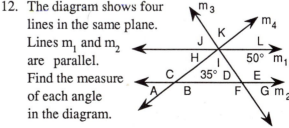

223

13. In the figure below line m₁ is parallel to line m₂ and m₃ is a transversal. Find the value of x and then find the measure of either angle.

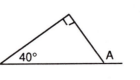

14. In the diagram, m₁ is parallel to m₂. Find m∠1.

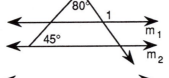

15. Find m∠1 if m₁ is parallel to m₂.

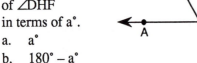

16. If lines AB and CD are parallel, express the measure of ∠DHF in terms of a°.
    a.   a°
    b.   180° – a°
    c.   a° – 180°   d.   90° – a°

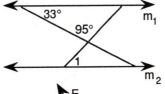

17. Find m∠x in the figure.

18. Find x and the measure of each of the angles of the triangle.

19. Find m∠x for the figure at right.

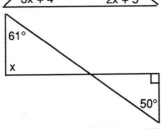

20. Find m∠A.

21. Find m∠1.

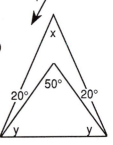

22. a. Find y in degrees. (Use the small triangle.)
    b. Find x in degrees. (Use the large triangle.)

23. Determine if the following are true or false for the figure shown.
    a. $\overline{AB} \perp \overline{BC}$
    b.   m∠2 + m∠3 = 90°
    c.   m∠2 + m∠3 + m∠4 = 180°
    d.   ∠1 and∠2 are complementary.
    e.   m∠1 = m∠3 + m∠4

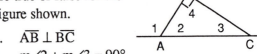

24. Which of the following statements is/are true for the figure at right?
    i.   ∠A ≅ ∠E
    ii. m∠D = 140°
    iii. ∠A is supplementary to ∠C
    a.   i only   b.   iii only
    c.   i and iii only   d.   ii and iii only

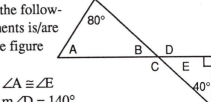

25. Find m∠R.

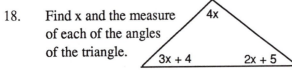

Topic 4

Congruent Triangles

This section defines congruent triangles and presents three methods for quickly determining when triangles are congruent. At the end of this section you should be able to show that angles or line segments are congruent by determining that triangles containing these angles or line segments are congruent.

As we know, angles are congruent if they have the same measure and line segments are congruent if they have the same length. Roughly speaking, two triangles are congruent if they have exactly the same size and shape.

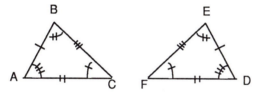

In the accompany diagram, $\triangle ABC$ is congruent to $\triangle FED$ (written $\triangle ABC \cong \triangle FED$) because $\triangle ABC$ could be moved onto $\triangle FED$ to create an exact fit. We should put A on D, C on F, and B on E, which would place $\overline{AB}$ on $\overline{DE}$, $\overline{BC}$ on $\overline{EF}$, and $\overline{AC}$ on $\overline{DF}$. Notice how we indicate the congruences between angles and line segments in the figure.

In short, when we write $\triangle ABC \cong \triangle DEF$, we mean six things

$$
\begin{array}{lll}
\overline{AB} \cong \overline{DE}, & \text{or} & AB = DE, \\
\overline{AC} \cong \overline{DF}, & \text{or} & AC = DF, \\
\overline{BC} \cong \overline{EF}, & \text{or} & BC = EF, \\
\angle A \cong \angle D, & \text{or} & m\angle A = m\angle D, \\
\angle B \cong \angle E, & \text{or} & m\angle B = m\angle E, \\
\angle C \cong \angle F, & \text{or} & m\angle C = m\angle F.
\end{array}
$$

In certain cases, given only three of these things, we can immediately establish that the triangles are congruent.

Determining Congruent Triangles

1. SAS

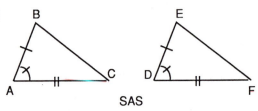

SAS

Two triangles are congruent when two sides and the included angle of the first triangle are congruent to two sides and the included angle of the second triangle. ("SAS" stand for "side angle side.")

2. ASA

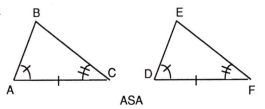

ASA

Two triangles are congruent when two angles and the included side of the first triangle are congruent to two angles and the included side of the second triangle. ("ASA" stands for "angle side angle.")

3. SSS

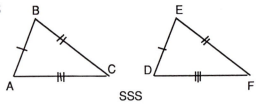

SSS

Two triangles are congruent when all three sides of one are congruent to the corresponding sides of the second. ("SSS" stands for "side side side.")

Many properties involving plane figures can be proved by using congruent triangles.

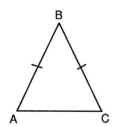

E
X
A
M
P
L
E

The accompanying figure is an **isosceles triangle**. By definition, an isosceles triangle has two congruent sides. ($\overline{AB} \cong \overline{CB}$). We can very quickly prove that the angles opposite these sides are congruent ($\angle A \cong \angle C$) by drawing $\overline{BM}$, where M is the midpoint of $\overline{AC}$.

As shown, $\overline{AM} \cong \overline{MC}$ (M is a midpoint), $\overline{AB} \cong \overline{CB}$ (given), and BM lies in both ΔI and ΔII. Hence, by SSS, ΔI ≅ ΔII. This means that $\angle A \cong \angle C$ by the definition of a congruence between the triangles.

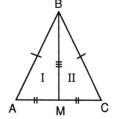

> Angles opposite congruent sides of an isosceles triangle are congruent.

One method of classifying triangles is in terms of lengths of the sides. The figure at the right shows an **equilateral triangle**. This type of triangle has three congruent sides. As the figure indicates, it also has three congruent angles and is sometimes called an **equiangular triangle**.

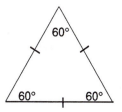

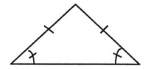

The figure at the left is an **isosceles triangle**. It has two congruent sides and the angles opposite the congruent sides are congruent. The converse is also true. If a triangle has two congruent angles, then the sides opposite those angles are congruent.

The figure at the right is a **scalene triangle**. A scalene triangle has no congruent sides and, consequently, no congruent angles.

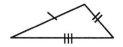

Problem 1

For the figure at the right, which of the
following is/are true?

i. $m\angle C = 70°$

ii. $m\angle A = m\angle B$

iii. $m\angle D = m\angle E = m\angle F$

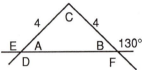

Solution

i.   To determine $m\angle C$, the sizes of $\angle A$ and $\angle B$ are needed. $m\angle B = 50°$
     because $\angle B$ is supplementary to the 130° angle. But $m\angle A = m\angle B$
     because the triangle is isosceles (two congruent sides and two congruent
     angles opposite those sides). Thus, $m\angle A = m\angle B = 50°$ and $m\angle C = 80°$
     because the sum of the triangle's angles is 180°. $m\angle C = 70°$ is, therefore,
     false.

ii. As shown in the solution of (i), $m\angle A = m\angle B$ is true.

iii. $\angle D$ and $\angle E$ are vertical angles and, therefore, congruent. Also, $\angle A$ and
     $\angle D$ are supplementary angles and since $m\angle A = 50°$ this means
     $m\angle D = 130°$. Angle F is a vertical angle with a 130° angle and, therefore,
     $m\angle F = 130°$. Thus, $m\angle D = m\angle E = m\angle F$ is true.

E
X
A
M
P
L
E

The **parallelogram** shown below is a four-sided plane figure in which both
pairs of opposite sides are parallel.

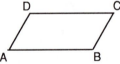

$(\overline{AB} \parallel \overline{DC}$ and $\overline{AD} \parallel \overline{BC})$

We can show that both pairs of opposite sides are congruent by drawing
diagonal $\overline{AC}$. With $\overline{AB} \parallel \overline{DC}$, congruent alternate interior
angles are designated with a single demarkation, and
with $\overline{AD} \parallel \overline{BC}$, congruent alternate interior angles are
designated with two demarkations. Since $\overline{AC}$ is in
both ΔI and ΔII, $\Delta I \cong \Delta II$ by ASA. This means that
$AB = DC$ and $AD = BC$ by the definition of a congruence
between the triangles.

> Opposite sides of a parallelogram are equal in length.

Problem Set 4

1.

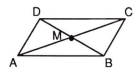

If ABCD is a parallelogram, why is
ΔCDM ≅ ΔABM? Why does AM = MC and
BM = MD? What does this tell us about a
parallelogram's diagonals?

2.

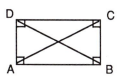

A rectangle is a parallelogram with four right
angles. Why is Δ ABC congruent to ΔABD?
What does this mean about diagonals $\overline{AC}$ and
$\overline{BD}$ of the rectangle?

3.

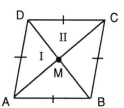

A rhombus is a parallelogram containing
congruent adjacent sides. Why is ΔI ≅ ΔII?
(Hint: Look back at problem 1.) Why does
this show that $\overline{DB} \perp \overline{AC}$? What does this tell us
about the diagonals of a rhombus?

4. Make a sketch and use congruent triangles to
explain why the following statement is true. If
two line segments bisect each other (have the
same midpoint), then the line segments joining
the ends of the given line segments are congruent.

5. Given the figure as marked,
explain why ΔMNK is
isosceles.

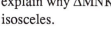

6. In the accompanying figure XU = XV and
$m\angle 1 = m\angle 2 = m\angle 3 = m\angle 4$.
Which one of the following
is true?

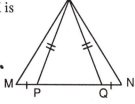

   a. $m\angle 5 \neq m\angle 6$
   b. $\angle 1 \cong \angle 7$
   c. $\angle 7 \cong \angle 8$
   d. The diagram contains
      exactly one pair
      of congruent triangles.

7. Which one of the
following is true in
the accompanying
diagram?

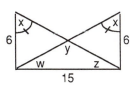

   a. m < y = m < x   b. m < x = m < w
   c. m < w = m < y   d. m < w = m < z

Similar Triangles

This section presents the concept of similar triangles. At the end of this section you need to be able to tell when triangles are similar and set up correct proportions for the corresponding sides of similar triangles.

Consider the two triangles shown at the right. Suppose they both have the same exact shape, even though they are not identical in size. We say that $\triangle ABC$ and $\triangle DEF$ are **similar triangles**. We write:

$$\triangle ABC \sim \triangle DEF.$$

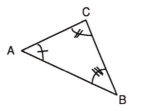

In a more formal approach, knowing that $\triangle ABC \sim \triangle DEF$ means that corresponding angles are congruent ($m\angle A = m\angle D$, $m\angle C = m\angle F$, $m\angle B = m\angle E$) and that corresponding sides are **proportional**, namely:

$$\frac{AC}{DF} = \frac{AB}{DE} = \frac{CB}{FE}$$

In certain cases, given only some of these things, we can immediately establish that the triangles are similar, implying that all corresponding angles are congruent and corresponding sides are proportional.

Determining Similar Triangles

1. **AA**

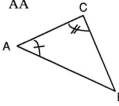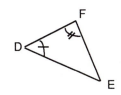

Two triangles are similar (same shape) if two angles of the first triangle are congruent to two angles of the second triangle.

2. **SSS**

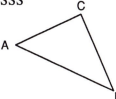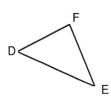

Two triangles are similar if corresponding sides are proportional.

$$\frac{AC}{DF} = \frac{AB}{DE} = \frac{CB}{FE}$$

3. **SAS**

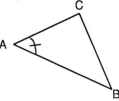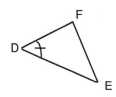

Two triangles are similar if two pairs of corresponding sides are proportional and the angle included between these sides in the first triangle is congruent to the angle included between these sides in the second triangle.

$$\frac{AC}{DF} = \frac{AB}{DE} \text{ and } m\angle A = m\angle D$$

Problem 1

Given that $\overline{AC} \parallel \overline{DE}$. Explain why $\triangle ABC$ and $\triangle DFE$ are similar.

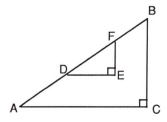

Solution

Both triangles contain 90° angles. Thus $\angle ACB \cong \angle DEF$. Since we have parallel lines, the corresponding angles are congruent. Thus $\angle CAB \cong \angle EDB$. The triangles are similar because of these two congruent angle pairs. (AA)

Problem 2

Consider the accompanying triangles, and find the length of side x.

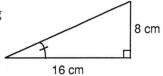

Solution

The two triangles are similar since two angles of one are congruent to two angles of the other as indicated by the angle markings. Hence, the corresponding sides are proportional.

$$\frac{x}{8} = \frac{12}{16} \text{ or } \frac{x}{8} = \frac{3}{4} \text{ gives } 4 \cdot x = 8 \cdot 3 \text{ or } 4x = 24 \text{ or } x = 6 \text{ cm.}$$

Problem 3

Consider the following figure in which $\overline{AB} \parallel \overline{CD}$. Find AB.

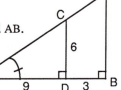

Solution

$\triangle ABE$ is similar to $\triangle CDE$ because two angles of the smaller triangle are congruent to two angles of the larger triangle. Both triangles share $\angle E$, and both triangles contain right angles. Thus, corresponding sides are proportional.

$$\frac{AB}{CD} = \frac{BE}{DE} \text{ or } \frac{AB}{6} = \frac{12}{9} \text{ or } \frac{AB}{6} = \frac{4}{3}$$

Thus, we obtain: $3 \cdot AB = 6 \cdot 4$ or $3 \cdot AB = 24$ or $AB = 8$.

Problem 4

The sun is shining in a way that a 5 foot tall pole casts a shadow of 2 feet. Find the height of a pole that casts a shadow of 50 feet.

Solution

A drawing for this type of problem makes the similarity of the triangles easier to see and the pairs of matching sides easier to select.

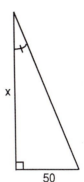

$$\frac{x}{5} = \frac{50}{2} \text{ or } \frac{x}{5} = \frac{25}{1}$$

Solving gives $x \cdot 1 = 5 \cdot 25$ or $x = 125$.
Thus, the height of the pole is 125 feet.

Problem 5

Consider the similar triangles shown at the right. Which of the following proportions is incorrect?

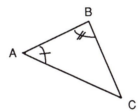

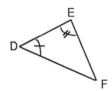

1) $\frac{AB}{DE} = \frac{AC}{DF}$ 2) $\frac{AB}{AC} = \frac{DE}{DF}$ 3) $\frac{AB}{DF} = \frac{AC}{DE}$

Solution

To be correct, both ratios of a proportion must make the same comparison of corresponding sides.

1) $\dfrac{AB \text{ (corresponds to DE)}}{DE} = \dfrac{AC \text{ (corresponds to DF)}}{DF}$ is a correct proportion.

Notice that the ratio on the left of the correct proportion above compares corresponding sides of $\triangle ABC$ to $\triangle DEF$, and the ratio on the right also compares corresponding sides of $\triangle ABC$ to $\triangle DEF$.

2) $\dfrac{AB \text{ (corresponds to DE)}}{AC \text{ (corresponds to DF)}} = \dfrac{DE}{DF}$ is a correct proportion.

Notice that the ratio on the left of the correct proportion above compares two sides of $\triangle ABC$, and the ratio on the right compares the corresponding sides of $\triangle DEF$.

233

3) $\dfrac{AB \text{ (corresponds to DE)}}{DF} = \dfrac{AC \text{ (corresponds to DF)}}{DE}$ is not correct.

Notice that the ratio on the left makes a different comparison than the ratio on the right. To be correct, the two ratios must follow exactly the same pattern.

Problem 6

Find the length of $\overline{CD}$ in the figure where $\overline{CD} \parallel \overline{AB}$.

Solution

The solution depends upon establishing that $\triangle ECD$ is similar to $\triangle EAB$ which, in turn, depends upon showing that the triangles have congruent angles. As the figure at the right indicates, the line of $\overline{AC}$ serves as a transversal for the given parallel lines. Therefore, the corresponding angles are congruent. $\angle E$ is shared by both triangles. $\triangle EDC$ is similar to $\triangle EAB$. (AA) Now a proportion comparing corresponding sides is:

$$\frac{AB}{CD} = \frac{BE}{DE} \text{ or } \frac{10}{x} = \frac{9}{5}$$

Hence $9x = 50$ and $x = \dfrac{50}{9} = 5\frac{5}{9}$ ft.

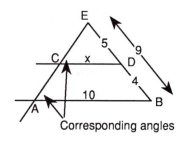

Corresponding angles

Although we have used AA to determine similar triangles, similarity can also be determined by SSS and SAS.

E
X
A
M
P
L
E
S

1. The triangles at the right are similar because they have three pairs of proportional sides. (SSS)

   $$\frac{3}{12} = \frac{4}{16} = \frac{2}{8}$$

2. The triangles at the right are similar because they have two pairs of proportional sides.

   $$\frac{3}{9} = \frac{4}{12}$$

   Also, the vertical angles included between these sides are congruent. (SAS)

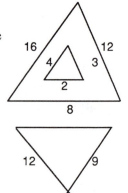

234

Since similar triangles have the same shape, but not necessarily the same size, and congruent triangles have the same size and shape, observe that **all congruent triangles are similar**. Congruent triangles have congruent corresponding sides, so that the ratio of corresponding sides will always reduce to $\frac{1}{1}$.

Problem Set 5

1. In the figure shown, $\triangle ABC$ is similar to $\triangle DEC$. Find DE.

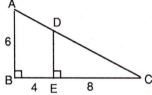

2. In the figure shown, $\triangle ABC$ is similar to $\triangle DEC$. Find AB.

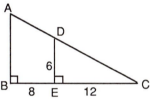

3. Which statement is true for the pictured triangles?

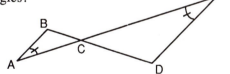

   a. $\dfrac{BC}{CD} = \dfrac{ED}{AB}$

   b. $\dfrac{BC}{BA} = \dfrac{CE}{ED}$

   c. If AB = 4 ft, AC = 5 ft and CE = 7.5 ft, then DE = 6 ft.

   d. $\angle BCA \cong \angle CED$

4. Which statement is true for the pictured triangles?

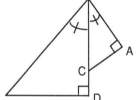

   a. $\dfrac{ED}{EB} = \dfrac{CB}{CA}$

   b. $\angle BDE \cong \angle BCA$

   c. $\dfrac{EB}{CB} = \dfrac{AC}{ED}$

   d. $\dfrac{AB}{BD} = \dfrac{BC}{EB}$

5. A flagpole casts a shadow 56 feet long at the same time that a fence post casts a shadow 8 feet long. If the post is 3 feet high, how tall is the flagpole?

6. Explain why $\triangle ABC$ is similar to $\triangle EDC$.

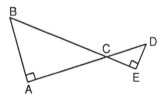

7. In problem 6 above, if AB = 16 cm, ED = 12 cm, CE = 15 cm, find AC.

8. Find the length of x. The line of $\overline{DE}$ is parallel to the line of $\overline{AB}$.

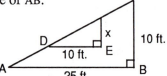

10 ft.

9. In the figure shown, $\overline{AB} \parallel \overline{DE}$. If AC = 12, CD = 4 and CE = 8, find BC.

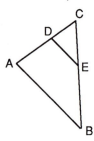

10. Which of the sets of pictured triangles contain(s) similar triangles?

i.

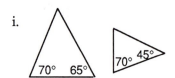

ii.

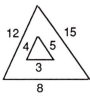

iii.

a. i only
b. ii only
c. iii only
d. i and iii only

11. Which statement is true for the pictured triangles?

a. $\dfrac{AD}{AC} = \dfrac{AE}{AB}$

b. $\dfrac{AD}{AB} = \dfrac{AC}{AE}$

c. $\dfrac{AD}{AB} = \dfrac{AE}{AC}$

d. $\dfrac{AD}{AE} = \dfrac{AC}{AB}$

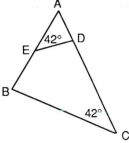

12. In the accompanying figure, is $\overline{PQ} \parallel \overline{AB}$? Explain.

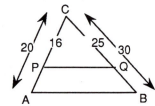

13. Given the accompanying figure, find x so

14.

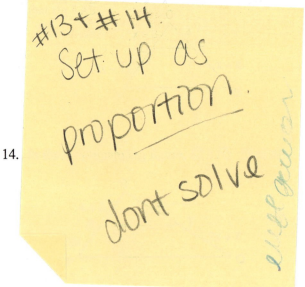

#13 + #14.
Set up as
proportion.
dont solve

Topic 6

The Pythagorean Theorem For The Right Triangle

One of the most powerful and useful theorems of geometry is the Pythagorean Theorem. At the end of this section you need to know the theorem and be able to use it to find the missing side of a right triangle.

We earlier classified triangles based on their sides (equilateral, isosceles, scalene).

Another method of classifying triangles is in terms of the size of the triangle's angles. Earlier, the equiangular (three congruent angles) and isosceles (two congruent angles) triangles were presented. Three more types of angle-classified triangles are described below.

A triangle with three acute angles (less than 90°) is an **acute triangle**.

acute triangle

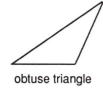

obtuse triangle

A triangle with one obtuse angle (more than 90°) is an **obtuse triangle**.

The triangle shown at the right is a **right triangle**. The side opposite the right angle is called the **hypotenuse**. The other two sides are called **legs**.

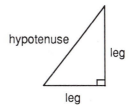

The **Pythagorean Theorem** states:

In any right triangle, the sum of the squares of the legs is equal to the square of the hypotenuse.

Informal Geometry

In the accompanying figure the Pythagorean
Theorem may be stated symbolically as:

$$a^2 + b^2 = c^2$$

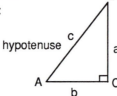

We can prove the Pythagorean Theorem using properties of congruent triangles and
formulas for the areas of a rectangle and a triangle. This will be done in Topic 8 when
we discuss area.

Problem 1

Use the Pythagorean Theorem to determine the
missing side (c) in the right triangle in which $\angle C$
is the right angle, side a is 3 feet, and side b is 4 feet.

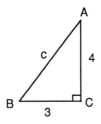

Solution

Substitute the values into the statement of the theorem.

Thus, $a^2 + b^2 = c^2$ when a = 3 and b = 4
becomes: $3^2 + 4^2 = c^2$
which gives: $9 + 16 = c^2$
$$25 = c^2$$
$$5 = c \text{ because } \sqrt{25} = 5$$

The missing side, c, measures 5 feet.

Problem 2

Use the Pythagorean Theorem and the principles
for solving equations to determine the missing side in
the right triangle in which $\angle C$ is the right angle, side b
is 5 inches, and side c is 13 inches.

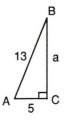

Solution

The missing side to be determined is side a.

Thus, $a^2 + b^2 = c^2$ when b = 5 and c = 13

becomes: $a^2 + 5^2 = 13^2$

$$a^2 + 25 = 169$$

$$a^2 + 25 - 25 = 169 - 25$$

$$a^2 = 144$$

$$a = 12 \text{ because } \sqrt{144} = 12$$

The missing side, a, measures 12 inches.

Problem 3

Find side b in the right triangle with hypotenuse 4 and one side (leg) $\sqrt{7}$.

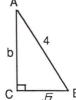

Solution

$$a^2 + b^2 = c^2$$

$$(\sqrt{7})^2 + b^2 = 4^2$$

$$7 + b^2 = 16 \qquad \text{If a is positive, } (\sqrt{a})^2 = a; \text{ thus, } (\sqrt{7})^2 = 7.$$

$$b^2 = 9$$

$$b = 3$$

Problem 4

A 26 foot ladder is placed against a wall. The bottom of the ladder is 24 feet away from the wall. How high up does the ladder reach?

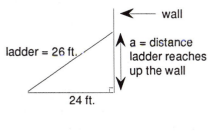

Solution

$$a^2 + b^2 = c^2$$

$$a^2 + 24^2 = 26^2$$

$$a^2 + 576 = 676$$

$$a^2 = 100$$

$$a = 10$$

Thus, the ladder reaches 10 feet up the wall.

Problem 5

A general leaves headquarters and walks 7 miles
due east and then 4 miles due north.
How far is the general
from headquarters?

General

c

4 miles
north

Headquarters

7 miles east ⟶

Solution

$$7^2 + 4^2 = c^2$$
$$49 + 16 = c^2$$
$$65 = c^2$$
$$c = \sqrt{65}$$

$\sqrt{65}$ is slightly more than 8. The general is $\sqrt{65}$ miles from headquarters.

Problem Set 6

1. Use the accompanying right triangle
   in which $\angle C$ is the right angle.

   B

   c a

   A b C

   a. Find c if b = 8 inches
      and a = 15 inches.
   b. Find b if a = 24
      feet and c = 25 feet.
   c. Find a if c = 10 yards and b = 6 yards.
   d. Find c if b = $\sqrt{3}$ centimeters
      and a = 1 centimeter.
   e. Find b if c = $\sqrt{170}$ meters and a = 11
      meters.
   f. Find a if c = $\sqrt{2}$ inches and b = 1 inch.

2. Use the Pythagorean Theorem to solve each of
   the following. (Hint: Sketch a right triangle in
   each problem and assign values to the appropriate parts.)
   a. A sail boat leaves a dock sailing 9 miles
      due west and then 12 miles due north.
      How far away is the boat from the dock?

   b. How high up on a wall does a 26 foot
      ladder reach if the foot of the ladder is
      10 feet from the wall?
   c. What must be the length of a guy wire on
      a 24 foot flagpole if the wire is to be se-
      cured on the ground 7 feet from the base
      of the pole?
   d. An empty lot is 40 feet long and 30 feet
      wide. How many feet does a person save
      by walking diagonally across the lot
      instead of walking the length and width
      of the lot?
   e. Two flag poles are 42 feet and 49 feet high
      respectively and are 24 feet apart. How
      long is a wire from the top of one pole to
      the top of the second pole?

f. A builder wishes to test whether the walls at a corner of a building form a right angle. The builder measures 8 feet from the corner along one wall and 6 feet from the corner along the other wall, discovering the distance between the ends of these lines is 10 feet. Can the builder conclude that the walls form a right angle? (Hint: Show that the distances satisfy the Pythagorean theorem.)

3. In the sketch that is shown, find the cost of constructing the new street if construction costs $100 per linear foot.

new street

3 miles

4 miles

4. If a bicyclist averages 10 miles per hour, how long will it take to cover the distance represented by AB?

12 miles

B

9 miles

A

a. 1 hour b. $1\frac{1}{2}$ hours

c. $2\frac{1}{2}$ hours d. 3 hours

5. A balloon rises at the rate of 12 feet per minute when the wind is blowing horizontally at 9 feet per minute. After two minutes, how far away from the starting point, in a direct line, is the balloon?

6. What is the length of AB in the accompanying figure?

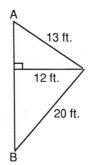

A

13 ft.

12 ft.

20 ft.

B

7. Find the perimeter of a right triangle with legs measuring 12 inches and 16 inches.

Quadrilaterals and Polygons

The emphasis of this section is on polygons and quadrilaterals. At the end of this section you need to know what is meant by polygon, regular polygon, convex polygon, quadrilateral, pentagon, hexagon and octagon. Also you need to know how to find the number of degrees in the sum of the measures of the angles of an n-sided polygon. Finally you should know the definitions and properties of each of the following quadrilaterals: parallelogram, rectangle, square, rhombus, and trapezoid.

A polygon is a figure formed by fitting together line segments end to end. Stated more formally, we have the following definition.

◊ **Definitions**

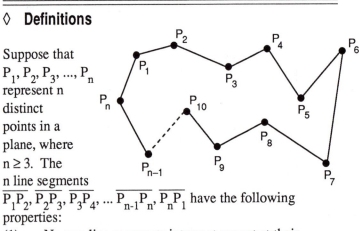

Suppose that $P_1, P_2, P_3, ..., P_n$ represent n distinct points in a plane, where $n \geq 3$. The n line segments $\overline{P_1P_2}, \overline{P_2P_3}, \overline{P_3P_4}, ... \overline{P_{n-1}P_n}, \overline{P_nP_1}$ have the following properties:

(1)   No two line segments intersect except at their end points.

(2)   No two line segments with a common endpoint lie on the same line.

The union of the n line segments is called a **polygon**. Points $P_1, P_2, P_3, ..., P_n$ are **vertices** of the polygon and segments $\overline{P_1P_2}, \overline{P_2P_3}, \overline{P_3P_4}, ... \overline{P_{n-1}P_n}, \overline{P_nP_1}$ are its **sides**. The sum of the lengths of the sides is the **perimeter**. A line segment whose endpoints are two nonconsecutive vertices of the polygon is called a **diagonal**.

E X A M P L E S

Each figure shown below is a polygon:

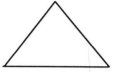  

There are names for polygons based upon the number of sides they contain.
Below are some of these different polygons and the shapes they could assume.
There are, of course, other possible shapes.

Triangle	**Quadrilateral**	**Pentagon**	**Hexagon**	**Heptagon**	**Octagon**
(three sides)	(four sides)	(five sides)	(six sides)	(seven sides)	(eight sides)

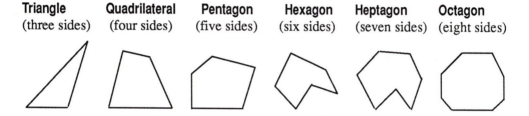

◊ **Definitions**

A polygon is **convex** if, for any two points A and B in
its interior, the line segment $\overline{AB}$ lies in the interior. A
convex polygon with all sides congruent and all angles
congruent is a **regular polygon**.

E X A M P L E S

1. This is not a convex polygon.
    Line segment $\overline{AB}$ does not lie
    within the polygon.

2. The following figures are examples of regular polygons. In each figure
    the sides are of equal length and the angles are of equal size.

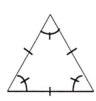 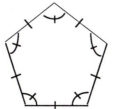 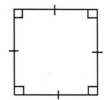

Informal Geometry

We know that the sum of the three interior angles of any triangle is 180°. What is the sum of the measures of the four interior angles in a rectangle, or indeed, any convex polygon?

Let us consider a convex quadrilateral and draw a diagonal from any vertex, as shown in the figure at the right. Observe that we obtain two triangles. The sum of the angle measures of the two triangles (360°) should equal the sum of the angle measures of the quadrilateral. Let us express this sum as $2 \cdot 180°$ or $(4 - 2) \cdot 180°$.

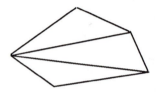

Now let us consider the convex pentagon shown at the left. Notice that we can draw two diagonals from one vertex. When this is done, we obtain three triangles. Thus, the sum of the measures of the interior angles of the convex pentagon is 540° or $3 \cdot 180°$ or $(5 - 2) \cdot 180°$.

We can find the sum of the measures of the interior angles of a convex polygon by drawing all the diagonals from any one vertex of the polygon. Consider the pattern below.

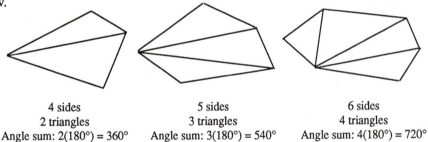

4 sides	5 sides	6 sides
2 triangles	3 triangles	4 triangles
Angle sum: $2(180°) = 360°$	Angle sum: $3(180°) = 540°$	Angle sum: $4(180°) = 720°$

This pattern leads to a generalization.

> The sum of the measures of the interior angles
> of a convex polygon of n sides is $(n - 2) \cdot 180°$.

Observe that in the case of a triangle ($n = 3$), the formula gives us:
$$(3 - 2) \cdot 180° \text{ or } 1 \cdot 180° \text{ or } 180°$$
Thus, this relationship verifies that the sum of the measures of the interior angles of a triangle is 180°.

The sum of the measures of the interior angles of a convex hexagon is:
$$(6 - 2) \cdot 180° \text{ or } 4 \cdot 180° \text{ or } 720°$$

Problem 1

In the accompanying figure, the octagon is regular. Find m∠A.

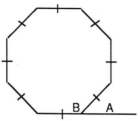

Solution

1. The sum of the measures of the interior angles

   = $(n - 2) \cdot 180°$
   = $(8 - 2) \cdot 180°$
   = $6 \cdot 180°$
   = $1080°$

2. Since all interior angles are congruent, $m\angle B = \frac{1080}{8} = 135°$.

3. Since ∠A is the supplement of ∠B, $m\angle A = 180° - 135° = 45°$.

Although we might refer to triangles and quadrilaterals as 3-gons and 4-gons, these terms are seldom used.

All convex quadrilaterals have four interior angles whose measures have a sum of $(4 - 2) \cdot 180°$ or $360°$. Let us consider some special kinds of quadrilaterals.

◊ Definitions

A **parallelogram** is a quadrilateral in which both pairs of opposite sides are parallel.
A **trapezoid** is a quadrilateral in which one and only one pair of opposite sides are parallel.
A **rhombus** is a parallelogram all of whose sides are congruent.
A **rectangle** is a parallelogram all of whose angles are right angles.
A **square** is a rectangle all of whose sides are congruent.

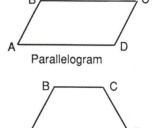

Parallelogram

Trapezoid

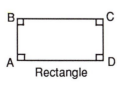

Rectangle

Square

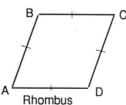

Rhombus

Informal Geometry

As we saw in Topic 4, we can use our knowledge about parallel lines and congruent triangles to prove many additional properties for the quadrilaterals. The list below includes the basic definitions along with many of these properties.

1. A parallelogram is a quadrilateral containing two pairs of congruent and parallel sides. The figure shown is an example of a parallelogram with diagonals. Any parallelogram is a quadrilateral and has the following properties:

    a. Opposite sides are equal in length.
    b. Opposite sides are parallel.
    c. All sides are not necessarily equal in length.
    d. Opposite angles are equal in measure.
    e. All angles are not necessarily equal in measure.
    f. Diagonals are not necessarily equal in length.
    g. Diagonals bisect each other (intersect each other at their midpoints).
    h. Consecutive angles are supplementary.

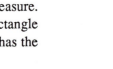

2. A rectangle is a parallelogram containing four angles that are equal in measure. These four angles are right angles. The figure shown is an example of a rectangle with diagonals. Any rectangle is a quadrilateral, a parallelogram, and has the following properties:

    a. Opposite sides are parallel and equal in length.
    b. All sides are not necessarily equal in length.
    c. Opposite angles are equal in measure.
    d. All angles are equal in measure, and each angle is a right angle.
    e. Diagonals are equal in length and bisect each other.

    Notice that a rectangle includes the properties of a parallelogram.

3. A square is a rectangle with four congruent sides. The square is the only regular polygon (all sides and angles congruent) among the quadrilaterals. The figure shown is an example of a square with diagonals. Any square is a quadrilateral, a parallelogram, a rectangle, and has the following properties:

    a. Opposite sides are parallel and equal in length.
    b. All sides are equal in length.
    c. Opposite angles are equal in measure.
    d. All angles are right angles.
    e. Diagonals are equal in length and bisect each other.
    f. Diagonals form right angles with each other.

    A square has the properties of a rectangle and a parallelogram and some additional properties.

4. A rhombus is a parallelogram containing four congruent sides. The figure shown is a rhombus with diagonals. (A square can be defined as a rhombus with four right angles.) Any rhombus is a quadrilateral, a parallelogram, and has the following properties:
   a. All sides are equal in length.
   b. Opposite sides are parallel and equal in length.
   c. All angles are not necessarily equal in measure.
   d. Diagonals are not necessarily equal in length.
   e. Diagonals form right angles with each other and bisect each other.

Notice that the rhombus includes the properties of a parallelogram.

5. A trapezoid is a quadrilateral that contains exactly one pair of parallel sides. The figure shown is an example of a trapezoid with diagonals. Any trapezoid is a quadrilateral and has the following properties:
   a. Exactly one pair of parallel sides
   b. Non-parallel sides are not necessarily equal in length.
   c. Parallel sides not equal in length.
   d. Opposite angles are not equal in measure.
   e. Diagonals are not equal in length.

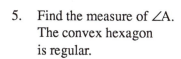

Problem Set 7

1. What is the sum of the measures of the angles of a convex hexagon? A convex octagon?

2. Three angles of a quadrilateral measure 64°, 121°, and 157°. What is the measure of the fourth angle?

3. Find m∠x in the diagram.

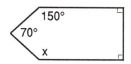

4. A plane geometric figure has 12 sides. How many degrees are there in the sum of the angles?

5. Find the measure of ∠A. The convex hexagon is regular.

6. Name the quadrilateral(s) that satisfy the following conditions.
   a. Opposite sides parallel; diagonals congruent.
   b. All sides congruent; diagonals perpendicular.
   c. Diagonals congruent.
   d. Diagonals perpendicular.
   e. Diagonals bisect each other.
   f. One pair of opposite sides parallel.
   g. Four right angles.
   h. Diagonals bisect each other, are congruent, and are perpendicular.

7. Which one statement is true for the parallelogram shown at the right?

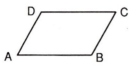

   a. $m \angle A \neq m \angle C$
   b. $AD = AB$
   c. $\angle A$ and $\angle B$ are supplementary.
   d. $\angle B$ and $\angle D$ are complementary.

8. Select the geometric figure that does not have opposite sides that are congruent.
   a. rhombus   b. square
   c. trapezoid   d. rectangle

9. Find the perimeter of the figure at the right. It consists of a square and 4 equilateral congruent triangles.

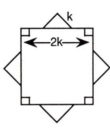

10. What is the perimeter of the figure shown below?

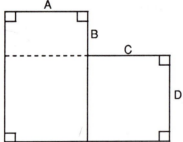

11. The diagram at the right shows the cross section of a house. The cross section consists of an isosceles triangle and a square. Line segment $\overline{AB}$ divides the base of the isosceles triangle in half. What is the length from the highest point on the roof to the bottom of the house?

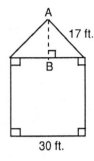

12. Select the geometric figure that does not have all sides equal in length.
   a. regular octagon
   b. parallelogram
   c. rhombus
   d. square

13. Select the geometric figure that does not have all angles congruent.
   a. rhombus
   b. square
   c. rectangle
   d. regular hexagon

14. Consider the accompanying parallelogram. Find $m\angle B$ and $m \angle C$.

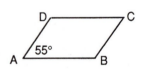

15. Which statement listed below is false?
   a. Opposite angles of a parallelogram are congruent.
   b. Consecutive angles of a rectangle are supplementary.
   c. A trapezoid has one pair of opposite sides that will intersect somewhere in the plane if extended.
   d. Every rhombus is a square.

248

16. Which statement listed below is true?
    a. All rectangles are parallelograms.
    b. Diagonals of a rhombus are congruent.
    c. The non-parallel sides of a trapezoid are congruent.
    d. Some squares have non-congruent adjacent sides.

17. What is the perimeter, in centimeters, of a parallelogram having two adjacent sides that measure 8 meters and 4 meters?
    a. 0.24 cm   b. 1200 cm
    c. 2400 cm   d. 24 cm

18. In a rhombus, which one of the following is not necessarily true?
    a. All four sides are congruent.
    b. Diagonals are perpendicular.
    c. The sum of the measures of the four interior angles is 360°.
    d. Diagonals are congruent.

19. The quadrilateral in the accompanying diagram is a parallelogram. Find the measures of the four angles.

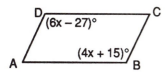

20. Two consecutive angles of a parallelogram have measures (x + 30) and (2x − 60), respectively. Find the measure of each angle of the parallelogram.

21. In the accompanying diagram, GMKH is a parallelogram. MQ = HP. Use congruent triangles to show that $\overline{GK}$ and $\overline{PQ}$ bisect each other.

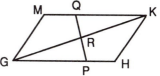

22. Find the measure of each angle in the accompanying figure.

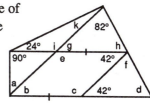

23. If both quadrilaterals in the accompanying figure are parallelograms, what is the relationship of ∠D to ∠R and ∠R to ∠C?

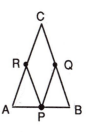

24. In the accompanying figure, ΔABC is isosceles with AC = BC. P, Q, and R are midpoints. Show that PQ = PR.

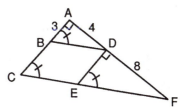

25. In the diagram find BD, EF, DE, and AC.

Topic 8

Area

This section summarizes formulas for finding the area of polygons and circles. At the end of the section you should be able to solve problems based upon these formulas.

Often we are interested in measuring the interior surface that is enclosed by a region. In this section, we consider a very important concept in measurement. We use the word **area** to refer to the measure of the interior surface of a closed curve.

We must select a basic unit of measure to determine the area of a region. We want to be able to completely cover the region by placing the units so they touch but do not overlap.

The most conveniently shaped unit is a **square unit**. A square unit is a square with sides that measure one unit in length.

square unit

1 unit

Our task is to determine how many square units are contained in a region. Thus, **area is always measured in terms of square units**.

Consider the rectangular region ABCD at the right. Our unit of measure will be the square unit of measure shown by the figure.

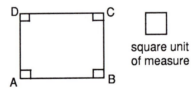

square unit of measure

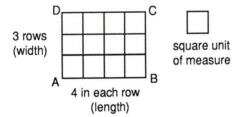

3 rows (width)

4 in each row (length)

square unit of measure

We simply count the square units to find the area. Observe that it takes 12 square units to cover this region. Using the basic unit, we say that the area of the region is 12 square units.

Notice there are 3 rows with 4 units in each row. We call the 3 rows the **width** of the region and the 4 units in each row the **length** of the region. The length and width of the rectangular region are its **dimensions**. Can you see that the area may simply be determined by finding the product of the length and the width? Thus, Area = 4 • 3 or A = 12 square units.

> ### Note
>
> People frequently refer to the area of a rectangle when what they really mean is the area of a rectangular region. We will continue this practice also.

> The area (A) of a rectangle is the product of the length (L) and the width (W). (A = L • W).

There are various standard square units used to measure area. The **square inch** (in^2) is a square with sides that are one inch in length. A square with sides one foot in length is called a **square foot** (ft^2). A square with sides that are one yard in length has an area of one **square yard** (yd^2).

Some important relationships exist among the square units:

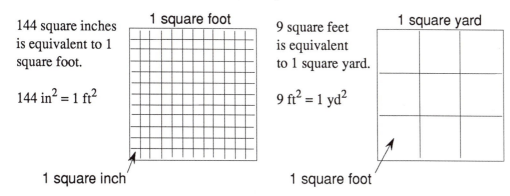

144 square inches is equivalent to 1 square foot.

$144\ in^2 = 1\ ft^2$

1 square foot

1 square inch

9 square feet is equivalent to 1 square yard.

$9\ ft^2 = 1\ yd^2$

1 square yard

1 square foot

To find the area of a rectangle, the length and width must be stated in the same units. Thus, we state the dimensions of a rectangle that measures 3 ft. by 24 in. as 3 ft. by 2 ft. or 36 in. by 24 in.

Problem 1

What will it cost to carpet a rectangular room measuring 12 feet by 15 feet if the carpet costs $18.50 per square yard?

Solution

Since the cost is given in square yards, it is a good idea to change the dimensions to yards before finding area. Since 12 feet = 4 yards (3 feet = 1 yard) and 15 feet = 5 yards, we have:

$$A = LW = 4 \cdot 5 = 20$$

Since the area is 20 yd^2, the cost is $(18.5)(20) = 370$. It will cost $370.

Problem 2

An 8 ft. by 11 ft. rectangular wall can be painted for $13. Find the cost to paint a rectangular wall 12 ft. by 11 ft.

Solution

Set up a proportion as: $\dfrac{\text{original area}}{\text{new area}} = \dfrac{\text{original cost}}{\text{new cost}}$

$\begin{matrix}\text{original area} \\ \text{new area}\end{matrix}$ $\quad \dfrac{8 \cdot 11}{12 \cdot 11} = \dfrac{13.00}{x} \quad$ $\begin{matrix}(\$) \text{ original cost} \\ (\$) \text{ new cost}\end{matrix}$

Reduce before solving for x. $\quad \dfrac{8 \cdot \cancel{11}}{12 \cdot \cancel{11}} = \dfrac{13.00}{x} \quad$ becomes $\quad \dfrac{2}{3} = \dfrac{13}{x}$

The proportion is solved as:

$$2x = 3 \cdot 13 \qquad \text{Recall: If } \tfrac{a}{b} = \tfrac{c}{d} \text{ then } ad = bc.$$
$$2x = 39$$
$$x = \tfrac{39}{2} = 19.5$$

Since x stands for dollars, the cost is $19.50.

It is possible to find the **surface area** of a rectangular solid. The surface area refers to the area of all the polygons that make up the solid figure. The surface area is always measured in square units.

Problem 3

Find the surface area of the accompanying rectangular solid.

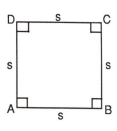

4 cm

3 cm

5 cm

Solution

To find the surface area, we must find the areas of the six rectangles that make up the solid and add them.

Area of base	$= 5 \cdot 3 = 15$ cm^2
Area of top	$= 15$ cm^2
Area of front	$= 5 \cdot 4 = 20$ cm^2
Area of back	$= 20$ cm^2
Area of side	$= 4 \cdot 3 = 12$ cm^2
Area of opposite side	$= 12$ cm^2

Surface area $= 15 + 15 + 20 + 20 + 12 + 12 = 94$ cm^2

We now discuss the formulas for areas of other polygons.

Consider the square region ABCD shown in which the letter s represents the length of any of the four congruent sides. Since a square is a rectangle, the area can be determined by using the formula for the area of a rectangle.

$A = L \cdot W$. Thus, we obtain: $A = L \cdot W$ or $A = s \cdot s$ or $A = s^2$

> The area (A) of a square is the square of the length of a side (s). $(A = s^2)$

Problem 4

Consider the square ABCD shown in which the measure of a side is 5 feet. Find its area.

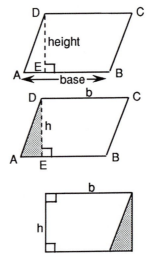

Solution

Using the formula $A = s^2$ and substituting 5 for s gives:
$$A = s^2 = 5^2 = 25$$

Thus, the area is 25 square feet (25 ft^2).

Consider the parallelogram ABCD shown at the right. The line segment DE, drawn from a vertex and perpendicular to the base, is called the **height** or the **altitude**.

It can be demonstrated that the area of the parallelogram is the same as the area of a rectangle. In the figure at the right, if $\triangle AED$ is removed from the left of the parallelogram and attached to the right, the result is seen to be a rectangle with the same base (length) and height (width) as the original parallelogram. Since the length of the rectangle equals the base (b) of the parallelogram and the width equals the height (h), the formula for the area of the rectangle can be transformed into a formula for the area of the parallelogram.

$A = L \cdot W$ becomes $A = b \cdot h$ or $A = bh$

> The area (A) of a parallelogram equals the product of its base (b) and height (h).
> $(A = b \cdot h)$

Problem 5

Find the area of the parallelogram shown.

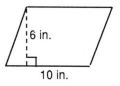

6 in.

10 in.

Solution

Since the base (b) is 10 in. and the height (h) is 6 in., the formula

$$A = bh \text{ becomes } A = 10 \cdot 6 = 60.$$

Thus, the area of the parallelogram is 60 square in. (60 in^2).

Consider the accompanying parallelogram ABCD in which DE is the height (h) and AB is the base (b). The diagonal BD forms △ABD.

Since △ABD ≅△BDC, the area of a triangle is one-half the area of a parallelogram. Since the area of a parallelogram is A = b • h or A = bh, the area of △ABD is $\frac{1}{2}$ this area or

$$A = \frac{1}{2} \cdot b \cdot h \text{ or } A = \frac{1}{2}bh.$$

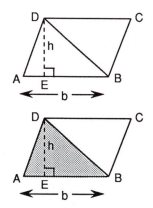

> The area (A) of a triangle equals half the product of the base (b) and the height (h). $(A = \frac{1}{2}bh)$

There is only one formula for the area of a triangle, but three figures are shown below to aid in applying the formula. In all cases the formula is:

$$A = \frac{1}{2}bh$$

where b is the length of the side called the base and h is the height (the perpendicular distance from the vertex to the base or extended base).

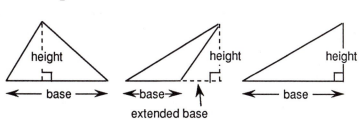

Problem 6

What is the cost to cover a triangular plot with a base of 3 yards and a height of 4 feet with shrubs if shrubs cost $25 per square foot?

Solution

The base, 3 yards, measures $3 \cdot 3 = 9$ feet. Thus:
$$A = \tfrac{1}{2}bh = \tfrac{1}{2} \cdot 9 \cdot 4 = 18 \text{ ft}^2$$
The cost is $18 \cdot 25 = 450$. The cost is $450.

Problem 7

Find the area of the accompanying figure representing a parallelogram and a triangle.

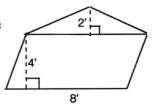

Solution

The figure above needs to be seen as a parallelogram and a triangle which do not overlap. The area of the entire figure is found by adding the area of the parallelogram to the area of the triangle.

Area of parallelogram $= b \cdot h = 8 \cdot 4 = 32 \text{ ft}^2$

Area of triangle $= \tfrac{1}{2} \cdot b \cdot h = \tfrac{1}{2} \cdot 8 \cdot 2 = 8 \text{ ft}^2$

Total area $= 32 + 8 = 40 \text{ ft}^2$

Consider the accompanying trapezoid ABCD with height DE (indicated as h). If the lower base AB is a and the upper base DC is b, it is possible to develop the formula for the area of the trapezoid.

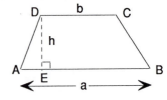

Draw a diagonal BD and form two triangles. Thus,
area (A) of trapezoid = (A) of triangle I + (A) of triangle II

$$
\begin{aligned}
A &= \tfrac{1}{2}ah &+& \tfrac{1}{2}bh \\
A &= \tfrac{1}{2}h(a + b)
\end{aligned}
$$

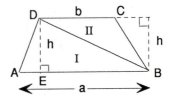

> The area (A) of a trapezoid equals half the product of the height (h) and the sum of the bases (a and b).
>
> $$A = \tfrac{1}{2}h(a + b)$$

Problem 8

Find the area of the region shown at the right consisting of a trapezoid and a right triangle.

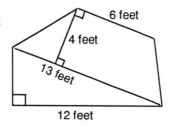

6 feet

4 feet

13 feet

12 feet

Solution

Area of trapezoid $= \tfrac{1}{2}h(a + b) = \tfrac{1}{2} \cdot 4 \cdot (13 + 6) = \tfrac{1}{2} \cdot 4 \cdot 19 = 38$ ft^2

Area of triangle $= \tfrac{1}{2}bh = \tfrac{1}{2} \cdot 12 \cdot h$

We can find h using the Pythagorean theorem.

$$12^2 + h^2 = 13^2$$
$$144 + h^2 = 169$$
$$h^2 = 25$$
$$h = 5$$

Thus, area of triangle $= \tfrac{1}{2} \cdot 12 \cdot 5 = 30$ ft^2

Total area $=$ area of trapezoid + area of triangle
$$= 38 + 30 = 68 \text{ ft}^2$$

Up to this point we have considered the areas of polygons. We now turn our attention to the circle.

◊ Definition

A **circle** is a set of points in the plane equally distant from a given point called its center.

Informal Geometry

The **radius** of a circle is a line segment that joins the center of the circle to a point on the circle. The **diameter** of a circle is a line segment that passes through the center of a circle and joins two points on the circle. The diameter (d) is twice the length of the radius (r). Thus, d = 2 • r.

The distance around a circle is the **circumference**. To determine the circumference of a circle, its diameter or radius must be known.

The ratio of the circumference of a circle to its diameter is always the same regardless of the size of the circle. This result is the number π (the Greek letter "pi"), an irrational number approximated by 3.14 or $\frac{22}{7}$, but closer to 3.14159.

Thus $\pi = \dfrac{\text{circumference (C)}}{\text{diameter (d)}}$ or $\pi = \dfrac{C}{d}$

This relationship implies that C = πd.

The area (A) of a circle is the product of π and the square of the radius (r). $(A = \pi r^2)$

The circumference (C) of a circle is the product of π and the diameter. $(C = \pi d)$
The circumference (C) of a circle is the product of 2π and the radius. $(C = 2\pi r)$

Problem 9

How much fencing is required to enclose a circular garden that measures 10 yards across?

Solution

The enclosure of the garden refers to circumference of the circle. Since the diameter is 10 yards, C = π d = π • 10. The circumference is 10π yards. Approximately 10 • 3.14 or 31.4 yards of fencing is required.

Unless otherwise indicated, circumference and area of a circle should be expressed in terms of π.

Problem 10

How much sod is required to cover a circular garden that measures 10 yards across?

Solution

Covering the garden with sod implies the area of the circle. Since the diameter is 10 yards, the radius is $\frac{1}{2} \cdot 10$ or 5 yards.

$$\text{Thus, } A = \pi r^2 = \pi \cdot 5^2 = 25\pi.$$

25π square yards of sod is required, which is approximately $(25)(3.14)$ or 78.5 square yards.

Problem 11

The figure at the right shows two smaller semicircles, each with a diameter of 4 yards, drawn inside a larger semicircle. Find the area of the shaded region.

4 yds.   4 yds.

Solution

The area of the shaded region equals:

the area of the larger semicircle – the area of the two smaller semicircles.

The area of the larger semicircle $= \frac{1}{2}\pi r^2$

$$= \frac{1}{2} \cdot \pi \cdot 4^2$$
$$= 8\pi \text{ yd}^2$$

The area of each smaller semicircle $= \frac{1}{2}\pi r^2$

$$= \frac{1}{2} \cdot \pi \cdot 2^2$$
$$= 2\pi \text{ yd}^2$$

The shaded area $= 8\pi - (2\pi + 2\pi)$

$$= 8\pi - 4\pi$$
$$= 4\pi \text{ yd}^2$$

Informal Geometry

Now that we know about areas, it is not too difficult to prove the Pythagorean Theorem.

The Pythagorean Theorem

In a right triangle, the sum of the squares of the legs is equal to the square of the hypotenuse.

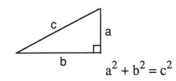

$$a^2 + b^2 = c^2$$

Proof

1. Consider the square with each side measuring a + b. As shown in the square we draw four right triangles with legs a and b.
2. By SAS, each of the four triangles is congruent to the given triangle. Therefore they all have hypotenuse equal to c, as shown in the figure.
3. Since a triangle has an angle sum of 180°, r + s + 90 = 180. This means that r + s = 90. Looking at the diagram, r + s + t = 180, so t = 90. Thus the quadrilateral formed by the four hypotenuse is a square.
4. The area of the large square is equal to the area of the small (unshaded) square, plus the sum of the areas of the four congruent triangles. This gives:

$$(a + b)^2 = c^2 + 4 \cdot \tfrac{1}{2}ab$$
$$a^2 + 2ab + b^2 = c^2 + 2ab$$

Subtracting 2ab from both sides, we obtain:
$$a^2 + b^2 = c^2,$$

which is the Pythagorean Theorem that was to be proved.

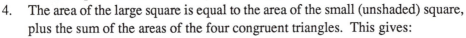

Problem Set 8

1. A rectangular room measures 9 feet by 21 feet. What is the cost of carpeting the room at $12.98 per square yard?

2. If the smaller rectangle in the diagram has dimensions 10 ft by 30 ft and the larger rectangle has dimensions 20 ft by 60 ft, find the area of the shaded region.

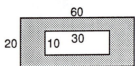

260

3. Find the area of the shaded region.

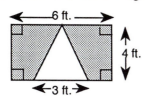

4. Find the area of the shaded region.

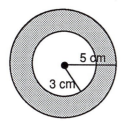

5. Find the surface area of the rectangular solid.

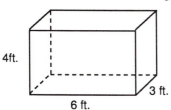

6. Find the area of right triangle ABC.

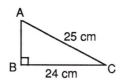

7. Find the area of the trapezoid. Each unit on the graph paper represents one meter.

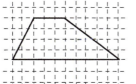

8. A large rectangle has dimensions 4 ft by 3 ft. A smaller rectangle has dimensions $3\frac{1}{3}$ ft by $2\frac{1}{2}$ ft. How much larger is the area of the large rectangle?

9. Determine the formula for computing the surface area of the accompanying solid figure which is composed of three attached cubes whose edges each measure x.
   a. $10x^2$
   b. $12x^2$
   c. $14x^2$
   d. $16x^2$

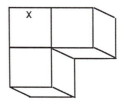

10. Find the area of the region showing a parallelogram and a triangle.

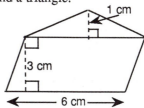

11. How many yards of fencing will it take to go around a circular flower bed that measures 6 yards across?

12. What is the formula for finding the surface area of the solid shown below? The triangles at both ends are equilateral. The other regions are rectangles.

261

13. What is the formula for the area of the shaded region? Express the answer in terms of π and r.

14. Find the area of the figure consisting of a square and four semicircles. Use 3.14 for π.

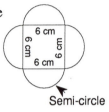

Semi-circle

15. Find the shaded area using 3.14 for π.

14 ft.

16. a. If the radius of a circle is doubled, what happens to the area?
    b. A pizza with radius 4 inches sells for $1.50. Find the proportional charge for a pizza of radius 8 inches.

Find the total areas for the figures in problems 17 and 18. Use 3.14 for π.

17.

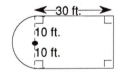

30 ft.
10 ft.
10 ft.

18.

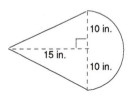

10 in.
15 in.
10 in.

19. A rectangular wall measures 14 feet by 10 feet and has a triangular opening with base 10 feet and height 4 feet. The wall, except for the triangular opening, is to be covered with wallpaper. The wallpaper come in rolls measuring 40 feet by $1\frac{1}{2}$ feet and sells for $12 per roll. The paper hanger will charge $20 for the labor. Find the total cost of papering the wall.

20. A photograph collection is mounted on pages measuring 2 feet by $2\frac{1}{2}$ feet. A particular photograph measures 21 inches by $2\frac{1}{6}$ feet. Find the area of the margin of the page in square inches.

21. A square has a perimeter of 20 feet. What is the area of the square?

22. Find the area outside the trapezoid and inside the square in the figure shown below.

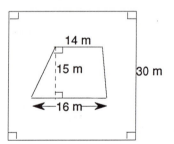

14 m
15 m
30 m
16 m

23. Writing paper that measures 8 inches by 11 inches contains margins of $\frac{1}{6}$ foot at the top and at each side and $\frac{1}{12}$ foot at the bottom. What is the total area, in square inches, on which one may write?

24. A circular target has a radius of 1 foot with a circular bullseye whose radius measures 2 inches. What is the ratio of the area of the bullseye to the total target area?

25. Round:
    a. 2476 cm² to the nearest hundred cm².
    b. 76.43 m² to the nearest m².
    c. 27.453 cm² to the nearest tenth cm².

26. The Pythagorean theorem for the right triangle is one of the best known ideas in mathematics. Several hundred different proofs of this theorem have been recorded. James Garfield, the twentieth president of the United States, used his knowledge of polynomials and the trapezoid shown in the diagram to prove the theorem. See if you can reproduce Garfield's proof by finding the area of the trapezoid in two ways, establishing that $c^2 = a^2 + b^2$.

    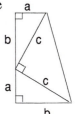

    Hint: Find the area of the trapezoid using

    $A = \frac{1}{2} \cdot$ height $\cdot$ (sum of the two parallel sides).

    Set this equal to the sum of the areas of the three triangles shown in the figure.

Topic 9

Volume

This section summarizes formulas for finding the volume of geometric solid figures. At the end of the section you should be able to solve problems based upon these formulas.

Volume refers to the amount of space enclosed by a solid figure. The basic unit for the measurement of volume is the **unit cube**, a rectangular solid composed of six square faces. Each edge of the unit cube measures 1 linear unit in length. Notice in the figure at the right that a cube has three dimensions: length, width and height. Cubic units must be counted to obtain the volume of a solid. Thus, **volume is always measured in terms of cubic units**.

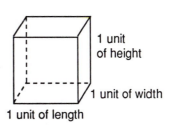

The figure at the right shows a rectangular solid which is next to the basic unit cube. Notice that the solid occupies as much space as 12 units. Thus, the volume of this solid is 12 cubic units, written 12 cubic units or 12 units^3.

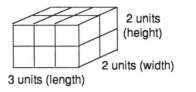

unit cube

A cubic inch (in^3) is a very common unit of measurement. It is the volume of a cube that is one inch long, one inch wide, and one inch high. The cubic foot (ft^3) and the cubic yard (yd^3) are other common basic units of measurement.

Because solid figures have three dimensions, drawings to represent them on a piece of paper usually use dashed lines to create the illusion of depth. Four drawings of space figures are shown below.

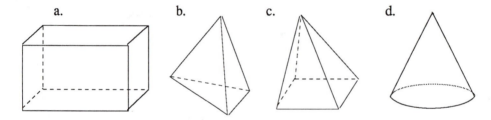

a.   b.   c.   d.

Figures a, b, and c have surfaces that are polygons. These solid figures are called polyhedrons. Figure d contains a surface that is not a polygon, the circular bottom. Figure d does not represent a polyhedron.

◊ Definitions

Any closed surface formed by the union of polygonal regions is called a **polyhedron**. Each polygonal region is called a **face** of the polyhedron. A **regular polyhedron** is one whose faces are all made up of one kind of regular polygon. The line segment formed by the intersection of two faces is called an **edge**. Each endpoint of the line segment is called a **vertex**.

Problem 1

The polyhedron shown at the right is a regular
polyhedron since all six faces are squares of the
same size. This polyhedron is called a hexahedron,
but more commonly referred to as a **cube**.

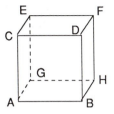

a.   Name the edges of the cube.

Solution

There are 12 edges:

$\overline{AB}$, $\overline{BH}$, $\overline{GH}$, $\overline{AG}$, $\overline{AC}$, $\overline{GE}$, $\overline{CE}$, $\overline{CD}$, $\overline{DF}$, $\overline{EF}$, $\overline{HF}$ and $\overline{BD}$.

b.   Name the vertices.

Solution

There are 8 vertices: A, B, H, G, C, D, F and E.

The polyhedron at the right is called a **rectangular solid**
or a **rectangular parallelepiped**. Each of the six faces is
a rectangle. The cube is a special case of the rectangular
solid in which each face is a square.

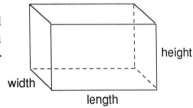

> The volume (V) of a rectangular solid is the
> product of the length (L) and width (W) and
> height (H). $(V = L \cdot W \cdot H)$

Problem 2

Find the volume of the accompanying rectangular solid.

Solution

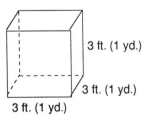

Notice that this rectangular solid is a cube with an
edge that measures 3 feet or 1 yd. Thus,

$$V = L \cdot W \cdot H = 3 \cdot 3 \cdot 3 = 27 \text{ cubic ft } (27 \text{ ft}^3)$$
$$V = L \cdot W \cdot H = 1 \cdot 1 \cdot 1 = 1 \text{ cubic yd } (1 \text{yd}^3)$$

Observe that $1 \text{ yd}^3 = 27 \text{ ft}^3$.

Problem 3

A rectangular solid measuring 21 ft by 6 ft by 9 ft is completely filled with dirt. A truck is capable of carrying 7 cubic yards. How many trips will it take to empty the rectangular solid of its contents?

Solution

Because the capability of the truck is given in cubic yards, it would be best to convert feet to yards before finding the volume.

Thus, 21 ft = 7 yd, 6 ft = 2 yd and 9 ft = 3 yd.

We have

$$V = LWH = 7 \cdot 2 \cdot 3 = 42.$$

Since the solid contains 42 cubic yards of dirt, $\frac{42}{7} = 6$ trips are necessary to remove its contents.

The polyhedron at the right is called a **rectangular pyramid** or a **right pyramid**. Notice that there are four triangular faces and one rectangular face. The base of the rectangular pyramid is a rectangle.

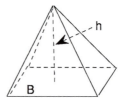

> The volume (V) of a rectangular pyramid is $\frac{1}{3}$ the product of the area of the base (B) and the height (h). $(V = \frac{1}{3} \cdot B \cdot h)$

Problem 4

A granite monument has the shape of a pyramid with a rectangular base measuring 10 feet by 3 feet. The height is 6 feet. Find the weight of the monument if the granite weighs 160 pounds per cubic foot.

Solution

Since the base is a rectangle, the area of the base (B) is:

$$B = L \cdot W$$
$$B = 10 \cdot 3$$

Thus, $B = 30$ sq. ft.

The formula for the volume of the pyramid is now applied:

$$V = \frac{1}{3} \cdot B \cdot h$$
$$V = \frac{1}{3} \cdot 30 \cdot 6$$
$$V = 60$$

Thus, the volume of the pyramid is 60 cubic ft (60 ft^3). Its weight is $(60)(160) = 9{,}600$ pounds.

The polyhedron shown at the right is called a **right triangular prism**. Two faces are triangles. The remaining faces are rectangles.

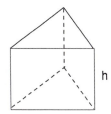

The volume (V) of a right triangular prism is the product of the area of the base (B) and the height (h). $(V = B \cdot h)$

Problem 5

How many cubic feet of space is available in the tent shown in the accompanying diagram?

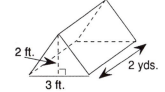

2 ft. 3 ft. 2 yds.

Solution

Since the base is a triangle, the area (B) of the triangle is :

$$B = \frac{1}{2} \cdot b \cdot h$$
$$B = \frac{1}{2} \cdot 3 \cdot 2$$
$$B = 3$$

Thus, the area of the base is 3 square feet. The height measures 2 yards or 6 feet. To find the volume of the right triangular prism, we have:

$$V = B \cdot h$$
$$V = 3 \cdot 6$$
$$V = 18$$

Thus, there are 18 cubic feet of space available in the tent.

We now consider geometric solids not entirely composed of faces that are polygons. These solids are not polyhedrons. Formulas for volume are given in terms of π.

The solid at the right is a **right circular cylinder**. Circular regions make up the top and bottom. The side, if unrolled, is a rectangle. One dimension of this rectangle is the height of the cylinder. The other dimension of this rectangle is the circumference of the circle at the top or the bottom of the cylinder.

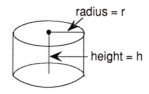

> The volume (V) of a right circular cylinder is the product of the area of the circular base and the height (h). $(V = \pi r^2 h)$

Problem 6

A hot water tank has the shape of a cylinder with a diameter of 48 inches and a height of 2 yards. Each cubic foot holds 8 gallons of water. How many gallons of water will the tank hold?

Solution

All dimensions should be changed to feet. Since
$$\text{diameter} = 48 \text{ inches, the radius} = 24 \text{ inches} = 2 \text{ feet.}$$
The height is 2 yards = 6 feet.
$$V = \pi r^2 h$$
$$V = \pi \cdot 2^2 6$$
$$V = 24\pi$$
The volume is 24π ft^3, so the tank holds $(24\pi)(8) = 192\pi$ gallons. This is approximately $(192)(3.14)$ or 602.88 gallons. As in the previous section, all answers should be given in terms of π unless otherwise indicated.

The solid figure shown at the right is a **right circular cone**.

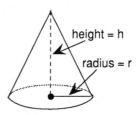

> The volume (V) of a right circular cone is $\frac{1}{3}$ the product of the area of the circular base and the height (h).   ($V = \frac{1}{3} \cdot \pi r^2 h$)

Problem 7

What is the weight of a statue in the shape of a cone having a circular base with a diameter of 144 inches and a height of 10 feet if each cubic foot weighs $\frac{8}{\pi}$ pounds?

Solution

The diameter is 144 inches or 12 feet, so the radius is $\frac{12}{2}$ or 6 feet.

$$
\begin{aligned}
V &= \tfrac{1}{3}\pi r^2 h \\
&= \tfrac{1}{3} \cdot \pi \cdot 6^2 \cdot 10 \\
&= \tfrac{1}{3} \cdot \pi \cdot 36 \cdot 10 \\
&= 120\,\pi
\end{aligned}
$$

The volume is 120π ft^3. The weight is the number of cubic feet (120π) multiplied by the weight of each cubic foot ($\frac{8}{\pi}$ pounds). The weight is:

$$120\pi \cdot \tfrac{8}{\pi} = 120 \cdot 8 = 960.$$

The statue weighs 960 pounds.

◊ **Definition**

A **sphere** is a set of points in space equally distant from a given point, called the center.

A sphere may be represented as shown at the right.

> The volume (V) of a sphere is $\frac{4}{3}$ the product of π and the cube of the radius (r).   ($V = \frac{4}{3} \cdot \pi \cdot r^3$)

Problem 8

A spherical tank of radius 1 meter can be filled with a liquid for $12. How much would it cost to fill a spherical tank of radius 3 meters with the same liquid?

Solution

We set up a proportion: $\dfrac{\text{original volume}}{\text{new volume}} = \dfrac{\text{original cost}}{\text{new cost}}$

$$\text{Volume} = \tfrac{4}{3}\pi r^3$$

$$\begin{array}{l}\text{original volume} \\ \text{new volume}\end{array} \quad \dfrac{\tfrac{4}{3}\pi 1^3}{\tfrac{4}{3}\pi 3^3} = \dfrac{12}{x} \quad \begin{array}{l}\text{original cost} \\ \text{new cost}\end{array}$$

$$\dfrac{\tfrac{4}{3}\pi 1}{\tfrac{4}{3}\pi 27} = \dfrac{12}{x}$$

We obtain: $\dfrac{1}{27} = \dfrac{12}{x}$ or $x = 27 \cdot 12$ or $x = 324$ or $324

Thus, the new cost is $324.

In summary, be aware that:
1. Line segments are measured in linear units, such as inches and centimeters.
2. Area is measured in square units, such as square inches and cm^2.
3. Volume is measured in cubic units, such as cubic inches and cm^3.

The basic metric unit for measuring volume is the liter (l). One liter is approximately 1.05 quarts. Again, the metric prefixes apply, so that 1 kiloliter (kl) = 1000 liters. Since volume is also measured in cubic units, there is a relationship between liters and cubic centimeters given by:

1 liter = 1000 cubic centimeters.

E
X
A
M
P
L
E

The volume of a 1.37 liter flask is (1.37)(1000) or 1,370 cubic centimeters.

Problem Set 9

1. Find the volume of a rectangular solid with length 6 ft, width 9 ft and height 48 in. Express the answer in terms of cubic yards.

2. A family is moving to Florida. The mover estimates their possessions will take up 750 cubic feet of space. Would a truck with a container 8 feet wide, 6 feet high, and 16 feet long hold all the possessions?

3. Compare the volumes of three 4-inch cubes and four 3-inch cubes, and indicate which is greater.

4. Find the volume and the surface area of a cube whose edge measures 4 yards.

5. Find the volume of a rectangular solid with $L = \frac{5}{24}$ feet, $W = \frac{8}{3}$ feet and $H = \frac{21}{16}$ feet.

6. For each item, identify the appropriate measure (cm, cm^2, cm^3) needed for the figure.

    a. segment BF
    b. the area of plane region BFGC
    c. the interior of the solid region.

7. A granite monument has the shape of a pyramid with a rectangular base measuring 18 yards by 9 feet. The height is 96 inches. Find the weight of the monument if the granite weighs 160 pounds per cubic foot.

8. A right triangular prism has a triangular base of 9 yards and a height of 4 yards. The height of the prism is 20 yards. Find the volume of the prism.

9. A hot water heater has the shape of a cylinder with a diameter of 72 inches and a height of 4 yards. Each cubic foot holds 8 gallons of water. How many gallons of water will the tank hold?

10. What is the weight of a statue in the shape of a cone having a circular base with a diameter of 72 inches and a height of 30 feet if each cubic foot weighs $\frac{13}{\pi}$ pounds?

11. Find the volume of a sphere whose diameter measures 12 meters.

12. A spherical tank of radius 2 meters can be filled with liquid for $6.00. How much would it cost to fill a spherical tank of radius 10 meters with the same liquid?

13. A right circular cylinder of radius 2 yd and height 1 yd can be filled with a liquid for $6. How much would it cost to fill a cylinder of radius 4 yd and height 3 yd?

14. A patio measuring 3 feet by 6 feet by 4 inches is to be filled with concrete that costs $36 per cubic yard. What will it cost to fill the patio?

15. Find the volume of the solid formed by the two cubes in the accompanying figure. Express the answer in terms of B.

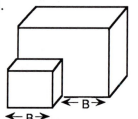

16. Find the total surface area of the right circular cylinder. Express the answer in terms of π.

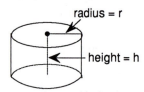

17. Round:
    a. 18.56 yd^3 to the nearest cubic yard.
    b. 2437 cm^3 to the nearest hundred cm^3.
    c. 2637 cm^3 to the nearest thousand cm^3.
    d. 17.37 m^3 to the nearest tenth m^3.

18. What is the volume in cubic centimeters of an 8.62 liter flask?

Chapter 3 Summary

1. Measurement

a. Line segments are measured in linear units, area in square units, and volume in cubic units or liters. 1 liter = 1,000 cm ^{3}

b. Common metric units for length include:

millimeter (mm) = $\frac{1}{1000}$ of a meter

centimeter (cm) = $\frac{1}{100}$ of a meter

decimeter (dm) = $\frac{1}{10}$ of a meter

kilometer (km) = 1,000 meters

c. Notations:
Line AB: $\overleftrightarrow{AB}$
Line segment AB: $\overline{AB}$
Length of $\overline{AB}$: AB
$\overline{AB} \cong \overline{CD}$ means AB = CD

2. Angles

a. Angles are measured in degrees. Acute angles measure less than 90°, right angles measure exactly 90°, obtuse angles measure more than 90° but less than 180°, and straight angles measure exactly 180°.

b. Complementary angles have a sum of their measures of 90°, and supplementary angles have a sum of their measures of 180°.

c. $\angle A \cong \angle B$ means that m $\angle A$ = m $\angle B$.

d. Vertical angles are congruent.

3. Parallel Lines

a. Parallel lines lie in the same plane and do not intersect.

b. Two lines are parallel if and only if alternate interior or alternate exterior or corresponding angles are congruent.

c. Two lines are parallel if and only if interior or exterior angles on the same side of the transversal are supplementary.

d. Notations:
$\overleftrightarrow{AB} \parallel \overleftrightarrow{CD}$ (Line AB is parallel to line CD.)
$\overleftrightarrow{AB} \perp \overleftrightarrow{CD}$ (Line AB is perpendicular to line CD.)

4. Triangles

a. The sum of the measures of the interior angles is 180°.

b. Any exterior angle has a measure equal to the sum of the measures of the two remote interior angles.

c. Equilateral triangles have three congruent sides, isosceles triangles have two congruent sides (and two congruent angles opposite these sides), and scalene triangles have no congruent sides.

d. The Pythagorean Theorem states that in a right triangle the sum of the squares of the legs is equal to the square of the hypotenuse.

5. Congruent Triangles

a. Two triangles are congruent means that corresponding sides and angles are congruent.

b. The conditions SAS, ASA, and SSS determine congruent triangles. Once congruency is established, all other corresponding parts are congruent.

c. Notation:

$\triangle ABC \cong \triangle DEF$ ($\triangle ABC$ is congruent to $\triangle DEF$.)

6. Similar Triangles

a. Two triangles are similar means that corresponding angles are congruent and corresponding sides are proportional.

b. Two triangles are similar if and only if:
1. two angles of one triangle are congruent to two angles of the other triangle, or
2. all three pairs of corresponding sides are proportional, or
3. two corresponding pairs of sides are proportional and the angles included between these sides are congruent.

c. When similarity is determined by two congruent angle pairs, corresponding sides of similar triangles are proportional.

7. Polygons

a. Regular polygons have congruent sides and congruent angles.

b. The sum of the measures of the interior angles of a convex polygon of n sides is $(n - 2) \cdot 180°$.

8. Quadrilaterals

a. Trapezoid: Exactly one pair of parallel sides.

b. Parallelogram: Opposite sides are congruent and parallel. Consecutive angles are supplementary. Diagonals bisect each other. Opposite angles are congruent.

c. Rectangle: A parallelogram with four right angles. Diagonals are congruent and bisect.

d. Rhombus: A parallelogram with four congruent sides. Diagonals are perpendicular and bisect.

e. Square: A rectangle with four congruent sides or a rhombus with four right angles. Diagonals are congruent, perpendicular and bisect.

9. Geometric Formulas for Area

a. Rectangle $A = LW$

b. Square $A = s^2$

c. Parallelogram $A = bh$

d. Triangle $A = \frac{1}{2}bh$

e. Trapezoid $A = \frac{1}{2}h(a + b)$

f. Circle $A = \pi r^2$ (also: $C = \pi d = 2\pi r$)

g. Rectangular Solid

The surface area is found by finding the area of the six rectangles that form the solid and taking the sum of these six numbers.

10. Geometric Formulas for Volume

a. Rectangular Solid $V = LWH$

b. Rectangular Pyramid $V = \frac{1}{3}Bh$

c. Right Triangular Prism $V = Bh$

d. Right Circular Cylinder $V = \pi r^2 h$

e. Right Circular Cone $V = \frac{1}{3}\pi r^2 h$

f. Sphere $V = \frac{4}{3}\pi r^3$

Sample Examination – Geometry

1. Round 78.349 cubic feet to the nearest tenth of a cubic foot.
   a. 78.3 ft^3
   b. 78.35 ft^3
   c. 78.4 ft^3
   d. 80 ft^3

2. Use the protractor to find m∠ABC. Then classify the angle by its measure.

   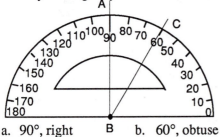

   a. 90°, right
   b. 60°, obtuse
   c. 30°, obtuse
   d. 30°, acute

3. Round 14.645 cubic yards to the nearest ten cubic yards.
   a. 10 yd^3
   b. 14.6 yd^3
   c. 14.7 yd^3
   d. 20 yd^3

4. What is the perimeter of a rectangle that is 500 meters wide and 700 meters long?
   a. 2.4 km
   b. 350 km
   c. 350,000 m^2
   d. 2,400,000 km

5. What is the formula for the total surface area of the rectangular solid shown below with a base measuring A feet by 3A feet and a height measuring A feet?

   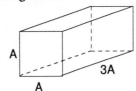

   a. 3A^3 ft^3
   b. 3A^3 ft^2
   c. 13A^2 ft^2
   d. 14A^2 ft^2

6. The two circles shown below have the same center. The smaller, unshaded circle has a diameter of 4 inches. The larger circle has a diameter of 2 feet. What is the area of the shaded ring?

   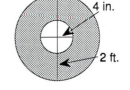

   a. 20π in^2
   b. 140π in^2
   c. 160π in^2
   d. 560π in^2

7. Which one of the following names a polygon having no two sides equal in length?
   a. parallelogram
   b. scalene triangle
   c. quadrilateral
   d. isosceles triangle

8. The solid shown at right is made up by attaching 3 identical cubes whose edges each measure 12 feet.

   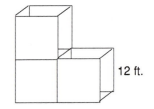

   The solid is completely filled with dirt. The dirt is to be removed by trucks that can carry 8 cubic yards per trip. If there is a charge of $10 for each truckload to haul the dirt away, what will it cost to remove all the dirt from the solid?
   a. $240
   b. $1,920
   c. $1,940
   d. $2,160

9. How much fencing is needed to enclose a circular garden that measures 20 yards across?
   a. 400π yd
   b. 100π yd^2
   c. 100π yd
   d. 20π yd

10. What is the volume of a cone that is 15 meters high if the circular base is 10 meters in diameter?
    a. 500π m^3
    b. 187.5π m^3
    c. 125π m^3
    d. 50π m^3

11. Select the formula that correctly expresses the area inside the trapezoid and outside the square in the accompanying diagram. The trapezoid has bases of 10A and 6A and a height of 2A. One side of the square is represented by A.

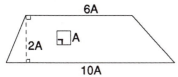

a. $9A^2$ b. $15A^2$ c. $19A^2$ d. $31A^2$

12. Find the volume of the solid shown below consisting of a cylinder and a cone. The circular top of the cylinder is the circular base of the cone.

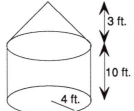

a. $213\frac{1}{3}\pi$ ft^3

b. 208π ft^3

c. 176π ft^3

d. $69\frac{1}{3}\pi$ ft^3

13. Which statement listed below is true of polygons?
   a. Diagonals of a parallelogram are congruent.
   b. Every rhombus is a square.
   c. Each interior angle of a regular octagon measures 135°.
   d. Opposite angles of a trapezoid are congruent.

14. What is the cost to cover a triangular plot with a base of 9 feet and a height of 4 feet with shrubs if shrubs cost $25 per square foot?
   a. $900   b. $450   c. $420   d. $325

15. Round 7 ft. 5 in. to the nearest foot.
   a. 7 ft   b. 7.5 ft   c. 8 ft   d. 9 ft

16. What is the measure of an interior angle of a regular pentagon, a five-sided polygon?

   a. 108°   b. 135°   c. 144°   d. 180°

17. Find the perimeter of the figure shown below composed of a square and four identical equilateral triangles. One side of the square measures 2k and one side of each triangle measures k.

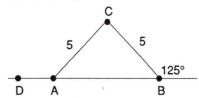

a. $6k^2$ b. 8k   c. 12k   d. 16k

18. An empty rectangular lot measures 12 miles long and 16 miles wide. How long will it take a person to walk diagonally across the lot if the person averages 2 miles per hour?

   a. 10 hours   b. 14 hours
   c. 28 hours   d. 40 hours

19. Which one of the following is true for the accompanying figure?

   a. Triangle ABC is an isosceles right triangle.
   b. m∠DAC = 55°
   c. ∠ABC is the complement of the 125° angle.
   d. m∠C = 70°

20. What will it cost to cover a rectangular floor measuring 40 feet by 50 feet with square tiles that measure 2 feet on each side if a package of 10 tiles costs $13 per package?

   a. $13,000   b. $6,500
   c. $1,300   d. $650

21. The figure below shows a metal casting 10 cm square and 2 cm thick with a hole in the center 5 cm square. What is the volume of the metal casting?

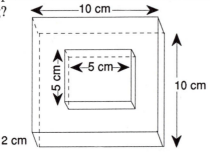

a. 50 cm³
b. 75 cm³
c. 150 cm³
d. 175 cm³

22. If one sphere has a radius of 2 cm and a second sphere has a radius of 3 cm, what fraction will result if the volume of the smaller sphere is divided by the volume of the larger sphere?

a. $\frac{2}{3}$　b. $\frac{4}{9}$　c. $\frac{4}{9\pi}$　d. $\frac{8}{27}$

23. Round the measure of AB to the nearest $\frac{1}{4}$ inch.

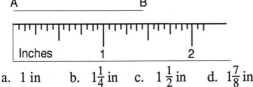

a. 1 in　b. $1\frac{1}{4}$ in　c. $1\frac{1}{2}$ in　d. $1\frac{7}{8}$ in

24. What is the perimeter of an isosceles triangle whose congruent sides measure 6 meters each and whose third side measures 6 centimeters?

a. 12.6 m
b. 18 m
c. 126 cm
d. 1,206 cm

25. How many cubic feet of space is available in the tent, a prism, shown below? The triangles at both ends have a base of 3 ft and height measuring 2 ft. The tent is 2 yards long.

a. 6 ft³
b. 12 ft³
c. 18 ft³
d. 36 ft³

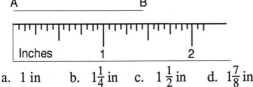

278

26. Sue travels 16 miles south and then 12 miles east. Her travel costs $0.15 per mile. What would Sue save if she had traveled directly from her starting point to her point of destination?

a. $1.20
b. $3.00
c. $4.20
d. None of these

27. The accompanying figure consists of a square with an equilateral triangle and a semicircle attached. One side of the square measures 2A linear units. What is the distance around this figure?

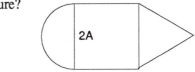

a. $8A + \pi A$
b. $12A + \pi A$
c. $8A + 2\pi A$
d. $12A + 2\pi A$

28. Which statement is true for the pictured triangles?

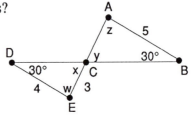

a. $m\angle z \neq m\angle w$
b. $\frac{CE}{CA} = \frac{CB}{CD}$
c. $AC = 3.75$
d. $m\angle x = 30°$

29. The outside dimensions of a picture frame are 2 feet by 30 inches. If its inside dimensions are $1\frac{1}{4}$ feet by 25 inches, what is the area of the frame?

a. 28.75 ft²
b. 50.125 ft²
c. 300 in²
d. 345 in²

30. The figure below shows a hemisphere (a half-sphere) on top of a cylinder. What is the volume of the resulting solid?

    a. 738π ft^3
    b. 864π ft^3
    c. $1,008\pi$ ft^3
    d. None of these

    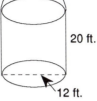

    20 ft.

    12 ft.

31. Which statement listed below is true of quadrilaterals?
    a. Not all quadrilaterals have a sum of measures of the four interior angles equal to 360°.
    b. Some rhombuses are not parallelograms.
    c. Consecutive angles of a parallelogram are supplementary.
    d. Opposite sides of a trapezoid are congruent.

32. Which of the following names a geometric figure that must contain at least one angle measuring 45°?
    a. equilateral triangle
    b. rhombus
    c. isosceles right triangle
    d. parallelogram

33. Which statement is true for the figure shown, given that $\overleftrightarrow{AB} \parallel \overleftrightarrow{CD}$?

    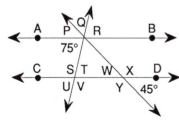

    a. m∠Q = 60°
    b. m∠V = m∠R
    c. ∠T ≅ ∠W
    d. None of these statements is true.

34. Which statement is true for the pictured triangles?

    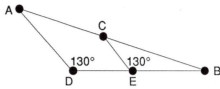

    a. m∠DAB = m∠DBC
    b. $\frac{CE}{AD} = \frac{AB}{CB}$
    c. m∠DAB = m∠BCE
    d. None of these statements is true.

35. Which of the following pairs of angles are complementary?

    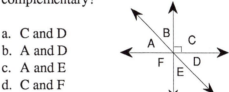

    a. C and D
    b. A and D
    c. A and E
    d. C and F

36. Which of the following could be used to report the distance around a circular swimming pool?
    a. meters   b. degrees
    c. square meters   d. cubic feet

37. Which one of the following would not be used to report the amount of water in an aquarium?
    a. cubic feet   b. liters
    c. gallons   d. meters

38. Which statement is true for the pictured triangles below?

    a. CB = $10\sqrt{13}$ b. $\frac{CB}{FE} = \frac{3}{2}$
    c. $\frac{AB}{DE} = \frac{2}{3}$ d. m∠ACB ≠ m∠DEF

    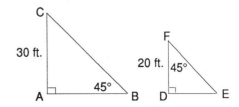

39. Consider the figure shown below.

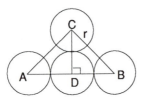

There are four circles. Each circle has a radius of r. The three outside circles each touch the circle whose center is D at exactly one point. The outside circles have centers at A, B, and C, which also serve as vertices for △ABC.

Which statement is true for this figure?
a. The perimeter of △ABC is 8r.
b. The area of △ABC is $8r^2$.
c. The area of △ABC is $4r^2$.
d. AC = 3r.

40. Which statement is true for the figure shown, given that quadrilateral PQRS is a parallelogram?

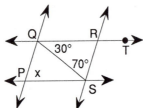

a. m∠x = 70°   b. m∠x = m∠SRT
c. m∠SRT = 100°
d. None of the above is true.

41. What type of triangle is shown below?

a. scalene   b. isosceles
c. equilateral   d. acute

42. Study the information given showing the areas of three figures of the same type.

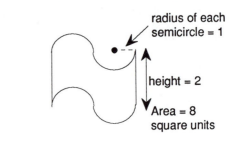

radius of each semicircle = 1
height = 2
Area = 8 square units

radius of each semicircle = 2
height = 3
Area = 24 square units

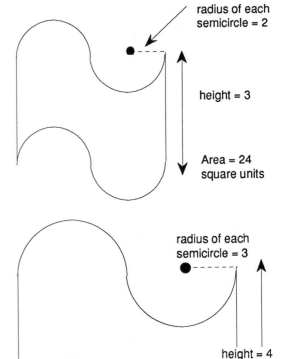

radius of each semicircle = 3
height = 4
Area = 48 square units

What is the area of the same type of figure with a radius of 9 and a height of 10?
a. 80   b. 360   c. 810   d. 900

43. Select the geometric figure that does not possess all of the following characteristics:
    i.   quadrilateral
    ii.   opposite sides parallel
    iii.   all angles equal in measure

   a. rhombus   b. square
   c. rectangle   d. none of these

44. Which of the sets of pictured triangles contain(s) similar triangles?

   i.

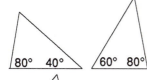

   ii.   iii.

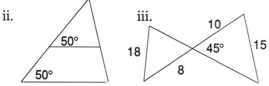

   a. i only   b. ii only
   c. i and ii only   d. ii and iii only
   e. All of the sets contain similar triangles.

45. Figure (1) below shows one face of a cube which contains a circular hole. The hole goes completely through the cube. The resulting solid is shown in figure (2). Find the volume of the solid in terms of π.

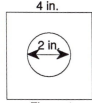

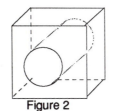

Figure 1   Figure 2

   a. $(32 - 4\pi)\text{in}^3$ b. $(64 - 2\pi)\text{in}^3$
   c. $(64 - 4\pi)\text{in}^3$ d. None of these

46. What is the volume in centiliters of a 4.35 liter bottle?
   a. 4.35 cl   b. 43.5 cl
   c. 435 cl   d. 4350 cl

47. Which one of the following is true for the accompanying diagram?

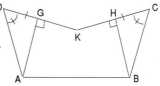

   a. AD = BC
   b. m∠ADG = m∠DAG
   c. m∠DAG ≠ m∠CBH
   d. GK + KH = AB

48. In the accompanying diagram, MG = KG and R is the midpoint of $\overline{MK}$. Which one of the following is true?

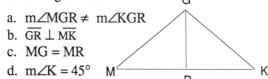

   a. m∠MGR ≠ m∠KGR
   b. $\overline{GR} \perp \overline{MK}$
   c. MG = MR
   d. m∠K = 45°

49. Given that $\overline{AB} \parallel \overline{CD}$, which one of the statements is not true for the figure shown? (The measure of angle ABD is represented by x, with the lower-case letters representing the measures of the various angles.)
   a. $v + w = 180°$
   b. $u = w$
   c. $\overleftrightarrow{AB} \perp \overleftrightarrow{BE}$
   d. $\overleftrightarrow{AC}$ and $\overleftrightarrow{BE}$ intersect somewhere in the plane.

50. In the accompanying diagram, AC = BC and ∠CAE ≅ ∠CBD. Which one of the following is true?

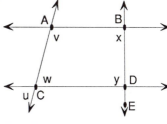

   a. BD = AE
   b. m∠BAE ≠ m∠ABD
   c. The picture contains exactly one isosceles triangle.
   d. None of the above is true.

Algebra

The year is 1700 B.C. The place: Egypt. A brief sentence in a 3600-year-old Egyptian papyrus reads, "Aha, its whole, its seventh, it makes 19."

From the time of the Pharaohs, humankind has been intrigued by solving mathematical problems involving an unknown number. The explosive-sounding Egyptian "aha" is not an exclamation but instead a word representing "a heap" or a "quantity." In modern algebra we equivalently say: "Let x equal ..." Indeed, we can reformulate the Egyptian problem of "aha, its whole, its seventh, it makes 19" in twentieth-century notation. The problem becomes $x + \frac{1}{7}x = 19$, using symbolic notation to establish the relationship between known and unknown in an equation.

Solving problems with equations is the focal theme of algebra. The word "algebra" is related to the steps we employ in order to solve equations. The word first appeared in the title of a book, *Hisab aljabr w' al-muqabalah*, written in Baghdad about A.D. 825 by the Arab mathematician Mohammed al-Khowarizmi. The title of the treatise, translated as the "science of transposition and opposition," is commonly referred to as Al-jabr. The Latin variant of the Arabic word al-jabr is, naturally, algebra.

Many people, of course, get through life without needing to solve algebraic equations. This is not the case in the vastly complicated world just beyond our reach. Algebraic equations are indispensable for reducing complicated problems to simple terms. As scientists grasp at the possibilities of nature, they cannot avoid algebraic symbols and equations to enhance what they are saying. Past experiments and future possibilities lie implicitly in equations scribbled on chalkboards or cafeteria napkins.

Algebra

It took thousands of years before mathematical problems could be solved using the marvelous notation and precise logic of modern algebra. In this chapter we review some of the more important topics of algebra including linear and quadratic equations, inequalities, properties of exponents, graphing, systems of equations, and verbal problems. Since our aim throughout the book has been to increase your ability to reason logically and solve problems, we've included some challenging algebraic word problems that should give you something to think about and further enhance your problem-solving skills.

Topic 1

Real Numbers and Their Properties

In this section the real numbers are defined. The basic properties for the real numbers are reviewed. Also reviewed is the order-of-operations agreement for the real numbers. At the end of this section you need to be able to solve problems that utilize the basic vocabulary of number theory, identify a property that illustrates an algebraic statement, recognize incorrect applications of the basic properties, and apply the order-of-operations agreement to both numerical and algebraic expressions.

◊ Definitions

The **natural numbers** consist of the set $\{1,2,3,4,5,...\}$.
A **prime number** is a natural number greater than 1 whose only natural number divisors are 1 and the number itself. A natural number greater than 1 that is not a prime number is called a **composite number**.

E X A M P L E S

3 is a prime number because its only natural number divisors are 1 and 3. 4 is a composite number because, in addition to being divisible by 1 and 4, it is also divisible by 2. 5 is a prime number because its only natural number divisors are 1 and 5. 6 is a composite number; in addition to being divisible by 1 and 6, its other divisors include 2 and 3.

Problem 1

How many prime numbers less than 25 and greater than 10 will yield a remainder of 3 when divided by 5?

Solution

Prime numbers between 10 and 25 include 11, 13, 17, 19 and 23. Each of these five numbers should be divided by 5 to see which give remainders of 3. Both 13 and 23 yield a remainder of 3 when divided by 5, so the answer is two.

Although there are many ways to factor a given composite number, there is only one way to factor it into prime numbers.

◊ Definition

The factorization of a composite number into prime numbers is called its **prime factorization**.

Problem 2

Find the prime factorization of 180.

Solution

By inspection,
$$180 = 2 \cdot 90 = 2 \cdot 2 \cdot 45 = 2 \cdot 2 \cdot 3 \cdot 15 = 2 \cdot 2 \cdot 3 \cdot 3 \cdot 5.$$

Notice that the last factorization of 180 contains nothing but prime factors. Thus, the prime factorization of 180 is $2 \cdot 2 \cdot 3 \cdot 3 \cdot 5$ which can also be written $2^2 \cdot 3^2 \cdot 5$.

Problem 3

Find the greatest common divisor of 98 and 84.

Solution

Find the prime factorization of 98 and 84.
$98 = 2 \cdot 49 = 2 \cdot 7 \cdot 7$
$84 = 2 \cdot 42 = 2 \cdot 7 \cdot 6 = 2 \cdot 7 \cdot 3 \cdot 2$
Two prime factors of 84, namely 2 and 7, are also prime factors of 98.
We use these shared prime factors to find the largest natural number that divides both 98 and 84. The greatest common divisor is $2 \cdot 7$ or 14.

◊ Definitions

The **whole numbers** consist of the set $\{0,1,2,3,...\}$.
The **integers** consist of the set
$\{..., -3, -2, -1, 0, 1, 2, 3, ...\}$. If a and b represent integers and there exists an integer c such that $a = b \cdot c$, then b is a **factor** of a and a is a **multiple** of b.

**E
X
A
M
P
L
E
S**

1. Since $24 = 4 \cdot 6$, 4 is a factor of 24 and 6 is a factor of 24. (4 and 6 are not prime factors.) 24 is a multiple of 4. 24 is a multiple of 6.
2. Positive factors of 18 are 1, 2, 3, 6, 9, 18.
3. The first four positive multiples of 5 are 5, 10, 15, 20.

Problem 4

How many positive factors of 20 are even and divisible by 5?

Solution

Positive factors of 20 are 1, 2, 4, 5, 10, 20. Even factors are 2, 4, 10, 20. Only 10 and 20 are divisible by 5, so the answer is two.

Problem 5

Find the smallest positive multiple of 4 which yields a remainder of 1 when divided by 5.

Solution

Positive multiples of 4 are 4, 8, 12, 16, 20, 24,... . Observe that 16 is the smallest number from this collection that yields a remainder of 1 when divided by 5.

◊ Definition

Rational numbers are numbers of the form $\frac{a}{b}$ where a and b are integers and $b \neq 0$.

Problem 6

How many rational numbers in the form $\frac{a}{b}$ can be written if the rational number must be less than 2, a cannot equal b, and a and b can only be 2, 3, or 5?

Solution

Positive fractions that satisfy the conditions of the problem include $\frac{2}{3}, \frac{2}{5}, \frac{3}{2},$ $\frac{3}{5},$ and $\frac{5}{3}$. (Observe that $\frac{5}{2}$ is not permissible because $\frac{5}{2} = 2.5$ and 2.5 is not less than 2.) The answer is five.

Problem 7

Which one of the following is true for every integer x?

a. $\frac{1}{x^2 + 1}$ is an integer.

b. $\frac{1}{x + 1}$ is a rational number.

c. $\frac{1}{x^2 + 1}$ is a rational number.

Solution

Consider each statement and substitute a few specific integers for x.
Statement **a** is not true for every integer.

If $x = 3$, $\frac{1}{3^2 + 1} = \frac{1}{9 + 1} = \frac{1}{10}$ and $\frac{1}{10}$ is not an integer. $\frac{1}{10}$ is a rational number.

Statement **b** is not true for every integer.

The expression $\frac{1}{x + 1}$ is undefined when $x = -1$. Division by 0 is undefined.

Statement **c** is true for every integer x.

$\frac{1}{x^2 + 1}$ becomes $\frac{1}{3^2 + 1}$ or $\frac{1}{10}$ when $x = 3$, and $\frac{1}{10}$ is a rational number.

When $x = -3$, $\frac{1}{x^2 + 1}$ becomes $\frac{1}{(-3)^2 + 1}$ or $\frac{1}{10}$.

When $x = 0$, $\frac{1}{x^2 + 1}$ becomes $\frac{1}{0^2 + 1}$ or $\frac{1}{1}$ and $\frac{1}{1}$ is a rational number.

When expressed in decimal form, a rational number either comes to an end or has a repeating pattern. For example, $\frac{1}{2} = 0.5$ (terminates or comes to an end) and $\frac{1}{3} = 0.333\ldots$, written $0.\overline{3}$. The line over the digit indicates that this is the repeating portion.

Recall that the rational number $\frac{3}{11}$ can be changed to its decimal equivalent by dividing 11 into 3.000 ... . $\frac{3}{11} = 0.272727\ldots = 0.\overline{27}$.

◊ Definition

Irrational numbers are numbers that, when expressed in decimal form, neither terminate nor repeat.

E
X
A
M
P
L
E
S

Numbers such as $\sqrt{3}$ and $\sqrt{7}$ are irrational numbers. Not every square root, however, is an irrational number. $\sqrt{25} = 5$ and 5 is a rational number. π (pi) is an irrational number and only approximately equal to 3.14.

Since a number cannot be both rational and irrational, irrational numbers cannot be expressed as the ratio of two integers.

◊ Definition

The set of **real numbers** is the union of the set of rational numbers and the set of irrational numbers.

The following diagram illustrates the subsets that make up the real numbers.

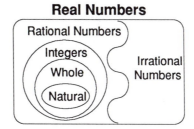

Basic Properties for the Real Numbers: a, b and c represent real numbers.

1. Closure of Addition. When adding any two real numbers, the result (sum) is one real number.

2. Closure of Multiplication. When multiplying any two real numbers, the result (product) is one real number.

3. Commutative of Addition. $a + b = b + a$

4. Commutative of Multiplication. $ab = ba$

5. Associative of Addition. $(a + b) + c = a + (b + c)$

6. Associative of Multiplication. $(ab)c = a(bc)$

7. Distributive. $a(b + c) = ab + ac$
    $$(b + c)a = ba + ca$$
    $$a(b + c + d + \ldots + f) = ab + ac + ad + \ldots + af$$
    $$(b + c + d + \ldots + f)a = ba + ca + da + \ldots + fa$$

8. Zero is the identity of addition. $a + 0 = a$

Algebra

9. Inverses of Addition. Corresponding to each real number there is another real number such that their sum is zero. $a + (-a) = 0$ $(-a)$ is called the additive inverse of a. Additive inverses enable us to return to zero (the identity of addition).

10. One is the identity of multiplication. $a \cdot 1 = a$

11. Inverses of multiplication. Corresponding to each real number except zero there is another real number such that their product is one. $a \cdot \frac{1}{a} = 1$ $(a \neq 0)$. $\frac{1}{a}$ is called the multiplicative inverse or **reciprocal** of a.

    Multiplicative inverses enable us to return to 1 (the identity of multiplication).

Problem 8

Determine whether each statement is true or false.
(a) $5(3 + 7) = 15 + 35$
(b) $3(6 \cdot 4) = 18 \cdot 12$
(c) $17y + y = (17 + 1)y = 18y$
(d) $(5 + x) \cdot 4 = 5 + 4x$
(e) The multiplicative inverse of -3 is $-\frac{1}{3}$.
(f) Every real number has a multiplicative inverse.

Solution

(a) True. This is an application of the distributive property.
(b) False. This is not an application of the distributive property. We distribute multiplication over addition, so that

$$3(6 + 4) = 3 \cdot 6 + 3 \cdot 4$$

In the case of $3(6 \cdot 4)$, the parentheses indicate to first find the product of 6 and 4. Thus

$$3(6 \cdot 4) = 3 \cdot 24 = 72$$

(c) True. Since 1 is the identity of multiplication, $1y = y$.
$17y + 1y = (17 + 1)y$ by the distributive property.

(d) False. The distributive property requires that each term within the parentheses be multiplied by 4:

$$(5 + x) \cdot 4 = 20 + 4x$$

(e) True. This is true because $(-3)(-\frac{1}{3}) = 1$.

(f) False. The number 0 has no multiplicative inverse.

The distributive property enables us to combine terms whose variable factors are identical by combining their numerical coefficients.

EXAMPLES

(a) $4x + 15x = (4 + 15)x = 19x$

(b) $3x^2y - 7x^2y = (3 - 7)x^2y = -4x^2y$

(c) $-5ab^3 - ab^3 = (-5 - 1)ab^3 = -6ab^3$

(d) $2x - 5x + 13x = (2 - 5 + 13)x = 10x$

(e) $7a^3 + 2b^3 - 3a^3 = 7a^3 - 3a^3 + 2b^3 = (7 - 3)a^3 + 2b^3 = 4a^3 + 2b^3$

(f) $5x^2y - 3xy^2 + 6xy$ cannot be simplified because there are no similar terms.

Problem 9

Simplify: $3(x + y) + 5(y - 4x)$.

Solution

$3(x + y) + 5(y - 4x)$ — Use the distributive property to remove the parentheses.
$= 3x + 3y + 5y - 20x$
$= -17x + 8y$ — Combine like terms.

Problem 10

Simplify: $-4(5x - z) - (z - 2y) + 6(x + 2y - z)$.

Solution

$-4(5x - z) - (z - 2y) + 6(x + 2y - z)$ — Use the distributive property to remove the parentheses.
$= -20x + 4z - z + 2y + 6x + 12y - 6z$
$= -14x + 14y - 3z$ — Combine like terms.

Problem 11

Simplify: $7 - 5[4x - 3y - 2(1 - 3x - y)]$.

Solution

$$7 - 5[4x - 3y - 2(1 - 3x - y)].$$
$$= 7 - 5[4x - 3y - 2 + 6x + 2y]$$
$$= 7 - 5[10x - y - 2]$$

Use the distributive property to remove parentheses.
Combine like terms.

$$= 7 - 50x + 5y + 10$$

Use the distributive property to remove brackets.

$$= -50x + 5y + 17$$

Combine like terms.

Order of Operations

Mathematicians have agreed to the following order of operations for computing problems with more than one operation.
1. Working from left to right, do all operations in the **grouping symbols**.
2. Working from left to right, do all **exponents** (powers).
3. Working from left to right, do all **multiplication** and **division**.
4. Working from left to right, do all **addition** and **subtraction**.

Problem 12

Compute the answer for $1 + 2(-3) + 8 \div 2$

Solution

There are no operations in grouping symbols and no exponents, so the first computing is accomplished by doing all multiplication and division.

$$1 + 2(-3) + 8 \div 2 = 1 + -6 + 8 \div 2 = 1 + -6 + 4.$$

Now do all addition and subtraction.

$$1 + -6 + 4 = -5 + 4 = -1$$

Problem 13

Find the answer for $\frac{1}{5} - 6 \div \frac{1}{3} \cdot \frac{1}{9}$

Solution

There are no operations in grouping symbols. Nor are there exponents. Begin with multiplication and division.

$$\frac{1}{5} - 6 \div \frac{1}{3} \cdot \frac{1}{9} = \frac{1}{5} - 18 \cdot \frac{1}{9} = \frac{1}{5} - 2$$

Now complete the subtraction.

$$\frac{1}{5} - 2 = \frac{1}{5} - \frac{10}{5} = -\frac{9}{5} = -1\frac{4}{5}$$

Problem 14

Find the answer for $\frac{1}{4} - 6(2 + 8) \div \left(-\frac{1}{3}\right)\left(-\frac{1}{9}\right)$

Solution

First complete the operation in grouping symbols.

$$\frac{1}{4} - 6(2 + 8) \div \left(-\frac{1}{3}\right)\left(-\frac{1}{9}\right) = \frac{1}{4} - 6(10) \div \left(-\frac{1}{3}\right)\left(-\frac{1}{9}\right)$$

Next do all multiplication and division.

$$\frac{1}{4} - 6(10) \div \left(-\frac{1}{3}\right)\left(-\frac{1}{9}\right) = \frac{1}{4} - 60 \div \left(-\frac{1}{3}\right)\left(-\frac{1}{9}\right)$$
$$= \frac{1}{4} - (-180)\left(-\frac{1}{9}\right)$$
$$= \frac{1}{4} - (+20)$$

Finally we do all addition and subtraction.

$$\frac{1}{4} - (+20) = \frac{1}{4} + (-20) = \frac{1}{4} + \left(-\frac{80}{4}\right) = -\frac{79}{4} = -19\frac{3}{4}$$

Problem 15

The formula for finding the dealer's cost for a car (C) having list price (L) and shipping charge (S) is $C = 0.8(L–S) + S$. Find the dealer's cost for a car having a list price of $14,950 and a shipping charge of $600.

Solution

$$\begin{aligned}
C &= 0.8(L - S) + S \\
&= 0.8(14,950 - 600) + 600 \\
&= 0.8(14,350) + 600 \\
&= 11,480 + 600 = 12,080
\end{aligned}$$

Thus, the dealer's cost is $12,080.

Problem 16

Evaluate $2(x - 5)^2 + 2x(y - z)$ if $x = -2$, $y = 3$ and $z = -1$.

Solution

$$
\begin{aligned}
2(x - 5)^2 + 2x(y - z) &= 2(-2 - 5)^2 + 2(-2)[3 - (-1)] \\
&= 2(-7)^2 + 2(-2)[3 + 1] \\
&= 2(-7)^2 + 2(-2)(4) \\
&= 2(49) + 2(-2)(4) \\
&= 98 + (-16) \\
&= 82
\end{aligned}
$$

Problem 17

The equality $f(x) = 3x^2 - 5x + 2$ is read "f at x equals $3x^2 - 5x + 2$" and gives the value of the function f for every specified value of x. Substitute -4 for x to find f(-4).

Solution

$$
\begin{aligned}
f(-4) &= 3(-4)^2 - 5(-4) + 2 \\
&= 3(16) - 5(-4) + 2 \\
&= 48 + 20 + 2 \\
&= 70
\end{aligned}
$$

We say that f at -4 is 70. When the value of the independent variable (or domain) is -4, the value of the dependent variable (or range) is 70. Observe that a function is a relationship between two variables such that for each value of the independent variable there corresponds exactly one value of the dependent variable. The set of all values of the independent variable is called the domain of the function. The set of all values taken on by the dependent variable is called the range of the function.

The order-of-operations agreement can be applied to expressions including variables.

Problem 18

Simplify $8y - 3y \cdot 2 + 14y^2 \div 7 \cdot 2$.

Solution

$$
\begin{aligned}
8y - 3y \cdot 2 + 14y^2 \div 7 \cdot 2 \quad &= 8y - 6y + 2y^2 \cdot 2 \\
&= 8y - 6y + 4y^2 \\
&= 2y + 4y^2
\end{aligned}
$$

Problem Set 1

1. How many prime numbers less than 29 and greater than 17 will yield a remainder of 3 when divided by 4?

2. Find the prime factorization of 630.

3. How many distinct prime factors of 378 are also prime factors of 162?

4. What is the greatest common divisor of 385 and 105?

5. How many positive factors of 42 are even, less than 42 and also divisible by 3?

6. Find the smallest positive multiple of 7 which yields a remainder of 1 when divided by 3 and a remainder of 3 when divided by 5.

7. Which number has a divisor of 5 and a factor of 25?
   a. 20   b. 55
   c. 75   d. 105

8. List all rational numbers in the form $\frac{a}{b}$, $a \neq b$ if $\frac{a}{b}$ is greater than 3 and a and b can only be 2, 3, or 10.

9. Which one of the following is true for every integer x?
   a. $\frac{1}{x^2 + 5}$ is an integer.
   b. $x^2 + 1$ is greater than zero.
   c. $\sqrt{x}$ is an irrational number.
   d. $\frac{1}{x + 3}$ is a rational number.

10. Which one of the following is false for every integer x?
   a. $\frac{1}{x^2 + 1}$ is greater than zero.
   b. $\frac{6}{x^2 + 3}$ is an integer.
   c. $(x + 1)^2 = 0$
   d. $\frac{1}{x^2}$ is less than zero.

11. The number $\frac{a}{b}$ continues to get larger as the numerator a gets larger and the denominator b gets smaller. If a is between $2\frac{1}{5}$ and $3\frac{2}{5}$ inclusively, and b is between $1\frac{1}{2}$ and 3 inclusively, what is the largest fraction possible?

12. An **arithmetic progression** is a sequence of numbers each of which, after the first, is obtained from the preceding one by adding a constant number to it. For example, the following is an arithmetic progression with first number 5 and constant addend 3. 5, 8, 11, 14, 17, etc. What is the next term in this arithmetic sequence?

13. Consider the arithmetic progression -7, -3.9, -0.8, 2.3, etc. What is the next real number in this sequence?

14. A **geometric progression** is a sequence of numbers each of which, after the first, is obtained from the preceding one by multiplying by a constant number. For example, the following is a geometric progression with first number 5 and constant multiplier 2. 5, 10, 20, 40, 80, etc. What is the next term in this geometric sequence?

Algebra

15. Find the missing rational number in the following geometric progression:

$9, -6, 4, \underline{\hspace{1cm}}, \frac{16}{9}$

16. Name the property that shows why each statement is true.

  a. $(2 \cdot 3) \cdot 5 = 2 \cdot (3 \cdot 5)$
  b. $\sqrt{7} + 0 = \sqrt{7}$
  c. $3(7 + 4) = 3 \cdot 7 + 3 \cdot 4$
  d. $3 \cdot \sqrt{7} = \sqrt{7} \cdot 3$
  e. $(5) + (-5) = 0$
  f. $1x = x$
  g. $7 \cdot \frac{1}{7} = 1$
  h. $8x + 3x = (8 + 3)x$
  i. $\frac{2}{3} \cdot \frac{3}{2} = 1$
  j. $(a + b) + c = (b + a) + c$
  k. $a(bc) = a(cb)$

Determine whether each statement is true or false.

17. $\pi \cdot 5 = 5\pi$
18. $3 \cdot 0 \cdot 7 = 21$
19. $7[5 + (-5)] = 0$
20. $-(7 + 4) = (-7) + (-4)$
21. $-(7 \cdot 4) = (-7)(-4)$
22. $2(3 + 8) = 2 \cdot 3 + 2 \cdot 8$
23. $2(3 \cdot 8) = (2 \cdot 3) \cdot (2 \cdot 8)$
24. $2 + (3 \cdot 8) = (2 + 3) \cdot (2 + 8)$
25. $14x + x = (14 + 1)x$
26. $(7 + y) \cdot 3 = 7 + 3y$
27. Every real number has an additive inverse.
28. $[b + (-c)] + c = b$
29. $(-y) + (-y) = 0$

Perform each of the following operations.

30. $(-8\frac{2}{3}) + (-1\frac{1}{3})$

31. $(+57) + (-93)$

32. $4 - (-3\frac{3}{5})$

33. $(-\frac{1}{4}) - (+5\frac{3}{4})$
34. $(-3\frac{1}{5}) - (-2\frac{2}{3})$
35. $(-7)(-4)(-\frac{1}{2})$
36. $\frac{-15}{-3}$
37. $2 + 4(-5) + 6 \div 3$
38. $2\frac{1}{4} - 7 \div \frac{1}{4} \cdot \frac{1}{2}$
39. $\frac{2}{3} - 4(3 + 5) \div (-\frac{1}{2})(-\frac{1}{8})$
40. $5(6 - 4)^3 - 5$
41. $(\frac{1}{2} - \frac{7}{4}) \div (1 - \frac{3}{8})$
42. $(7 - 2 \cdot 3)^3$
43. $-36(\frac{1}{9} - \frac{1}{6})$
44. $5[3 - (-4)] + 65$
45. $36 - 24 \div 4 \times 3 - 1$
46. $3(4 + 3 \div 2 - 8)$

47. The formula for finding what an investment (P) at a fixed interest rate (R) is worth after one year is given by the formula W = P(R + 1), where W represents the worth of the investment. What will an investment of $12,500 at 14% be worth after one year?

48. The formula for changing a Fahrenheit temperature (F) to a Celsius temperature (C) is $C = \frac{5}{9}$ (F – 32). What is the Celsius temperature when the Fahrenheit temperature is 50°?

49. The formula for the sales price (P) of an article with dealer's cost (D) and markup (M) is P = D + MD. What is the sales price of an article costing a dealer $12 with a markup of 40%?

50. The formula used to find rate of speed (R) in miles per hour for the distance (D) in miles and the time (T) in hours is $R = \frac{D}{T}$. Find the rate of speed of an object that travels 164 miles in $1\frac{1}{3}$ hours.

51. Evaluate $2x^2 + 5xy$ if $x = -3$ and $y = 2$.

52. Evaluate $3(x - 1)^2 + 2x(y - z)$ if $x = -3$, $y = 2$ and $z = -4$.

53. If $f(x) = x^2 + 2x - 1$, find $f(-6)$.

54. Given the function defined by $f(x) = x^3 - 2x^2 - x$, find $f(-3)$.

55. Study the examples:
$$a^4 * a^3 = a^{-5}$$
$$a^2 * a^7 = a^3$$
$$a^1 * a^2 = a^0$$
Which equality below is compatible with these examples?
   a. $a^x * a^y = a^{x+y-12}$
   b. $a^x * a^y = a^{xy-11}$
   c. $a^x * a^y = a^{xy-2}$
   d. $a^x * a^y = a^{y-2x}$

56. Study the examples:

   If $A = 7$ and $B = 5$ then $C = \frac{49}{5}$.
   If $A = 8$ and $B = 2$ then $C = 32$.

   What is the formula for finding C in terms of A and B?

57. The mathematical model $P = (25t^2 + 125t) \div (t^2 + 1)$ describes systolic blood pressure P (measured in millimeters of mercury) t seconds after blood leaves the heart. Find systolic pressure 3 seconds after the blood moves from the heart.

58. In a study of the winter moth in Nova Scotia, the number of eggs (N) in a female moth depended on her abdominal width (W, in millimeters). The exact relationship was described by $N = 14W^3 - 17W^2 - 16W + 34$. How many eggs are there in a moth with an abdominal width of 2 millimeters?

59. A rock on the moon and on Earth is thrown into the air by a 6-foot person with a velocity of 48 feet per second. The height reached by the rock (in feet) after t seconds is described by

$$h_{moon} = -2.7t^2 + 48t + 6$$

$$h_{earth} = -16t^2 + 48t + 6$$

After 3 seconds, how much higher is the rock on the moon than on Earth? (The acceleration of gravity on the moon is approximately one-sixth of that on Earth.)

60. The formula $T = 3(A - 20)^2 \div 50 + 10$ describes the time (T, in seconds) for a person who is A years old to run the 100-yard dash. Find the percent increase in time from age 30 to age 40.

Simplify each of the following.

61. $7 - 3(x - 2y)$
62. $6y - 3y \cdot 2y + y$
63. $8a - 2a \cdot 5a + 6a^2 \div 3 \cdot 2$
64. $7t - 4t \cdot 3 + 6t^2 \div 3 \cdot 2$
65. $-3x + 4(2x - 4y) + y$
66. $-2(3 - 2x) - (6 - 5x)$
67. $6x - [3x - 2(x - 5)]$
68. $(x^2y + 9xy - 4xy^2) - (2xy^2 - x^2y + 9xy)$
69. $4x[2x^2 - 2x(x + 3) - 5]$
70. $x^2z - x[xy - x(y - z)]$

Topic 2

Operations Involving Square Roots

In this section addition, subtraction, multiplication, division and rationalization of the denominator are considered for expressions involving square roots. At the end of this section, if you are given any of these operations you should be able to obtain an answer in its simplest form.

An expression involving a square root is also called a **radical expression with index 2**.

The basic justification for most square root simplifications is the following equality:

If x and y are positive, $\sqrt{xy} = \sqrt{x} \cdot \sqrt{y}$.

Problem 1

a. Simplify $\sqrt{75}$

Solution

$$\sqrt{75} = \sqrt{25 \cdot 3} = \sqrt{25} \cdot \sqrt{3} = 5\sqrt{3}$$

b. Simplify $\sqrt{18}$

Solution

$$\sqrt{18} = \sqrt{9 \cdot 2} = \sqrt{9} \cdot \sqrt{2} = 3\sqrt{2}$$

c. Simplify $\sqrt{15}$

Solution

The only whole number factors of 15 are 1, 3, 5, and 15. Except for 1, none of these factors is a perfect square.

$\sqrt{15}$ cannot be simplified.

> **To Simplify Addition/Subtraction Expressions with Radicals:**
>
> 1. If possible, simplify the radicals.
> 2. Combine terms with the same radical factor.

Problem 2

a. Simplify $3\sqrt{2} - 4\sqrt{50} + \sqrt{32}$

Solution

$$
\begin{aligned}
3\sqrt{2} - 4\sqrt{50} + \sqrt{32} &= 3\sqrt{2} - 4(\sqrt{25} \cdot \sqrt{2}) + (\sqrt{16} \cdot \sqrt{2}) \\
&= 3\sqrt{2} - 4 \cdot 5\sqrt{2} + 4\sqrt{2} \\
&= 3\sqrt{2} - 20\sqrt{2} + 4\sqrt{2} \\
&= -13\sqrt{2}
\end{aligned}
$$

b. Simplify $\sqrt{2} + \sqrt{8} + \sqrt{75}$

Solution

$$
\begin{aligned}
\sqrt{2} + \sqrt{8} + \sqrt{75} &= \sqrt{2} + (\sqrt{4} \cdot \sqrt{2}) + (\sqrt{25} \cdot \sqrt{3}) \\
&= \sqrt{2} + 2\sqrt{2} + 5\sqrt{3} \\
&= 3\sqrt{2} + 5\sqrt{3}
\end{aligned}
$$

> **To Simplify Multiplication Expressions Involving Radicals:**
>
> 1. If possible, simplify radicals.
> 2. Multiply using $\sqrt{x} \cdot \sqrt{y} = \sqrt{xy}$. (x and y are positive.)
> 3. If possible, simplify.

Problem 3

a. Multiply $\sqrt{3} \cdot \sqrt{6}$

Solution

$$
\sqrt{3} \cdot \sqrt{6} = \sqrt{18} = \sqrt{9} \cdot \sqrt{2} = 3\sqrt{2}
$$

b. Simplify $\sqrt{8} \cdot \sqrt{2}$

Solution

$$\sqrt{8} \cdot \sqrt{2} \quad \begin{aligned} &= (\sqrt{4} \cdot \sqrt{2}) \cdot \sqrt{2} \\ &= 2\sqrt{2} \cdot \sqrt{2} \\ &= 2(\sqrt{2} \cdot \sqrt{2}) \\ &= 2\sqrt{4} \\ &= 2 \cdot 2 \\ &= 4 \end{aligned}$$

In this case the problem might be more easily done as:
$$\sqrt{8} \cdot \sqrt{2} = \sqrt{16} = 4$$

However, the ease of this solution was dependent upon the numbers being relatively small.

c. Simplify $(3\sqrt{6})(-5\sqrt{2})$

Solution

$$(3\sqrt{6})(-5\sqrt{2}) \quad \begin{aligned} &= (3 \cdot -5)(\sqrt{6} \cdot \sqrt{2}) \\ &= -15\sqrt{12} \\ &= -15\sqrt{4} \cdot \sqrt{3} \\ &= -15 \cdot 2\sqrt{3} \\ &= -30\sqrt{3} \end{aligned}$$

d. Simplify $4\sqrt{3}(2\sqrt{6} + 5\sqrt{3})$

Solution

Begin by removing the parentheses using the distributive property.

$$4\sqrt{3}(2\sqrt{6} + 5\sqrt{3}) \quad \begin{aligned} &= 8\sqrt{18} + 20\sqrt{9} \\ &= 8(\sqrt{9} \cdot \sqrt{2}) + 20 \cdot 3 \\ &= 8 \cdot 3\sqrt{2} + 60 \\ &= 24\sqrt{2} + 60 \end{aligned}$$

$24\sqrt{2}$ and 60 do not have identical radical factors and cannot be combined.

> **To Simplify the Division of Radicals:**
>
> 1. Use the fact that $\dfrac{\sqrt{x}}{\sqrt{y}} = \sqrt{\dfrac{x}{y}}.$ (x and y are positive.)
> 2. Reduce the fraction if possible.

Problem 4

a.   Divide $\sqrt{20} \div \sqrt{5}$

Solution

$$\sqrt{20} \div \sqrt{5} = \frac{\sqrt{20}}{\sqrt{5}} = \sqrt{\frac{20}{5}} = \sqrt{4} = 2$$

b.   Simplify $\dfrac{\sqrt{36}}{\sqrt{3}}$

Solution

$$\frac{\sqrt{36}}{\sqrt{3}} = \sqrt{\frac{36}{3}} = \sqrt{12} = \sqrt{4} \cdot \sqrt{3} = 2\sqrt{3}$$

The process of **rationalizing the denominator** refers to rewriting a radical fraction so that there is no radical in the denominator.
To accomplish this:

1. Multiply numerator and denominator of the fraction by a square root that yields a result of the form $\sqrt{a^2}$ in the denominator.

2. Simplify the denominator and the numerator, if possible.

Problem 5

a. Rationalize the denominator of $\dfrac{1}{\sqrt{5}}$.

Solution

$$\frac{1}{\sqrt{5}} = \frac{1}{\sqrt{5}} \cdot \frac{\sqrt{5}}{\sqrt{5}} = \frac{\sqrt{5}}{\sqrt{25}} = \frac{\sqrt{5}}{5}$$

By multiplying both numerator and denominator by the same number, $\sqrt{5}$, we are, in fact, multiplying by 1 (the identity of multiplication) and consequently not changing the value of the irrational number.

b. Rationalize the denominator of $\dfrac{6}{\sqrt{2}}$.

Solution

$$\frac{6}{\sqrt{2}} = \frac{6}{\sqrt{2}} \cdot \frac{\sqrt{2}}{\sqrt{2}} = \frac{6\sqrt{2}}{\sqrt{4}} = \frac{6\sqrt{2}}{2} = 3\sqrt{2}$$

c. Rationalize the denominator of $\sqrt{\dfrac{3}{7}}$.

Solution

$$\sqrt{\frac{3}{7}} = \frac{\sqrt{3}}{\sqrt{7}} = \frac{\sqrt{3}}{\sqrt{7}} \cdot \frac{\sqrt{7}}{\sqrt{7}} = \frac{\sqrt{21}}{\sqrt{49}} = \frac{\sqrt{21}}{7}$$

d. Rationalize the denominator of $\dfrac{1}{\sqrt{8}}$.

Solution

We can multiply numerator and denominator by $\sqrt{8}$. However, if we multiply by $\sqrt{2}$ this would result in $\sqrt{16}$ in the denominator. It would keep the numbers smaller and easier to simplify.

$$\frac{1}{\sqrt{8}} = \frac{1}{\sqrt{8}} \cdot \frac{\sqrt{2}}{\sqrt{2}} = \frac{\sqrt{2}}{\sqrt{16}} = \frac{\sqrt{2}}{4}$$

Problem Set 2

Simplify each expression.

1. $\sqrt{50}$

2. $\sqrt{12}$

3. $\sqrt{108}$

4. $5\sqrt{3} + 7\sqrt{3} - 5\sqrt{2}$

5. $3\sqrt{50} - 2\sqrt{32}$

6. $2\sqrt{96} - 3\sqrt{24}$

7. $\sqrt{18} + \sqrt{50} - \sqrt{72}$

8. $\sqrt{3} \cdot \sqrt{12}$

9. $\sqrt{10} \cdot \sqrt{8}$

10. $\sqrt{12} \cdot \sqrt{2}$

11. $(4\sqrt{3})(-2\sqrt{12})$

12. $(-3\sqrt{2})(-5\sqrt{22})$

13. $2\sqrt{5}(3\sqrt{10} + 4\sqrt{15})$

14. $2\sqrt{3}(\sqrt{15} - 2\sqrt{3})$

15. $\sqrt{150} \div \sqrt{6}$

16. $\sqrt{24} \div \sqrt{3}$

Rationalize the denominator of each expression.

17. $\dfrac{3}{\sqrt{7}}$

18. $\sqrt{\dfrac{1}{2}}$

19. $\dfrac{3}{\sqrt{6}}$

20. $\dfrac{1}{\sqrt{50}}$

21. $\sqrt{\dfrac{2}{7}}$

22. $\dfrac{3}{\sqrt{8}}$

23. $\dfrac{4}{\sqrt{32}}$

Topic 3

Exponents and Scientific Notation

In this section basic properties of exponents are reviewed. Also discussed are place values for a base 10 numeral and the role of exponents in scientific notation. At the end of this section you should be able to simplify exponential expressions, determine the place value of a digit in a base ten numeral, write a place value numeral when given its expanded notation, and use scientific notation in calculations.

As you know, exponents represent a convenient shorthand to indicate repeated multiplication.

◊ Definitions

$x^1 = x$ (x to the first power is x.)

$x^n = x \bullet x \bullet x \bullet ... \bullet x$

x is used as a factor n times with n = 2, 3, 4, etc.

x^n is read as "x to the nth power" and means that x is to be used n times in a multiplication. x is called the **base** and n the **power** or **exponent**.

We can add to these definitions the definitions for zero and negative integer exponents.

◊ Definitions

$x^0 = 1$ when $x \neq 0$ and 0^0 is undefined.

$x^{-n} = \dfrac{1}{x^n}$ for any natural number n.

---

a. $5^2 = 5 \cdot 5 = 25$

b. $(-8)^3 = (-8)(-8)(-8) = -512$

c. $7^0 = 1$

d. $(-2)^5 = (-2)(-2)(-2)(-2)(-2) = -32$

e. $3^{-4} = \frac{1}{3^4} = \frac{1}{81}$

f. $(-2)^{-3} = \frac{1}{(-2)^3} = \frac{1}{(-2)(-2)(-2)} = -\frac{1}{8}$

g. $10^{-2} = \frac{1}{10^2} = \frac{1}{100}$

h. $10^{-4} = \frac{1}{10^4} = \frac{1}{10000}$

Problem 1

Which of the following equals $(4^3)(3^2)$?

    a. $(4 + 4 + 4)(3 + 3)$
    b. $(4 \cdot 4 \cdot 4)(3 \cdot 3)$
    c. $(4 \cdot 3)(3 \cdot 2)$
    d. $(4 \cdot 3)^6$

Solution

By definition $(4^3)(3^2)$ means $(4 \cdot 4 \cdot 4)(3 \cdot 3)$, which is choice **b**.

Problem 2

Which of the following equals $2^2 + 7^2$?

    a. $(2 + 7)^2$
    b. $(2 + 7)^4$
    c. $2 \cdot 2 + 7 \cdot 2$
    d. $2 \cdot 2 + 7 \cdot 7$

Solution

By definition $2^2 + 7^2 = 2 \cdot 2 + 7 \cdot 7$, which is choice **d**.
Notice that $(2 + 7)^2 = 9^2 = 81$ and $2^2 + 7^2 = 4 + 49 = 53$.
In general $(x + y)^a$ is not equal to $x^a + y^a$.
Similarly $(x - y)^a$ is not equal to $x^a - y^a$.

Basic Properties of Exponents

1. $x^a \cdot x^b = x^{a+b}$

   When multiplying with the same base, retain the common base and add the exponents. Use this sum as the exponent of the common base.

2. $\dfrac{x^a}{x^b} = x^{a-b}$

   When dividing with the same base, subtract the exponent in the denominator from the exponent in the numerator, retaining the common base. Use this difference as the exponent of the common base.

3. $(x^a)^b = x^{ab}$

   When an exponential expression is raised to a power, multiply the exponents.

4. $(xy)^a = x^a y^a$

5. $\left(\dfrac{x}{y}\right)^a = \dfrac{x^a}{y^a}$

E X A M P L E S

a. $4^3 \cdot 4^2 = 4^5$ (Keep the base the same and add the exponents. The answer is not 16^5.)

b. $\dfrac{4^7}{4^2} = 4^{7-2} = 4^5$

c. $(4^3)^2 = 4^{3 \cdot 2} = 4^6$

d. $(4 \cdot 3)^5 = 4^5 \cdot 3^5$

e. $\left(\dfrac{4}{3}\right)^5 = \dfrac{4^5}{3^5}$

Problem 3

Which of the following is equal to $(5^3)^2$?

a. 5^5 b. 5^9 c. $(5 \cdot 3)^2$ d. $5^3 \cdot 5^3$

Solution

By the third property of exponents $(5^3)^2 = 5^{3 \cdot 2} = 5^6$.
This is not one of the choices. However $5^3 \cdot 5^3 = 5^6$.
The correct answer is **d**.

EXAMPLES

a. $x^3 \cdot x^7 = x^{3+7} = x^{10}$

b. $\dfrac{x^7}{x^3} = x^{7-3} = x^4$

c. $\dfrac{x^3}{x^7} = x^{-4} = \dfrac{1}{x^4}$

d. $(x^{-3})^{-4} = x^{(-3)(-4)} = x^{12}$

e. $(x^2 y^3)^4 = (x^2)^4 (y^3)^4 = x^8 y^{12}$

f. $\left(\dfrac{x^2}{y^5}\right)^3 = \dfrac{(x^2)^3}{(y^5)^3} = \dfrac{x^6}{y^{15}}$

g. $x^2 \cdot y^3$ cannot be simplified because the bases are different.

h. $3x^4 (2x^2 + y) = (3x^4)(2x^2) + (3x^4)(y) = 6x^6 + 3x^4 y$

Our next problem incorporates exponential properties with the agreed-upon order of operations.

Problem 4

Simplify $2 - (2y)(3y^2) + \dfrac{(4y^2)^2}{2y}$

Solution

Step 1

$(2y)(3y^2) = (2)(3)(y^{1+2}) = 6y^3$

Step 2

$\dfrac{(4y^2)^2}{2y} = \dfrac{4^2(y^2)^2}{2y} = \dfrac{16y^4}{2y} = 8y^{4-1} = 8y^3$

Step 3

$2 - (2y)(3y^2) + \dfrac{(4y^2)^2}{2y}$

$= 2 - 6y^3 + 8y^3$

$= 2 + 2y^3$

Algebra

Exponents with base 10 are used in numerals, a name for a number. Place values for numerals in base 10 are based upon powers of 10.

Place Values for a Base 10 Numeral
$$\ldots 10^3 \; 10^2 \; 10^1 \; 10^0 \; . \; 10^{-1} \; 10^{-2} \; 10^{-3} \ldots$$
$\updownarrow$
decimal point

Problem 5

Express the numeral 643.25 in expanded form.

Solution

$$643.25 = (6 \cdot 10^2) + (4 \cdot 10^1) + (3 \cdot 10^0) + (2 \cdot 10^{-1}) + (5 \cdot 10^{-2})$$

Thus the place value of the digit 5 is 10^{-2} or $\frac{1}{100}$ or hundredths. The place value of the digit 2 is 10^{-1} or $\frac{1}{10}$ or tenths.

Problem 6

What place value numeral is represented by the following expression?
$$(3 \cdot 10^1) + (4 \cdot 10^0) + (5 \cdot 10^{-1})$$

Solution

Evaluate the expression in each grouping.
$(3 \cdot 10^1) = 3 \cdot 10 = 30$ and $(4 \cdot 10^0) = 4 \cdot 1 = 4$ and $(5 \cdot 10^{-1}) = 5 \cdot \frac{1}{10} = 0.5$
Thus, $(3 \cdot 10^1) + (4 \cdot 10^0) + (5 \cdot 10^{-1}) = 30 + 4 + 0.5 = 34.5$.

Exponents are also extremely useful to represent large and small numbers. The table on the following page indicates the names of some fairly large numbers.

Exponents and Large Numbers
Names of Large Numbers

10^2	hundred	10^{18}	quintillion
10^3	thousand	10^{21}	sextillion
10^6	million	10^{24}	septillion
10^9	billion	10^{27}	octillion
10^{12}	trillion	10^{30}	nonillion
10^{15}	quadrillion	10^{100}	googol

The number of snow crystals necessary to form the ice age was approximately 10^{30}. If the entire universe were filled with protons and electrons, the total number would be 10^{110}.

The number of grains of sand on the beach at Coney Island is about 10^{20}.

Although people do a great deal of talking, the total output since the beginning of gabble to the present day, including all baby talk, love songs, and congressional debates, totals about 10^{16} (10 million billion) words.

A googol is 10^{100}. The number of raindrops falling on New York in a century is much less than a googol.

A googol times a googol is $10^{100} \cdot 10^{100}$ or 10^{200}, which is much less than a googolplex! A googolplex is 10 to the googol power, or $10^{10^{100}}$ or 1 with a googol of zeros! If you tried to write a googolplex without using exponential notation, there would not be enough room to write it, if you went to the farthest star, touring all the nebulae and putting down zeros every inch of the way.

Large and small numbers are frequently expressed in scientific notation.

◊ Definition

A number written in **scientific notation** appears as the product of two factors:

$$\left(\begin{matrix} \text{A number greater} \\ \text{than or equal to 1} \\ \text{but less than 10} \end{matrix} \right) \quad \text{x} \quad (10^{\text{some power}})$$

Each of the following is written in scientific notation and then changed to its usual decimal notation.

a. $2.5 \times 10^3 = 2.5 \times 1000 = 2,500$

b. $3.7 \times 10^0 = 3.7 \times 1 = 3.7$

c. $1.43 \times 10^{-2} = 1.43 \times \frac{1}{100} = 0.0143$

d. $7.16 \times 10^{-4} = 7.16 \times \frac{1}{10000} = 0.000716$

Notice that if we multiply any number by 10 to a power, it is done by moving the decimal point the same number of places as the exponent of 10.

If the exponent is **positive**, we move the decimal to the **right**.
If the exponent is **negative**, we move the decimal to the **left**.

Steps in Writing a Number in Scientific Notation

1. Move the decimal point so that the number written has only one non-zero digit to the left of the decimal point. This is equivalent to writing the first factor as a number greater than or equal to 1 and less than 10.

2. The second factor involves 10 raised to a power. The magnitude of this power is the number of places between the decimal point in the original number and the decimal point in the factor used in step 1.
    a. If the original number is greater than 10, the power on 10 is positive.
    b. If the original number is less than 1, the power on 10 has a negative sign of description.

Problem 7

a.   Write 47,000,000 in scientific notation.

Solution

Using the two steps listed on the preceeding page,

1.   The first factor is 4.7, a number greater than or equal to 1, but less than 10.

2.   The second factor involves 10 to a power.
$$47,000,000 = 4.7 \times 10^{?}$$
There are 7 places between the decimal point in 47,000,000 and 4.7. Since the original number (47,000,000) is greater than 10, the power will be positive 7. Thus, $47,000,000 = 4.7 \times 10^{7}$.

b.   Write 0.00000274 in scientific notation.

Solution

1. $0.00000274 = 2.74 \times 10^{?}$

2.   There are 6 places between the decimal point in 0.00000274 and 2.74. Since the original number (0.00000274) is less than 1, the power will be negative 6. Thus $0.00000274 = 2.74 \times 10^{-6}$.

c.   Write 1.3 in scientific notation.

Solution

1. $1.3 = 1.3 \times 10^{?}$

2.   There are no decimal places between the decimal point in the first factor of $1.3 \times 10^{?}$ and the original number 1.3. The power is 0.
Thus $1.3 = 1.3 \times 10^{0}$.

Problem 8

Multiply 0.00074 x 8,300,000,000 and write the product in scientific notation.

Solution

1. Write each number in scientific notation.
$$0.00074 = 7.4 \times 10^{-4}$$
$$8,300,000,000 = 8.3 \times 10^{9}$$

2. The problem can now be written as:
$$(7.4 \times 10^{-4}) \times (8.3 \times 10^{9})$$

3. $$(7.4) \times (8.3) = 61.42$$
$$(10^{-4}) \times (10^{9}) = 10^{-4+9} = 10^{5}$$

4. $$0.00074 \times 8,300,000,000 = 61.42 \times 10^{5}.$$
We now must write 61.42 in scientific notation.

5. $$61.42 = 6.142 \times 10^{1}(\text{or } 6.142 \times 10)$$

6. The problem now becomes
$$0.00074 \times 8,300,000,000 = 61.42 \times 10^{5}$$
$$= 6.142 \times 10^{1} \times 10^{5}$$
$$= 6.142 \times 10^{6}$$

Problem 9

Use scientific notation to find the quotient and write the answer in scientific notation. $(0.00025) \div (500,000)$

Solution

$$\frac{0.00025}{500,000} = \frac{2.5 \times 10^{-4}}{5 \times 10^{5}}$$
$$= 0.5 \times 10^{-4-5}$$
$$= 0.5 \times 10^{-9}$$
$$= 5 \times 10^{-1} \times 10^{-9}$$
$$= 5 \times 10^{-10}$$

We can convert the answer to usual decimal notation by moving the decimal point ten places to the left. Thus, $5 \times 10^{-10} = 0.0000000005$

Problem 10

Use scientific notation to compute:
Write the answer in scientific notation.

$$\frac{(8{,}000{,}000)(0.0009)}{12{,}000}$$

Solution

$$\frac{(8{,}000{,}000)(0.0009)}{12{,}000} = \frac{(8 \times 10^6)(9 \times 10^{-4})}{1.2 \times 10^4}$$

$$= \frac{7.2}{12} \times \frac{10^2}{10^4}$$

$$= 60 \times 10^{-2}$$

$$= 6.0 \times 10^1 \times 10^{-2}$$

$$= 6 \times 10^{-1}$$

Problem Set 3

1. Use the laws of exponents to simplify the following and express the answers with positive exponents.

   a. $a^4 \cdot a^7$
   b. $x^5 \cdot x$
   c. $2x^4 \cdot x^5$
   d. $(3x^3)(2x^4)$
   e. $y^4 \cdot y^{-7}$
   f. $x^{-2} \cdot x^{-5}$
   g. $\dfrac{x^7}{x^4}$
   h. $\dfrac{x^5}{x^5}$
   i. $\dfrac{x^{-3}}{x^4}$
   j. $\dfrac{-12x^6}{4x^2}$
   k. $(x^{-3})^6$
   l. $(2 \cdot a)^4$
   m. $\left(\dfrac{x}{y}\right)^3$

2. Is it true that $a^x \cdot a^y = a^{xy}$?

3. Is it true that $2^2 \cdot 2^3 = 4^5$?

4. Simplify each of the following.

   a. $(x^5 y^3)^4$
   b. $\left(\dfrac{x^3}{y^7}\right)^2$
   c. $(4y^2)^3$
   d. $(3y^3)^2 - (2y^2)^3$
   e. $\dfrac{(10y^4)^3}{25y}$
   f. $\dfrac{3(3b^2)^3}{3b^4}$

5. Choose the expression that is equivalent to $4a^3(a^3b^4)$.

   a. $5a^3b^4$
   b. $4a^3(b^3a^4)$
   c. $4a^9b^4$
   d. $(2a^3b^2)^2$

6. Choose the expression that is equivalent to $5x^2y(3x + y^2)$.

   a. $15x^2y + 5x^2y^2$
   b. $8x^3y + 5x^2y^3$
   c. $3x(5x^2y + y^2)$
   d. $5x^2y(y^2 + 3x)$

313

Algebra

7. Choose the expression that is equivalent to $2a^3(a^2b)^4$.

    a. $2a^3(a^6b^4)$ b. $2a^3(b^2a)^4$

    c. $2a^{11}b^4$ d. $(2a^5 + 2a^3b)^4$

8. Choose the expression that is not true for all real numbers.

    a. $4x^3y^2(5x - 2y^7) = 20x^4y^2 - 8x^3y^9$

    b. $(3x^3)(2y^4) = 6(xy)^7$

    c. $5x^3y^2(4x + y^7) = (y^7 + 4x)5x^3y^2$

    d. $4x^3(x^2y^7) = (4x^3x^2)y^7$

Determine the place value numeral represented by each of the following.

9. $(5 \cdot 10^2) + (3 \cdot 10^1) + (2 \cdot 10^0) + (3 \cdot 10^{-1})$
    $+ (6 \cdot 10^{-2})$

10. $(8 \cdot 10^2) + (4 \cdot 10^0) + (3 \cdot 10^{-2})$

11. $(3 \cdot 10^{-1}) + (6 \cdot 10^{-2}) + (7 \cdot 10^{-3})$

12. $(3 \cdot 10^{-2}) + (5 \cdot 10^{-3}) + (4 \cdot 10^{-4})$

13. Select the expanded notation for 3006.002.

    a. $(3 \cdot 10^4) + (6 \cdot 10) + (2 \cdot \frac{1}{10^3})$

    b. $(3 \cdot 10^3) + (6 \cdot 10^0) + (2 \cdot \frac{1}{10^2})$

    c. $(3 \cdot 10^4) + (6 \cdot 10^7) + (2 \cdot 10^9)$

    d. $(3 \cdot 10^3) + (6 \cdot 10^0) + (2 \cdot \frac{1}{10^3})$

14. Select the expanded notation for 500.03.

    a. $(5 \cdot 10^2) + (3 \cdot \frac{1}{10^2})$

    b. $(5 \cdot 10^3) + (3 \cdot \frac{1}{10})$

    c. $(5 \cdot 10^3) + (3 \cdot \frac{1}{10^2})$

    d. $(5 \cdot 10^2) + (3 \cdot \frac{1}{10})$

15. Write each of the following in scientific notation.

    a.   376   b.   0.0057

    c.   1.4   d.   0.057

    e.   5.7   f.   37,600

16. Multiply and write the answer in scientific notation.
$$(3)(10^5)(7)(10^{-3})$$

17. Divide and write the answer in scientific notation.
$$\frac{(66)(10^5)}{(3)(10^9)}$$

In problems 18-23 use scientific notation to compute each of the following. Write the answer in scientific notation.

18. 0.00047 x 9,200,000

19. (2,800,000,000,000) ÷ (14,000)

20. (0.0000124) ÷ (3,100,000)

21. 840,000 x 0.00000000000071

22. (1,200,000,000,000) ÷ (4,800,000)

23. $\dfrac{(5{,}000)(0.004)}{40{,}000}$

24. $82{,}000 + 6{,}000 =$
    a. 8.8×10^3
    b. 8.8×10^4
    c. 8.8×10^{-3}
    d. 8.8×10^{-4}

25. The chirp of a cricket releases 9000 ergs of energy. The energy release of a 100-megaton H-bomb is approximately

    $10{,}000{,}000{,}000{,}000{,}000{,}000{,}000{,}000{,}000$ ergs

    How many times greater than the cricket's chirp is the energy released by the H-bomb? **Note:** To put these numbers into perspective, when you pronounce an average syllable of a word, you release 200 ergs of energy.

26. Pouiseville's law states that the speed of blood (S, in centimeters per second) located r centi-meters from the central axis of an artery is

    $$S = (1.76 \cdot 10^5)[(1.44 \cdot 10^{-2}) - r^2]$$

    Find the speed of blood at the central axis of this artery.

27. As we observe celestial bodies, we see them not as they exist in the present but rather as they did exist sometime in the past. If the distance from the Earth to the Sun is $9.3 \cdot 10^7$ miles and if light travels $1.86 \cdot 10^5$ miles per second, when one sees the Sun in the present, how many seconds ago in the past are we really observing it?

28. Among the planets of the solar system, Pluto is the most distant from the Sun, approximately $4.6 \cdot 10^9$ miles. How many seconds does it take the light of the Sun to reach Pluto if light travels $1.86 \cdot 10^5$ miles per second?

29. Which one of the following is not true for all real numbers?
    a. $7x^2(y + x) = 7x^2y + 7x^3$
    b. $(2x + 3y^2)(4x + y) = (y + 4x)(3y + 2x^2)$
    c. $5(xy) = (5x)y$
    d. $5x - 10y = -5(2y - x)$

30. Choose the expression that is equivalent to $8x^2 + 2y^3$
    a. $2x^2 + 8y^3$
    b. $2(y^3 + 4x^2)$
    c. $2x^3 + 8y^2$
    d. $(2x)^2 + 2y^3$

Solving First Degree Equations

Methods for solving first degree equations are reviewed in this section. Algebraic properties used to solve equations are summarized. At the end of the section you need to be able to correctly solve first degree equations. Furthermore, if you are given a step in the solution of an equation, you should be able to determine the property used in that step.

◊ **Definitions**

A **first degree equation** involves an equality in which the variable is raised to the first power. The **solution** of the equation is the value that will make the equation a true statement when it replaces the variable. The **solution set** of the equation is the set of all possible solutions.

Procedure For Solving First Degree Equations

1. Simplify each side or member of the equation. (The sides are separated by the equal sign.) This is usually accomplished by using the distributive property and then adding or subtracting like terms.

2. Add or subtract the same term from both members of the equation in order to get all terms containing the variable on one side of the equation and all numbers on the other side of the equation.

3. Solve for the variable by dividing both members of the equation by the numerical coefficient of the variable.

4. Check the solution in the original equation.

Problem 1

Solve $2x - (4x + 2) = 5x + 12$.

Solution

Step 1

Eliminate the parentheses in the equation using the distributive property and multiplying each term of $(4x + 2)$ by -1.

$$2x - (4x + 2) = 5x + 12$$

becomes

$$2x - 4x - 2 = 5x + 12$$

Step 2

Combine similar terms.

$$-2x - 2 = 5x + 12$$

Step 3

Subtract 5x from both members.

$$-2x - 2 - 5x = 5x + 12 - 5x$$

$$-7x - 2 = 12$$

Step 4

Add 2 to both members.

$$-7x - 2 + 2 = 12 + 2$$

$$-7x = 14$$

Step 5

Divide both members by -7.

$$\frac{7x}{-7} = \frac{14}{-7}$$

$$x = -2$$

Step 6

Check -2 as the solution.

$$
\begin{aligned}
2x - (4x + 2) &= 5x + 12 \\
2(-2) - [4(-2) + 2] &= 5(-2) + 12 \\
-4 - [-8 + 2] &= -10 + 12 \\
-4 - [-6] &= 2 \\
-4 + 6 &= 2 \\
2 &= 2
\end{aligned}
$$

Thus, -2 is the solution, and {-2} is the solution set.

Problem 2

Solve $2(x + 3) = 3[x - (1–x)]$.

Solution

Step 1

Eliminate the innermost grouping symbols (parentheses) first.

$$2(x + 3) = 3[x - (1 - x)]$$
becomes
$$2(x + 3) = 3[x - 1 + x]$$

Step 2

Combine similar terms within the brackets.

$$2(x + 3) = 3[x - 1 + x]$$
becomes
$$2(x+ 3) = 3[2x - 1]$$

Step 3

Eliminate the remaining grouping symbols using the distributive property.

$$2(x + 3) = 3[2x - 1]$$
becomes
$$2x + 6 = 6x - 3$$

Step 4

Isolate all the terms with the variable x in one member of the equation and all the terms without the variable in the other member.

$$-4x = -9 \text{ or } 9 = 4x$$

Step 5

The two equations obtained in Step 4 are equivalent. In either case, divide both members by the number multiplying x.

$$x = \frac{9}{4}$$

Step 6

Check $\frac{9}{4}$ as the solution.

$$2(x + 3) = 3[x -(1 - x)]$$
$$2(\tfrac{9}{4} + 3) = 3[\tfrac{9}{4} - (1 - \tfrac{9}{4})]$$
$$2(\tfrac{21}{4}) = 3[\tfrac{9}{4} - (-\tfrac{5}{4})]$$
$$\frac{42}{4} = 3[\tfrac{7}{2}]$$
$$\frac{21}{2} = \frac{21}{2}$$

Thus, $\frac{9}{4}$ is the solution, and $\{\frac{9}{4}\}$ is the solution set.

Problem Set 4

Solve each of the following equations using the set of real numbers as replacements for the variable.

1. $x + 6x + 5 = 2(x + 5) + 4x - 1$

2. $7y - (3y + 5) = 6y + 8$

3. $3(a + 4) + 5(2a - 1) = 7a - 9$

4. $8 - 4(p - 1) = 2 + 3(4 - p)$

5. $(b - 1) - (b + 2) - (b - 3) = -2$

6. $3(k + 1) = 2[k + 3(k - 2)]$

7. $3[x - 2(2x - 1)] = x - 4$

8. $7(x + 1) = 4[x - (3 - x)]$

9. $3(2x - 1) = 5[3x - (2 - x)]$

10. $x(x - 5) - 2(x - 5) - 3 = x(x + 2) + (x + 2)$

11. Select the property that justifies the following statement:
    If $-3x = 6$ then $x = -2$.

    a. If $a = b$ then $a + c = b + c$.
    b. If $ac = bc$ and $c \neq 0$ then $a = b$.
    c. $a(b + c) = ab + ac$
    d. If $a = b$ and $b = c$ then $a = c$.

12. Select the property that justifies the following statement:
    If $2x - 7 = 13$ then $2x = 20$.

    a. If $a = b$ then $a + c = b + c$.
    b. If $ac = bc$ and $c \neq 0$ then $a = b$.
    c. $a(b + c) = ab + ac$
    d. If $a = b$ and $b = c$ then $a = c$.

Topic 5

Verbal Problems

In this section we consider a variety of algebraic verbal problems that give rise to first degree equations. After completing the section, you should be able to solve these problems by translating verbal conditions into an algebraic equation.

Problem solving is the central theme of algebra. The problems, of course, are presented in English. We must use the words to translate from the ordinary language of English into the language of algebraic equations. In order to translate, we must understand the English prose and also be familiar with the forms of algebraic language. Following are some general steps we will follow in solving word problems.

Strategy for Solving Word Problems

Step 1 Read the problem and determine the quantities that are involved. Let x (or any variable) represent the quantity asked for in the problem.

Step 2 If necessary, write expressions for any other unknown quantities in the problem in terms of x.

Step 3 Write an equation, in x, that describes the verbal conditions of the problem.

Step 4 Solve the equation written in step 3.

Step 5 Check the solution in the original wording of the problem, not in the equation obtained from the words.

The most difficult step in this process is Step 3, since it involves translating verbal conditions into an algebraic equation. In some situations the conditions are given explicitly. In other instances, the conditions are only implied, making it necessary to use one's knowledge about the type of word problem to generate an English sentence that must then be translated into an equation.

Translations of some commonly used English phrases are listed in the accompanying table.

Algebraic Translations of English Phrases

English Phrase	Algebraic Expression
The sum of a number and 7	$x + 7$
Twice the sum of a number and 7	$2(x + 7)$
The sum of twice a number and 7	$2x + 7$
8 more than a number	$x + 8$
A number increased by 8	$x + 8$
The difference of x and 5	$x - 5$
7 less than a number	$x - 7$
7 minus a number	$7 - x$
A number decreased by 5	$x - 5$
5 times a number	$5x$
The product of 3 and a number	$3x$
$\frac{3}{4}$ of a number (used with fractions)	$\frac{3}{4}x$
A number multiplied by 13	$13x$
The quotient of 7 and a number	$\frac{7}{x}$
A number divided by 7	$\frac{x}{7}$

Problem 1

When 9 is subtracted from 8 times a number, the result is 3 times the sum of 1 and twice that number. Find the number.

Solution

Let x = the number.

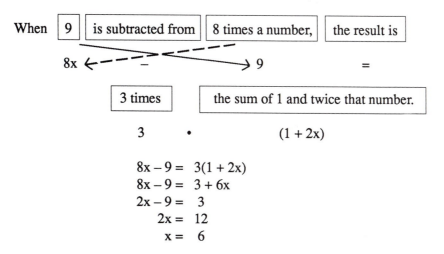

$$8x - 9 = 3(1 + 2x)$$
$$8x - 9 = 3 + 6x$$
$$2x - 9 = 3$$
$$2x = 12$$
$$x = 6$$

The number is 6.

Check

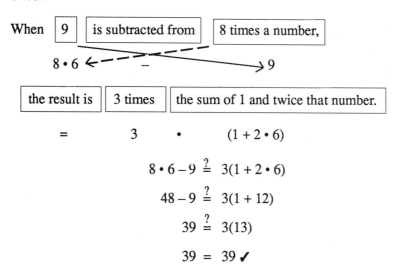

$$8 \cdot 6 - 9 \overset{?}{=} 3(1 + 2 \cdot 6)$$
$$48 - 9 \overset{?}{=} 3(1 + 12)$$
$$39 \overset{?}{=} 3(13)$$
$$39 = 39 \checkmark$$

Problem 2

8% of what number is 64?

Solution

Let x represent the number.

Therefore: $0.08 \cdot x = 64$ or $x = \frac{64}{0.08}$ or $x = 800$.

Thus, 8% of 800 is 64.

Problem 3

What percent of 60 is 15?

Solution

Let x represent the desired percent.

Therefore $x \cdot 60 = 15$ or $x = \frac{15}{60} = \frac{1}{4} = 0.25 = 25\%$

Thus, 25% of 60 is 15.

Problem 4

John spends 35% of his income on rent. One month he spent $420 on rent. What was his income that month?

Solution

Let x represent John's income. 35% of his income = money spent on rent. Therefore,

$$0.35x = 420 \quad \text{or} \quad x = \frac{420}{0.35} \quad \text{or} \quad x = 1,200$$

John's income was $1,200.

We now consider problems involving **consecutive integers**, such as 8, 9, and 10 or 23, 24, and 25. If we let x represent the first integer in a series of consecutive integers, the accompanying table should be helpful in solving consecutive integer problems.

Consecutive Integers

English Phrase	Algebraic Expression	Example
Two consecutive integers	x, x + 1	13, 14
Three consecutive integers	x, x + 1, x + 2	-8, -7, -6
Two consecutive even integers	x, x + 2	40, 42
Two consecutive odd integers	x, x + 2	-37, -35
Three consecutive even integers	x, x + 2, x + 4	30, 32, 34
Three consecutive odd integers	x, x + 2, x + 4	9, 11, 13

Problem 5

Find three consecutive even integers such that the sum of the first and third, increased by 4, is 20 more than the second.

Solution

Let

x = the first even integer
$x + 2$ = the second consecutive even integer
$x + 4$ = the third consecutive even integer

Then

Sum of the first and third	increased by 4	is	20 more than the second.
$x + (x + 4)$	$+4$	$=$	$(x + 2) + 20$

$$x + x + 4 + 4 = x + 2 + 20$$
$$2x + 8 = x + 22$$
$$x + 8 = 22$$
$$x = 14$$

The integers are 14, 16, and 18.

Check

Sum of the first and third	increased by 4	is	20 more than the second.
$14 + 18$	$+4$	$\overset{?}{=}$	$16 + 20$

$$36 = 36$$

Algebra

Many number problems focus on the digits of a two-digit number. If t represents the tens digit and u the units digit, the accompanying table should be helpful in solving digit problems.

Algebraic Translations of English Phrases

English Phrase	Algebraic Translation	Example
Tens digit	t	$83; t = 8$
Units digit	u	$u = 3$
Sum of digits	$t + u$	$8 + 3$
The number	$10t + u$	$10(8) + 3$ (or 83)

Problem 6

The tens digit of a two-digit number is 1 more than two times the units digit. If the sum of the digits is 13, what is the number?

Solution

Let u = the units digit.
Thus, $2u + 1$ = the tens digit (1 more than two times the units digit).
The sum of the digits is 13.

$$u + (2u + 1) = 13$$
$$3u + 1 = 13$$
$$3u = 12$$
$$u = 4$$

The units digit is 4 and the tens digit is $2u + 1$ or $2(4) + 1 = 9$.
The number is 94.

Problem 7

The tens digit of a two-digit number is 3 more than the units digit. If the number itself is 17 times the units digit, what is the number?

Solution

Let u = the units digit.
Thus, $u + 3$ = the tens digit (3 more than the units digit).
The number $= 10t + u$
$\qquad = 10(\text{tens digit}) + \text{units digit}$
$\qquad = 10(u + 3) + u$

We now translate:

The number	is	17 times the units digit.
$10(u + 3) + u$	=	$17 \cdot u$

We now solve the equation.

$$10(u + 3) + u = 17u$$
$$10u + 30 + u = 17u$$
$$11u + 30 = 17u$$
$$30 = 6u$$
$$5 = u$$

The units digit is 5 and the tens digit is u + 3 or 5 + 3 = 8.
The number is 85.

Many verbal problems involve a variety of unknown quantities. However, the conditions in the problem relate the unknowns in such a way that we can call one of them x and then represent the others in terms of x. We are then ready to translate from English into an algebraic equation. As usual, once we solve this equation we should be sure to state exactly what the problem asks for and check our solution with the conditions of the original verbal problem. Let's develop these ideas in a variety of illustrative examples.

Problem 8

Two numbers have a sum of 16. If twice the second is subtracted from 3 times the first, the result is 28. Find the numbers.

Solution

Let x = first number
Then 16 – x = second number (since their sum is 16)
Therefore:

3 times the first	–	twice the second number	is	28.
3x	–	2(16 - x)	=	28

Solving $3x - 2(16 - x) = 28$ gives

$$3x - 32 + 2x = 28$$
$$\text{or} \quad 5x - 32 = 28$$
$$\text{or} \quad 5x = 60$$
$$\text{or} \quad x = 12$$

The first number is 12 and the second is (16 – 12) or 4.

Problem 9

An estate of $60,000 was left to a wife, son, and daughter. The wife received $10,000 more than twice the daughter's share. The son received $10,000 less than the daughter's share. How much did each receive?

Solution

Let

$$x = \text{the daughter's share}$$

$$2x + 10{,}000 = \text{the wife's share}$$
($10,000 more than twice the daughter's share)

$$x - 10{,}000 = \text{the son's share}$$
($10,000 less than the daughter's share)

The total of the estate was $60,000.

| Daughter's share | + | wife's share | + | son's share | = | 60,000. |

$$x \quad + \quad 2x + 10{,}000 \quad + \quad x - 10{,}000 = 60{,}000$$
$$4x = 60{,}000$$
$$x = 15{,}000$$

Daughter's share = x = $15,000
Wife's share = 2x + 10,000 = 2(15,000) + 10,000 = $40,000
Son's share = x − 10,000 = 15,000 − 10,000 = $5,000

The daughter's share is $15,000, the wife's share is $40,000, and the son's share is $5000.

Check: 15,000 + 40,000 + 5000 = 60,000.

Problem 10

The larger of two numbers is 1 more than 3 times the smaller. The difference between 8 times the smaller and 2 times the larger is 10. Find the numbers.

Solution

Let

$$x = \text{the smaller number}$$
$$3x + 1 = \text{the larger number}$$

The larger number is <u>1 more than</u> <u>3 times the smaller.</u>

The difference between	8 times the smaller	and	2 times the larger	is	10.

$$8x \qquad - \qquad 2(3x + 1) \quad = \quad 10$$

$$8x - 2(3x + 1) = 10$$
$$8x - 6x - 2 = 10$$
$$2x - 2 = 10$$
$$2x = 12$$
$$x = 6$$

Smaller number = x = 6
Larger number = 3x + 1 = 3 • 6 + 1 = 19

The smaller number is 6 and the larger number is 19.

Check

The difference between	8 times the smaller	and	2 times the larger	is	10.

$$8 \cdot 6 \qquad - \qquad 2 \cdot 19 \qquad = \quad 10$$

$$8 \cdot 6 - 2 \cdot 19 = 10$$
$$48 - 38 = 10$$
$$10 = 10$$

Algebra

Problem Set 5

1. If 3 is added to 5 times a number, the result is 43. What is the number?

2. 3 less than a number equals 42. What is the number?

3. In a mathematics class there are 4 more men than women. If there are 30 students in the class, how many men are there?

4. If a certain number is multiplied by 3 and then 7 is added, the result is 11 less than 5 times the original number. What is the original number?

5. If 4 times a number is increased by 30, the result is the same as when 9 times the number is decreased by 10. What is the number?

6. If a second number is twice a first number and 3 times the first equals 12 increased by the second number, what are the numbers?

7. If Jim is 3 years younger than Ken and twice Jim's age decreased by 5 years equals Ken's age increased by two years, what are their ages?

8. 15% of what number is 75?

9. What percent of 50 is 20?

10. One number is 4 times another number. If the larger number is diminished by 3, the result is 6 more than the smaller number. Find the numbers.

11. Yoko's monthly budget allows 25% for housing, 35% for rent, 10% for clothing, and the rest on miscellaneous. One particular month Yoko spent $615 in the miscellaneous category. What was her income that month?

12. The difference between two numbers is 7 and their product is 44. If x represents the greater number, what equation could be used to find x?
   a. $x(x-7) = 44$
   b. $x(7-x) = 44$
   c. $x - (x-7) = 44$
   d. $x + (x-7) = 44$

13. The sum of three consecutive integers is 30. What are the integers?

14. The sum of three consecutive integers is 234. Find the integers.

15. The sum of three consecutive even integers is 198. Find the integers.

16. The sum of three consecutive odd integers is 51. Find the integers.

17. The sum of four consecutive odd integers is 216. Find the integers.

18. The sum of four consecutive even integers is 180. Find the integers.

19. The sum of three consecutive integers is 25. Find the integers.

20. The sum of three consecutive odd integers is 186. Find the integers.

21. The largest of three consecutive even integers is 6 less than twice the smallest. Find the integers.

22. Find three consecutive odd integers such that the largest is 13 less than twice the smallest.

23. Find three consecutive even integers such that the sum of the first and the third exceeds one-half of the second by 15.

24. Find three consecutive odd integers such that the sum of three times the first and twice the second exceeds three times the third by 26.

25. Find three consecutive even integers such that twice the second is equal to the sum of the first and the third.

26. Find three consecutive odd integers such that twice the second is equal to the sum of the first and the third increased by one.

27. The square of a number, decreased by 6 times the number, is 18 more than the number. Which equation should be used to find x, the number?
    a. $(x-6)^2 = x + 18$
    b. $x^2 - 6x^2 = x + 18$
    c. $x^2 - 6x + 18 = x$
    d. $x^2 - 7x = 18$

28. A molecule contains 1 more atom of carbon than twice the number of atoms of oxygen and 1 less atom of hydrogen than carbon. If the molecule contains a total of 21 atoms, how many atoms of carbon are there?

29. The library fees for a borrowed book are $.70 for the first day and $.30 for each additional day. If the loan of a book came to $4.30, for how many days was the book borrowed?

30. The tens digit of a two-digit number is 1 more than three times the units digit. If the sum of the digits is 9, what is the number?

31. The tens digit of a two-digit number is 4 less than the units digit. If the sum of the digits is 14, what is the number?

32. The tens digit of a two-digit number is 2 more than the units digit. If the number itself is 16 times the units digit, what is the number?

33. The tens digit of a two-digit number is 6 more than the units digit. If the number itself is 31 times the units digit, what is the number?

34. A two-digit integer is equal to 4 times the sum of its digits. Which equation should be used to find the number if t represents its tens digit and u represents its units digit?
    a. $4(10t + u) = t + u$
    b. $tu = 4(t + u)$
    c. $10t + u = 4(t + u)$
    d. $4tu = t + u$

35. The tens digit of a two-digit number is 3 more than the units digit. If the number is 16 times its units digit, what equation can be used to find t, the tens digit?
    a. $10(t + 3) + (t - 3) = 16t$
    b. $10(t + 3) + (t - 3) = 16$
    c. $10t + (t - 3) = 16$
    d. $10t + (t - 3) = 16(t - 3)$

36. In a community of 600 people, candidates A and B ran for mayor. Candidate B received 121 more votes than candidate A. Both candidates together received 493 votes. How many votes were received by candidate A?

37. Choose the algebraic description that equivalently translates the following verbal situation: For any three consecutive positive odd integers, the square of the middle integer is greater than the product of the smallest integer, x, and the largest integer.

   a. $(x + 1)^2 > x(x + 2)$

   b. $x(x + 4) < (x + 2)^2$

   c. $x^2 > (x + 2)(x + 4)$

   d. $x^2 + 4 > x(x + 4)$

38. The sum of 5 more than a certain number and 10 more than twice the number is equal to the product of 2 and the number increased by 8. Find the number.

39. The difference between two numbers is 2 and the sum of their reciprocals is $\frac{5}{12}$. If x represents the greater number, what equation could be used to find x?

   a. $\frac{1}{x} + \frac{1}{2 - x} = \frac{5}{12}$

   b. $\frac{1}{x + (x - 2)} = \frac{5}{12}$

   c. $x + (x - 2) = \frac{12}{5}$

   d. $\frac{1}{x} + \frac{1}{x - 2} = \frac{5}{12}$

40. The first three digits of Sophie's telephone number are 279. If 70 is added to Sophie's age, this sum is 5939 less than 3 times the number formed by the last four digits of Sophie's telephone number. If Sophie is 30 years old, what is her telephone number?

41. At a gathering, there are five times as many Democrats as Republicans. If 12 more Republicans arrive, there will be twice as many Democrats as Republicans. How many Democrats are at the gathering?

Contest Problems

Problems 42 through 49 are brain teasers.

42. Twenty years ago Tom took a course in how to get rich by investing in condominiums. Tom now owns condos throughout the country. One-half of his condos are in Miami, an eighth are in Atlanta, a twelfth in New York, a twentieth in Chicago, a thirtieth in San Francisco, and the remaining 50 are in Boulder. How many condominiums does Tom own?

43. Carla attends three bingo games. At the first she doubles her money and spends $30 in celebration. At the second she triples her money and spends $54 in celebration. At the third she quadruples her money and spends $72 in celebration. Finally, feeling bingoed out, Carla returns home with $48. How much money did she originally have?

44. Nathan has incredible luck. He just found 2 dollars on the sidewalk. His friend Adelaide remarked, "Now you've got 5 times as much as you'd have had if you'd lost 2 bucks." How much did Nathan have before finding 2 dollars?

45. Kay, working all day, grew incredible oranges by the bay. Her favorite orange weighs nine-tenths of its weight plus nine-tenths of a pound. What does Kay's orange, grown during the day by the bay, weigh?

46. If you spend $\frac{1}{3}$ of your money and then lose $\frac{2}{3}$ of what you still have left, leaving you with only $12, how much money did you originally have?

47. Suppose that we agree to pay you 8¢ for every problem in this chapter that you solve correctly and fine you 5¢ for every problem done incorrectly. If at the end of 26 problems, we do not owe each other any money, how many problems did you solve correctly?

48. A man passed one-sixth of his life in childhood, one-twelfth in youth, and one-seventh in childless marriage. After five years of marriage, the man had a child. Alas! late-born wretched child; after attaining half her father's life, cruel fate overtook her, leaving the man to spend his last 4 years solving algebraic word problems. What was the man's final age?

49. A thief steals a number of rare plants from a nursery. On the way out, the thief meets three security guards, one after another. To each security guard the thief is forced to give one-half the plants that he still has, plus 2 more. Finally, the thief leaves the nursery with 1 lone palm. How many plants were originally stolen?

Topic 6

Inequalities

In this section we consider statements in which one member is greater than, less than, or not equal to another member. Such statements are called inequalities. At the end of this section you need to be able to place the correct symbol of equality or inequality between two given numbers, solve inequalities and graph solution sets on the number line, select properties that justify statements involving inequalities, and determine whether or not a given number satisfies an equation or an inequality.

> The symbols used to express inequalities are:
> $\neq$ "is not equal to"
> $>$ "is greater than"
> $\geq$ "is greater than or equal to"
> $<$ "is less than"
> $\leq$ "is less than or equal to"

The order of real numbers can be considered on the real number line, a sort of "infinite ruler" with positive numbers represented to the right of zero and negative numbers to the left of zero. There is a one-to-one correspondence between real numbers and points on the number line. A number x is greater than a number y if x is to the right of y. Also, a number x is less than a number y if x is to the left of y on the number line.

E X A M P L E S

On the number line, the following order relations are true.

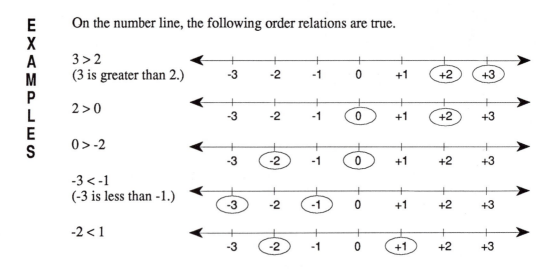

3 > 2
(3 is greater than 2.)

2 > 0

0 > -2

-3 < -1
(-3 is less than -1.)

-2 < 1

Observe that the inequality symbol (> or <) branches open in the direction of the larger number.

Problem 1

In each of the following choose the correct symbol (=, <, >) to make a true statement.

a. $\frac{9}{21} [\ ] \frac{3}{7}$

Solution

The rational numbers are equal. The correct symbol is =.

b. $0.20 [\ ] \frac{1}{4}$

Solution

$$\frac{1}{4} = 0.25 \text{ and } 0.20 < 0.25.$$

c. $3.2\overline{4} [\ ] 3.\overline{24}$

Solution

$$3.2\overline{4} = 3.24444 \ldots \quad 3.\overline{24} = 3.242424 \ldots \quad 3.2\overline{4} > 3.\overline{24}$$

d. $7.21 [\ ] 7.207$

Solution

$$7.21 > 7.207$$

e. $\frac{5}{12} [\ ] \frac{3}{7}$

Solution

We can either find a common denominator and compare numerators or change each fraction to a decimal.

Since $\frac{5}{12} = \frac{35}{84}$ and $\frac{3}{7} = \frac{36}{84}, \frac{5}{12} < \frac{3}{7}.$

Algebra

The process of solving an inequality for a variable is nearly identical to the process of solving equations presented in Topic 4. One major difference, however, exists.

> If both members of an inequality are divided or multiplied by the same negative real number, the direction of the inequality must be reversed.

E
X
A
M
P
L
E
S

1. If $6 > 4$ then $\frac{6}{-2} < \frac{4}{-2}$ or $-3 < -2$.

2. If $-2 < 4$ then $\frac{-2}{-2} > \frac{4}{-2}$ or $1 > -2$.

Problem 2

Solve for x: $3x - 2 > x + 2$

Solution

Step 1
The solution method is nearly identical to the procedure used in solving $3x - 2 = x + 2$. We begin by eliminating x from the right member.

$$3x - 2 > x + 2$$
$$3x - 2 - x > x + 2 - x$$
$$2x - 2 > 2$$

Step 2
We now collect all numerical terms on the right by adding 2 to both members.

$$2x - 2 > 2$$
$$2x - 2 + 2 > 2 + 2$$
$$2x > 4$$

Step 3
We solve for x by dividing both members by 2. Division by a positive number will not reverse the direction of the inequality.

$$\frac{2x}{2} > \frac{4}{2}$$
$$x > 2$$

All real numbers greater than 2 satisfy the inequality $3x - 2 > x + 2$.

The graph of the solution set, the set of all real numbers greater than 2, can be shown on the number line. The open dot (o) over the 2 indicates that 2 is not part of the solution set and excludes this value.

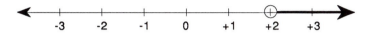

Using set-builder notation, the solution set is $\{x \mid x > 2\}$ ("the set of all real numbers x such that x is greater than 2").

Problem 3

Solve $2(x + 5) \geq 6(x + 1)$.

Solution

Step 1

First eliminate the parentheses using the distributive property.

$$2(x + 5) \geq 6(x + 1)$$
becomes
$$2x + 10 \geq 6x + 6$$

Step 2

Eliminate 6x from the right member of the inequality.

$$2x + 10 - 6x \geq 6x + 6 - 6x$$
becomes
$$-4x + 10 \geq 6$$

Step 3

Isolate -4x in the left member of the inequality.

$$-4x + 10 - 10 \geq 6 - 10$$
becomes
$$-4x \geq -4$$

Step 4

Divide both members by -4 and reverse the direction of the inequality because of division by a negative number.

$$\frac{-4x}{-4} \leq \frac{-4}{-4}$$
becomes
$$x \leq 1$$

All real numbers less than or equal to 1 satisfy the inequality $2(x + 5) \geq 6(x + 1)$. The graph of the solution set, the set of real numbers less than or equal to 1, can again be shown on the number line. The closed dot (•) over the 1 indicates that 1 is a part of the solution set.

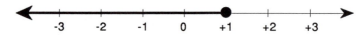

The solution set is $\{x \mid x \leq 1\}$.

Problem 4

A salesperson is paid a monthly commission of 25% on all sales over $2000. What monthly sales will generate a commission greater than $800?

Solution

Let x represent monthly sales in dollars.

25%　of　sales over $2000　must be greater than　$800.

0.25　•　(x - 2000)　　　>　　　800

We solve the resulting inequality.

$$0.25(x - 2000) > 800$$
$$0.25x - 500 > 800$$
$$0.25x > 1300$$
$$x > 5200$$

Monthly sales must be greater than $5200 to generate more than $800 in commission.

Problem 5

Solve $4 < 3x + 7 \leq 13$ and graph the solution set.

Solution

If we read the inequality from the perspective of the middle expression, it states that $3x + 7$ is greater than 4 and less than or equal to 13. Our goal is to obtain an equivalent inequality that has only x as the middle expression.

Step 1
Subtract 7 from all three members of the inequality.

$$4 - 7 < 3x + 7 - 7 \leq 13 - 7$$

becomes

$$-3 < 3x \leq 6$$

Step 2

Divide all three members by 3.

$$-\frac{3}{3} \;<\; \frac{3x}{3} \;\leq\; \frac{6}{3}$$

becomes

$$-1 \;<\; x \;\leq\; 2$$

All real numbers greater than -1 but less than or equal to 2 satisfy the inequality. The graph of the solution set is at the right.

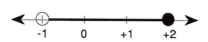

The solution set is $\{x \mid -1 < x \leq 2\}$.

Three important algebraic properties are used to solve inequalities. These properties enable us to write a series of equivalent inequalities that each have the same solution.

Properties Used to Solve Inequalities

1. If $a > b$ then $a + c > b + c$. Since c can be positive or negative, this property states that the same real number c can be added to or subtracted from each member of an inequality while maintaining the inequality.

2. If $ac > bc$ and $c > 0$ then $a > b$. This property states that the same positive number c can divide each member of an inequality while maintaining the inequality.

3. If $ac > bc$ and $c < 0$ then $a < b$. This property states that the same negative number c can divide each member of an inequality, but the inequality must be reversed.

E X A M P L E S

1. If $x + 7 > 10$ then $x > 3$. Since we have subtracted 7 (or added negative 7) from both members of $x + 7 > 10$, this step illustrates property (1) listed in the preceding table. $x + 7 > 10$ and $x > 3$ are equivalent inequalities because they have the same solution set.

2. If $4x > 20$ then $x > 5$. Since we have divided both sides of $4x > 20$ by positive 4, maintaining the inequality, this step illustrates property (2) listed in the preceding table. Once again $4x > 20$ and $x > 5$ are equivalent inequalities with the same solution set.

3. If $-4x > 20$ then $x < -5$. Since we have divided each member of $-4x > 20$ by negative 4, reversing the inequality, property (3) listed above is illustrated. $-4x > 20$ and $x < -5$ are equivalent inequalities.

Problem 6

Which choice listed below has (-2) as a solution?

a. $(t + 5)(t - 1) < -9$
b. $|x - 2| = -4$
c. $y + 4 \leq 0$
d. $z^2 + 3z + 20 \geq 17$

Solution

Substitute (-2) into each equation or inequality. If a true statement results, (-2) is a solution. If a false statement results, (-2) is not a solution.

a. $(t + 5)(t - 1) < -9$ becomes

$$(-2 + 5)(-2 - 1) < -9$$
$$(3)(-3) \quad < -9$$
$$-9 \quad\quad < -9$$

This false statement indicates that (-2) is not a solution.

b. $|x - 2| = -4$ becomes

$$|-2 - 2| = -4$$
$$|-4| = -4$$

Since the absolute value of -4 is 4, we have 4 = -4, a false statement. Again, (-2) is not a solution.

c. $y + 4 \leq 0$ becomes

$$-2 + 4 \leq 0$$
$$2 \quad \leq 0$$

Since 2 is not less than or equal to 0 (2 > 0), -2 is not a solution of $y + 4 \leq 0$.

d. $z^2 + 3z + 20 \geq 17$ becomes

$$(-2)^2 + 3(-2) + 20 \geq 17$$
$$4 + (-6) + 20 \geq 17$$
$$18 \quad \geq 17$$

This true statement indicates that (-2) is a solution to the inequality listed in option d.

Problem Set 6

1. Insert the correct symbol (>, <, or =) between the two given numbers.

   a. $\frac{3}{4}[\ ]\frac{2}{3}$ b. $-\frac{3}{4}[\ ]-\frac{2}{3}$

   c. $-\frac{5}{6}[\ ]-0.1$ d. $-\frac{5}{2}[\ ]-2$

   e. $0.3[\ ]\frac{1}{3}$ f. $\frac{1}{8}[\ ]\frac{13}{16}$

   g. $2[\ ]-5{,}000{,}000$ h. $\frac{3}{4}[\ ]\frac{12}{16}$

   i. $8.31[\ ]8.309$ j. $5.8\overline{7}[\ ]5.\overline{87}$

In problems 2-4 solve for the variable and graph the solution set on the number line.

2. $4x + 2x + 7 > 3x + 10$

3. $3x + 8 + 4 < 7x + 28$

4. $3(2x - 1) \geq 8(x + 3)$

In problems 5-10 solve for the variable.

5. $1 - 2x > 5$

6. $2(3 + x) + 5x \geq 8x - 3(x - 2)$

7. $14 < 5x + 4 \leq 29$

8. $3 \leq 2x + 3 < 11$

9. $y < y - (8 - 2y)$

10. $a \geq a - (9 - 3a)$

For each statement in problems 11-16, select the property used to justify that statement. Select from the following four properties.

   a. If $a > b$ then $a + c > b + c$.
   b. If $ac > bc$ and $c > 0$ then $a > b$.
   c. If $ac > bc$ and $c < 0$ then $a < b$.
   d. If $a > b$ and $b > c$ then $a > c$.

11. If $3x > 21$ then $x > 7$.

12. If $3x + 5 > 26$ then $3x > 21$.

13. If $x + 2 > 5$ and $5 > 3$ then $x + 2 > 3$.

14. If $-7x > 35$ then $x < -5$.

15. If $4 \leq 3x + 7 < 13$ then $-3 \leq 3x < 6$.

16. If $-7x < 35$ then $x > -5$

17. Which choice listed below has $\frac{2}{3}$ as a solution?

   a. $x^2 = \frac{4}{3}$ b. $8y - 5\frac{1}{3} \leq 0$

   c. $x - \frac{2}{3} > 3$ d. $(x + 3)(x - 1) = \frac{11}{9}$

18. Which of the following has/have (-5) as a solution?

   i. $|x - 5| = 10$
   ii. $(x + 4)(x - 3) < 7$
   iii. $\frac{y}{5} + 1 > 0$

   a. i only   b. ii only
   c. iii only   d. i and ii only

19. Which of the following has/have (-7) as a solution?

   i. $(x - 7)(x + 1) = 0$
   ii. $x + 7 < 5$
   iii. $2y^2 - 3y + 1 = 120$

   a. i only   b. ii only
   c. iii only   d. ii and iii only

20. Which one of the following is true for every integer x?

   a. $\frac{1}{x^2} > 0$ b. $x^2 + 1 > 0$

   c. $(x + 1)^2 > x^2$ d. $x^3 \leq 0$

Algebra

21. In order to be listed on "The Top 50 Mutual Funds," a fund must have assets greater than $320 million. If a growth fund has current assets of $140 million and grows steadily at the rate of $9 million per year, how long will it take to make the list of the top 50 funds?

22. Membership in a fitness club costs $500 yearly plus $1 for each hour spent working out. A competing club charges $440 yearly plus $1.75 per hour for use of their equipment. How many hours must a person work out yearly to make membership in the first club cheaper than membership in the second club?

23. If $b < 0$, then $b^2 < ab + b$ is equivalent to which of the following?
    a. $b < a + 1$
    b. $b > a + 1$
    c. $b < -a - 1$
    d. $b > -a - 1$

24. If $b < 0$, then $ab^3 > ab^4 + b^2$ is equivalent to which of the following?
    a. $ab^2 < ab^3 + b^2$
    b. $ab^2 > ab^3 + b^2$
    c. $ab^2 < ab^3 + b$
    d. $ab^2 < -ab^3 - b$

25. If $x > 0$, then $x^2 > x + xy$ is equivalent to which of the following?
    a. $x < x + y$
    b. $x < 1 + y$
    c. $x > 1 + y$
    d. $x > x + y$

26. Choose the inequality that is equivalent to $4 - 2y > 12$.
    a. $-2y > 8$
    b. $-2y < 8$
    c. $2y > 8$
    d. $2y < 8$

27. Choose the inequality that is equivalent to $-5x > 25$.
    a. $x < 5$
    b. $x < -5$
    c. $x > -5$
    d. $x > 5$

28. Choose the inequality that is equivalent to $7 < x + 3 < 12$.
    a. $12 < x < 15$
    b. $4 < x < 9$
    c. $21 < x < 36$
    d. $4 > x > 9$

29. Choose the inequality that is equivalent to $14 < 2x < 20$.
    a. $12 < x < 18$
    b. $16 < x < 22$
    c. $7 < x < 10$
    d. $28 < x < 40$

30. Choose the inequality that is equivalent to $18 < -3x < 24$.
    a. $-8 < x < -6$
    b. $-6 < x < -8$
    c. $21 < x < 27$
    d. $6 > x > 8$

Topic 7

Ratio and Proportion

This section explains ratios and proportions. At the end of this section you need to be able to set up and solve proportions based upon verbal problems.

◊ **Definition**

A **ratio** of two numbers, x and y, is a comparison of x to y by division. The **ratio** of x to y is written as $\frac{x}{y}$ or x:y ($y \neq 0$).

A ratio expressed as a fraction should be reduced to lowest terms.

A class contains 20 female students and 24 male students. The ratio of female students to male students may be expressed as:

$$\frac{\text{female students}}{\text{male students}} = \frac{20}{24} = \frac{5}{6} \text{ or } 5{:}6$$

◊ **Definition**

A **proportion** is a statement that one ratio equals another.

A proportion appears symbolically in the following form:

$$\frac{a}{b} = \frac{c}{d} \quad (b \neq 0 \text{ and } d \neq 0)$$

This proportion is read "a is to b as c is to d."

When one ratio equals another, the four quantities are said to be **in proportion** or **proportional**.

Algebra

A most important principle for working with proportions is:

If $\frac{a}{b} = \frac{c}{d}$, then a • d = b • c. (b ≠ 0 and d ≠ 0)

Problem 1

Solve the proportions using the principle cited above.

a.   Solve $\frac{4}{9} = \frac{8}{x}$.

Solution

$$\frac{4}{9} = \frac{8}{x} \text{ becomes } 4 \bullet x = 9 \bullet 8 \text{ or } 4x = 72.$$

Dividing both sides by 4 solves the proportion. x = 18

b.   Solve $\dfrac{3\frac{1}{3}}{2\frac{1}{2}} = \dfrac{x}{4\frac{1}{4}}$.

Solution

$$2\tfrac{1}{2} \bullet x \ = \ 3\tfrac{1}{3} \bullet 4\tfrac{1}{4} \ \text{ or } \ \tfrac{5}{2}x \ = \tfrac{10}{3} \bullet \tfrac{17}{4}$$

Dividing both sides by $\frac{5}{2}$ gives

$$x \ = \frac{170}{12} \div \frac{5}{2} = \frac{170}{12} \bullet \frac{2}{5} \ = \frac{340}{60} = \frac{17}{3} = 5\tfrac{2}{3}$$

Problem 2

A forest service catches, tags and then releases 72 deer back into a park. Two weeks later they select a sample of 336 deer, 21 of which were found to be tagged. Assuming that the ratio of tagged deer in the sample holds for all deer in the park, approximately how many deer are in the park?

Solution

Set up a proportion comparing tagged deer with the total number of deer.

$$\frac{\text{tagged deer}}{\text{total number}} : \quad \frac{72}{x} = \frac{21}{336}$$

Reducing gives: $\quad \dfrac{72}{x} = \dfrac{1}{16}$

$$1x = (72)(16)$$
$$x = 1152$$

Since x stands for the total number of deer in the park, there are approximately 1,152 deer.

Problem 3

On a map $\frac{1}{4}$ inch represents 60 miles. How many miles are represented by $1\frac{1}{2}$ inches?

Solution

Setting up a proportion comparing inches to miles gives

$$\frac{\text{inches per 60 miles}}{60 \text{ miles}} = \frac{\text{inches per ? miles}}{? \text{ miles}}$$

$$\frac{\frac{1}{4}}{60} = \frac{1\frac{1}{2}}{x}$$

This gives: $\qquad \dfrac{1}{4} \cdot x = 60 \cdot 1\dfrac{1}{2} \quad$ or $\quad \dfrac{1}{4}x = 90.$

Multiplying both members by 4 gives x = 360.
Since x stands for unknown miles, the answer is 360 miles.

Problem 4

The ratio of Jan's weight to Bob's weight is 4 to 3. If Jan's weight is 120 pounds, find Bob's weight.

Solution

The ratio of Jan's weight to Bob's weight is

$$\frac{\text{Jan's weight}}{\text{Bob's weight}} = \frac{4}{3}$$

This ratio is equal to $\frac{120}{x}$, where x represents Bob's weight.
Using the cross products of the proportion

$$\frac{4}{3} = \frac{120}{x} \quad \text{gives} \quad 4x = 360 \quad \text{or} \quad x = 90.$$

Thus, Bob weighs 90 pounds.

Problem 5

Two machines can complete 5 tasks every 8 days. Let t represent the number of tasks these machines can complete in 30 days. Which of the following proportions accurately represents this situation?

a. $\frac{8}{5} = \frac{30}{t}$

b. $\frac{8}{5} = \frac{t}{30}$

c. $\frac{t}{5} = \frac{8}{30}$

Solution

It is not necessary to write all correct proportions. If we write one proportion that is correct and multiply the cross products, any other correct choice must give us an identical result when the cross products are multiplied.

Let us compare tasks to days. (Observe that we can also compare days to tasks.)

$$\frac{\text{Tasks (in 8 days)}}{8 \text{ days}} = \frac{\text{Tasks (in 30 days)}}{30 \text{ days}}$$

$$\frac{5}{8} = \frac{t}{30}$$

We now multiply cross products. Since this proportion is correct, any given choice that results in $8t = 5 \cdot 30$ is also correct.

Choice a, $\frac{8}{5} = \frac{30}{t}$, becomes $8t = 5 \cdot 30$, so a is correct.

Choice b, $\frac{8}{5} = \frac{t}{30}$, becomes $5t = 8 \cdot 30$, so b is incorrect.

Choice c, $\frac{t}{5} = \frac{8}{30}$, becomes $30t = 5 \cdot 8$, so c is incorrect.

Problem Set 7

1. Solve for x. $\frac{3}{5} = \frac{7}{x}$

2. Solve for x. $\frac{2\frac{1}{5}}{3\frac{1}{4}} = \frac{x}{2\frac{1}{3}}$

3. On a map, $\frac{1}{3}$ inch represents 50 miles. How many miles are represented by $2\frac{2}{3}$ inches?

4. A photograph that measures 4 inches wide and 7 inches high is to be enlarged so that the height will be 10 inches. What will be the width of the enlargement?

5. To find an estimate of the number of bass in a pond, rangers tagged 135 bass and released them in the pond. Later they netted 140 bass and found that 30 of them were tagged. Approximately how many bass are in the pond?

6. In an effort to estimate the number of deer in a forest, rangers trapped 108 deer and found that 27 of them were tagged. Previously they had tagged 50 deer and released them. Approximately how many deer are in the forest?

7. An object that weights 17.6 kg on the moon has a weight of 110 kg on the earth. Find the earth weight of an object that weights 28.8 kg on the moon.

8. Fran builds 3 boats in 2 days.
   a. If Bill works at the same rate, in how many days will Bill build 9 boats?
   b. If Belinda works half as fast as Fran, in how many days will Belinda build 9 boats?

Algebra

9. Five cans of a product cost \$3. Let y be the cost of 11 cans. Select the correct statement of the given conditions.

a. $\frac{5}{3} = \frac{y}{11}$ b. $\frac{5}{11} = \frac{3}{y}$

c. $\frac{3}{5} = \frac{11}{y}$ d. $\frac{5}{y} = \frac{3}{11}$

10. The ratio of men to women in a class is 9 to 4. If there are 27 men in the class, how many women are there?

11. If the ratio of dogs to cats in a pet store is 5 to 2, determine how many cats there are if there are 20 dogs in the store.

12. If 13 pounds of fertilizer will cover 2,000 square feet of lawn, how much fertilizer is needed to cover 3,200 square feet?

13. Suppose 3 long distance runners cover 51 miles. Let x represent how many runners are needed to cover 85 miles. Select the correct statement of the given conditions.

a. $\frac{3}{51} = \frac{85}{x}$ b. $\frac{3}{x} = \frac{51}{85}$

c. $\frac{3}{x} = \frac{85}{51}$ d. $\frac{51}{3} = \frac{x}{85}$

Topic 8

Direct and Inverse Variation

The cephalic index is used by anthropologists to study differences among races of human beings. The index varies directly as the width of the head and inversely as the length of the head. The area of a circle varies directly as the square of its radius. The illumination of light varies inversely as the square of the distance from the source of the light. The number of hours required to accomplish a job varies directly with the number of tasks in the job and inversely as the number of people doing the job.

Statements like these, involving direct and inverse variation, appear in the natural and social sciences. This section explains the ideas of direct and inverse variation. At the end of this section you need to be able to correctly solve problems involving both types of variation.

English Statement	Algebraic Equation
y varies directly as x. y is proportional to x.	$y = kx$
y varies inversely as x. y is inversely proportional to x.	$y = \dfrac{k}{x}$

Procedure for Solving a Variation Problem

1. Translate the English statement into an equation.
2. Find the value for the constant k by substituting paired values for the variables.
3. Use the equation of step (1) with the value of k found in step (2).
4. Substitute the value of the unmatched variable and solve the equation.

Problem 1

y varies directly as x. When $y = 6$, then $x = 3$. Find y when $x = 10$.

Solution

The problem is solved using the four steps listed above.

Step 1
y varies directly as x translates as the equation $y = kx$.

Step 2
$y = kx$ when $y = 6$ and $x = 3$ becomes $6 = k \cdot 3$ or $k = 2$.

Step 3
Since $k = 2$, $y = kx$ becomes $y = 2x$.

Step 4
$y = 2x$ and $x = 10$ becomes $y = 2 \cdot 10$. Thus $y = 20$.

Problem 2

y varies inversely as x squared. When x = 5, y = 3. Find y when x = 10.

Solution

Step 1

"y varies inversely as x squared" implies $y = \frac{k}{x^2}$

Step 2

When x = 5 and y = 3, $y = \frac{k}{x^2}$ becomes

$3 = \frac{k}{x^2}$ or $3 = \frac{k}{5^2}$ or $3 = \frac{k}{25}$ or k = 75.

Step 3

$y = \frac{k}{x^2}$ becomes $y = \frac{75}{x^2}$.

Step 4

When x = 10, $y = \frac{75}{x^2}$ becomes $y = \frac{75}{10^2} = \frac{75}{100} = \frac{3}{4}$.

Problem 3

The force, F, required to stretch a spring is proportional to the elongation, E.

If 24 pounds stretches a spring 3 inches, find the force required to stretch the spring $4\frac{1}{2}$ inches.

Solution

Step 1

The phrase "is proportional to" gives the equation F = kE.

Step 2

F = kE when F = 24 and E = 3 becomes 24 = k • 3 or k = 8.

Step 3

Since k = 8, F = kE becomes F = 8E.

Step 4

F = 8E and $E = 4\frac{1}{2}$ becomes $F = 8 \cdot 4\frac{1}{2} = 36$.

Thus, the required force is 36 pounds.

Problem 4

The electrical resistance (R) of a wire is directly proportional to the length (L) of the wire and inversely proportional to the square of the diameter (D) of the wire. An 8-foot wire with a diameter of 1 inch has a resistance of 8 ohms. Predict the resistance of a 27-foot wire having a diameter of 3 inches.

Solution

$R = \dfrac{kL}{D^2}$ Translate "R is directly proportional to L and inversely proportional to the square of D."

$8 = \dfrac{k(8)}{1^2}$ Find K. When L = 8 and D = 1, R = 8.

$8 = k \cdot 8$

$1 = k$

$R = \dfrac{L}{D^2}$ Substitute 1 for k in the original equation.

$R = \dfrac{27}{3^2}$ Find R when L = 27 and D = 3.

$R = \dfrac{27}{9}$

$R = 3$

Thus the resistance of a 27-foot wire having a diameter of 3 inches is 3 ohms.

Problem Set 8

1. y varies directly as x. When y = 10, x = 2. Find y when x = 7.

2. y varies inversely as x. When y = 9, x = 3. Find y when x = 54.

3. y varies directly as x squared. When y = 3, x = 2. Find y when x = 6.

4. y varies inversely as x squared. When y = 1, x = 2. Find y when x = 5.

Algebra

5. The amount of paint required to paint a circular floor varies directly as the square of the radius. If it takes 4 liters of paint for a floor of radius 10 meters, find the amount of paint required for a floor of radius 16 meters.

6. The current I flowing in an electrical circuit varies inversely as the resistance R in the circuit. When R = 4 ohms then I = 24 amperes. What is the current I when the resistance is 6 ohms?

7. The time T required to do a job is inversely proportional to the product of the number of workers W and the number of hours they work per day H. Nine workers working 10 hours a day can do a job in 14 days. (When W = 9 and H = 10, T = 14.) Find how long it would take 12 workers working 7 hours per day to do the job.

8. The distance required to stop a car (d) varies directly as the square of its speed (r). If 200 feet are required to stop a car traveling 60 miles per hours, how many feet are required to stop a car traveling 100 miles per hour?

9. The distance that a body falls (d) varies directly as the square of the time (t) in which it falls. A body falls 64 feet in 2 seconds. Predict the distance that the same body will fall in 10 seconds.

10. The volume of a gas (V) in a container at a constant temperature varies inversely as the pressure (p). If the volume is 32 cubic centimeters at a pressure of 8 pounds, find the pressure when the volume is 40 cubic centimeters.

11. The intensity of illumination on a surface varies inversely as the square of the distance of the light source from the surface. The illumination from a source is 25 footcandles at a distance of 4 feet. What is the illumination when the distance is 6 feet?

12. The gravitational force with which the Earth attracts an object varies inversely with the square of the distance from the center of Earth. If a gravitational force of 160 pounds acts on an object 4000 miles from Earth's center, predict the force of attraction on an object 6000 miles from the center of Earth.

13. The volume of a gas is directly proportional to its temperature and inversely proportional to the pressure. At a temperature of 100 Kelvin and a pressure of 15 kilograms per square meter, the gas occupies a volume of 20 cubic meters. Find the volume at a temperature of 150 Kelvin and a pressure of 30 kilograms per square meter.

14. The cephalic index is used by anthropologists to study differences among races of human beings. The index varies directly as the width of the head and inversely as the length of the head. If the cephalic index is 75 for a width of 6 inches and a length of 8 inches, find the index for a head width of 7 inches and a length of 10 inches.

Topic 9

Factoring Quadratic Expressions

In this section factoring quadratic expressions is discussed. At the end of this section you should be able to correctly factor quadratic expressions.

◊ **Definition**

An expression in the form $ax^2 + bx + c$, where $a \neq 0$, is called a **quadratic expression** or a **second degree expression**.

E
X
A
M
P
L
E

$3x^2 + 5x - 2$ is a quadratic expression in which
$a = 3$,
$b = 5$ and
$c = -2$.

The multiplication of two **binomials** (expressions containing two terms) frequently gives rise to a quadratic expression.

Problem 1

Find the product of $2x + 3$ and $4x + 7$.

Solution

The multiplication can be done in a horizontal format using the distributive property. We will multiply each term in the second binomial $(4x + 7)$ by each term in the first binomial $(2x + 3)$.

$$
\begin{aligned}
(2x + 3)(4x + 7) &= 2x(4x + 7) + 3(4x + 7) \\
&= (2x)(4x) + (2x)(7) + (3)(4x) + (3)(7) \\
&= 8x^2 + 14x + 12x + 21 \\
&= 8x^2 + 26x + 21
\end{aligned}
$$

Algebra

Because the multiplication of binomials occurs so frequently in algebra, we need to further examine the multiplication process used in Problem 1. In general, we have $(A + B)(C + D)$.

We distribute A and then B to each term in the second factor.

$$(A + B)(C + D) = A(C + D) + B(C + D)$$
$$= AC + AD + BC + BD$$

The product $(AC + AD + BC + BD)$ can be computed by:

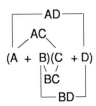

a. multiplying **FIRST** terms of each binomial: AC
b. multiplying **OUTSIDE** terms of each binomial: AD
c. multiplying **INSIDE** terms of each binomial: BC
d. multiplying **LAST** terms of each binomial: BD

The word "FOIL" is a memory device for the multiplication of binomials. The word contains the first letter of the words FIRST, OUTSIDE, INSIDE and LAST. The "FOIL" method is often a way to quickly multiply two binomials.

Problem 2

Find the product of $(3x + 4)$ and $(2x + 1)$ using the "FOIL" method.

Solution

Step 1
Multiply First terms. $(3x)(2x) = 6x^2$

Step 2
Multiply Outside terms. $(3x)(1) = 3x$

Step 3
Multiply Inside terms. $(4)(2x) = 8x$

Step 4
Multiply Last terms $(4)(1) = 4$

Thus, $(3x + 4)(2x + 1) = 6x^2 + 3x + 8x + 4$.
Combining like terms, the product becomes $6x^2 + 11x + 4$.

We will now discuss a general method for factoring a quadratic expression. We will begin with $ax^2 + bx + c$ and arrive at the equivalent **product**. This is the factoring process, and the distributive property is the basis for it.

In our previous work we multiplied $(3x + 4)$ and $(2x + 1)$, obtaining $6x^2 + 11x + 4$. We will now employ the reverse process, starting with $6x^2 + 11x + 4$ and obtaining $(3x + 4)$ and $(2x + 1)$. We call $(3x + 4)$ and $(2x + 1)$ the **factors** of $6x^2 + 11x + 4$. Since each factor involves only x raised to the first power, these factors are referred to as **linear factors**.

Since factoring is the reverse of multiplication, we know that
$$6x^2 + 11x + 4 = (3x + 4)(2x + 1)$$
or that
$$6x^2 + 11x + 4 \text{ factors into } (3x + 4)(2x + 1).$$

Observe the following relationships:

1. The first terms in each binomial factor (3x and 2x) are factors of the first term of the quadratic expression ($6x^2$). Thus, $(3x)(2x) = 6x^2$. In a product like $6x^2$, the number 6 is called the **numerical coefficient**.

2. The last terms in each binomial factor (4 and 1) are factors of the last term of the quadratic expression. Thus, $(4)(1) = 4$.

3. The sum of the outer product (3x) and the inner product (8x) equals the middle term of the quadratic expression (11x).

These observations lead us to a general procedure for factoring $ax^2 + bx + c$.

To factor a quadratic expression $ax^2 + bx + c$:

1. Find the pairs of factors of the numerical coefficients of the first term and the last term of the quadratic expression.

2. By trial and error, position the pairs of factors in such a way that the sum of the outer product and the inner product will equal the middle term of the quadratic expression.

Problem 3

Factor $2x^2 + 7x + 3$.

Solution

Step 1

The pairs of factors of the coefficient of the first term (2) are
$$2 \text{ and } 1 \text{ or } -2 \text{ and } -1.$$

The pairs of factors of the last term (3) are
$$3 \text{ and } 1 \text{ or } -3 \text{ and } -1.$$

The first term in each factor must contain x so that the product $(x \cdot x)$ will result in x^2, the letter portion of the first term $2x^2$. Let us agree that when the first term in the quadratic expression is positive we will use only positive factors of that first term. Thus, we will not use -2x and -x even though $(-2x)(-x) = 2x^2$. Thus, we have: $(2x \quad)(x \quad)$.

Step 2

Since the signs in this quadratic expression are all positive, the sign in each factor is positive.

The quadratic expression has the possible factors:
$(2x + 3)(x + 1) = 2x^2 + 5x + 3$ (wrong middle term)
$(2x + 1)(x + 3) = 2x^2 + 7x + 3$ (correct)

Since only $(2x + 1)(x + 3) = 2x^2 + 7x + 3$, then $2x^2 + 7x + 3$ factors as $(2x + 1)(x + 3)$ or $(x + 3)(2x + 1)$. Observe that in the expression $(2x + 1)(x + 3)$ the sum of the outer product $(6x)$ and the inner product (x) equals the middle term of the quadratic expression $(7x)$. We can check using the "FOIL" method, showing that :
$$(2x + 1)(x + 3) = 2x^2 + 7x + 3.$$

Problem 4

Factor $15x^2 - 17x - 4$.

Solution

Step 1
The pairs of positive factors of 15 are: [15 and 1] or [5 and 3].

We have the possibilities: $(15x \quad)(x \quad)$ or $(5x \quad)(3x \quad)$.

The pairs of factors of -4 are: [4 and -1], [-4 and 1], [2 and -2], or [-2 and 2].

Step 2
We must position these factors in such a way that the sum of the outer product and inner product equals -17x, the middle term.

The list below shows all possible factorizations:

$(15x + 4)(x - 1)$	$(5x + 4)(3x - 1)$
$(15x - 4)(x + 1)$	$(5x - 4)(3x + 1)$
$(15x + 1)(x - 4)$	$(5x - 1)(3x + 4)$
$(15x - 1)(x + 4)$	$(5x + 1)(3x - 4)$ (correct answer)
$(15x - 2)(x + 2)$	$(5x + 2)(3x - 2)$
$(15x + 2)(x - 2)$	$(5x - 2)(3x + 2)$

Since only $(5x + 1)(3x - 4)$ has a sum of outer and inner products equal to -17x, then $15x^2 - 17x - 4$ factors as $(5x + 1)(3x - 4)$. Thus, $5x + 1$ and $3x - 4$ are the linear factors of the quadratic expression $15x^2 - 17x - 4$.

Problem Set 9

Factor the quadratic expressions in problems 1-15.

1. $3x^2 + 8x + 5$
2. $2x^2 + 9x + 7$
3. $5x^2 + 56x + 11$
4. $4x^2 + 9x + 2$
5. $8x^2 + 10x + 3$
6. $6x^2 - 23x + 15$
7. $16x^2 - 6x - 27$
8. $8x^2 - 18x + 9$
9. $4x^2 - 27x + 18$
10. $12x^2 - 19x - 21$
11. $4x^2 - x - 18$
12. $6x^2 + 11x + 3$
13. $4x^2 - 12x + 9$
14. $8x^2 - 26x + 21$
15. $6x^2 + 19x - 7$

Quadratic Equations

Methods for solving quadratic equations are discussed in this section. At the end of the section you need to be able to solve quadratic equations using factoring and, if necessary, the quadratic formula.

◊ Definition

A **quadratic equation** is an equation of the form $ax^2 + bx + c = 0$, where $a \neq 0$ and a,b, and c are real numbers.

Examples of quadratic equations include:

$x^2 - 2x - 15 = 0$ (a = 1, b = -2, and c = -15), and
$3x^2 - 7x - 6 = 0$ (a = 3, b = -7 and c = -6).

These equations and many other quadratic equations can be solved by factoring. We will use a property of real numbers that states:

If a product is zero, then at least one of the factors must be zero.

Symbolically, we can write:

If $AB = 0$, then $A = 0$ or $B = 0$.

We can use this property and factoring to solve many quadratic equations.

Problem 1

Solve $x^2 - 2x - 15 = 0$.

Solution

Step 1
Factor $x^2 - 2x - 15$. We obtain $(x + 3)(x - 5) = 0$. We now have the product of two factors equal to zero. Consequently, at least one factor is zero.

Step 2

Set each factor equal to zero.
$$x + 3 = 0 \quad \text{or} \quad x - 5 = 0$$

Step 3

Solve the equations in step 2.
$$x + 3 = 0 \quad \text{or} \quad x - 5 = 0$$
$$x = -3 \qquad x = 5$$
These two values are solutions of $x^2 - 2x - 15 = 0$.

Step 4

We can check each solution in the original equation.

If $x = -3$, we obtain
$$\begin{aligned} x^2 - 2x - 15 &= (-3)^2 - 2(-3) - 15 \\ &= 9 + 6 - 15 \\ &= 0 \end{aligned}$$

If $x = 5$, we have
$$\begin{aligned} x^2 - 2x - 15 &= 5^2 - 2(5) - 15 \\ &= 25 - 10 - 15 \\ &= 0 \end{aligned}$$

We can also say that -3 and 5 are **roots** of the equation $x^2 - 2x - 15 = 0$. The solution set is $\{-3, 5\}$.

Problem 2

Solve $x(3x - 7) = 6$.

Solution

We must begin by writing the equation in the form $ax^2 + bx + c = 0$.

$$\begin{aligned} x(3x - 7) &= 6 \\ 3x^2 - 7x &= 6 \\ 3x^2 - 7x - 6 &= 0 \end{aligned}$$

Step 1

Factor.

$$\begin{aligned} 3x^2 - 7x - 6 &= 0 \\ (3x + 2)(x - 3) &= 0 \end{aligned}$$

Step 2

Set each factor equal to zero. $3x + 2 = 0$ or $x - 3 = 0$

Step 3

Solve for x.

$$3x + 2 = 0 \text{ or } x - 3 = 0$$
$$3x = -2 \qquad x = 3$$
$$x = \frac{-2}{3}$$

Step 4

We can easily check the two values in the original equation. Thus, $\frac{-2}{3}$ and 3 are roots of the quadratic equation. The solution set is $\{-\frac{2}{3}, 3\}$.

There are many quadratic equations that cannot be solved by factoring. Indeed, not every quadratic expression $ax^2 + bx + c$ is factorable. Consequently, a second technique is needed to solve quadratic equations. This method will work whether or not the equation can be factored.

This second method involves a formula that is traditionally proved in intermediate algebra using a process called completing the square. The derivation of the formula can be found in any intermediate algebra textbook. We will consider this important result without its derivation.

If $ax^2 + bx + c = 0$, then $x = \dfrac{-b + \sqrt{b^2 - 4ac}}{2a}$ or $x = \dfrac{-b - \sqrt{b^2 - 4ac}}{2a}$.

We can abbreviate by writing $x = \dfrac{-b \pm \sqrt{b^2 - 4ac}}{2a}$.

This formula is called the **quadratic formula**.

Problem 3

Use the quadratic formula to solve $12x^2 - 5x - 3 = 0$.

Solution

Since the equation is in the form $ax^2 + bx + c = 0$, a = 12, b = -5, and c = -3. Observe that a is the coefficient of x^2, b is the coefficient of x, and c is the constant term.

We now substitute these values in the formula. $\quad x = \dfrac{-b \pm \sqrt{b^2 - 4ac}}{2a}$

$$x = \frac{-(-5) \pm \sqrt{(-5)^2 - 4(12)(-3)}}{2(12)}$$

$$x = \frac{5 \pm \sqrt{25 + 144}}{24}$$

$$x = \frac{5 \pm \sqrt{169}}{24}$$

$$x = \frac{5 \pm 13}{24}$$

$$x = \frac{18}{24} = \frac{3}{4} \quad \text{or} \quad x = \frac{-8}{24} = \frac{-1}{3}$$

The roots of the equation are $\frac{3}{4}$ and $\frac{-1}{3}$. The solution set is $\left\{ \frac{-1}{3}, \frac{3}{4} \right\}$.

The following problem illustrates a quadratic equation with irrational roots.

Problem 4

Use the quadratic formula to solve $3x^2 = 2 - 4x$.

Solution

We begin by writing the equation $\qquad 3x^2 = 2 - 4x.$
in the form $ax^2 + bx + c = 0.$ $\qquad 3x^2 + 4x - 2 = 0$
We now see that: $\qquad a = 3, \ b = 4, \ \text{and} \ c = -2.$

Since $x = \frac{-b \pm \sqrt{b^2 - 4ac}}{2a}$, we obtain

$$x = \frac{-4 \pm \sqrt{4^2 - 4(3)(-2)}}{2(3)}$$

$$x = \frac{-4 \pm \sqrt{16 + 24}}{6}$$

$$x = \frac{-4 \pm \sqrt{40}}{6}$$

$$x = \frac{-4 \pm 2\sqrt{10}}{6} = \frac{2(-2 \pm \sqrt{10})}{6} = \frac{-2 \pm \sqrt{10}}{3}$$

Thus, the roots of the equation are $\frac{-2 + \sqrt{10}}{3}$ and $\frac{-2 - \sqrt{10}}{3}$.

The solution set is $\left\{ \frac{-2 + \sqrt{10}}{3}, \frac{-2 - \sqrt{10}}{3} \right\}$.

Problem Set 10

Find the roots of the quadratic equations in problems 1-12 using factoring.

1. $3x^2 + 10x - 8 = 0$
2. $2x^2 - 5x - 3 = 0$
3. $5x^2 - 8x + 3 = 0$
4. $7x^2 - 30x + 8 = 0$
5. $x^2 - x = 2$
6. $x^2 + 8x = -15$
7. $3x^2 - 17x = -10$
8. $4x^2 - 11x = -6$
9. $x(x - 3) = 54$
10. $x(2x - 5) = -3$
11. $x(2x + 1) = 3$
12. $x(x - 6) = 16$

13. The product of a number and the number decreased by 8 is -15. Find the number(s).

14. The product of a number and 2 less than 7 times the number is 5. Find the number(s).

Find the roots of the quadratic equations in problems 15-24 using the quadratic formula.

15. $5x^2 + 9x + 4 = 0$
16. $12x^2 + x - 1 = 0$
17. $x^2 + 2x - 4 = 0$
18. $3x^2 - 2x - 2 = 0$
19. $4x^2 - 3x - 2 = 0$
20. $x^2 = 1 - 7x$
21. $x^2 = 1 - x$
22. $x(x - 6) = 7$
23. $x(x - 4) = 45$
24. $25x^2 + 10x = -1$

25. Study the following sequence of equations:
$(x - 5)(x + 4) = 0$
$(x - 6)(x + 5) = 0$
$(x - 7)(x + 6) = 0$
etc.
Which pairs of numbers will appear as solutions to one of the equations that eventually emerges in this sequence?
a. 12 and -11   b. 7 and -8
c. -8 and -7   d. -8 and -9

Graphing

Principles for graphing lines and related regions are discussed in this section. At the end of this section you need to be able to correctly graph equations in the form $Ax + By = C$, inequalities and the intersection of linear inequalities.

The rectangular (or Cartesian) coordinate system consists of two number lines that are perpendicular and intersect at the point 0 on both lines. Each number line is called an **axis.** The horizontal line is called the **x-axis** and the vertical line is called the **y-axis.** The point of intersection of the two axes is called the **origin.** The axes divide the plane into four regions, called **quadrants**, which are numbered I through IV in a counter-clockwise direction.

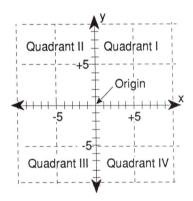

The x and y axes can be used to associate ordered pairs of numbers with points in the plane. Each point in the plane will have an ordered pair of real numbers associated with it. Locating a point in a plane is called **plotting the point.** The ability to correctly plot points is essential to the graphing process.

In an ordered pair (x,y) the **x-number indicates horizontal movement right or left.** If the x-number is positive, the point is to the right of the origin. If the x-number is negative, the point is to the left of the origin. The **y-number indicates vertical movement up or down**. If the y-number is positive, the point is above the origin. If the y-number is negative, the point is below the origin.

Problem 1

Plot the point represented by the ordered pair (-1,-2).

Solution

The point (-1,-2) is plotted by:
    1)   Starting at the origin,
    2)   Moving 1 unit left, and
    3)   Moving 2 units down.

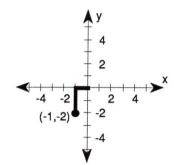

The graph at the right shows
the process used to plot (-1,-2).
The point lies in Quadrant III.

Observe that every point on the x-axis has an ordered pair (x,0). Examples are (2,0) and (-1,0). Every point on the y-axis has an ordered pair (0,y). Examples are (0,4) and (0,-2). The ordered pair associated with the origin is (0,0). A point on either axis does not lie in any quadrant. Also observe that for every ordered pair there is precisely **one** point in the rectangular coordinate system.

Let us now discuss the process for graphing an equation of the form $Ax + By = C$. Such an equation is called a **first degree equation** because the exponent of each variable is 1. Such an equation is also called a **linear equation in two variables** or a **linear equality.**

E
X
A
M
P
L
E
S

1. $2x + 3y = 7$ is a linear equation with two variables, x and y.

2. $x^2 + 2y = 9$ is not a linear equation. This is not a first degree equation because not all the exponents of the variables are 1.

3. $x = 7$ is a linear equation, but only one variable appears. To write $x = 7$ with two variables, use the fact that $0y = 0$. Thus, $x = 7$ is equivalent to $x + 0y = 7$.

The graph of a linear equation in two variables is always a straight line. Since a straight line is determined by any two points on it, it is possible to find the graph by finding any two ordered pair solutions of the equation. As a check, it is generally wise to find **three** ordered pairs of the solution set. If they lie on the same straight line, then in all likelihood the work has been done correctly, and the line is the correct graph of the equation.

In the next two problems we will see that it is possible to graph a linear equation in either of two ways.

Problem 2

Graph $x + 2y = 6$ by plotting points. The variables may be replaced by real numbers.

Solution

Three ordered pair solutions need to be found, but **any three** solutions will work. Consequently, any three numbers can be chosen to replace x, and the matching numbers for y will provide the three ordered pair solutions.

Let $x = 0$. Then, $x + 2y = 6$ gives $0 + 2y = 6$ or $y = 3$. Thus, $(0,3)$ is an ordered pair solution.

Let $x = 2$. Then, $x + 2y = 6$ gives $2 + 2y = 6$. Solving for y leads successively to $2y = 4$ and then to $y = 2$. Therefore, $(2,2)$ is another ordered pair solution.

Let $x = 4$. Then $x + 2y = 6$ gives $4 + 2y = 6$. Solving for y leads successively to $2y = 2$ and then to $y = 1$. $(4,1)$ is a third ordered pair solution for the equation.

Notice that we have completed a table of values as follows:

x	0	2	4
y	3	2	1

The three solutions, $(0,3)$, $(2,2)$ and $(4,1)$, are plotted on the graph shown at the right. Notice that all three points are on the same straight line. This line is the graph of all the solutions of $x + 2y = 6$ and represents the solution set for the equation.

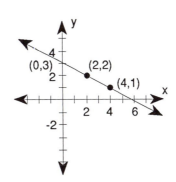

363

Algebra

It is also possible to graph a linear equation by finding only **two** points and drawing the line that contains them. The two points where the line crosses the axes are most easily found.

In the previous problem, the graph crossed the y-axis at (0,3). Thus, 3 is called the **y-intercept**. The graph crosses the x-axis at (x,0). Thus, x is called the **x-intercept**. The intercepts are useful for graphing linear equations.

To graph a linear equation using the intercepts:

1. Find where the graph crosses the x-axis by letting y = 0 and solving the equation to find (x,0).

2. Find where the graph crosses the y-axis by letting x = 0 and solving the equation to find (0,y).

3. Draw the straight line through the two points.

Problem 3

Graph 2x + 3y = 6 by first finding the intercepts.

Solution

Let y = 0.

$$2x + 3 \cdot 0 = 6$$
$$2x + 0 = 6$$
$$2x = 6$$
$$x = 3$$

The x-intercept is 3, so the graph crosses the x-axis at the point (3,0).

Let x = 0.

$$2 \cdot 0 + 3y = 6$$
$$3y = 6$$
$$y = 2$$

The y-intercept is 2, so the graph crosses the y-axis at the point (0,2). The graph is correctly drawn at the right.

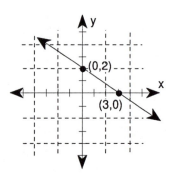

Problem 4

Graph y = -x by finding the intercepts.

Solution

Let y = 0. Then   0 = -x or x = 0. The x-intercept is 0, so the graph crosses the x-axis at the point (0,0).

Let x = 0. Then y = -0 or y = 0.

The y-intercept is also 0, so the graph crosses the y-axis also at the point (0,0).

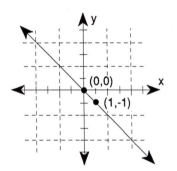

Since only one point, (0,0), of the line has been found, a second, different, point is needed. Select any value of x.

Let x = 1. Then y = -1.

The point (1,-1) is a second point on the line.

The graph of the line appears at the right.

It is possible to graph the solution set for an inequality in two variables such as x < y + 1. We will see that the solution set is a region of the plane.

Problem 5

Graph the solution set for x < y + 1.

Solution

Step 1
Graph the linear **equation** x = y + 1. The equation is the **boundary** for the graph and is obtained from the inequality by replacing the inequality symbol with an equal sign.

Any three ordered pair solutions of x = y + 1 (or simply the two intercepts) are needed. Three solutions are (0,-1), (1,0) and (2,1) because their x and y values make x = y + 1 true.

For (0,-1) 0 = -1 + 1   For (1,0), 1 = 0 + 1   For (2,1), 2 = 1 + 1

Step 2

Use the three solutions, (0,-1), (1,0), and(2,1) to graph the straight line of x = y + 1, but use a **dashed line** to indicate < rather than =. A dashed line is used because the points on the boundary line do not belong to the solution set of the given inequality. Inequalities with the symbols ≤ and ≥ would use a **solid line** because the points on the boundary line would be part of the solution set.

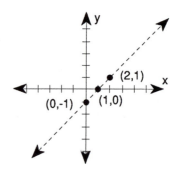

Step 3

The graph of x < y + 1 is the region above the dashed line or it is the region below it. To decide which is correct, select any ordered pair that does not lie on the straight line. Frequently (0,0) is a selection that will make this step simple. Use the selected ordered pair to test whether the given inequality is true or false.

For (0,0), x < y + 1 is 0 < 0 + 1 or 0 < 1 which is true.

Step 4

Since the point (0, 0) tested in Step 3 made the inequality true, all points on the same side of the dashed line graphed in Step 2 will also make the inequality true. The solution set of the inequality x < y + 1 is, therefore, the shaded region shown at the right.

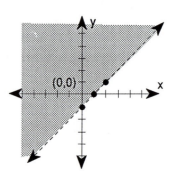

Problem 6

Graph the solution set for x ≥ y.

Solution

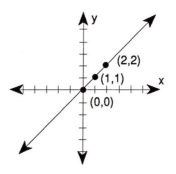

Step 1

Find any three solutions of the equation x = y. Three such solutions are (0,0), (1,1), and (2,2).

Step 2

Graph the boundary line of $x = y$ using the three solutions found in Step 1. A solid line is used because solutions of $x = y$ are also solutions of $x \geq y$.

Step 3

The graph of $x \geq y$ is the region above the line or the region below the line. To decide which region is correct, select any ordered pair for a point not on the line. The origin, (0,0), cannot be used in this case because (0,0) is a point on the line.

The point (2,3) is selected and tested in $x \geq y$. The result is $2 \geq 3$ and false. Therefore, (2,3) and all other points on the same side of the line of $x = y$ make the inequality $x \geq y$ false.

Step 4

The testing of (2,3) in $x \geq y$ indicates that the solution set of the inequality is on the opposite side of the line from (2,3). The shaded portion of the graph at the right represents the solution set. The solid line is part of this solution set.

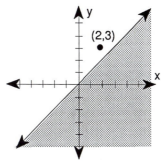

The graphs of some equations are horizontal or vertical lines. The table following describes these graphs and their related regions.

The graph of $x = c$ is:
    a line parallel to the y-axis
    and c units from it.

The graph of $x \geq c$ is:
    the region to the right of $x = c$
    and also includes the line.

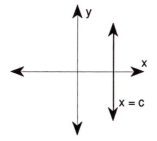 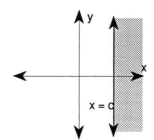

367

Algebra

The graph of x > c is:
    the region to the right of x = c,
    but not the line itself.

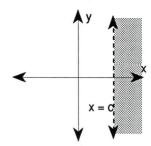

The graph of y = c is:
    a line parallel to the x-axis
    and c units from it.

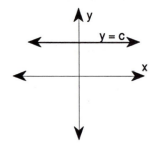

The graph of y ≥ c is:
    the region above y = c
    and also includes the line.

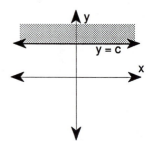

The graph of y > c is:
    the region above y = c,
    but not the line itself.

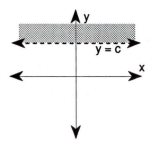

You may find it useful to remember that the graph of any equation of the form x = c is a line parallel to the y-axis and the graph of any equation of the form y = c is a line parallel to the x-axis. Furthermore the graph of x = 0 is the y-axis and the graph of y = 0 is the x-axis.

Problem 7

a.   Graph x = -2.

Solution

The graph of x = -2 is a vertical line parallel to the y-axis and 2 units to the left of it.

The graph appears at the right.

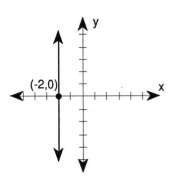

b.   Graph y = 3.

Solution

The graph of y = 3 is a horizontal line parallel to the x-axis and 3 units above it.

The graph appears at the right.

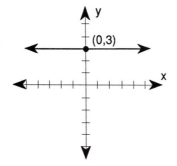

c.   Graph x < -1.

Solution

The graph of x = -1 is the line parallel to the y-axis and 1 unit to the left of it.

x < -1 is the region to the left of the line, but does not include the line.

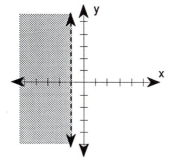

d.   Graph y ≥ -3.

Solution

The graph of y = -3 is the line parallel to the x-axis and 3 units below it.

y ≥ -3 includes the line of y = -3 and the region above it.

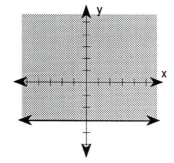

e.   Graph x ≥ -1 and y ≤ 0.

Solution

The graph numbered (1) uses a series of horizontal lines to represent the graph of x ≥ -1.

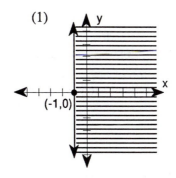

The graph numbered (2) uses a series of vertical lines to represent the graph of $y \leq 0$. The graph consists of the x-axis ($y = 0$) and the region below the x-axis ($y < 0$).

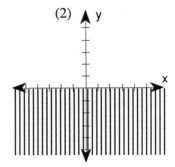

The word "and" in $x \geq -1$ and $y \leq 0$ indicates that the intersection of the two graphs is needed. This intersection is shown in the graph numbered (3).

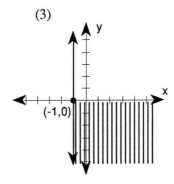

Problem 8

Identify the conditions that correspond to the shaded region.

Solution

The solid vertical line parallel to the y-axis has $x = -2$ as its equation. Since the shaded region is to the left of this line, $x \leq -2$. The dashed line parallel to the x-axis has $y = 1$ as its equation. Since the line is dashed, but the shaded region is above the line, $y > 1$. The graph shows the intersection of these two conditions. Thus, $x \leq -2$ and $y > 1$ are the conditions that describe the shaded region of the plane.

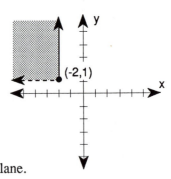

Problem 9

Graph the solution of the system of
$y \geq x + 1$ and $x \geq 0$.

Solution

Step 1

To graph $y \geq x + 1$ we must first graph
$y = x + 1$. Two solutions, $(-1,0)$ and $(0,1)$ are
found and plotted. The **solid line** through these
two points is shown at the right.

Step 2

The point $(0,0)$ is tested in $y \geq x + 1$.
Since $0 \geq 0 + 1$ or $0 \geq 1$ is false, the region
representing the solution of $y \geq x + 1$
appears as horizontal lines as shown
at the right.

Step 3

The graph of $x \geq 0$ is imposed by the use
of vertical lines.

Step 4

The set of points such that $y \geq x + 1$ and
$x \geq 0$ is the region at the right.

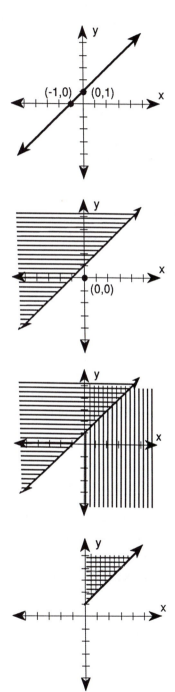

Problem 10

Graph the solution of $x \geq y$, $x \geq 3$ and $y \geq 0$.

Solution

Step 1
Graph $x \geq y$. In the figure at the right, the solution set is indicated by horizontal lines.

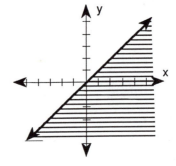

Step 2
Graph $x \geq 3$. In the figure at the right, the solution set of $x \geq 3$ is indicated by the vertical lines.

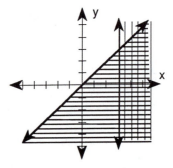

Step 3
Graph $y \geq 0$. The solution set is shown by slanted lines in the figure at the right.

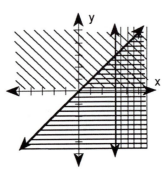

Step 4
The solution of the system is the set of points common to all three regions.

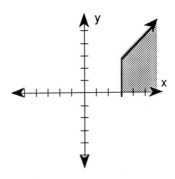

Problem 11

Which of the condition(s) listed below corresponds to the graph at the right?

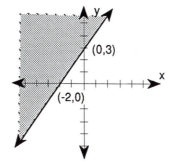

a. $x < 2$ and $y > 3$

b. $y = -x$

c. $x < 2$, $y > 3$, and $y > x$

d. $y > \frac{3}{2}x + 3$

Solution

Try to eliminate each choice.

Choice a   The graph of $x < 2$ would include all points to the left of the vertical line $x = 2$. Therefore, choice a is incorrect.

Choice b $y = -x$ is an equation. Its graph is a straight line — not a region. Choice b is incorrect.

Choice c   Again, $x < 2$ eliminates this option just as it did in choice a. Choice c is incorrect.

Choice d   Let us confirm that this is the correct option. The dashed line crosses the axes at (-2,0) and (0,3), and both pairs should be checked in the equation

$$y = \frac{3}{2}x + 3$$

$$0 = \frac{3}{2} \cdot -2 + 3 \text{ is true.}$$

$$3 = \frac{3}{2} \cdot 0 + 3 \text{ is true.}$$

Finally, test a point in the shaded region to see if it satisfies the inequality. The point (0,4) is tested in the steps below.

$$y > \frac{3}{2}x + 3$$

$$4 > \frac{3}{2} \cdot 0 + 3 \text{ or } 4 > 3 \text{ is true.}$$

The test confirms the fact that choice d is correct.

Problem Set 11

Graph:

1. $3x - 2y = 6$

2. $2x - 4y \leq 4$

3. $x < y + 1$

4. $x - 2y = -4$

5. $x < y$

6. $x < -2$

7. $y > 2$

8. $x \geq 0$ and $y \geq 0$

9. $y \geq 0$ and $y \leq 2$

10. $y \leq x + 2$ and $x \leq 0$

11. $x \geq 0$ and $x \leq 2$

12. $x - y > 2$ and $x + y > 2$

13. Which option gives the condition(s) that correspond to the shaded region of the plane shown at the right?

    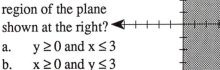

    a. $y \geq 0$ and $x \leq 3$

    b. $x \geq 0$ and $y \leq 3$

    c. $x + y \leq 3$

    d. $y \geq 0$ and $y \leq 3$

14. Which option gives the conditions that correspond to the shaded region of the plane shown at the right?

    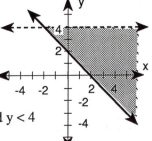

    a. $2x + 2y \geq 2$ and $y < 4$

    b. $x \geq 2$ and $y \geq 2$

    c. $x + y \geq 2$ and $x < 4$

    d. $x + y \geq 2$ and $y < 4$

15. Use three inequalities to describe the shaded region of the plane shown at the right.

    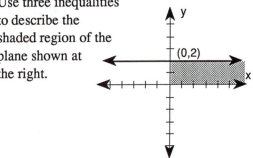

16. Which option gives the condition(s) that correspond to the shaded region of the plane shown at the right?

    a. $3x + y > 6$

    b. $3x + y < 6$

    c. $y \geq 6$ and $x \geq 2$

    d. $y > 6$ and $x > 2$

17. Which option gives the conditions that correspond to the shaded region of the plane shown at the right?

    a. $1 \leq x \leq 2$

    b. $1 \leq |x| \leq 2$

    c. $1 \leq y \leq 2$

    d. $1 \leq |y| \leq 2$

    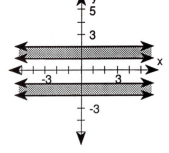

Topic 12

Solving Two Equations in Two Variables

In this topic we consider systems of equations in two variables. At the end of this section you should be able to solve such systems by the substitution and elimination methods, identifying systems that have no solution or infinitely many solutions.

We now turn our attention to solving a system of two equations in two variables. An example of such a system is:

$$2x - y = 4$$
$$3x + y = 6$$

> The solution set of a system of equations in two variables is the set of all ordered pairs of values (a, b) that satisfy every equation in the system.

Problem 1

Show that (2, 0) is a solution of the system $2x - y = 4$ and $3x + y = 6$.

Solution

Using substitution we can show that (2, 0) satisfies both equations.

$$
\begin{array}{ll}
2x - y = 4 & \qquad 3x + y = 6 \\
2(2) - 0 = 4 & \qquad 3(2) + 0 = 6 \\
\qquad\quad 4 = 4 & \qquad\qquad\quad 6 = 6
\end{array}
$$

In set notation, the solution set to this system is $\{(2, 0)\}$ – that is, the set consisting of the ordered pair (2, 0).

> The solution to a system of equations in two variables corresponds to the point(s) of intersection of their graphs.

Algebra

In the diagram at the right, we see that the graphs of $2x - y = 4$ and $3x + y = 6$ intersect at $(2, 0)$, which was precisely the solution of the system.

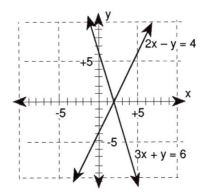

Now let us consider a strictly algebraic approach. To solve a system of equations algebraically, we want to transform the system into an equivalent system that can be solved by inspection. **Equivalent systems** of equations are systems that have the same solution set.

The following systems of equations

$$\begin{cases} 2x - y = 4 \\ 3x + y = 6 \end{cases} \quad \text{and} \quad \begin{cases} x = 2 \\ y = 0 \end{cases}$$

are equivalent because they both have the same solution set, $\{(2, 0)\}$. The system on the right can be solved by inspection.

When solving a linear system, we will begin with

$$a_1 x + b_1 y = c_1$$
$$a_2 x + b_2 y = c_2$$

and end with an equivalent system in the form

$$x = x_1$$
$$y = y_1$$

which gives the solution set explicitly as $\{(x_1, y_1)\}$. One way to transform the original system into $x = x_1$ and $y = y_1$ involves **substitution**. We can substitute for one variable in any equation either an equivalent expression for that variable obtained from another equation in the system or the actual value for the variable.

Let's see exactly what this means. In the original system that we considered,

$$2x - y = 4$$
$$3x + y = 6$$

we can work with either equation, obtain an expression for y in terms of x (or x in terms of y) and then substitute this expression for y (or for x) into the other equation. This means that we are faced with four possibilities: Solve the first equation for x in terms of y, solve the first equation for y in terms of x, solve the second equation for x in terms of y, or solve the second equation for y in terms of x. When possible, **solve for the variable that has a coefficient of 1 or -1**.

376

In the example,
$$2x - y = 4$$
$$3x + y = 6$$
we will solve for y in terms of x in the second equation. We obtain
$$y = -3x + 6$$

We now substitute $-3x + 6$ for y in the other equation. Thus $2x - y = 4$ becomes
$$2x - (-3x + 6) = 4$$
and we have transformed the system to one equation in one variable. We now solve this equation.

$$2x - (-3x + 6) = 4$$
$$2x + 3x - 6 = 4$$
$$5x = 10$$
$$x = 2$$

Since we must still find y, we should ideally substitute 2 into either of the original equations. However, since we initially solved the second equation for y in terms of x, many students prefer to use this transformation of the second equation. Thus,
$$y = -3x + 6$$
$$y = -3(2) + 6$$
$$y = 0$$

Our original system has now been transformed to
$$x = 2 \qquad y = 0$$
and we see that (2, 0) appears to be the solution of the system.

To check that (2, 0) is indeed a solution to both equations, we substitute 2 for x and 0 for y as we did in Problem 1.

Since (2, 0) satisfies both equations, we say that (2, 0) is the solution to the system and consequently the solution set is {(2, 0)}. You should get into the habit of checking ordered pair solutions to both equations of the system.

Before considering additional illustrative examples, let us summarize the steps used in the substitution method.

> **Solving Systems of Two Equations in Two Variables (x and y) by the Substitution Method**
>
> 1. Solve one equation for x in terms of y or for y in terms of x.
> 2. Substitute this expression for that variable into the other equation.
> 3. Solve the resulting equation in one variable.
> 4. Substitute the solution from step 3 into either original equation to find the value of the other variable.
> 5. Check the solution in both of the given equations.

Problem 2

Solve by the substitution method.

$$3x - 2y = -5$$
$$4x + y = 8$$

Solution

Step 1

Solve for y in the second equation, obtaining

$$y = 8 - 4x$$

Step 2

Substitute $(8 - 4x)$ for y in the first equation.

$$3x - 2y = -5$$
$$3x - 2(8 - 4x) = -5$$

Step 3

Solve this equation in one variable.

$$3x - 2(8 - 4x) = -5$$
$$3x - 16 + 8x = -5$$
$$11x - 16 = -5$$
$$11x = 11$$
$$x = 1$$

Step 4

Substitute 1 for x in either original equation.

$$4x + y = 8$$
$$4(1) + y = 8$$
$$y = 4$$

Step 5

Check that $(1, 4)$ is a solution by substituting 1 for x and 4 for y in both original equations.

$$3x - 2y = -5 \qquad\qquad 4x + y = 8$$

$$3(1) - 2(4) \overset{?}{=} -5 \qquad\qquad 4(1) + 4 \overset{?}{=} 8$$

$$3 - 8 \overset{?}{=} -5 \qquad\qquad 4 + 4 \overset{?}{=} 8$$

$$-5 = -5 \qquad\qquad 8 = 8$$

The solution set is $\{(1, 4)\}$.

The second algebraic method we will consider for solving systems of equations is the **elimination method,** sometimes called the addition method. This method is particularly useful for linear systems in which none of the variables has a coefficient of 1 or -1, such as

$$3x + 2y = 2$$
$$8x - 5y = -5$$

Using the substitution method we saw that our aim in solving a system of linear equations was to transform the system into equivalent equations of the form

$$x = x_1$$
$$y = y_1$$

explicitly giving a solution set of $\{(x_1, y_1)\}$. Consider the system

$$3x + 2y = 2 \qquad (1)$$
$$8x - 5y = -5 \qquad (2)$$

Using properties of equality, we can multiply both sides of equation (1) by the same nonzero number, say 5, and similarly multiply both sides of equation (2) by the same nonzero number, say 2, obtaining the **equivalent system**

$$15x + 10y = 10 \qquad (3)$$
$$16x - 10y = -10 \qquad (4)$$

Equations (1) and (3) are equivalent, and so are equations (2) and (4). The sum of equations (3) and (4),

$$31x = 0 \qquad (3) + (4)$$

obtained by adding left and right sides of the equations, is called a **linear combination** of the two equations. Notice that the linear combination $31x = 0$ is an equation that is free of the variable y, making it possible to solve for x, resulting in $x = 0$.

Algebra

The concept of a linear combination can be used to solve a system by choosing appropriate multipliers so that the **coefficients** of one of the variables, x or y, are **additive inverses**. This will result in an equation free of one of the variables. Let's see exactly what this means by considering an illustrative example.

Problem 3

Solve the system
$$3x + 2y = 48 \quad (1)$$
$$9x - 8y = -24 \quad (2)$$

Solution

Step 1

We must rewrite one or both equations in equivalent forms so that the coefficients of the same variable (either x or y) will be additive inverses of one another. We can accomplish this in a number of ways. If we wish to eliminate x, we can multiply each term of the first equation by -3 and then add the equations.

$$3x + 2y = 48 \quad \text{multiply by -3}$$
$$9x - 8y = -24$$

We obtain the equivalent system
$$-9x - 6y = -144 \qquad (3)$$
$$9x - 8y = -24 \qquad (4)$$

Add the corresponding members of (3) and (4). We get
$$-14y = -168 \quad \text{(a linear combination of the original equations)}$$
$$y = 12$$
which contains in its solution set any solution common to the solution sets of the original equations in the system. The solution is in the form (x, 12).

Step 2

Substitute 12 for y in either (1) or (2) to determine the x-component for the ordered pair (x, 12) that satisfies both equations. If (1) is used, we obtain
$$3x + 2y = 48$$
$$3x + 2(12) = 48$$
$$3x + 24 = 48$$
$$3x = 24$$
$$x = 8$$

If (2) is used we obtain

$$9x - 8y = -24$$
$$9x - 8(12) = -24$$
$$9x - 96 = -24$$
$$9x = 72$$
$$x = 8$$

The ordered pair (8, 12) satisfies both (1) and (2), so the solution set is {(8, 12)}.

Notice that we could have made the decision to eliminate y instead of x. To accomplish this it would have been necessary to multiply the first equation by 4 and then add the equations.

The goal of this method, then, is to transform the original system into an equivalent system so that the coefficients of one of the variables are additive inverses. We then add the equations to eliminate this variable. For this reason, we call the method the **elimination** or **addition** method.

As we noted in problem 3, we can usually make a number of decisions regarding how to eliminate a variable. This is illustrated below.

Eliminate x:

$2x + y = 2$	multiply by -1	$-2x - y = -2$
$2x - 6y = 30$	no change	$2x - 6y = 30$
	Add:	$-7y = 28$

Eliminate y:

$2x + y = 2$	multiply by 6	$12x + 6y = 12$
$2x - 6y = 30$	no change	$2x - 6y = 30$
	Add:	$14x = 42$
$x + y = 3$	no change	$x + y = 3$
$x - y = 1$	no change	$x - y = 1$
	Add:	$2x = 4$

Eliminate x:

$x + y = 3$	no change	$x + y = 3$
$x - y = 1$	multiply by -1	$-x + y = -1$
	Add:	$2y = 2$

Problem 4

Solve by the elimination method.

$$7x = 5 - 2y$$
$$3y = 16 - 2x$$

Solution

Step 1

We first arrange the system so that variable terms appear on the left and constants appear on the right. We obtain:

$$7x + 2y = 5$$
$$2x + 3y = 16$$

We can eliminate x or y. Let us eliminate y by multiplying the first equation by 3 and the second equation by -2.

$$7x + 2y = 5 \text{ multiply by 3} \qquad 21x + 6y = 15$$
$$2x + 3y = 16 \text{ multiply by -2} \qquad \underline{-4x - 6y = -32}$$
$$\text{Add:} \quad 17x \qquad = -17$$
$$x = -1$$

(This is the x-coordinate of the solution to our system.)

Step 2

Substitute -1 for x in either original equation to find the y-coordinate.

$$3y = 16 - 2x$$
$$3y = 16 - 2(-1)$$
$$3y = 16 + 2$$
$$3y = 18$$
$$y = 6$$

The solution (-1, 6) can be shown to satisfy both equations in the system. Consequently, the solution set is {(-1, 6)}.

Before considering additional illustrative examples, let us summarize the steps involved in the solution of a system of two equations in two variables by the elimination method.

Solving Systems by Elimination

1. Write the system in the form

$$a_1x + b_1y = c_1$$
$$a_2x + b_2y = c_2$$

2. If necessary, multiply either equation or both equations by appropriate numbers so that the coefficients of x or y will have a sum of zero.
3. Add the equations in step 2. The sum is an equation in one variable.
4. Solve the equation from step 3.
5. Substitute the value obtained in step 4 into either of the given equations and solve for the other variable.
6. Check the solution in both of the original equations.

Problem 5

Solve by the elimination method.
$$x - 10y = 64$$
$$3x - 14y = 90$$

Solution

Step 1
We can eliminate x by multiplying the first equation by -3 and leaving the second unchanged.

$x - 10y = 64$	multiply by -3	$-3x + 30y = -192$
$3x - 14y = 90$	no change	$\underline{3x - 14y = 90}$
	Add:	$16y = -102$
		$y = -\dfrac{102}{16}$

Reducing the fraction, the y-coordinate of our solution is $-\dfrac{51}{8}$.

Step 2

Substitution of this value back into either original equation in the system results in cumbersome arithmetic. Another option is to go back to the equations with integral coefficients and this time eliminate y instead of x.

$$x - 10y = 64 \qquad \text{multiply by -7} \qquad -7x + 70y = -448$$
$$3x - 14y = 90 \qquad \text{multiply by 5} \qquad \underline{15x - 70y = 450}$$
$$\text{Add:} \quad 8x = 2$$
$$x = \frac{2}{8} = \frac{1}{4}$$

The solution to our system is $(\frac{1}{4}, \frac{-51}{8})$ and its solution set is $\{(\frac{1}{4}, \frac{-51}{8})\}$.

As we shall now see, some systems of equations have no solution and others have infinitely many solutions.

Problem 6

Solve the system.
$$2x + 3y = 5$$
$$4x + 6y = 11$$

Solution

We will use the elimination method, eliminating x by multiplying the first equation by -2. We obtain the equivalent system

$$-4x - 6y = -10$$
$$4x + 6y = 11$$

Adding, we have $0 = 1$. Since this is a **contradiction**, the false statement $0 = 1$ indicates there is no solution to the system. The solution set for the system is the empty set, $\emptyset$. If we graph the two equations, the resulting lines would be parallel. Whenever both variables have been eliminated and the resulting statement is false, the solution set for the system is $\emptyset$. Such a system is called an **inconsistent system**.

Problem 7

Solve the system.

$$y = 3 - 2x \quad (1)$$
$$4x + 2y = 6 \quad (2)$$

Solution

Using the substitution method and substituting the expression $3 - 2x$ for y in the second equation, we obtain

$$4x + 2(3 - 2x) = 6$$
$$4x + 6 - 4x = 6$$
$$6 = 6$$

Both variables have been eliminated and the resulting statement $6 = 6$ is true. This identity indicates that the system has infinitely many solutions. Such a system is called a **dependent system**. The lines representing the graphs of the equations coincide. Any ordered pair that satisfies the first equation also satisfies the second equation. Such ordered pairs include (0, 3), (1, 1), (2, -1), and so on. Thus the solution set consists of all ordered pairs that satisfy either equation. We write this as $\{(x, y) \mid y = 3 - 2x\}$ [the set of all ordered pairs (x, y) such that $y = 3 - 2x$] or $\{(x, y) \mid 4x + 2y = 6\}$ [the set of all ordered pairs (x, y) such that $4x + 2y = 6$].

Problem Set 12

Solve each system by the substitution method.

1. $x = 2y - 5$
    $x - 3y = 8$

2. $x = 2y - 2$
    $2x - 2y = 1$

3. $4x + y = 5$
    $2x - 3y = 13$

4. $x - y = 4$
    $2x - 5y = 8$

5. $x + y = 0$
    $3x + 2y = 5$

6. $3x - 2y = 4$
    $2x - y = 1$

7. $7x - 3y = 23$
    $x + 2y = 13$

Solve each system by the elimination method.

8. $x + y = 7$
    $x - y = 3$

9. $2x + y = 3$
    $x - y = 3$

10. $12x + 3y = 15$
    $2x - 3y = 13$

11. $2x + y = 3$
    $2x - 3y = -41$

12. $x - 2y = 5$
    $5x - y = -2$

13. $4x - 5y = 17$
    $2x + 3y = 3$

14. $2x - 9y = 5$
    $3x - 3y = 11$

15. $3x - 4y = 4$
    $2x + 2y = 12$

Algebra

16. $3x - 7y = 1$
    $2x - 3y = -1$

17. $2x - 3y = 2$
    $5x + 4y = 51$

18. $4x + y = 2$
    $2x - 3y = 8$

19. $3x + 4y = 16$
    $5x + 3y = 12$

Classify each system
as inconsistent or
dependent.

20. $x + 2y - 3 = 0$
    $12 = 8y + 4x$

21. $3x + 3y = 2$
    $2x + 2y = 3$

22. $0.2x - 0.5y = 0.1$
    $0.4x = y - 0.2$

23. $2x - y = -2$
    $4x - 2y = 5$

24. $3x - 2y = -2$
    $6x - 4y = 2$

25. $\frac{x}{3} + \frac{y}{5} = 15$
    $10x + 6y = 5$

26. $x + 2y = 3$
    $4x + 8y = 12$

Chapter 4 Summary

1. **The Real Numbers**
    a. Natural (Counting) Numbers
        $\{1,2,3,\ldots\}$
    b. Whole Numbers
        $\{0,1,2,\ldots\}$
    c. Integers
        $\{\ldots,-3,-2,-1,0,1,2,3,\ldots\}$
    d. Rational Numbers
        Numbers in the form $\frac{x}{y}$ where x and y are integers, $y \neq 0$.
    e. Irrational Numbers
        Numbers that, when expressed as decimals, neither terminate nor repeat.

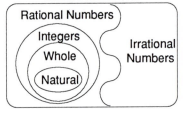

Real Numbers

2. **Properties of the Real Numbers**

    In each of the following properties, x, y, and z represent real numbers.
    a. Closure of Addition $x + y$ is a unique real number.
    b. Closure of Multiplication xy is a unique real number.
    c. Commutative of Addition $x + y = y + x$
    d. Commutative of Multiplication $xy = yx$
    e. Associative of Addition $(x + y) + z = x + (y + z)$
    f. Associative of Multiplication $(xy)z = x(yz)$

g. Identity of Multiplication $\qquad$ $x \cdot 1 = 1 \cdot x = x$

h. Identity of Addition $\qquad$ $x + 0 = 0 + x = x$

i. Inverses of Addition $\qquad$ $x + (-x) = 0$

j. Inverses of Multiplication $\qquad$ $\frac{x}{y} \cdot \frac{y}{x} = 1, x \neq 0, y \neq 0$

k. Distributive $\qquad$ $x(y + z) = xy + xz$

3. Basic Vocabulary of Number Theory

a. Let a and b represent integers. If there exists an integer c such that $a = b \cdot c$, b is a **factor** of a, b **divides** a, a is **divisible** by b, and a is a **multiple** of b.

b. Prime Number:
A natural number greater than 1 whose only positive factors are 1 and itself.

c. Composite Number:
A natural number greater than 1 which is not prime.

4. Order of Operations

a. Work all operations within grouping symbols, working within innermost grouping symbols first.

b. Work all multiplication and division from left to right.

c. Work all addition and subtraction from left to right.

5. Operations With Square Roots

a. Addition-Subtraction
If possible, simplify each radical expression. Then combine like terms.

b. Multiplication
Use the fact that $\sqrt{a} \cdot \sqrt{b} = \sqrt{ab}$ (a and b are non-negative).

c. Division
Use the fact that $\frac{\sqrt{a}}{\sqrt{b}} = \sqrt{\frac{a}{b}}$ (a and b are non-negative and $b \neq 0$.)

d. Rationalization of the Denominator
If possible, simplify the radical expression in the denominator. Multiply numerator and denominator by the radical expression in the denominator.

Algebra

6. Definitions involving Exponents

a. x^n means that x is used as a factor n times, where n is a counting number greater than or equal to 1.

b. $x^1 = x$ c. $x^0 = 1, x \neq 0$ d. $x^{-a} = \dfrac{1}{x^a}$

7. Laws of Exponents

a. $x^a \cdot x^b = x^{a+b}$ b. $\dfrac{x^a}{x^b} = x^{a-b}, \; x \neq 0$ c. $(x^a)^b = x^{ab}$

d. $(xy)^a = x^a y^a$ e. $\left(\dfrac{x}{y}\right)^a = \dfrac{x^a}{y^a}, \; y \neq 0$

8. Scientific Notation

a. The original number is written as a product of a decimal number greater than or equal to 1, but less than 10, and a power of ten.

b. The first two laws of exponents are used to perform multiplication and division problems in scientific notation. The base is always 10.

9. Principles Used to Solve Equations

a. $a = b$ if and only if $a + c = b + c$.
The same real number can be added to or subtracted from both members of an equation.

b. $a = b$ if and only if $ac = bc, \; c \neq 0$.
The same non-zero real number can multiply or divide both members of an equation.

c. Some quadratic equations (equations of the form $ax^2 + bx + c = 0$, where $a \neq 0$ and a, b, and c are real numbers) can be solved by factoring, using the property that if a product is zero, then at least one of the factors is zero. If $AB = 0$, then $A = 0$ or $B = 0$.

d. All quadratic equations can be solved using the quadratic formula in which
$$x = \frac{-b \pm \sqrt{b^2 - 4ac}}{2a} \; .$$

10. Principles Used to Solve Inequalities

a. $a > b$ if and only if $a + c > b + c$.
The same real number can be added to or subtracted from both members of an inequality.

b. $a > b$ if and only if $ac > bc$ and $c > 0$.
The same positive real number can multiply or divide both members of an inequality without affecting the direction of the inequality.

c. $a > b$ if and only if $ac < bc$ and $c < 0$.
The same negative real number can multiply or divide both members of an inequality, reversing the direction of the inequality.

11. Solving Verbal Problems

a. Represent the unknown quantity by some variable, usually x.
b. If there are additional unknown quantities, if possible represent these in terms of x.
c. Formulate an equation expressing the given verbal relationships.
d. Solve the equation.
e. Consecutive integer problems can be solved by representing the integers by x, x + 1, x + 2, and so on. Consecutive even or consecutive odd integers are represented by x, x + 2, x + 4, and so on.
f. If t represents the tens digit and u the units digit of a two-digit number, t + u is the sum of the digits and 10t + u is the number.

12. Principle For Working With Proportions

If $\frac{a}{b} = \frac{c}{d}$, $b \neq 0$, $d \neq 0$, then $a \cdot d = b \cdot c$.

13. Variation

a. $y = kx$ translates as y varies directly as x or y is proportional to x.

b. $y = \frac{k}{x}$ translates as y varies inversely as x or y is inversely proportional to x.

14. Graphing

a.   The graph of $Ax + By = C$ ($A \neq 0$ and $B \neq 0$) is a line that is neither horizontal nor vertical. The equation can be graphed by finding the x-intercept (set $y = 0$) and the y-intercept (set $x = 0$) and then drawing the straight line through these two points. If these points are both the origin, another point is necessary to graph the equation.

b. $x = C$ has a vertical line as its graph.

c. $x = 0$ has the y-axis as its graph.

d. $y = C$ has a horizontal line as its graph.

e. $y = 0$ has the x-axis as its graph.

15. Solving Two Equations in Two Variables (x and y)

a.   The substitution method works well when one of the variables has a coefficient of 1. Solve for this variable in terms of the other variable and substitute this expression into the other equation.

b.   The elimination method involves adding the equations in order to eliminate a variable. It is often necessary to multiply one or both equations by a nonzero number to create the situation where coefficients of a variable are additive inverses.

c.   If either method results in a contradiction, such as $0 = 3$, the system has no solution and is called inconsistent. The solution set is $\emptyset$.

d.   If either method results in a statement of the form $a = a$, such as $3 = 3$, the system has infinitely many solutions and is called dependent.

Sample Examination – Algebra

1. Which statement illustrates the commutative property of multiplication?
   a. $c + (a \cdot b) = c + (b \cdot a)$
   b. $(a + b) \cdot 5 = a(5) + b(5)$
   c. $a + b = b + a$
   d. $a(8) = a(3 + 5)$
   e. None of these

2. Which statement illustrates the associative property of addition?
   a. $[a + (b + c)] + d = a + [(b + c) + d]$
   b. $(a \cdot b) \cdot c = a \cdot (b \cdot c)$
   c. $(a + b) + c = a + (c + b)$
   d. $5(a + b) = 5a + 5b$
   e. None of these

3. Select the property or properties that could be used to simplify the following numerical expression in the least number of computational steps.
   $$.37(26.5) + .37(65.2) = ?$$
   a. Associative property of addition and commutative property of addition
   b. Distributive property and associative property of addition
   c. Distributive property only
   d. Distributive property and commutative property of addition

4. Select the property or properties illustrating the following relationship:
   $$3(4 + 5) = 3 \cdot 5 + 3 \cdot 4$$
   a. Associative property of multiplication only
   b. Commutative property of addition
   c. Distributive property and associative property of multiplication

   d. Distributive property only
   e. Distributive property and commutative property of addition

5. Identify the property of operations illustrated by $2(x) + 2(y) = 2(x + y)$.
   a. Commutative property of addition
   b. Associative property of addition
   c. Commutative property of multiplication
   d. Associative property of multiplication
   e. Distributive property of multiplication over addition

6. Choose the equivalent expression for $3(5) + 3(a)$.
   a. $18a$
   b. $3(5 \cdot a)$
   c. $(3)(3) + (5)a$
   d. $3(5 + a)$
   e. $(3 + 3)(5 + a)$

7. Select the multiplicative inverse for the real number $\frac{2}{3}$.
   a. $\frac{-2}{3}$ b. $\frac{3}{2}$ c. 0 d. 1
   e. None of these

8. Select the correct answer for $36 - 12 \div 4 \cdot 3 - 1$.
   a. 34 b. 28 c. 17 d. 1
   e. None of these

9. Select the correct answer for $3[\frac{2}{3} - 3(\frac{1}{3} + 1)]$.
   a. $\frac{14}{3}$ b. $\frac{-10}{3}$ c. $\frac{2}{3}$ d. -10
   e. None of these

Algebra

10. Select the correct answer
    for $4b^2 \cdot 2 \cdot 3 \div 12 + 12b^2 \div 3 - b^2$.
    a. $6b^2$ b. $4b^2$ c. $35b^2$ d. $5b^2$
    e. None of these

11. Choose the correct answer for $5\pi + 8\pi - 3$.
    a. $13\pi^2 - 3$ b. 10π
    c. $13\pi - 3$ d. $4\pi^2 - 3$
    e. None of these

12. Choose the correct answer for $-2\sqrt{5} - \sqrt{3} + \sqrt{5}$.
    a. $-3\sqrt{5} - \sqrt{3}$ b. $-2 - \sqrt{3}$
    c. $-\sqrt{5} - \sqrt{3}$ d. $-\sqrt{5} + \sqrt{3}$
    e. None of these

13. Choose the correct answer for $\sqrt{3} + \sqrt{12}$.
    a. $3\sqrt{3}$ b. $5\sqrt{3}$ c. 6   d. $\sqrt{15}$
    e. None of these

14. Choose the correct answer for $\sqrt{3} \cdot \sqrt{8}$.
    a. 24   b. $4\sqrt{6}$ c. 73   d. $2\sqrt{6}$
    e. None of these

15. Choose the correct answer for $\dfrac{9}{\sqrt{3}}$.
    a. $\dfrac{\sqrt{3}}{3}$ b. $3\sqrt{3}$ c. $9\sqrt{3}$ d. $\sqrt{3}$
    e. None of these

16. The difference of two whole numbers is an odd
    number. Which of the following statements is
    true about these two numbers?
    a. Both of the numbers may be odd.
    b. Both of the numbers may be even.
    c. Only one of the numbers is even.
    d. The sum of the numbers may be even.

17. If $x \# y * z = \dfrac{yz}{x}$, $p \# q * r = \dfrac{qr}{p}$,
    and $a \# b * c = \dfrac{bc}{a}$, then $k \# m * n =$ _____
    a. $\dfrac{km}{n}$ b. $\dfrac{kn}{m}$ c. $\dfrac{mn}{k}$ d. kmn
    e. None of these

18. Which whole number is divisible by 5 and also
    a factor of 20?
    a. 10   b. 15   c. 55   d. 60
    e. None of these

19. Find the smallest positive multiple of 8 which
    yields a remainder of 2 when divided by 5.
    a. 16   b. 24   c. 32   d. 40
    e. None of these

20. How many prime factors of 126 are also factors
    of 15?
    a. one   b. two   c. three   d. four
    e. five

21. Choose the expression equivalent to $7(x + y)$.
    a. $7xy$ b. $7x + y$
    c. $7x + 7y$ d. $7 + (x + y)$

22. Choose the expression equivalent to
    $(2a + 6b)(2a - 6b)$.
    a. $2(a + 3b)(a - 3b)$
    b. $(2a - 6b)(6b + 2a)$
    c. $8ab(2a - 6b)$
    d. $(2a + 6b)(6b - 2a)$

23. Choose the expression equivalent to $12y + 4x$.
    a. $16xy$ b. $y(12 + 4x)$
    c. $3y + x$ d. $4(x + 3y)$

24. Choose the expression equivalent to 6x + 4y.
    a. 4x + 6y
    b. 4y – 6x
    c. 10(x + y)
    d. 4y + 6x

25. Choose the equation that is not true for all real numbers.
    a. 8x + 8y = 8(x + y)
    b. 4xy(3x + y) = 4xy(3y + x)
    c. (x – y)(x + y) = (y + x)(x – y)
    d. (5x)y = 5(xy)

26. Choose the equation that is not true for all real numbers.
    a. 7ab(x – 4y) = 7abx – 28aby
    b. (5 + x) + y = 5 + (x + y)
    c. 3(xy) = (3x)(3y)
    d. 5a – 10b = -5(2b – a)

27. How many prime numbers less than 30 and greater than 10 will yield a remainder of 2 when divided by 3?
    a. five
    b. four
    c. three
    d. two

28. $36 – 12 \div 4 \cdot 3 – 2 =$
    a. 33
    b. 25
    c. 16
    d. 0

29. If f(x) = 200 + x + 0.4(200 + x), find f(50).
    a. 1250
    b. 500
    c. 350
    d. 260

30. How many factors of 12 are divisible by 3?
    a. two
    b. three
    c. four
    d. five

31. Find f(-3) given that $f(x) = 4x^2 – 5x – 6$.
    a. 45
    b. 33
    c. 15
    d. -27

32. $7 – 5(2a – b) =$
    a. 7 – 10a + 5b
    b. 7 – 10a – 5b
    c. 4a – 2b
    d. 4a – b

33. $\sqrt{36} + \sqrt{3} =$
    a. $\sqrt{39}$
    b. $6\sqrt{3}$
    c. $36\sqrt{3}$
    d. $\sqrt{3} + 6$

34. Which whole number is divisible by 3 and is also a factor of 45?
    a. 7
    b. 9
    c. 18
    d. 90

35. If $y = (2x + 3)^2$, find y when x = 5.
    a. 169
    b. 121
    c. 109
    d. 26

36. Select the equivalent expression for $(2^3)(5^2)$.
    a. 10^6
    b. (2 + 2 + 2)(5 + 5)
    c. $(2 \cdot 2 \cdot 2)(5 \cdot 5)$
    d. $(2 \cdot 5)^6$
    e. None of these

37. Select the equivalent expression for $3^2 + 4^2$.
    a. $(3 + 4)^2$
    b. $(3 + 4)^4$
    c. (3)(2) + (4)(2)
    d. (3)(3) + (4)(4)
    e. None of these

38. Select the equivalent expression for $(3^2)^3$.
    a. 9^6
    b. $3^2 \cdot 3^2 \cdot 3^2$
    c. 3^5
    d. 3^8
    e. None of these

39. Select the equivalent expression for $2(3)^2$.
    a. 6^2
    b. $2^2 \cdot 3^2$
    c. $2 \cdot 3^2$
    d. $(2 \cdot 3)^2$
    e. None of these

40. Select the equivalent expression for $3^4 – 2^2$.
    a. (3)(3)(3)(3) – (2)(2)
    b. 1^2
    c. $(3 – 2)^2$
    d. (3 + 3 + 3 + 3) – (2 + 2)
    e. None of these

Algebra

41. Select the equivalent expression for $\frac{4^5}{4^2}$.
    a. 3
    b. $(4 + 4 + 4 + 4 + 4) \div (4 + 4)$
    c. 1^3 d. 4^3
    e. None of these

42. Select the equivalent expression for $\frac{4^4}{2^2}$.
    a. 2^2
    b. $(4 \cdot 4 \cdot 4 \cdot 4) \div (2 \cdot 2)$
    c. $(4 \cdot 4 \cdot 4 \cdot 4) - (2 \cdot 2)$
    d. 4^2 e.   None of these

43. Select the equivalent expression for $(5 - 3)^2$.
    a. $5^2 - 3^2$ b. $(5)(2) - (3)(2)$
    c. 2^2 d. $(5)(5)(3)(3)$
    e. None of these

44. Use scientific notation to compute
    $0.00250 \div 1,250,000$.

    a. $2 \cdot 10^{-9}$ b. $2 \cdot 10^3$
    c. $2 \cdot 10^9$ d. $2 \cdot 10^{-2}$
    e. None of these

45. Use scientific notation to compute
    $(2.1 \cdot 10^5)(1.3 \cdot 10^{-6})$.
    a. 0.273   b.   0.0273
    c. 2.73   d.   -0.273
    e. None of these

46. Select the place value associated with the
    underlined digit in 3.01$\underline{5}$6 (base ten).

    a. $\frac{1}{10^0}$ b. $\frac{1}{10^1}$

    c. $\frac{1}{10^2}$ d. $\frac{1}{10^3}$

    e. None of these

47. Study the following examples:
    $$a^2 \mathbin{\#} a^4 = a^{10} \qquad\qquad a^3 \mathbin{\#} a^2 = a^7$$
    $$a^5 \mathbin{\#} a^3 = a^{11}$$
    Select the statement that is compatible with
    the data.
    a. $a^x \mathbin{\#} a^y = a^{2x+y}$
    b. $a^x \mathbin{\#} a^y = a^{x+2y}$
    c. $a^x \mathbin{\#} a^y = a^{x+y+4}$
    d. $a^x \mathbin{\#} a^y = a^{xy+2}$

48. Study the following examples:
    $$a^5 * a^3 * a^2 = a^5 \qquad\qquad a^3 * a^7 * a^2 = a^6$$
    $$a^2 * a^4 * a^8 = a^7$$
    Select the statement that is compatible with the
    data.
    a. $a^x * a^y * a^z = a^{x+y+z}$

    b. $a^x * a^y * a^z = a^{\frac{xyz}{2}}$

    c. $a^x * a^y * a^z = a^{\frac{x+y+z}{2}}$

    d. $a^x * a^y * a^z = a^{\frac{xy}{2}+z}$

49. For r = .03, n = 4, p = 100, I = $(1.03)^4 \cdot 100$
    For r = .05, n = 6, p = 400, I = $(1.05)^6 \cdot 400$
    For r = .07, n = 5, p = 600, I = $(1.07)^5 \cdot 600$
    For r = .06, n = 7, p = 200, I = _____

    a. $(1.06)^6 \cdot 200$ b. $(1.06)^7 \cdot 200$
    c. $(1.07)^6 \cdot 200$ d. $(1.07)^7 \cdot 200$

50. Select the expanded notation for 2007.0005.
    a. $(2 \cdot 10^4) + (7 \cdot 10) + (5 \cdot 10^{-4})$
    b. $(2 \cdot 10^3) + (7 \cdot 10) + (5 \cdot 10^{-4})$
    c. $(2 \cdot 10^3) + (7 \cdot 10^0) + (5 \cdot 10^{-4})$
    d. $(2 \cdot 10^8) + (7 \cdot 10^5) + (5 \cdot 10^1)$

51. Select the numeral for
    $(5 \cdot 10^3) + (1 \cdot 10) + (7 \cdot 10^{-2})$.
    a. 51.7   b.   5001.007
    c. 5010.007   d.   5010.07

52. Select the numeral for $(2 \times \frac{1}{10}) + (2 \times \frac{1}{10^4})$.
    a. 0.02002
    b. 0.20020
    c. 0.20002
    d. 2.00002

53. Choose the expression that is equivalent to $6y^3(y^3z^8)$.
    a. $7y^3z^8$
    b. $6y^3(z^3y^8)$
    c. $6y^9z^8$
    d. $6(y^3z^4)^2$

54. Choose the expression that is equivalent to $4xy^2(5x + y^4)$.
    a. $20x^2y^2 + 4xy^8$
    b. $4xy^2(5y^4 + x)$
    c. $4xy^6 + 20x^2y^2$
    d. $(4xy^2 + 5x)y^4$

55. Choose the statement that is not true for all non-zero real numbers.
    a. $a^3 + b^3 = (a + b)^3$
    b. $(b^2)^3 = b^2 \cdot b^2 \cdot b^2$
    c. $\frac{(4b^2)2}{2b} = 8b^3$
    d. $(7x^3)y^7 = 7(x^3y^7)$

56. $4 + 2 \cdot 5b - \frac{2(3b)2}{2b} =$
    a. $b + 4$
    b. $21b$
    c. $19b + 4$
    d. $4 + 7b$

57. If $21 - (13 - 2x) = 16 - (13x - 7)$, then
    a. $x = \frac{1}{11}$
    b. $x = -\frac{15}{11}$
    c. $x = \frac{15}{11}$
    d. $x = 1$

58. If $3(2b - 1) \geq 9b - 15$, then
    a. $b \geq 4$
    b. $b \leq 4$
    c. $b \leq \frac{14}{3}$
    d. $b \leq \frac{6}{5}$

59. If $2[x - 3(2x - 1)] = x - 2$, then
    a. $x = -\frac{4}{11}$
    b. $x = -\frac{8}{11}$
    c. $x = \frac{5}{11}$
    d. $x = \frac{8}{11}$

60. If $y \geq y - (6 - 2y)$, then
    a. $y \leq 3$
    b. $y \geq 3$
    c. $y \leq -3$
    d. $y \geq -3$

61. Choose the inequality equivalent to $-4y - 4 > 6$.
    a. $-4y > 10$
    b. $-4y < 10$
    c. $-4y > 2$
    d. $-4y < 2$

62. Choose the inequality equivalent to $-3x < -12$.
    a. $x < -4$
    b. $x > -4$
    c. $x < 4$
    d. $x > 4$

63. Choose the equation equivalent to $4x - 7 = 3x - 9$.
    a. $4x = 3x - 16$
    b. $7x - 7 = -9$
    c. $x - 7 = -9$
    d. $4x + 9 = 3x - 7$

64. Choose the inequality equivalent to $-12 < x - 5 < 9$.
    a. $-17 < x < 14$
    b. $-7 > x > 14$
    c. $-7 < x < 14$
    d. $-17 < x < 4$

65. If $y < 0$, then $y^3 < xy^2 + y$ is equivalent to which of the following?
    a. $y^2 > xy + 1$
    b. $y^2 < xy + 1$
    c. $y^2 > xy + y$
    d. $y^2 < xy + y$

66. Identify the symbol that should be placed in the brackets to form a true statement.
    $$-\frac{5}{6} \; [\;] -0.1$$
    a. $=$
    b. $>$
    c. $<$

67. Identify the symbol that should be placed in the brackets to form a true statement.
    $$4.12[\;] \sqrt{15}$$
    a. $=$
    b. $>$
    c. $<$

68. Identify the symbol that should be placed in the brackets to form a true statement.

$$2.6\overline{8} \ [\ ] \ 2.\overline{68}$$

a. $=$ b. $>$ c. $<$

69. Which is a linear factor of the following expression?

$$8x^2 - 22x + 15$$

a. $2x - 5$ b. $4x - 5$
c. $8x - 3$ d. $4x + 3$

70. Find the correct solutions to this equation:
$4x^2 = 8x - 1$

a. $1 + \sqrt{3}$ and $1 - \sqrt{3}$

b. $\dfrac{2 + \sqrt{3}}{2}$ and $\dfrac{2 - \sqrt{3}}{2}$

c. $1 + 4\sqrt{3}$ and $1 - 4\sqrt{3}$

d. $\dfrac{-2 + \sqrt{3}}{2}$ and $\dfrac{-2 - \sqrt{3}}{2}$

71. Find the correct solutions to this equation:
$6y^2 = 7y + 3$

a. $\dfrac{7 + \sqrt{120}}{12}$ and $\dfrac{7 - \sqrt{120}}{12}$

b. $\dfrac{-7 + \sqrt{120}}{12}$ and $\dfrac{-7 - \sqrt{120}}{12}$

c. $\dfrac{3}{2}$ and $-\dfrac{1}{3}$

d. $-\dfrac{3}{2}$ and $\dfrac{1}{3}$

72. Which of the following has/have $\frac{1}{4}$ as a solution?

i. $y^2 = \dfrac{1}{8}$ ii. $5x - \dfrac{5}{4} = 0$ iii. $8y - 2 \le 0$

a. i only b. ii only
c. iii only d. ii and iii only

73. Which of the following has/have (-2) as a solution?

i. $2x - 4 = 0$ ii. $(x + 4)(x + 2) < 0$
iii. $3x^2 + 5x + 6 = 8$

a. i only b. ii only
c. iii only d. ii and iii only

74. The difference between two numbers is 7 and their product is 120. What equation can be used to find one of the numbers x?

a. $x(x - 7) = 120$ b. $x(7 - x) = 120$
c. $x - (x - 7) = 120$
d. $x + (x - 7) = 120$

75. The sum of three consecutive odd integers is five more than twice the middle integer. Select the equation that can be used to find x, the smallest integer.

a. $x + (x + 2) + (x + 4) = 2(x + 2) + 5$
b. $x + (x + 2) + (x + 4) + 5 = 2(x + 2)$
c. $x + (x + 1) + (x + 2) = 2(x + 1) + 5$
d. $x + (x + 1) + (x + 2) + 5 = 2(x + 1)$

76. Choose the algebraic description that is equivalent to the verbal description: For any three consecutive positive integers, the cube of the middle integer is greater than the product of the smallest integer, x, and the largest integer.

a. $(x + 2)^3 > x(x + 1)$
b. $x^3 + 1 > x(x + 2)$
c. $(x + 1)^3 > x^2 + 2x$
d. $(x + 1)(x + 2) > x^3$

77. A two-digit positive integer is equal to 5 times the sum of its digits. If t represents the tens digit and u the units digit, which equation is equivalent to this verbal description?

a. $5(10t + u) = t + u$
b. $tu = 5(t + u)$
c. $10t + u = 5(t + u)$
d. $5tu = t + u$

78. The tens digit of a two-digit number is 3 more than the units digit. If the number itself is 21 times the units digit, what equation can be used to find t, the tens digit?
    a. $10(t + 3) + (t - 3) = 21t$
    b. $10t + (t - 3) = 21(t - 3)$
    c. $10(t + 3) + (t - 3) = 21$
    d. $10t + (t - 3) = 21$

79. Jerry spends 45% of his monthly income on housing. One particular month he spent $3,150 on housing. What was his income that month?
    a. $1,417.50   b. $8,000.00
    c. $10,150.00
    d. The correct answer is not given.

80. 32 is 60% of what number?
    a. 1.92   b. 19.2
    c. $53.\overline{3}$ d. 192

81. Two machines can complete 9 tasks every 6 days. Let t represent the number of tasks these machines can complete in a 30-day month. Select the correct statement of the given condition.
    a. $\dfrac{6}{9} = \dfrac{t}{30}$ b. $\dfrac{t}{9} = \dfrac{6}{30}$
    c. $\dfrac{t}{6} = \dfrac{9}{30}$ d. $\dfrac{9}{6} = \dfrac{t}{30}$

82. A seamstress can sew 3 dresses in 2 days. An assistant works half as fast. In how many days can the assistant sew 9 dresses?
    a. 3   b. 6   c. 9   d. 12

83. A forest service catches, tags, and then releases 19 bears back into a park. Two weeks later they select a sample of 156 bears and find that 13 of them are tagged. Assuming that the ratio of tagged bears in the sample is proportional to the actual ratio in the park, approximately how many bears are in the park?
    a. 114   b. 200   c. 228   d. 456

84. The lift of an airplane wing varies directly as the square of its width. A wing whose width is 5 inches has a lift of 35 pounds. Find the lift when the wing's width is 20 inches.
    a. 70 pounds   b. 140 pounds
    c. 540 pounds   d. 560 pounds

85. The number of pens sold varies inversely as the price per pen. If 4,000 pens are sold at a price of $1.50 each, how many pens will be sold at a price of $1.20?
    a. 2,000   b. 3,000
    c. 5,000   d. 6,000

86. Which shaded region identifies the portion of the plane in which $x \geq 2$ and $y \leq 0$?
    a. 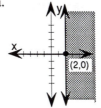   b.

    c. 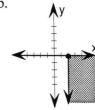   d.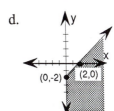

Algebra

87. Which option gives the condition(s) that correspond(s) to the shaded region of the plane illustrated at right?

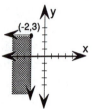

   a. $x \le -2$ and $y \le -3$
   b. $x \ge -2$ and $y \le 3$
   c. $x \le -2$ and $y \le 3$
   d. $x \ge -2$ and $y \le -3$

88. Which option gives the condition(s) that correspond(s) to the shaded region of the plane illustrated at the right?

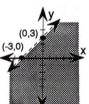

   a. $y < x + 3$
   b. $y \le x + 3$
   c. $x < 3$ and $y > 3$
   d. $x < 3$, $y > 3$, and $y > x$

89. Identify the conditions which correspond to the shaded region of the plane.

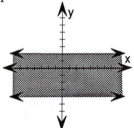

   a. $x \ge -4$ and $x \ge 2$
   b. $y \ge -4$ and $y \ge 2$
   c. $-4 \le x \le 2$
   d. $-4 \le y \le 2$

90. Choose the correct solution set for the system of linear equations.
$$y = 4x - 5$$
$$5x - y = 11$$
   a. $\{(-6, -41)\}$ b. $\{(6, 19)\}$
   c. $\{(\frac{2}{3}, \frac{-23}{3})\}$ d. $\emptyset$

91. Choose the correct solution set for the system of linear equations.
$$3x - 2y = -7$$
$$2x - 5y = -12$$
   a. $\{(1, -2)\}$ b. $\{(2, -1)\}$
   c. $\{(-1, 2)\}$ d. $\emptyset$

92. Choose the correct solution set for the system of linear equations.
$$3x + y = -7$$
$$2y = -14 - 6x$$
   a. $\{(1, -10)\}$ b. $\{(2, -13)\}$
   c. $\{(x, y) \mid y = \frac{1}{2}(-14 - 6x)\}$
   d. $\emptyset$

93. Choose the correct solution set for the system of linear equations.
$$2x - 3y = 1$$
$$-4x + 6y = 5$$
   a. $\{(1, \frac{1}{3})\}$ b. $\{(\frac{1}{2}, \frac{7}{6})\}$
   c. $\{(x, y) \mid 2x - 3y = 1)\}$

   d. $\emptyset$

Appendix 1

Solved Problems in Arithmetic Involving Fractions, Decimals and Percents —A Review

Adding mixed numbers: $\quad 6\frac{1}{5} + \frac{1}{2} + 5\frac{7}{10}$

Solution

$$
\begin{aligned}
6\frac{1}{5} &= 6\frac{2}{10} \\
\frac{1}{2} &= \frac{5}{10} \\
5\frac{7}{10} &= 5\frac{7}{10} \\
\hline
&\quad 11\frac{14}{10} = 11 + 1\frac{4}{10} = 12\frac{2}{5}
\end{aligned}
$$

Subtracting mixed numbers: $\quad 6 - 2\frac{5}{7}$

Solution

$$
\begin{aligned}
6 &= 5\frac{7}{7} \\
-2\frac{5}{7} &= -2\frac{5}{7} \\
\hline
&\quad 3\frac{2}{7}
\end{aligned}
$$

Subtracting mixed numbers: $\quad 5\frac{1}{2} - 2\frac{3}{4}$

Solution

$$
\begin{aligned}
5\frac{1}{2} &= 5\frac{2}{4} = 4\frac{6}{4} \\
-2\frac{3}{4} &= -2\frac{3}{4} = -2\frac{3}{4} \\
\hline
&\qquad\qquad\quad 2\frac{3}{4}
\end{aligned}
$$

Multiplying mixed numbers: $\quad 3\frac{1}{3} \times 1\frac{3}{4}$

Solution $\quad 3\frac{1}{3} \times 1\frac{3}{4} = \frac{10}{3} \times \frac{7}{4} = \frac{5}{3} \times \frac{7}{2} = \frac{35}{6} = 5\frac{5}{6}$

Dividing mixed numbers: $\quad 1\frac{2}{3} \div 6\frac{2}{3}$

Solution $\quad 1\frac{2}{3} \div 6\frac{2}{3} = \frac{5}{3} \div \frac{20}{3} = \frac{\overset{1}{\cancel{5}}}{\underset{1}{\cancel{3}}} \times \frac{\overset{1}{\cancel{3}}}{\underset{4}{\cancel{20}}} = \frac{1}{4}$

Appendix 1

Adding decimal numerals: Add 1.7, 0.039, 93, and 0.13.

Solution   1.7   Attach zeros.   1.700
              0.039   0.039
              93.   93.000
              0.13   0.130
                                          94.869

Subtracting decimal numerals: Subtract 0.834 from 2.

Solution   2.000   Check: 1.166
             − 0.834   + 0.834
               1.166   2.000   Correct

Multiplying decimal numerals: 1.4 x 0.009

Solution   1.4   1 decimal place
               x 0.009   3 decimal places
                .0126   4 decimal places in the product

Dividing decimal numerals: 2.8 ÷ 0.0004

Solution   7 0 0 0.   = 7,000.0 = 7,000
                   .0004) 2.8 0 0 0.
                            2 8
                              0

Converting a fraction to a decimal: Change $\frac{3}{7}$ to its decimal form.

Solution   .428571428 … (blocks of digits repeat forever)
                   7) 3.000000000

                   Write the answer as $0.\overline{428571}$ with a line over the block of digits
                   that have an infinite repeating pattern.

To round a decimal:

1. Look at the digit to the right of the place the rounding is to occur.
2. If this digit is 5 or greater, add 1 to the place-digit to be rounded and drop the digits to the right.
3. If the digit is less than 5, drop the digits to the right and do not change the digit in the place to be rounded.

Example: Round 27.93 to the nearest tenth.
Solution   27.93 rounded to the nearest tenth is 27.9 as the digit right of the 9, (3), is less than 5.

Example: Round 18.76 to the nearest tenth.
Solution   18.76 rounded to the nearest tenth is 18.8 as the digit right of the 7, (6), is greater than or equal to 5.

Example: Round 2.0585 to the nearest thousandth.
Solution   2.0585 rounded to the nearest thousandth is 2.059 as the digit right of the digit 8, (5), is greater than or equal to 5.

To change a decimal to a percent:

1. Put the decimal point two places to the right in the new numeral.
2. Add a % sign.

Examples:
$$0.83 = 83\%$$
$$0.06 = 6\%$$
$$0.009 = 0.9\%$$
$$1 = 100\%$$
$$0.6 = 60\%$$

Appendix 1

To convert a percent to a decimal:

1. Put the decimal point two places to the left in the new numeral.
2. Drop the % sign.

Examples:

$$23\% = 0.23$$
$$2\% = 0.02$$
$$1.7\% = 0.017$$
$$37.3\% = 0.373$$
$$3\tfrac{4}{5}\% = 3.8\% = 0.038$$
$$8\tfrac{1}{4}\% = 8.25\% = 0.0825$$

To change a fraction to a percent:

1. Change the fraction to a decimal by dividing the denominator into the numerator. Add a decimal point and zeros as needed.
2. Change the decimal to a percent.

Examples:

$$\tfrac{3}{4} = 0.75 = 75\%$$
$$\tfrac{1}{5} = 0.2 = 20\%$$
$$\tfrac{37}{1000} = 0.037 = 3.7\%$$

To change a percent to a fraction: Put the percent over 100, drop the % sign and simplify if possible.

Example: Write $8\tfrac{1}{3}\%$ as a fraction.

Solution $8\tfrac{1}{3}\% = \dfrac{8\tfrac{1}{3}}{100} = \dfrac{\overset{1}{\cancel{25}}}{3} \times \dfrac{1}{\underset{4}{\cancel{100}}} = \dfrac{1}{12}$

Example: Write 30% as a fraction.

Solution $30\% = \dfrac{30}{100} = \dfrac{3}{10}$

402

Example: Write 107.6% as a fraction.

Solution $107.6\% = \frac{107.6}{100} = 1.076 = 1\frac{76}{1000}$

Solving percent increase (or decrease) problems:
1.   Set up a fraction equal to the amount of increase (or decrease) divided by the original amount.
2.   Change the fraction to a percent.

Example: If 20 is increased to 25, what is the percent increase?

Solution $\frac{\text{Amount of increase}}{\text{Original amount}} = \frac{5}{20} = \frac{1}{4} = 25\%$

Operations with signed numbers

a.   Addition: The sum of two numbers with like signs has the same sign as the two numbers and is found by adding their absolute values. If the two numbers have unlike signs, the sign of the sum is the sign of the original number having the larger absolute value and is found by subtracting the smaller absolute value from the larger absolute value.
b.   Subtraction: By definition, $a - b = a + (-b)$. To subtract real numbers, change the sign on the second number and follow the appropriate addition rule.
c.   Multiplication and division of two real numbers: The product or quotient of two numbers with the same sign is positive. The product or quotient of two numbers with different signs is negative. The multiplication or division is performed by multiplying or dividing the absolute values of the two numbers and giving the answer the proper sign.
d.   A multiplication problem involving an even number of negative factors has a positive product and one with an odd number of negative factors has a negative product.

Examples

$$(-6) + (2\tfrac{5}{7}) = -3\tfrac{2}{7}$$

$$(-5\tfrac{1}{2}) + (-2\tfrac{3}{4}) = (-5\tfrac{2}{4}) + (-2\tfrac{3}{4}) = -7\tfrac{5}{4} = -8\tfrac{1}{4}$$

$$(3\tfrac{1}{3})(-1\tfrac{3}{4}) = -5\tfrac{5}{6}$$

$$(-1\tfrac{2}{3}) \div (-6\tfrac{2}{3}) = \tfrac{1}{4}$$

Practice Problems in Arithmetic (Answers appear in the answer section.)

1. $5 + 2\frac{2}{3} + \frac{7}{10}$

2. $6\frac{1}{2} + 5\frac{2}{3} + 8\frac{3}{5}$

3. $18 - 3\frac{9}{11}$

4. $18\frac{3}{4} - 5\frac{5}{8}$

5. $9\frac{1}{10} - 5\frac{3}{4}$

6. $25 \times 2\frac{3}{10}$

7. $2\frac{2}{3} \times 2\frac{1}{4} \times \frac{1}{2}$

8. $\frac{7}{10} \div 6$

9. $19\frac{1}{2} \div 6\frac{1}{4}$

10. Add: 0.8, 3, 7.415 and 13.25

11. $0.02 - 0.0008$

12. $27.8 - 15.379$

13. 0.379×0.562

14. 0.803×2.05

15. $16 \div 0.004$

16. $15.6 \div 0.0013$

17. Change $\frac{3}{8}$ to a decimal.

18. Change $\frac{7}{18}$ to a decimal.

19. Round 3.6449 to the nearest tenth.

20. Round 8.6949 to the nearest hundredth.

21. Round 23.896 to the nearest hundredth.

22. Round 8.6945 to the nearest thousandth.

23. Round 317.2358 to the nearest thousandth.

24. Change to percents:
    a. 0.7295   b. 0.006
    c. 2.3

25. Change to decimals:
    a. 23%   b. 0.9%   c. 97.4%   d. $4\frac{1}{8}\%$

26. Change to percents:
    a. $\frac{4}{5}$ b. $\frac{1}{3}$ c. $\frac{7}{8}$

27. Write each of the following as a fraction in simplest terms:
    a. 75%   b. $12\frac{1}{2}\%$ c. $87\frac{1}{2}\%$ d. $66\frac{2}{3}\%$

28. An electronics distributor ordered 25 calculators which cost $30 each. Each calculator was to be sold for $35. If the distributor returned 3 calculators, for which $2 charge per calculator had to be paid, find the distributor's profit.

29. Juan has $250 to purchase new tires. Tire prices are:
    Brand A: $42 each + 5% tax
    Brand B: $65 each + 5% tax
    If Juan purchases two Brand A tires and two Brand B tires, how much change will he receive?

30. George weighed 180 pounds. After dieting, his weight went down to 162 pounds. What was the percent of decrease in his weight?

31. A small private school employs ten teachers with salaries ranging between $500 and $800 per week. Which of the following values could be a reasonable estimate of the semimonthly payroll for the teachers?
    a. $6,500 b. $10,000
    c. $13,000 d. $16,000

32. Use the circle graph at the right. If Marion earns $2000 per month, how much more does she spend on food than on bills?

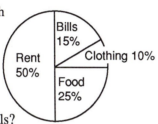

33. A team played 70 games and won 60% of the games. If there are 40 games left, how many of these 40 games must they win to ultimately win 70% of all the games they played?

34. An insurance company pays 100% emergency room treatment, 80% doctor bills with $100 deductible, and 90% medication. Barbara submitted the following bills: $125 emergency room, $175 doctor bills, and $95 medication. What does the insurance company pay?

35. Pencils were purchased at 65¢ per dozen and sold for 3 pencils for 20¢. Find the profit on 8 dozen pencils.

36. Maintaining weight can be accomplished by daily consumption of calories equal to 15 times one's body weight. Reduction of calorie intake by $\frac{1}{3}$ enables a person to lose one pound per week. If Liz weighs 200 pounds, how many calories should she consume on a daily basis in order to lose 52 pounds for the year?

37. $\frac{47}{1000} =$
    a. 0.047% b. 0.47%
    c. 4.7% d. 47%

38. 206.7% =
    a. $20\frac{67}{100}$ b. $20\frac{67}{1000}$
    c. $2\frac{67}{100}$ d. $2\frac{67}{1000}$

39. An item purchased for $2,000 is worth $650 after ten years. Assuming that the value depreciates linearly (steadily), what was it worth at the end of the seventh year?

40. The Sanchez home has an assessed valuation of $78,500. The tax rate is $3.40 per $100. A 3% discount is allowed if the tax is paid within the first quarter of the year. How much tax will Ms. Sanchez pay if she takes advantage of the discount?

41. Each day a small business owner sells 20 pizza slices at $1.50 per slice and 40 sandwiches at $2.50 each. If business expenses come to $60 per day, what is the owner's profit for a ten-day period?

42. A restaurant bill came to $60 before a 5% tax was added. How much money is saved by leaving a tip of 15% on the bill before the tax is added instead of 15% on the final bill inclusive of the tax?

43. Last year, Sarah Rosenberg earned $17,000 and her son Josh earned $7,000. Their total yearly income was $28,000. Based on the assumption that their only other source of income was from interest on Sarah's saving account, what fractional part of their income was from interest on the account?

44. A store received 200 containers of juice to be sold by April 1. Each container cost the store $0.75 and sold for $1.25. The store signed a contract with the manufacturer in which the manufacturer agreed to a $0.50 refund for every container not sold by April 1. If 150 containers were sold by April 1, how much profit did the store make?

45. At a masquerade party the judges eliminate $\frac{1}{4}$ of the eligible contestants after each half hour. If 256 contestants were present at the start of the party, how many would still be eligible for a prize after two hours?

46. A plant nursery offers free delivery on orders of $50 or more to one address. The nursery charges $5 for deliveries under $50. A delivery truck left with three palms for $100 each, four oak trees for $60 each, and six ficus trees for $40 each. Each tree was delivered to a different address. If the delivery person can keep 12% of all money collected, how much was kept after all trees were delivered?

47. Calculators costing $20 each are reduced by 30%. At the reduced rate, what is the cost of 25 calculators?

48. Imelda travels at a constant rate, traveling 110 miles at 11:45 A.M., 125 miles at 12:15 P.M. and 140 miles at 12:45 P.M. At what time will Imelda have traveled 200 miles?

49. Income tax for taxable income between $8,000 and $12,000 is $4,200 plus 38% of the excess over $8,000. How much tax must be paid on a taxable income of $9,500?

50. A motel offers the following special group rate: If 30 or less people stay at the motel, the cost per person per night is $22.75. However, for each person over the 30th, the cost per person for lodging for every participant decreases by $ .20. What is the amount spent for a group of 47 people for one night at the motel?

Appendix 2: Review Competencies Covering the Entire Text

Answers with brief explanations begin on page 424.

1. Sets A, B, C, and U are related as shown in the diagram below. Which of the following statements is true assuming none of the regions is empty?

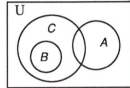

   a. All elements of set U are elements of set C.
   b. Some elements belong to all four sets A, B, C, and U.
   c. Some elements belong to A ∩ C but not to set B.
   d. Any element which is a member of set C must also be a member of set B.

2. If $3(t-1) = 2[t-3(t-2)]$, then:
   a. $t = \frac{7}{15}$ b. $t = \frac{-9}{7}$ c. $t = \frac{15}{7}$ d. $t = \frac{-7}{9}$

3. A box contains ten tennis balls, of which four are defective. If two balls are randomly selected without replacement, find the probability that at least one ball is defective.
   a. $\frac{2}{15}$ b. $\frac{1}{3}$ c. $\frac{2}{3}$ d. $\frac{13}{15}$

4. All of the following arguments have true conclusions, but one of the arguments is not valid. Select the argument that is not valid.
   a. All people who are outstanding athletes possess excellent eye-hand coordination. Only outstanding athletes are eligible for athletic scholarships. Therefore, to be eligible for an athletic scholarship, one must possess excellent eye-hand coordination.
   b. Prolonged periods of rain will damage desert plants. The cactus is a desert plant. Therefore, the cactus will be damaged by prolonged periods of rain.

   c. All multiples of 15 are multiples of 5. Twenty-one is not a multiple of 5. Therefore, 21 is not a multiple of 15.
   d. Clocks are designed to inform people of the time. Time-measuring devices are also designed to inform people of the time. Therefore, clocks are time-measuring devices.

5. For each of the statements below, determine which one(s) has/have -3 as a solution.
   i. $5x + 1 > -13$
   ii. $2y^2 + 7y = -3$
   iii. $\frac{4}{3}x - 4 = 0$
   a. i only   b. ii only
   c. iii only   d. ii and iii only

6. What is the area of the shaded region? The diameter of each small semi-circle is the radius of the larger semicircle.
   a. 25π sq. ft
   b. 50π sq. ft
   c. 75π sq. ft
   d. 100π sq. ft

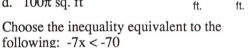

7. Choose the inequality equivalent to the following: $-7x < -70$
   a. $x < -10$ b. $x < 10$ c. $x > -10$ d. $x > 10$

8. The roots of the equation $x^2 = 4 - 4x$ are:
   a. $-2 + 4\sqrt{2}$ and $-2 - 4\sqrt{2}$
   b. $-2 + 2\sqrt{2}$ and $-2 - 2\sqrt{2}$
   c. $2 + 4\sqrt{2}$ and $2 - 4\sqrt{2}$
   d. $2 + 2\sqrt{2}$ and $2 - 2\sqrt{2}$

9. A college student can compute his or her grade point average by converting A to 4 points, B to 3 points, C to 2 points, D to 1 point, and F to 0 points. Bernie has so far accumulated 10 A's, 7 B's, 5 C's, and no D's or F's. What is his grade point average?
   a. 2.2   b. 3.1   c. 3.2   d. 22

10. To qualify for a rental lease at Lakeview-at-the-Hammocks, one must have a yearly income of at least $20,000, no more than 2 children, only 1 pet not in excess of 20 pounds, and at least $5,000 in some kind of savings. Read the qualifications of the three applicants listed below. Then identify who qualifies for the rental lease.

> Frank Martinez, single, earns $60,000 yearly, has no children, one German shepherd weighing 45 pounds, with $40,000 in a savings account.

> Dr. Selma Rubin, divorced, earns $200,000 yearly as an internist. Her three children live with her. They have no pets, and Dr. Rubin has nearly one million dollars in U.S. Govenment bonds.

> Bill and Roberta Raboid are husband and wife. Bill earns $14,000 yearly and Roberta earns $6,500 yearly. They have two cats, each weighing 11 pounds, with $6,000 in a savings account.

  a. Frank Martinez   b. Dr. Selma Rubin
  c. Bill and Roberta Raboid
  d. No one qualifies for the rental lease.

11. Select the numeral for $(2 \cdot \frac{1}{10}) + (2 \cdot \frac{1}{10^6})$.
  a. 0.020002   b. 0.200020
  c. 0.200002   d. 2.000002

12. $2[\frac{1}{2} - \frac{1}{2}(10 - 2 \cdot 3)] =$
  a. $\frac{-23}{2}$ b. -2   c. -3   d. $\frac{-3}{2}$

13. $\frac{1}{4} \cdot 12c + 6c \div \frac{1}{3} - c^2 + 4c =$
  a. $25c - c^2$ b. $9c - c^2$
  c. $25c$ d. $17c - c^2$

14. Find the median of the numbers in the list:
    5, 6, 7, 3, 7, 7, 4, 1, 3, 6

  a. 6   b. 7   c. 5.5   d. 5

15. Select the statement that is not logically equivalent to: If Sarah is in San Francisco, then she is in California.
  a. If Sarah is not in California, then she is not in San Francisco.
  b. If Sarah is in California, then she is in San Francisco.
  c. Sarah is in California when she is in San Francisco.
  d. Sarah is not in San Francisco or she is in California.

16. Select the statement that is the negation of: A Supreme Court nominee receives majority approval by the Senate or the nominee is not a judge on the Supreme Court.
  a. A Supreme Court nominee does not receive majority approval by the Senate or the nominee is a judge on the Supreme Court.
  b. A Supreme Court nominee does not receive majority approval by the Senate and the nominee is a judge on the Supreme Court.
  c. A Supreme Court nominee receives majority approval by the Senate and the nominee is a judge on the Supreme Court.
  d. If a Supreme Court nominee receives majority approval by the Senate, then the nominee is a judge on the Supreme Court.

17. The table below shows the percent of all car sales in the United States in 1979.

Manufacturer	Percent of All Car Sales
GM	46
Ford	20
Chrysler	9
AMC	2
Imports	23

If it is known that the manufacturer was not Ford or Chrysler, find the probability that the car was an import.

  a. $\frac{23}{71}$ b. $\frac{29}{71}$ c. $\frac{23}{100}$ d. $\frac{29}{100}$

Appendix 2

18. Which statement listed below is true?
   a. Opposite angles of a parallelogram are not necessarily congruent.
   b. Diagonals of a trapezoid are perpendicular.
   c. Consecutive angles of a rectangle are complementary.
   d. Adjacent sides of a rhombus have equal measure.

19. Simplify $\sqrt{36} + \sqrt{6}$

   a. $\sqrt{42}$ b. $\sqrt{6} + 6$ c. $6\sqrt{6}$ d. $7\sqrt{6}$

20. Simplify $\dfrac{12}{\sqrt{6}}$

   a. $2\sqrt{6}$ b. $\dfrac{\sqrt{6}}{2}$ c. $\sqrt{2}$ d. $\dfrac{\sqrt{72}}{6}$

21. For the following lists of numbers, the value of x represents the same type of measure of central tendency.

6,7,7,8:	x = 7
3,5,8,12:	x = 7
2,2,3,9:	x = 4

   What is the value for x in the list 1.1, 2.3, 3.8, 7.2, 8.1?
   a. 3.5   b. 3.8   c. 4.5   d. 7.0

22. Which shaded region below identifies the portion of the plane in which $x \le -1$ and $y \ge 0$?

   a.   b.
   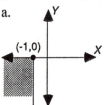   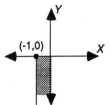

   c.   d.
   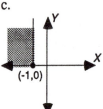   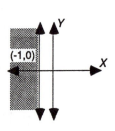

23. Which option gives the condition(s) that correspond(s) to the shaded region of the plane shown at the right?
   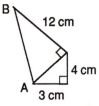
   a. $y - x < 2$
   b. $y - x > 2$
   c. $x > -2$ and $y < 2$
   d. $y > -2$ and $x < 2$

24. If $y > y - (16 - 2y)$, then:
   a. $y > 8$ b. $y < 8$ c. $y > -8$ d. $y < -8$

25. Select the statement that is the negation of the statement: If it is hot then at least one municipal pool is open.
   a. If it is not hot, then at least one municipal pool is not open.
   b. If all municipal pools are not open, then it is not hot.
   c. It is hot and no municipal pool is open.
   d. It is not hot and at least one municipal pool is not open.

26. $(-0.006) \div (-0.12) =$

   a. 0.0005%   b. 0.05%
   c. 5%   d. 50%

27. 108.7%
   a. $108\frac{7}{10}$ b. $10\frac{87}{100}$ c. $1\frac{87}{100}$ d. $1\frac{87}{1000}$

28. What is the length of AB in meters?
   a. 0.13 m
   b. 1300 m
   c. 0.17 m
   d. 1700 m

410

29. Study the examples:
$$x^9 + x^6 - x^3 = x^{18}$$
$$x^4 + x^6 - x^2 = x^{12}$$
$$x^5 + x^4 - x^2 = x^{10}$$

Select the equation which is compatible with the data.

a. $x^a + x^b - x^c = x^{a+b+c}$

b. $x^a + x^b - x^c = x^{bc}$

c. $x^a + x^b - x^c = x^{\frac{ac}{b}}$

d. $x^a + x^b - x^c = x^{\frac{ab}{c}}$

30. The formula for the sales price (P) of an article with cost (C) and mark-up (M) is $P = C + MC$. What is the sales price of an object costing \$12 at a 40% mark-up?

a. \$52   b. \$492   c. \$12.48   d. \$16.80

31. Choose the equation that is not true for all real numbers.

a. $7x + 14y = 7(2y + x)$

b. $6a^2b(3x + y) = (y + 3x)6ba^2$

c. $(x - y)(x + y) = (x + y)(y - x)$

d. $(6x^3)y^2 = 6(x^3y^2)$

32. Which whole number is divisible by 5 and is also a factor of 45?

a. 9   b. 15   c. 20   d. 90

33. In 1980, Joe earned \$20,000 and spent 15% of his income on car expenses. In 1981, Joe earned \$25,000 and spent 20% of his income on car expenses. Find the percent increase in the amount that Joe spent on his car from 1980 to 1981.

a. 5%   b. $66\frac{2}{3}$%   c. 40%   d. 60%

34. Two classes each have an enrollment of 40 students. On a certain day, $\frac{4}{5}$ of one class and $\frac{7}{8}$ of the other are present. How many students are absent from the two classes?

a. 8   b. 13   c. 26   d. 67

35. Given the function defined by $f(x) = x^3 - 6x^2 - x + 2$, find f(-2).

a. -32   b. -28   c. 16   d. 20

36. On a very difficult examination, half the students scored 45%. Most of the remaining students scored 75%. However, a few students had scores of 95% or better. Which of the following is true about this distribution?

a. The mean is less than the median.

b. The mean is greater than the median.

c. The mean and the median have identical values.

d. The mode is greater than the median.

37. Which one of the following is false for the accompanying figure?

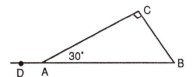

a. $(AC)^2 + (BC)^2 = (AB)^2$

b. $m \angle DAC = m \angle ABC + 90°$

c. $\triangle ABC$ is right and scalene.

d. $m \angle ABC \neq 60°$

38. A linear factor of the expression $8x^2 - 14x + 3$ is:

a. $2x - 3$ b. $2x + 3$ c. $4x + 1$ d. $8x + 3$

39. Use the table below to answer this question.

Standard deviations above mean	Proportion of area between mean and indicated standard deviation above mean
.00	.000
.25	.099
.50	.192
.75	.273
1.00	.341
1.25	.394
1.50	.433
1.75	.460
2.00	.477
2.25	.488
2.50	.494
2.75	.497
3.00	.499

Two hundred students took an examination having a mean of 60 and a standard deviation of 20. If the scores are normally distributed, approximately what proportion of the students scored between 30 and 85?

   a. 0.827   b. 0.866 c. 0.173   d. 0.039

40. Use scientific notation to find the answer:
$0.00073 \cdot 8{,}200{,}000 =$

   a. $5.986 \cdot 10^3$ b. $5.986 \cdot 10^2$

   c. $5.986 \cdot 10$ d. $1.55 \cdot 10^2$

41. In November, 40 people each purchased $30 worth of merchandise. In December, there were 10% fewer customers, but each customer increased their purchase by 20%. What is the change in sales from November to December?

   a. $96 increase   b. $98 increase

   c. $44 decrease   d. None of these

42. A dinner at a restaurant costs $60 before 5% sales tax was added to the bill. A customer left a tip equal to 25% of the final bill (the bill after the sales tax was added to the dinner bill). Afterwards, the customer decided that the tip should have been 25% of the dinner bill, not the final bill. What would have been saved by leaving a tip only on the dinner bill?

   a. $0.75   b. $1.25   c. $3.00   d. $5.00

43. Which statement is true for a set of scores that is normally distributed?

   a. The percent of scores above any score is equal to the percent of scores below that score.

   b. The probability of randomly selecting a score that falls between one standard deviation above or below the mean is approximately 0.68.

   c. All of the scores must fall within four standard deviations from the mean.

   d. The mean, median, and standard deviation all have the same value.

44. Study the premises below. Select a logical conclusion if one is warranted.

      All physicists are scientists. All biologists are scientists. All scientists are college graduates. Florence is a scientist.

   a. Florence is a physicist or a biologist.

   b. All biologists are college graduates.

   c. Florence is not a college graduate.

   d. None of the above is warranted.

45. All students who talk during lecture are rude. No lovable people are rude. Eubie is a lovable person. Which one of the following cannot be logically concluded from these premises?

   a. All students who talk during lecture are not lovable people.

   b. Eubie is not a student who talks during lecture.

   c. Some lovable people are students who talk during lecture.

   d. Eubie is not rude.

46. In a mathematics class consisting of 40 students, 15 students are older than 30, 11 students are majoring in business, and 5 students are business majors older than 30. If one student is selected at random, what is the probability that the selected student is older than 30 or a business major?

a. $\frac{15}{40}+\frac{11}{39}-\frac{5}{38}$ b. $\frac{15}{40}+\frac{11}{40}-\frac{5}{40}$

c. $\frac{15}{40}\cdot\frac{11}{39}-\frac{5}{38}$ d. $\frac{5}{40}+\frac{5}{40}$

47. A rectangular roof measuring 40 feet by 30 feet has a square porch 10 feet long on a side extending from it. The roof material cost is $70 for bundles covering 100 square feet and the labor cost for the roof is $275. What is the total cost of the labor and material to roof the building?

a. $345   b. $1,115   c. $1,185   d. $275

48. Five men and four women are trying out for a vocal group that will consist of two men and two women. How many different vocal groups can be selected?

a. 60   b. 20   c. 9   d. 4

49. Which one of the following is not valid?

a. If a person earns an A in finite mathematics, then that person does not miss more than two classroom lectures. Jacques missed five classroom lectures in finite mathematics. Thus, Jacques did not earn an A in finite mathematics.

b. Maggie does not have a good time when she listens to music whose lyrics are racist. At this moment Maggie is listening to a new rock album that contains racist lyrics throughout. Consequently, at this moment Maggie is not having a good time.

c. A Supreme Court nominee must receive majority approval by the Senate or the nominee is not a judge on the Supreme Court. Bork, a Reagan nominee, did not receive majority approval by the Senate. Therefore, Bork is not a judge on the Supreme Court.

d. If one is to answer question 28 correctly, then one must first find the correct length of the hypotenuse. Ana correctly found the length of the hypotenuse. Therefore, Ana got the right answer to question 28.

50. If there is a mathematics and English requirement, all college bookstores do a great business. The college bookstore at Tate College is not doing a great business. Tate College has an English requirement. What can be logically concluded?

a. Tate College has no mathematics requirement.

b. Tate College has a mathematics requirement.

c. If there is no mathematics requirement or no English requirement, some college bookstores do a great business.

d. If college bookstores do a great business, there is a mathematics and English requirement.

51. An executive decides to visit cities A, B, C, D, E, and F in random order. What is the probability that city E will be visited first, city D second, and city A last?

a. $\frac{1}{30}$ b. $\frac{1}{120}$ c. $\frac{1}{360}$ d. $\frac{1}{720}$

52. How much molten steel is needed to construct a solid spherical statue having a diameter of 6 feet?

a. 9π cubic ft   b. 36π cubic ft

c. 72π cubic ft   d. 288π cubic ft

Appendix 2

53. Suppose that a consumer protection agency wants to determine whether the citizens of Dade County think that Florida Power and Light company charges them fair rates for electricity. Which of the following is the most appropriate procedure to select an unbiased sample of Florida Power and Light company customers?
    a. Survey all the customers who pay their electric bills at Government Center in Miami on the third day of the month.
    b. Survey all Florida Power and Light customers who live in thirty randomly selected blocks within Dade County.
    c. Survey 100 individuals who are randomly selected from telephone directories of Dade, Broward and Monroe Counties.
    d. Survey a random sample of employees who work for Florida Power and Light in Dade County.

54. What is the volume of the combined cylinder and cone shown below if both have a diameter of 6 feet and a height of 3 feet?

    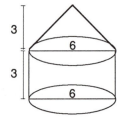

    a. 27π ft^3
    b. 36π ft^3
    c. 54π ft^3
    d. 144π ft^3

55. A building contractor is to dig a foundation 90 feet long, 60 feet wide, and 6 feet deep for an apartment's foundation. The contractor pays $12 per load for trucks to remove the dirt. Each truck holds 10 cubic yards. What is the cost to the contractor to have all the dirt hauled away?
    a. $1,440   b. $12,960
    c. $14,400   d. $129,600

56. Which one of the following is true for the accompanying figure showing four lines in the same plane?

    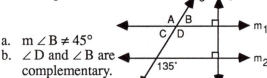

    a. m $\angle$ B $\neq 45°$
    b. $\angle$ D and $\angle$ B are complementary.
    c. m $\angle$ A $= 135°$
    d. None of the above is necessarily true.

57. Which one of the following statements is true for the triangles in the accompanying figure?
    a. m $\angle$ BAC $=$ m $\angle$ DEC
    b. $\dfrac{AC}{DC} = \dfrac{DE}{AB}$
    c. If CE $= 5$ ft, BE $= 4$ ft, and AB $= 10$ ft, the measure of DE is $5\frac{5}{9}$ ft.
    d. $\dfrac{CE}{DC} = \dfrac{AC}{BC}$

    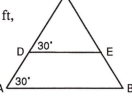

58. Which one of the following is false for the accompanying figure?

    a. m $\angle$ D $= 100°$
    b. m $\angle$ B $+$ m $\angle$ C $+$ m $\angle$ D $= 180°$
    c. m $\angle$ A $= 140°$ d. $8^2 + 8^2 = (BC)^2$

59. $\frac{1}{10}$ of a person's salary is spent for clothing, $\frac{1}{3}$ for food, and $\frac{1}{5}$ for rent. What percent of the salary is left?
    a. $46\frac{2}{3}\%$ b. $42\frac{1}{3}\%$ c. $37\frac{2}{3}\%$ d. $36\frac{2}{3}\%$

60. $2 - 5(a - 3b) =$
    a. $-3a - 9b$ b. $-3a + 9b$
    c. $2 - 5a + 15b$ d. $2 - 5a - 15b$

61. Select the symbol that shoud be placed in the box. $-\frac{5}{6}$ [ ] -0.84
   a. =   b. <   c. >

62. Study the figures shown below.

9 triangles in the interior

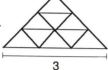

3

16 triangles in the interior

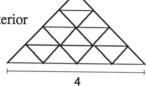

4

How many triangles are contained within the interior when the base measures 12?
   a. 36   b. 78   c. 124   d. 144

63. How many prime numbers less than 29 and greater than 17 will yield a remainder of 3 when divided by 4?
   a. one   b. two   c. three   d. four

64. An object that weighs 7 pounds on planet A weighs 11.27 pounds on planet B. Find the weight on planet B of an object that weighs 6 pounds on planet A.
   a. 3.73 lbs.   b. 9.46 lbs.
   c. 9.66 lbs.   d. 10.16 lbs.

65. $5\frac{1}{2} - 2\frac{3}{4} =$
   a. $3\frac{3}{4}$ b. $2\frac{3}{4}$ c. $2\frac{1}{4}$ d. $-2\frac{1}{4}$

66. If 420 is decreased by 13% of itself, what is the result?
   a. 126   b. 355.4   c. 365.4   d. 366.4

67. What is the area of a square, in square meters, with a side measuring 10 centimeters?
   a. $1m^2$ b. $0.4m^2$ c. $0.1m^2$ d. $0.01m^2$

68. Two common sources for finding out about new movies are television reviews and newspaper reviews. Thirty percent of American adults find out about new movies from television reviews but not newspaper reviews, while 5% find out about new movies from both television and newspaper reviews. What is the probability that a randomly selected American adult did not find out about a new movie from television?
   a. 0.25   b. 0.65   c. 0.7   d. 0.75

69. Select the statement that is the negation of the statement: All autumn days are cool.
   a. Some autumn days are not cool.
   b. Some autumn days are cool.
   c. No autumn days are cool.
   d. If it is not an autumn day, then it is not cool.

70. Select the statement that is not logically equivalent to: It is not true that both *Othello* and *Walden Pond* were written by Shakespeare.
   a. If Shakespeare wrote *Othello*, he did not write *Walden Pond*.
   b. Shakespeare did not write *Othello* or he did not write *Walden Pond*.
   c. If Shakespeare wrote *Walden Pond*, he did not write *Othello*.
   d. Shakespeare did not write *Othello* and he did not write *Walden Pond*.

71. The circle graph below shows how a student's weekday is spent. What category contains 25% of the weekday?

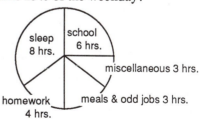

   a. School   b. Sleep
   c. Homework   d. Miscellaneous

415

72. The accompanying line graph indicates the temperature from Monday through Friday. Which of the following is true?

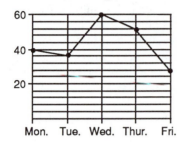

a. There is exactly one modal temperature for the five days.
b. The mean temperature for the five days is 42.2 degrees.
c. The median temperature for the five days is 60 degrees.
d. The percent increase in temperature from Tuesday to Wednesday is approximately 67%.

73. Select the rule of logical equivalence which directly (in one step) transforms statement i into statement ii.
    i. If a person studies, then that person does not fail.
    ii. If a person fails, then that person does not study.
    a. $(p \rightarrow \sim q) \equiv (q \rightarrow \sim p)$
    b. $(p \rightarrow \sim q) \equiv (\sim p \rightarrow q)$
    c. $\sim(p \rightarrow \sim q) \equiv (p \wedge q)$
    d. $(p \rightarrow \sim q) \equiv (\sim p \vee \sim q)$

74. $\frac{7}{14} =$
    a. 0.50% b. 20% c. 33.$\overline{3}$% d. 50%

75. A community offers homes in five different models, each available in four color schemes, each with or without a screened porch, and each with or without a pool. How many buying options are available?
    a. 13 b. 80 c. 120 d. 160

76. Select the conlusion that will make the following argument valid.
    If all people take exams honestly, then no supervision is needed. Some supervision is needed.
    a. Some people take exams honestly.
    b. If no supervision is needed, then all people take exams honestly.
    c. No people take exams honestly.
    d. Some people do not take exams honestly.

77. Five cans of juice cost $3. Let y be the cost of 11 cans of the same juice. Select the correct proportion reflecting the given conditions.
    a. $\frac{5}{3} = \frac{y}{11}$ b. $\frac{5}{3} = \frac{11}{y}$ c. $\frac{3}{5} = \frac{11}{y}$ d. $\frac{5}{11} = \frac{y}{3}$

78. Choose the correct solution set for the system of linear equations.
    $$6x + 5y = 9$$
    $$5x + 2y = 14$$
    a. $\{(-3, 4)\}$
    b. $\{(-4, \frac{33}{5})\}$
    c. $\{(4, -3)\}$
    d. $\emptyset$

79. After several tryouts, 20% of a football squad was discharged. The coach then had 32 players. How many players were on the squad at first?
    a. 80 b. 40 c. 39. d. 26

80. Which one of the following would not be used to describe the amount of water in an aquarium?
    a. cubic meters b. gallons
    c. liters d. square feet

81. Round 27.349 cm^3 to the nearest tenth of a cubic centimeter.
    a. 20 cm^3 b. 27.3 cm^3
    c. 27.4 cm^3 d. 30 cm^3

82. In the accompanying figure, round the measure of AB to the nearest $\frac{1}{4}$ inch.

   a. $1\frac{1}{4}$ inch   b. $1\frac{1}{2}$ inch

   c. $1\frac{7}{8}$ inch   d.   1 inch

83. Select the statement below which is logically equivalent to: Gene is an actor or a musician.
    a. If Gene is an actor, then he is not a musician.
    b. If Gene is not an actor, then he is a musician.
    c. It is false that Gene is not an actor or not a musician.
    d. If Gene is an actor, then he is a musician.

84. Ten percent of the pens that are made by a ballpoint pen manufacturer leak. If two pens are randomly selected with replacement, find the probability that neither pen leaks.

   a. $\frac{1}{100}$ b. $\frac{19}{100}$ c. $\frac{81}{100}$ d. $\frac{99}{100}$

85. The table below indicates scores on a 100-point exam and corresponding percentile ranks.

Score	Percentile Rank
90	99
80	87
70	72
60	49
50	26
40	8
30	1

What percentage of examinees scored between 60 and 80?

   a.   72%   b.   51%   c.   38%   d.   13%

86. The table below shows the distribution of the number of children in families of a community.

Number of Children	Proportion of Families
0	.35
1	.20
2	.25
3	.10
4	.08
5	.02

Which one of the following is true?
   a. The modal number of children per family is 2.
   b. The median number of children per family is 0.5.
   c. The mean number of children per family is 1.22.
   d. None of the above is true.

87. A room measures 12 feet by 15 feet. The entire room is to be covered with tiles that measure 3 inches by 2 inches. If the tiles are sold at 10 for 30¢, what will it cost to tile the room?
   a. $10.80   b. $108   c. $129.60   d. $1,296

88. If a person reads extensively, that person has an excellent vocabulary. If a person studies mathematics, that person is logical. Trisha has an excellent vocabulary, but is not logical. What can be validly concluded about Trisha?
     i.   Trisha reads extensively.
     ii.   Trisha does not study mathematics.
   a.   i only   b.   ii only
   c.   Both i and ii   d.   Neither i nor ii

89. Two representatives are chosen without replacement from a group of 40 people consisting of 20 men and 20 women. What is the probability that the two representatives selected are either both men or both women?

   a. $\frac{20}{40} \cdot \frac{19}{39}$ b. $\frac{19}{39}$

   c. $2 \cdot \frac{20}{40} \cdot \frac{19}{40}$ d. $\frac{2}{40} + \frac{2}{40}$

90. Select the statement below which is not logically equivalent to: Cassandra studies physics or calculus.
    a. If Cassandra studies physics, then she does not study calculus.
    b. If Cassandra does not study calculus, then she studies physics.
    c. If Cassandra does not study physics, then she studies calculus.
    d. It is false that Cassandra does not study physics and does not study calculus.

91. The tens digit of a two-digit number is 3 more than the units digit. If the number itself is 12 times the units digit, what equation can be used to find t, the tens digit?
    a. $10t + (t - 3) = 12$
    b. $10(t + 3) + (t - 3) = 12$
    c. $10t + (t - 3) = 12(t - 3)$
    d. $10(t + 3) + (t - 3) = 12t$

92. The lengths in feet of two sides of a rectangle are consecutive even integers. If ten more than half the length of the shorter side is increased by twice the length of the longer side, the result is 59 feet. If x represents the length of the shorter side, select the equation that can be used to find the area of the rectangle.
    a. $\frac{1}{2}x + 10 + 2(x + 1) = 59$
    b. $\frac{1}{2}x + 10 + 2x + 1 = 59$
    c. $x(x + 2) = 59$
    d. $10 + \frac{1}{2}x + 2(x + 2) = 59$

93. Because of the lake shown below, a road cannot directly connect B to C, but must instead connect B to A and then A to C. How long is the road from B to A and then from A to C?
    a. 28 miles
    b. 29 miles
    c. 30 miles
    d. 32 miles

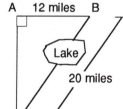

94. Find the area of the shaded region, the region outside the isosceles right triangle whose legs measure 1 foot each and inside the quadrilateral whose parallel sides measure 10 feet and 6 feet and whose height is 4 feet.
    a. 63.5 ft^2
    b. 63 ft^2
    c. 31.5 ft^2
    d. 31 ft^2

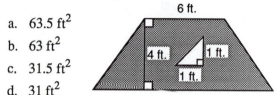

95. Let A = {1, 2}, B = {2, 3, 4} and U = {1, 2, 3, 4, 5}. Select the choice corresponding to $(A \cap B)'$.
    a. {2}
    b. {5}
    c. {3, 4}
    d. {1, 3, 4, 5}

96. Which option gives the conditions which correspond to the shaded region of the graph shown below?

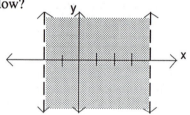

    a. x > -2 and x > 4
    b. -2 > x > 4
    c. -2 < x < 4
    d. y > -2 and y < 4

97. A person purchases eight gifts. The least expensive gift costs $6 and the most expensive gift costs $14. Which of the following is a reasonable estimate of the total amount spent on the eight gifts?
    a. $50   b. $92   c. $112   d. $126

98. Construct the truth table for $(p \rightarrow q) \land \neg q$ if the statements p and q occur in the following order:

p	q
T	T
T	F
F	T
F	F

Which one of the following represents the final column of truth values in the table?

	a.	b.	c.	d.
	F	F	F	T
	T	F	F	T
	F	F	T	T
	T	T	T	T

99. To be eligible for a scholarship, a student must have a grade point average of at least 3.6 and an activity index that exceeds .825. Marsha has a grade point average of 3.67 and an activity index of .83. Ethel has a grade point average of 3.7 and an activity index of .825. Paul has a grade point average of 3.8 and an activity index of .83. Who is not eligible for the scholarship?
   a. Marsha only   b. Ethel only
   c. Paul only
   d. Both Marsha and Paul

100. The box shown below, with length A, width B and height C, is constructed with no top. What is its surface area?

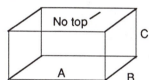

   a. 5ABC   b. AC + 2BC + 2AB
   c. 2AC + 2BC + 2AB
   d. 2AC + 2BC + AB

101. The accompanying figure consists of a square with an equilateral triangle and a semicircle attached. One side of the square measures 4B linear units. What is the distance around this figure?

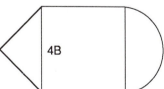

   a. $16B + 4\pi B$ b. $16B + 2\pi B$
   c. $24B + 4\pi B$ d. $24B + 2\pi B$

102. In how many ways can first, second and third prize be awarded to 5 people if no person can be given more than one prize?
   a. 125   b. 120   c. 60   d. 10

103. Seven cards, numbered 1 through 7, are put into a box. If one card is randomly selected, what is the probability of selecting an even number or a number greater than 5?
   a. $\frac{2}{7}$ b. $\frac{3}{7}$ c. $\frac{4}{7}$ d. $\frac{5}{7}$

104. The graph below depicts the number of fish caught (o) and the number of lobsters caught (x) by a group of six people on a number of outings in the Florida Keys.

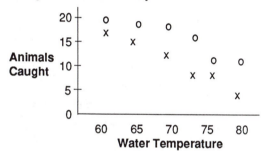

Which one of the following is true?
   a. Increased water temperature was responsible for the decrease in the number of fish and lobsters that were caught.
   b. There is an association between water temperature and animals caught only for the lobsters.
   c. Approximately 10 lobsters were caught when the water temperature was 60 degrees.
   d. Fewer fish and lobsters tend to be caught as the water temperature increases; a stronger relationship exists for the lobsters than for the fish.

105. Select the statement that is the negation of the statement: If it is cold, we will not go swimming.
    a. If it is not cold, then we will go swimming.
    b. It is cold and we do not go swimming.
    c. If we go swimming, then it is not cold.
    d. It is cold and we will go swimming.

106. Select the conclusion that will make the following argument valid: If vitamin C is effective, then I will not catch a cold. If I do not catch a cold, then I will not miss exercising.
    a. If vitamin C is not effective, then I will miss some exercising.
    b. If vitamin C is effective, then I will not miss exercising.
    c. If I do not catch a cold, then vitamin C was effective.
    d. If vitamin C is effective, then I will miss some exercising.

107. The table below shows the distribution of incomes in a community.

Income Level	Percent of People
$0 - 9,999	2
10,000 - 14,999	12
15,000 - 19,999	21
20,000 - 24,999	39
25,000 - 34,999	20
35,000 - 49,999	4
50,000 and over	2

What percentage of people in the community have incomes of at least $35,000?

    a. 6%   b. 26%   c. 74%   d. 94%

108. The graph below represents the distribution of ratings (1 = poor, 2 = fair, 3 = average, 4 = good, 5 = excellent) for a movie that recently opened.

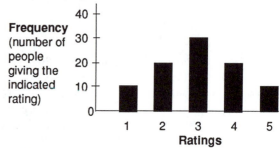

Select the statement that is true about the distribution of ratings.
    a. The mean, median, and mode have the same value.
    b. The mode is greater than the mean.
    c. The median is greater than the mode.
    d. The mode is less than the mean.

109. A recent survey indicated that 40% of the residents of Key Largo own boats. Of these, 5% use their boat four or more times per week. What is the probability that a randomly selected Key Largo resident will have a boat that is used four or more times per week?
    a. 0.45   b. 0.35   c. 0.2   d. 0.02

110. What is the volume in centiliters of a 3.25 liter bottle?
    a. 3.25 cl b. 32.5 cl c. 325 cl   d. 3250 cl

111. In the accompanying diagram $\overline{DA} \parallel \overline{CB}$ and $\overline{CD} \parallel \overline{BA}$. Lower-case letters indicate the measures of the various angles. (x = m < BCD, etc.)

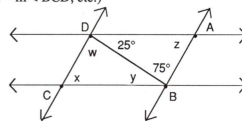

Which one of the following statements is true?
    a. z = 75° b. w = z   c. w = 25° d. x = 80°

112. 105 is 125% of what number?
   a. 8.4   b. 84   c. 86   d. 131.25

113. $(-0.73) + (0.296) =$
   a. 1.026   b. 0.434   c. -1.026   d. -0.434

114. What is the perimeter of a rectangle with dimensions of 50 centimeters and 6 meters?
   a. 13 cm   b. 112 cm
   c. 300 cm   d. 13 m

115. If Jason drives between 40 mph and 55 mph for 4 to 5 hours, estimate the distance traveled.
   a. 160 miles   b. 165 miles
   c. 217 miles   d. 265 miles

116. The electrical resistance of a wire varies directly as the length of the wire and inversely as the square of the wire's diameter. An 8-foot wire whose diameter is 1 inch has a resistance of 8 ohms. What is the resistance of a wire whose length is 6 feet and whose diameter is 2 inches?
   a. 1.5 ohms   b. 2.5 ohms
   c. 5 ohms   d. 12 ohms

117. The amount of floor surface that can be covered by the contents of a gallon of wood finishing liquid is given by which measure?
   a. square feet   b. cubic feet
   c. quarts   d. liters

118. A lending library charges a fee of 60¢ for the first day a book is borrowed and 30¢ for each additional day. A borrower paid $4.80 for loaning a book. For how many days was the book borrowed?
   a. 13   b. 14   c. 15   d. 16

119. Which one of the following correctly names a right triangle with one of its angles measuring 45°?
   a. scalene   b. isosceles
   c. equilateral   d. obtuse

120. $5\frac{4}{7} \div 1\frac{2}{7} =$
   a. $\frac{351}{49}$ b. $4\frac{1}{3}$ c. $4\frac{3}{7}$ d. $4\frac{1}{2}$

121. Which pairs of angles in the accompanying diagram are complementary?

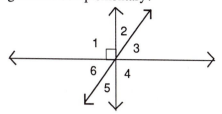

   a. 3 and 5   b. 1 and 4
   c. 2 and 5   d. 1 and 6

122. $\dfrac{6(3x-5y)}{2} - \dfrac{2(4x)^2}{2x} - (4x-3y) =$
   a. $-11x - 12y$ b. $-11x - 18y$
   c. $x - 12y$ d. none of these

123. $\dfrac{6^6}{2^3} =$
   a. 3^2 b. 3^3
   c. $\dfrac{6+6+6+6+6+6}{2+2+2}$ d. $\dfrac{6 \cdot 6 \cdot 6 \cdot 6 \cdot 6 \cdot 6}{2 \cdot 2 \cdot 2}$

124. Identify the missing term in the following geometric progression.
$$-16, 4, -1, \tfrac{1}{4}, \underline{\quad}, \tfrac{1}{64}$$
   a. $-\frac{1}{4}$ b. $-\frac{1}{8}$ c. $-\frac{1}{12}$ d. $-\frac{1}{16}$

125. Select the statement that is logically equivalent to: It is not true that both Jacksonville and Australia are cities.
   a. Jacksonville is not a city and Australia is not a city.
   b. If Australia is a city, then Jacksonville is a city.
   c. If Jacksonville is a city, then Australia is not a city.
   d. Jacksonville is a city or Australia is not a city.

126. Given that $\overline{BC} \parallel \overline{DE}$ and $\overline{AD} \perp \overline{DE}$, which one of the following statements is true for the figure shown? ($m\angle BAC = x$, etc.)

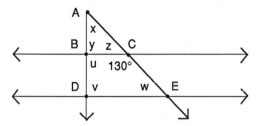

 a. $x = z$ b. $x = v$
 c. $\angle CBD$ and $\angle CED$ are supplementary angles.
 d. $w = 50°$

127. Look for a common relationship between the numbers in each pair. Then identify the missing term.

$(25, 5), (1, 1), (\frac{4}{9}, \frac{2}{3}), (0.16, 0.4), (4, \_\_)$

 a. 4 b. 2 c. $\frac{4}{3}$ d. $\frac{1}{2}$

128. Select the statement that is logically equivalent to: If it is July, it does not snow.
 a. If it snows, it is not July.
 b. If it is not July, it snows.
 c. If it does not snow, it is July.
 d. If it does not snow, it is not July.

129. If $b < 0$, then $b^2 < ab + b$ is equivalent to which of the following?
 a. $b < a + 1$ b. $b > -a - 1$
 c. $b < -a - 1$ d. $b > a + 1$

130. Choose the equation equivalent to the following: $4x - 7 = 3x + 4$
 a. $4x - 3 = 3x$ b. $7x - 7 = 4$
 c. $4x - 11 = 3x + 4$ d. $x - 7 = 4$

Appendix 2 Test Answers with Brief Explanations

1. $A \cap C$ is represented by the region where A and C intersect. This region is separate from circle B, so that elements in $A \cap C$ are not in set B. [c]

2. $3(t-1) = 2[t-3(t-2)]$
    $3t-3 = 2[t-3t+6]$
    $3t-3 = 2[-2t+6]$
    $3t-3 = -4t+12$
    $7t-3 = 12$
    $7t = 15$
    $t = \frac{15}{7}$ [c]

3. P(both are good) = P(first is good) • P(second is good)
    $= \frac{6}{10} \cdot \frac{5}{9} = \frac{1}{3}$

    P(at least defective) = 1 − P(both are good)
    $= 1 - \frac{1}{3} = \frac{2}{3}$ [c]

4. In option d, just because "clocks" and "time-measuring devices" are drawn inside the circle representing "things designed to inform people of the time," this does not mean that the "clocks" circle must be inside the "time-measuring devices" circle. [d]

5. i. $5(-3) + 1 > -13$
         $-14 > -13$, false

    ii. $2(-3)^2 + 7(-3) = -3$
         $18 + (-21) = -3$
         $-3 = -3$, true

    iii. $\frac{4}{3}(-3) - 4 = 0$
         $-4 - 4 = 0$
         $-8 = 0$, false   -3 is the solution to ii only   [b]

6. Area of shaded region = Area large semicircle − Area two smaller semicircles
    $= \frac{1}{2}\pi \cdot 10^2 - (\frac{1}{2}\pi \cdot 5^2 + \frac{1}{2}\pi \cdot 5^2)$
    $= 50\pi - (\frac{25\pi}{2} + \frac{25\pi}{2}) = 50\pi - 25\pi = 25\pi$ [a]

7. $-7x < -70$
    $\frac{-7x}{-7} > \frac{-70}{-7}$
    $x > 10$ [d]

8. $x^2 + 4x - 4 = 0$ ($a = 1, b = 4, c = -4$) for $x = \frac{-b \pm \sqrt{b^2 - 4ac}}{2a}$

    $x = \frac{-4 \pm \sqrt{16 - 4(1)(-4)}}{2(1)} = \frac{-4 \pm \sqrt{32}}{2} = \frac{-4 \pm \sqrt{16 \cdot 2}}{2} = \frac{-4 \pm 4\sqrt{2}}{2} = -2 \pm 2\sqrt{2}$ [b]

9. $GPA = \frac{(10)(4) + (7)(3) + (5)(2) + (0)(1) + (0)(0)}{10 + 7 + 5} = \frac{71}{22} \approx 3.2$ [c]

10. Frank Martinez: not eligible because of the weight of his dog.
    Dr. Selma Rubin: not eligible because of 3 children.
    Raboids: not eligible because of 2 pets. [d]

11. $(2 \cdot \frac{1}{10}) + (2 \cdot \frac{1}{10^6}) = 0.200002$ [c]

12. $2[\frac{1}{2} - \frac{1}{2}(10 - 2 \cdot 3)] = 2[\frac{1}{2} - \frac{1}{2}(10 - 6)] = 2[\frac{1}{2} - \frac{1}{2}(4)] = 2[\frac{1}{2} - \frac{4}{2}] = 2(-\frac{3}{2}) = -3$ [c]

13. $\frac{1}{4} \cdot 12c + 6c \div \frac{1}{3} - c^2 + 4c = 3c + 18c - c^2 + 4c = 25c - c^2$ [a]

14. Scores in order: 1, 3, 3, 4, 5, 6, 6, 7, 7, 7
    Position of median $= \frac{n+1}{2} = \frac{10+1}{2} = \frac{11}{2} = 5.5$

    median = average of scores of positions five and six $= \frac{5+6}{2} = 5.5$ [c]

15. p: Sarah is in San Francisco.
    q: Sarah is in California.
    Both $p \rightarrow q$ and $\sim p \rightarrow \sim q$ (converse and inverse) are not equivalent
    to $p \rightarrow q$. The converse appears in option b. [b]

16. p: A Supreme Court nominee receives majority approval.
    q: The nominee is a judge on the Supreme Court.
    $\sim(p \vee \sim q) \equiv \sim p \wedge q$ [b]

17. $\frac{\text{number of imports}}{\text{total number excluding Ford and Chrysler}} = \frac{23}{46 + 2 + 23} = \frac{23}{71}$ [a]

18. All sides of a rhombus are congruent. [d]

19. $\sqrt{36} + \sqrt{6} = 6 + \sqrt{6} = \sqrt{6} + 6$ [b]

20. $\frac{12}{\sqrt{6}} = \frac{12}{\sqrt{6}} \cdot \frac{\sqrt{6}}{\sqrt{6}} = \frac{12\sqrt{6}}{6} = 2\sqrt{6}$ [a]

21. Group 1: Mean = 7, median = 7, mode = 7, so x can be the mean or
    median or mode.
    Group 2: Mean = 7, median = 6.5, no mode; since x = 7, it must be the
    mean, and there is no need to consider group 3.
    x = the mean $= \frac{1.1 + 2.3 + 3.8 + 7.2 + 8.1}{5} = \frac{22.5}{5} = 4.5$ [c]

22. Graph of $x \leq -1$: The line of $x = -1$ (parallel to the y-axis) and the portion
    of the plane to the left of this vertical line. Graph of $y \geq 0$: The x-axis
    $(y = 0)$ and the half-plane above the x-axis. [c]

23. Eliminate c and d since the graphs of x = -2 and y = 2 are lines parallel to the y-axis and x-axis respectively, and no such dashed lines appear in the figure. The line of y − x = 2 has an x-intercept (set y = 0) of -2 and a y-intercept (set x = 0) of 2, which is verified by the diagram. The test point (0, 0) must satisfy the correct inequality since (0, 0) lies in the shaded region. y − x < 2 becomes 0 − 0 < 2, which is true. [a]

24. $y > y − (16 − 2y)$ or $y > y − 16 + 2y$ or $y > 3y − 16$ or $-2y > -16$
    Therefore, $y < 8$ [b]

25. p: It is hot
    q: Some municipal pool is open.
    ~(p → q) is p ∧~q. Since the negation of "some" is "no," the negation is: It is hot and no municipal pool is open. [c]

26. $.0060 \div .12 = .60 \div 12 = .05$ and $.05 = 5\%$ [c]

27. $108.7\% = 1.087 = 1\frac{87}{1000}$ [d]

28. Let C = hypotenuse of smaller triangle.
    $C^2 = 3^2 + 4^2; C^2 = 25; C = 5$
    Pythagorean Theorem in larger triangle:
    $5^2 + 12^2 = (AB)^2; 169 = (AB)^2; AB = 13$
    $13 \text{ cm} = 13(\frac{1}{100} \text{ m}) = 0.13 \text{ m}$ [a]

29. The pattern in all three examples is to multiply the first two numbers and divide this product by the third number. [d]

30. $P = C + MC = 12 + (.4)(12) = 12 + 4.8 = 16.8$ [d]

31. Since x − y is not equal to y − x (although x − y = -y + x), option c is not true for all real numbers. [c]

32. 15 is divisible by 5 and 45 = (15)(3), so 15 is also a factor of 45. [b]

33. 1980: (.15)(20,000) = 3000
    1981: (.2)(25,000) = 5000
    percent increase: $\frac{\text{increase}}{\text{original amount}} = \frac{2000}{3000} = \frac{2}{3} = .66\frac{2}{3} = 66\frac{2}{3}\%$ [b]

34. Class 1: $\frac{1}{5}$ absent $\quad \frac{1}{5} \cdot \frac{40}{1} = 8$
    Class 2: $\frac{1}{8}$ absent $\quad \frac{1}{8} \cdot \frac{40}{1} = 5$
    8 + 5 = 13 students absent [b]

35. $f(-2) = (-2)^3 − 6(-2)^2 − (-2) + 2$
    $= -8 − 6(4) + 2 + 2$
    $= -8 − 24 + 2 + 2$
    $= -28$ [b]

36. The mode is 45%. The few scores of 95% or better pull the mean up in this (extreme) direction. The median is either 45% or the average of 45% and 75% (60%). Mode < Mean, Median < Mean   [b]

37. $m\angle ABC = 180° - (90° + 30°) = 180° - 120° = 60°$ Option d is false. [d]

38. $8x^2 - 14x + 3 = (2x - 3)(4x - 1)$ [a]

39. $z(30) = \dfrac{\text{Score} - \text{Mean}}{\text{Standard Deviation}} = \dfrac{30 - 60}{20} = -\dfrac{30}{20} = -1.5$

   $z(85) = \dfrac{85 - 60}{20} = \dfrac{25}{20} = 1.25$ From the table: $.433 + .394 = .827$ [a]

40. $(7.3 \cdot 10^{-4}) \cdot (8.2 \cdot 10^6) = 59.86 \cdot 10^2 = 5.986 \cdot 10 \cdot 10^2 = 5.986 \cdot 10^3$
       [a]

41. November: $(40)(\$30) = \$1,200$
   December: $(40 - .1 \cdot 40)(30 + .2 \cdot 30) = (36)(\$36) = \$1,296$
   96 increase   [a]

42. Tax: $(.05)(\$60) = \$3.00$
   Save 25% of $3 = (.25)(3) = 0.75$ [a]

43. With approximately 34% of the scores between the mean and 1 standard deviation above the mean, and 34% of the scores between the mean and 1 standard deviation below the mean, option b is true.   [b]

44. Using Euler circles, physicists and biologists are shown inside the scientists' circle, and the scientists' circle is inside the college graduates' circle. Thus, the biologists' circle falls inside the college graduates' circle.
       [b]

45. Using Euler circles, talkers during lecture are inside the rude circle. The lovable people circle (containing Eubie) is separate from both these circles. We conclude that no lovable people talk during lecture. We cannot conclude that some lovable people talk during lecture.   [c]

46. P(over 30 or business) = P(over 30) + P(business) − P(over 30 ∩ business)
   $$= \dfrac{15}{40} + \dfrac{11}{40} - \dfrac{5}{40}$$ [b]

47. Area = $(40)(30) + (10)(10) = 1300 \text{ ft}^2$
   Bundles $= \dfrac{1300}{100} = 13$
   Cost = $(13)(\$70) + \$275 = \$1,185$ [c]

48. $\binom{5}{2} \cdot \binom{4}{2} = \dfrac{5!}{2!\,3!} \cdot \dfrac{4!}{2!\,2!} = 10 \cdot 6 = 60$ [a]

49. Consider option d. The form is:
   $p \rightarrow q$
   $\underline{q\quad\quad}$
   ∴ p, which is invalid (fallacy of the converse)   [d]

50. p: There is a mathematics requirement.
    q: There is an English requirement.
    r: College bookstores do a great business.

$(p \wedge q) \rightarrow r$ (given) $\sim p \vee \sim q$

$\dfrac{\sim r}{\therefore \sim(p \wedge q)}$ (given) $\dfrac{q}{\therefore \sim p}$ (given) (Tate has no math requirement.) [a]

51. $\dfrac{\text{Number of ways of visiting E first, D second, A last}}{\text{Total number of arrangements}} = \dfrac{1 \cdot 1 \cdot 3 \cdot 2 \cdot 1 \cdot 1}{6 \cdot 5 \cdot 4 \cdot 3 \cdot 2 \cdot 1} = \dfrac{1}{120}$ [b]

52. $V = \frac{4}{3}\pi\, r^3 = \frac{4}{3}\pi(3)^3 = \frac{4}{3}\pi \cdot \frac{27}{1} = 36\pi$ [b]

53. see answer to the right [b]

54. $V(\text{cone}) = \frac{1}{3}\pi\, r^2 h = \frac{1}{3}\pi\,(3)^2(3) = 9\pi \text{ ft.}^3$
    $V(\text{cylinder}) = \pi\, r^2 h = \pi\,(3)^2(3) = 27\pi \text{ ft.}^3$
    $9\pi + 27\pi = 36\pi \text{ ft.}^3$ [b]

55. $V = LWH = (30\text{yd})(20 \text{ yd})(2 \text{ yd}) = 1200 \text{ yd}^3$
    $\text{Trips} = \frac{1200}{10} = 120$
    $\text{Cost} = (120)(\$12) = \$1{,}440$ [a]

56. $m\angle A = 135°$ (congruent alternate exterior angles) [c]

57. Corresponding sides of similar triangles are proportional.
    $\frac{CE}{CB} = \frac{DE}{AB}$ or $\frac{5}{5+4} = \frac{DE}{10}$ or $9DE = 50$ and $DE = \frac{50}{9} = 5\frac{5}{9}$ [c]

58. $m\angle C = 180° - 140° = 40°$
    $m\angle B = 40°$ (isosceles triangle)
    $m\angle D = 180° - 80° = 100°$
    The triangle is not a right triangle, so the
    Pythagorean Theorem does not apply. [d]

59. $\frac{1}{10} + \frac{1}{3} + \frac{1}{5} = \frac{3 + 10 + 6}{30} = \frac{19}{30}$
    Fraction left $= 1 - \frac{19}{30} = \frac{11}{30} = .36\frac{2}{3} = 36\frac{2}{3}\%$ [d]

60. $2 - 5(a - 3b) = 2 - 5a + 15b$ [c]

61. $-\frac{5}{6} = -0.8\overline{3}$ Since $-0.8\overline{3}$ is farther to the right on the number line than
    -0.84, $-\frac{5}{6} > -0.84$ [c]

62. The pattern is that the number of triangles in the interior is the square
    of the base.
    $12^2 = 144$ [d]

63. Prime numbers greater than 17 and less than 29: 19, 23
Both yield a remainder of 3 when divided by 4. [b]

64. $\dfrac{\text{Planet A}}{\text{Planet B}}$: $\dfrac{7}{11.27} = \dfrac{6}{x}$ or $7x = (11.27)(6)$ or $7x = 67.62$ or $x = 9.66$ [c]

65. $5\frac{1}{2} = 5\frac{2}{4} = 4\frac{6}{4}$
$\underline{-2\frac{3}{4} = -2\frac{3}{4} = -2\frac{3}{4}}$
$\phantom{-2\frac{3}{4} = -2\frac{3}{4} = }2\frac{3}{4}$ [b]

66. $420 - (.13)(420) = 420 - 54.6 = 365.4$ [c]

67. $10 \text{ cm} = 10\left(\frac{1}{100}\text{ m}\right) = \frac{1}{10}\text{ m}$ Area $= \left(\frac{1}{10}\right)\left(\frac{1}{10}\right) = \frac{1}{100}\text{ m}^2$ [d]

68. P(television) $= 0.3 + 0.05 = 0.35$ p(not-television) $= 1 - 0.35 = 0.65$ [b]

69. The negation of "all" is "some...not." [a]

70. p: Shakespeare wrote *Othello*.
q: Shakespeare wrote *Walden Pond*.
$\sim(p \wedge q)$ is not equivalent to $\sim p \wedge \sim q$. [d]

71. 25% of the total $= (.25)(24) = 6$, school [a]

72. M(40), T(36), W(60), Th(52), F(28)
No temperature occurs most frequently, so there is no mode.
Mean $= \dfrac{40 + 36 + 60 + 52 + 28}{5} = 43.2$
Scores in order: 28, 36, 40, 52, 60   median = 40
T to W: $\dfrac{\text{increase}}{\text{original}} = \dfrac{24}{36} = \dfrac{2}{3} \approx .67 = 67\%$ [d]

73. p: A person studies.   q: A person fails. $(p \rightarrow \sim q) \equiv (q \rightarrow \sim p)$ [a]

74. $\dfrac{7}{14} = \dfrac{1}{2} = 0.5 = 50\%$ [d]

75. $5 \cdot 4 \cdot 2 \cdot 2 = 80$ [b]

76. p: All people take exams honestly. q: No supervision is needed.
$p \rightarrow q$
$\underline{\sim q}$ (The negation of "no" is "some.")
$\therefore \sim q$ (Some people do not take exams honestly)
          (The negation of "all" is "some...not.") [d]

77. $\dfrac{\text{cans}}{\text{cost}}$: $\dfrac{5}{3} = \dfrac{11}{y}$ [b]

78. $6x + 5y = 9$ Eliminate y by multiplying the $-12x - 10y = -18$
   $5x + 2y = 14$ equations by -2 and 5 respectively. $\underline{25x + 10y = 70}$
                                        Add: $13x$ $= 52$
                                                 x $= 4$

   $6x + 5y = 9$ becomes $6(4) + 5y = 9$ or $5y = -15$ or $y = -3$ $\{(4, -3)\}$ [c]

79. x: players originally on the team
   $x - .2x = 32$ simplifies to $.8x = 32$ or $x = \frac{32}{.8} = 40$ [b]

80. Volume cannot be measured in square feet. Square units are used to measure area.   [d]

81. $27.349 \text{ cm}^3 \approx 27.3 \text{ cm}^3$ [b]
          less than 5

82. The answer is either $1\frac{1}{4}$ or $1\frac{1}{2}$, and since the point B is more than midway between these options, the answer is $1\frac{1}{2}$.   [b]

83. p: Gene is an actor.   q: Gene is a musician.
   $p \vee q$ is logically equivalent to $\sim p \rightarrow q$.   [b]

84. P(does not leak) $= 1 - 0.1 = 0.9$
  P(neither leaks) $=$ P(first does not leak) $\cdot$ P(second does not leak)
            $= (0.9)(0.9) = 0.81 = \frac{81}{100}$ [c]

85. $87\% - 49\% = 38\%$ [c]

86. Mode $= 0$ (score with greatest proportion)
  Median $= 1$
  Mean $= \frac{(0)(35) + (1)(20) + (2)(25) + (3)(10) + (4)(8) + (5)(2)}{100} = \frac{142}{100} = 1.42$ [d]

87. Area of room $= (12 \cdot 12 \text{ in.})(15 \cdot 12 \text{ in.}) = 25{,}920 \text{ in}^2$
  Area of tile $= (3 \text{ in.})(2 \text{ in.}) = 6 \text{ in}^2$
  Number of tiles $= \frac{25{,}920}{6} = 4{,}320$
  Number of groups of 10 tiles $= \frac{4320}{10} = 432$
  Cost $= (432)(.3) = \$129.60$ [c]

88. p: Person reads extensively.
  q: Person has an excellent vocabulary.
  r: Person studies math.
  s: Person is logical.

  $p \rightarrow q$ $r \rightarrow s$
  $\underline{q\quad\quad}$ $\underline{\sim s\quad\quad}$
  $\therefore p$ (invalid) $\therefore \sim r$ (valid)

            (Trisha does not study math.)   [b]

89. P(both men) = P(man first) • P(man second) = $\frac{20}{40} \cdot \frac{19}{39} = \frac{19}{78}$

    Similarly, P(both women) = $\frac{19}{78}$

    P(both men or both women) = $\frac{19}{78} + \frac{19}{78} = \frac{38}{78} = \frac{19}{39}$ [b]

90. p: Cassandra studies physics. q: Cassandra studies calculus.
    $p \vee q$ is not equivalent to $p \rightarrow \sim q$.
    Cassandra can be studying both physics and calculus. [a]

91. t: tens digit. Then $t - 3$: units digit. And, $10t + (t - 3)$: the number.
    "Number is 12 times units digit" translates as:
    $$10t + (t - 3) = 12(t - 3)$$ [c]

92. Sides: x and $x + 2$
    (10 more than half the shorter side) + (twice the longer side)
    $$(\tfrac{1}{2}x + 10) + 2(x + 2) = 59$$ [d]

93. By the Pythagorean Theorem:
    $(AC)^2 + 12^2 = 20^2$ or $(AC)^2 + 144 = 400$ or $(AC)^2 = 256$ or $AC = 16$
    Thus, $AB + AC = 12 + 16 = 28$ [a]

94. Area of trapezoid – area of triangle = $\frac{1}{2} \cdot 4(10 + 6) - \frac{1}{2} \cdot 1 \cdot 1$
    $$= 32 - \tfrac{1}{2} = 31.5$$ [c]

95. $(A \cap B)' = \{2\}' = \{1, 3, 4, 5\}$ [d]

96. Equations of the dashed lines: $x = -2$ and $x = 4$
    Thus, $x > -2$ and $x < 4$. Equivalently: $-2 < x < 4$ [c]

97. Least amount spent: $8 \cdot \$6 = \$48$
    Most amount spent: $8 \cdot \$14 = \$112$
    Options a, c, and d are either too close to $48 and $112, or
    outside this range. [b]

98.

p	q	$p \rightarrow q$	$\sim q$	$(p \rightarrow q) \wedge \sim q$
T	T	T	F	F
T	F	F	T	F
F	T	T	F	F
F	F	T	T	T

[b]

99. Ethel's activity index (.825) does not exceed .825, so
    she is not eligible. [b]

100. Surface area = area bottom + area two sides + area front and back
     $$= AB + 2BC + 2AC$$ [d]

431

101. Perimeter = Length of four line segments that measure 4B each plus semicircle's circumference

$$= 4(4B) + \frac{1}{2}\pi\,(4B) = 16B + 2\pi B \qquad \text{[b]}$$

102. $5 \cdot 4 \cdot 3 = 60$ [c]

103. P(even or greater than 5)

$= $ P(even) + P(greater than 5) − P(even ∩ greater than 5)
$= $ P(even) + P(greater than 5) − P({6})
$= \frac{3}{7} + \frac{2}{7} - \frac{1}{7} = \frac{4}{7}$ [c]

104. As one variable increases (water temperature), the other variables decrease, but the degree of association between variables does not mean that changes in one cause changes in the other. [d]

105. p: It is cold.   q: We will not go swimming.
~(p → q) is p ∧~q, which translates as: It is cold and we will go swimming. [d]

106. p: Vitamin C is effective.   q: I will not catch a cold.
r: I will not miss exercising.

p → q
q → r
∴ p → r   (If vitamin C is effective, then I will not miss exercising.)   [b]

107. Percent of people with incomes of \$35,000 or more = 4% + 2% = 6% [a]

108. Mode = most frequent rating = 3   Median = middlemost rating = 3

Each rating of 4 is counterbalanced by a rating of 2, giving a rating of

$\frac{4 + 2}{2} = 3$. Similarly each 5 is counterbalanced by a 1. Thus, the mean

stays at 3. Mode = median = mean = 3. [a]

109. $(0.4)(0.05) = 0.02$ [d]

110. Just as a meter contains 100 centimeters, a liter contains 100 centiliters.
3.25 liters = 3.25(100 cl) = 325 cl [c]

111. $y = 25°$ and $w = 75°$ (congruent alternate interior angles)
$x = 180° − (25° + 75°) = 80°$ [d]

112. Let x = the number.
"125% of x = 105" translates as: $1.25x = 105$ or $x = \frac{105}{1.25} = 84$ [b]

113. The difference between 0.296 and 0.73 is:
$$\begin{array}{r} 0.730 \\ -\,0.296 \\ \hline 0.434 \end{array}$$

$(-0.73) + (0.296) = -0.434$ [d]

114. $P = 2L + 2W = 100$ cm $+ 12$ m $= 1$ m $+ 12$ m $= 13$ m   [d]

115. Distance = rate • time
Minimum distance $= 40 \cdot 4 = 160$ miles
Maximum distance $= 55 \cdot 5 = 275$ miles   [c]

116. R: resistance L: length D: diameter
$R = \frac{KL}{D^2}$ or $8 = \frac{K(8)}{1^2}$ or $8 = 8K$ and $1 = K$.
Thus, $R = \frac{(1)L}{D^2} = \frac{6}{2^2} = \frac{6}{4} = 1.5$ [a]

117. Floor surface refers to area, measured in square units.   [a]

118. x: number of days book was borrowed
$.6 + .3(x - 1) = 4.8$
$.6 + .3x - .3 = 4.8$
$.3 + .3x = 4.8$
$.3x = 4.5$
$x = \frac{4.5}{.3} = 15$ [c]

119. Angles measure $90°$, $45°$, and $90° - 45° = 45°$. With two congruent angles, the triangle has two sides of equal measure and is isosceles.   [b]

120. $5\frac{4}{7} \div 1\frac{2}{7} = \frac{39}{7} \div \frac{9}{7} = \frac{39}{7} \cdot \frac{7}{9} = \frac{39}{9} = 4\frac{3}{9} = 4\frac{1}{3}$ [b]

121. 2 and 3 are complementary. Since 2 and 5 have equal measure (congruent vertical angles), 5 and 3 are complementary.   [a]

122. $\frac{6(3x - 5y)}{2} - \frac{2(4x)^2}{2x} - (4x - 3y) = 3(3x - 5y) - \frac{16x^2}{x} - (4x - 3y)$
$= 9x - 15y - 16x - 4x + 3y$
$= -11x - 12y$ [a]

123. Exponents in numerator and denominator indicate repeated multiplication.   [d]

124. Since a geometric progression indicates that each number (after the first) is obtained from the previous number by multiplying by a constant number, in this progression the constant is $-\frac{1}{4}$. This can be seen most clearly from 4 to -1. The missing number is $(\frac{1}{4})(-\frac{1}{4}) = -\frac{1}{16}$.   [d]

125. p: Jacksonville is a city.
q: Australia is a city.
$\sim(p \wedge q)$ is equivalent to $\sim p \vee \sim q$.
$\sim(p \wedge q)$ is equivalent to $p \rightarrow \sim q$, which becomes:
If Jacksonville is a city, then Australia is not a city.   [c]

126. $u = 90°$ and $v = 90°$. Since the sum of the measures of the interior angles of a quadrilateral is 360°,
$$w = 360° - (90° + 90° + 130°) = 50°.$$
Equivalently: $z = 50°$ and $z = w$ (congruent corresponding angles), so $w = 50°$. [d]

127. The second number in each pair is the principal square root of the first number. $\sqrt{4} = 2$ [b]

128. p: It is July.
q: It does not snow.
$(p \rightarrow q) \equiv (\sim q \rightarrow \sim p)$
$\sim q \rightarrow \sim p$: If it snows, it is not July. [a]

129. $b^2 < ab + b$
$\dfrac{b^2}{b} > \dfrac{ab + b}{b}$
$b > \dfrac{ab}{b} + \dfrac{b}{b}$
$b > a + 1$ [d]

130. $4x - 7 = 3x + 4$
$4x - 7 + (-3x) = 3x + 4 + (-3x)$
$x - 7 = 4$ [d]

Answers

Answers for Chapter 1

Chp. 1, Topic 1,
Problem Set 1

1. a. {3,5,7,9,10}   b. {7,9}
   c. {3,5,7,9,10}   d. {5,10}
2. a. {d,i,c,e}   b. {e}
   c. {e}   d. {i,c,e}
3. a. {2}   b. {3}
   c. Ø   d. Ø
4. a. {1,2,4,6,8,9,10}   b. {2,3,4,5,8,9,10}
   c. {1,2,3,4,5,6,8,9,10}
   d. {1,2,3,4,5,6,8,9,10}
   e. {2,4,8,9,10}   f. {2,4,8,9,10}
   g. {2,3,4,5,7,8,9,10}   h. {1,6}
5. a. {d}   b. {a,c,d}   c. {a,c,d}   d. {a,c,d}
   e. {d}   f. {d}   g. {a,b,c,d}   h. {a,b,c}
   i. {a,b,c,d}   j. Ø
6. a. {11,12,13,14, . . .}   b. {5,6,7, . . .,19}
7. a. {1,3,5,7}   b. {1,2}
   c. {2,4,6,8}
8. a. false   b. true   c. true   d. false
9. a. {x};{y};{x,y};Ø
   b. {x};{y};{z};{x,y};{y,z};{x,z};{x,y,z};Ø
   c. {0};Ø
   d. {x};{y};{Ø};{x,y};{y,Ø};{x,Ø};{x,y,Ø};Ø
   e. Ø
10. a. Number of elements
    in a set.

0	1	2	3
1	2	4	8

    Number of subsets that
    can be formed.
    b. $2^4 = 16$; $2^5 = 32$
11. yes
12. Ø
13. a. The set of all Florida citizens who are
    employed.
    b. The set of all employed Florida citizens
    who are not registered Democrats.
    c. The set of all Florida citizens who are
    employed and registered Democrats.
14. a. $A \cup B = \{1,2,3,4,5,6,7,8\}$;
    $B \cup A = \{1,2,3,4,5,6,7,8\}$. Thus,
    $A \cup B = B \cup A$. The order in which the
    sets are combined under set union does
    not affect the result.
    b. $A \cap B = \{2,4,5,6\}$; $B \cap A = \{2,4,5,6\}$.
    Thus, $A \cap B = B \cap A$. The order in
    which the sets are combined under set
    intersection does not affect the result.
    c. $(A \cup B) \cup C = \{1,2,3,4,5,6,7,8\}$;
    $A \cup (B \cup C) = \{1,2,3,4,5,6,7,8\}$.
    Thus, $(A \cup B) \cup C = A \cup (B \cup C)$.
    Under set union the manner of
    grouping does not affect the result.
    d. $(A \cap B) \cap C = \{5,6\}$;
    $A \cap (B \cap C) = \{5,6\}$. Thus,
    $(A \cap B) \cap C = A \cap (B \cap C)$. Under set
    intersection the manner of grouping does
    not affect the result.
    e. $A \cup (B \cap C) = \{1,2,3,4,5,6,7,8\}$;
    $(A \cup B) \cap (A \cup C) = \{1,2,3,4,5,6,7,8\}$.
    Thus, $A \cup (B \cap C) = (A \cup B) \cap$
    $(A \cup C)$. This statement is a form of the
    distributive property. Note that both
    set union and set intersection are
    involved in this property.
    f. $A \cap (B \cup C) = \{1,2,3,4,5,6\}$;
    $(A \cap B) \cup (A \cap C) = \{1,2,3,4,5,6\}$.
    Thus, $A \cap (B \cup C) =$
    $(A \cap B) \cup (A \cap C)$. This statement is
    another form of the distributive property.

435

Answers

1. b
2. a
3. c
4. c
5. d
6. b
7. a
8. d
9. d
10. b
11. There are no quadrilaterals that are not polygons.
12. a
13. All triangles are not squares.

Chp. 1, Topic 3,
Problem Set 3

1. invalid argument
2. valid argument
3. valid argument
4. invalid argument
5. valid argument
6. invalid argument
7. valid argument
8. valid argument
9. invalid argument
10. invalid argument
11. valid argument
12. invalid argument
13. valid argument
14. invalid argument
15. valid argument
16. invalid argument
17. invalid argument
18. invalid argument
19. valid argument
20. valid argument
21. invalid argument

22. valid argument
23. b
24. c
25. c
26. d
27. a
28. a,b
29. b

Chp. 1, Topic 4,
Problem Set 4

1. a. Mary has it or Alice has not had it.
   b. Mary does not have it or Alice has had it.
   c. Mary does not have it and Alice has not had it.
   d. It is not true that both Mary has it or Alice has had it.
   e. It is not true that both Mary has it and Alice has not had it.
   f. It is false that Alice has not had it. This is equivalent to: Alice has had it.

2. a. $\sim p \lor q$ b. $\sim(p \land \sim q)$
   c. $\sim p \land \sim q$ d. $\sim p \land \sim q$

3. a. Hypothesis: I work hard.
      Conclusion: I will pass the course.
   b. Hypothesis: A polygon is a quadrilateral.
      Conclusion: A polygon has four sides.
   c. Hypothesis: The sky is not overcast.
      Conclusion: It is not raining. Notice the hypothesis appears at the end of the statement.

4. a. If you have long hair, then you will get dandruff.
   b. If you get dandruff, then you have long hair.
   c. If you do not have long hair, then you will not get dandruff.
   d. If you do not get dandruff, then you do not have long hair.

5. a. If George buys a television, then it is a Sony.
   b. If one is a soldier, then one is not afraid.
   c. If the bell rings, then the class is over.
   d. If one is a student, then one will pass this test.
   e. If it is a Corvette, then it will not enter this race.
   f. If one is a criminal, then one will be punished.
   g. If a person is your teacher, then the person is not dull.
   h. If a person is tall, then the person should play basketball.
   i. If the National Anthem is not being played, then no one remains standing.
   j. If a member is not excused, then he is required to attend the meeting.
6. c
7. a. If you have avoided a ticket, then you have observed the speed limit.
   b. If you are making the flowers grow, then you have watered them.
   c. If you attend class regularly, then you will pass the course.
   d. If I live in the North, then I can endure the winters.
   e. If you start the car, then you have turned on the ignition.
   f. If you miss the bus, then you will be late for class.

8. $(p \vee q) \rightarrow r$
   $\underline{r \wedge \sim q}$
   $\therefore p$

9. $(p \wedge q) \rightarrow r$
   $\underline{\sim r}$
   $\therefore \sim p \vee \sim q$

10. b
11. c
12. c

Chp. 1, Topic 5, Problem Set 5
1. false
2. true
3. true
4. true
5. true
6. false
7. true
8. false
9. a
10. false
11. true
12. true
13. true
14. a. true   b. false   c. true   d. true

Chp. 1, Topic 6, Problem Set 6
(Only the final column of the truth table is listed.)

1.	T	2.	F	3.	F	4.	F
	F		T		T		F
	T		F		T		F
	T		F		T		T

5.	F	6.	F	7.	T	8.	T
	F		F		F		F
	F		T		T		F
	T		F		T		F

9.	F	10.	F	11.	F
	T		F		F
	T		F		F
	T		F		T

Answers
12. F
    F
    F
    F
    T
    T
    F
    T

13. T   14. T   15. T   16. T
    T   T   T   F
    T   F   F   T
    F   T   T   T

17. The final column in each truth table, T, F, T, T is identical. These statements are logically equivalent.

18. T   19. T   20. T   21. T
    T   T   T   T
    T   T   F   T
    T   F   T   F

22. T   23. T
    T   T
    F   F
    T   T

Chp. 1, Topic 7, Problem Set 7

1. Converse: If Nigel is in England, then he is in London. Inverse: If Nigel is not in London, then he is not in England. Contrapositive: If Nigel is not in England, then he is not in London.

2. Converse: If it is yellow, then it is a banana. Inverse: If it is not a banana, then it is not yellow. Contrapositive: If it is not yellow, then it is not a banana.

3. Converse: If Joan is having a good time, then she is at the movies. Inverse: If Joan is not at the movies, then she is not having a good time. Contrapositive: If Joan is not having a good time, then she is not at the movies.

4. Converse: If Erin does not wear red clothing, then it is St. Patrick's Day. Inverse: If it is not St. Patrick's Day, then Erin wears red clothing. Contrapositive: If Erin wears red clothing, then it is not St. Patrick's Day.

5. Converse: If one does not advocate freedom, then one advocates censorship. Inverse: If one does not advocate censorship, then one advocates freedom. Contrapositive: If one advocates freedom, then one does not advocate censorship.

6. Converse: $\sim q \rightarrow p$; Inverse: $\sim p \rightarrow q$; Contrapositive: $q \rightarrow \sim p$

7. Converse: $\sim q \rightarrow \sim p$; Inverse: $p \rightarrow q$; Contrapositive: $q \rightarrow p$

8. Converse: If it is not allowed in the restaurant, then it is an animal. Inverse: If it is not an animal, then it is allowed in the restaurant. Contrapositive: If it is allowed in the restaurant, then it is not an animal.

9. Converse: If one is a scientist, then one is a chemist. Inverse: If one is not a chemist, then one is not a scientist. Contrapositive: If one is not a scientist, then one is not a chemist.

10. a. If Sherry lives in Palm Beach, then Sherry lives in Florida. (True)
    b. If Sherry lives in Florida, then Sherry lives in Palm Beach. (Not necessarily true)
    c. If Sherry does not live in Palm Beach, then Sherry does not live in Florida. (Not necessarily true)
    d. If Sherry does not live in Florida, then Sherry does not live in Palm Beach. (True)

11. Converse: If I am happy, then I pass the test. Inverse: If I do not pass the test, then I will not be happy.

12. Converse: If Erin wears green, then it is St. Patrick's Day. Inverse: If it is not St. Patrick's Day, then Erin does not wear green.

13. Converse: If one is a writer, then one is a poet. Inverse: If one is not a poet, then one is not a writer.

14. Converse: If a number is divisible by 3, then it is divisible by 6. Inverse: If a number is not divisible by 6, then it is not divisible by 3.

15. Converse: If it is not blue, then it is a banana. Inverse: If it is not a banana, then it is blue.

16. If a person succeeds, then that person works hard. A person works hard or that person does not succeed.

17. If it snows, the temperature is not above 32°. The temperature is not above 32° or it does not snow.

18. c

19. c

20. a. Barbara wins the election and I will not be sorry.
    b. You speak loudly and I cannot hear you.
    c. It is a nice day and I will not go to the beach.
    d. John is a criminal and he will not be punished.
    e. Bill is 18 and he is not eligible to vote.

21. a. If a number is a multiple of 2, then the number is even, and if the number is even, then the number is a multiple of 2.
    b. A number being even is necessary and sufficient for a number being a multiple of 2.
    c. A number being a multiple of 2 is necessary and sufficient for a number being even.

    d. A number is a multiple of 2 if and only if (iff) a number is even.
    e. A number is even if and only if (iff) the number is a multiple of 2.
    f. A number is a multiple of 2 is equivalent to a number is even.

22. The statement is false. "If you are a brilliant physicist, then you are Albert Einstein" is not necessarily true.

23. The statement is true since the conditional works in both directions.

24. True

25. True

26. False

27. True

28. False

Chp. 1, Topic 8, Problem Set 8

1. No people like baseball.

2. Some Floridians are not nice people.

3. Some parakeets weigh fifty pounds.

4. Some books do not have titles.

5. All teachers are interesting.

6. If some schools are not closed, then there is not a hurricane.

7. If some students fail the test, then the review session is not successful.

8. If no people suffer, then some corporations do not place profit above human need.

9. a. A person studies Latin and that person does not have an excellent vocabulary.
   b. It is hot and no city pool will be open.
   c. There is a lottery and some schools will not receive increased funding.

10. d

Answers

Chp. 1, Topic 9, Problem Set 9

1. Jim is not tall or John is not an athlete.
2. Mary does not live in Florida or Nancy does not live in Georgia.
3. Estelle is not loud or Estelle is not abrasive.
4. The Dolphins are not in the playoffs or the Buccaneers are not in the playoffs.
5. Clearwater is not in Georgia or Atlanta is in Florida.
6. The Strikers are Jacksonville's team or the Bandits are not Tampa's team.
7. All movies are exciting or some jokes are funny.
8. Vince is tall or Mike is wise.
9. Some dogs are not faithful or no cats are cute.
10. Frank does not appreciate rock music or Judy does not appreciate rock music.
11. b
12. London is not in England and Paris is not in France.
13. The bill does not pass and it is a law.
14. Dave does not visit San Francisco and he does not visit London.
15. It is hot and it is humid.
16. Some books do not have sample tests and they do get published.
17. Antonio is Prospero's brother and Romeo is not Juliet's lover.
18. Some people do not carry umbrellas and no people get wet.
19. If lines share a common point, then they are not parallel.
20. If the team does not win, then Jose does not play or Marsha does not play.
21. If one is not in the South, then one is not in Atlanta and one is not in New Orleans.
22. $(q \wedge \sim r) \rightarrow p$
23. $r \rightarrow (\sim p \vee q)$
24. a. If Joan is nervous, then she is not tense.
    b. If Pete is going to the movies, then he is not going to the beach.
    c. If Richard is rich, then he is not famous.
    d. If Joe is our driver, then he is not our guide.
25. a
26. d
27. b
28. d
29. c
30. b

Chp. 1, Topic 10, Problem Set 10

1. Valid since $[(p \vee q) \wedge \sim q] \rightarrow p$ is a tautology.
2. Valid since $[(\sim p \rightarrow \sim q) \wedge q] \rightarrow p$ is a tautology.
3. Invalid since $[(\sim p \rightarrow \sim q) \wedge \sim q] \rightarrow \sim p$ is not a tautology.
4. Invalid since $[(\sim p \rightarrow q) \wedge p] \rightarrow \sim q$ is not a tautology.
5. Valid since $[(\sim p \rightarrow q) \wedge \sim q] \rightarrow p$ is a tautology.
6. Valid since $[(\sim p \vee q) \wedge p] \rightarrow q$ is a tautology.

Chp. 1, Topic 11, Problem Set 11

1. c   2. a   3. b   4. d
5. c   6. c   7. a   8. b
9. d   10. d

Chp. 1, Topic 12, Problem Set 12

1. Some people do not obey the rules.
2. Some people smoke cigarettes.
3. Joel does not study mathematics.
4. Kathy does not have a knowledge of theatre.
5. Angie appreciates language.
6. We watched television on Friday.
7. Marco does not study biology.
8. Susan is not studying.

440

9. Fran did no homework problems.
10. If it is Tuesday, then Javier contemplates the meaning of existence.
11. If the medication is effective, then I will not fall behind.
12. If one lives in Tampa, then one lives in North America.
13. South Africa has no peace and must spend a great deal of money building jails.
14. An outstanding baseball player can hit and throw a ball.
15. It did not rain and it did not snow on Friday.
16. Samir does not study mathematics and he appreciates language.
17. We will watch television and we will not pass the exam.

Chp. 1, Topic 13, Problem Set 13

1. c 2. d 3. d
4. He first takes the goat across. He then returns and picks up the wolf. He leaves the wolf off and takes the goat back. He then leaves the goat at the starting place and takes the cabbage over to where the wolf is. He then returns and picks up the goat and goes where the wolf and the cabbage are waiting.
5. The man furthest from the wall either sees 2 tan hats or a black and a tan hat. If he saw 2 black hats, he would have known he had to have a tan hat. The middle man sees a tan hat because if he saw a black hat, he would know he must be wearing a tan hat from the first response. Therefore, the man facing the wall concludes he can only be wearing the tan hat the middle man sees.
6. Two letters (A,B) are left and one (C) is removed; three letters (D,E,F) are left and two (G,H) are removed, etc.

7. 276. The middle digit is not the sum of the other two digits.
8. Joan cannot be the art critic or architect. The aviator must be a man, so Joan must be the acrobat. Hence, Jane, the only other woman, must be the art critic. John cannot be the aviator, who is happily married, so he must be the architect.

Sample Examination — Sets and Logic

1. c
2. b
3. d
4. c
5. c
6. b
7. d
8. b
9. b
10. d
11. c
12. e
13. d
14. d
15. b
16. d
17. d
18. d
19. c
20. b
21. b
22. c
23. d
24. d
25. a
26. b
27. c
28. d
29. b
30. d
31. a
32. b
33. b
34. a
35. c
36. a
37. c
38. b
39. c
40. c
41. d
42. d
43. b
44. b
45. c

Answers

Answers for Chapter 2

Chp. 2, Topic 1,
Problem Set 1
1. 720
2. 120
3. 625
4. 96
5. 72
6. 9,000,000
7. a. 125   b. 25
8. 3,276,000
9. a. 18   b. 15
10. 12
11. 720
12. 120
13. 720
14. 24
15. 120
16. 210
17. 360
18. 3,024

Chp. 2, Topic 2,
Problem Set 2
1. No. It is meaningless to consider 3 objects 4 at a time.
2. a. 15   b. 56   c. 210   d. 1
   e. 1
3. a. 21   b. 56   c. 1   d. 1
   e. 5
4. 70
5. 56
6. 35
7. 10
8. 35
9. 56
10. 1,4,6,4,1
11. a. 30   b. 5
12. a. 105   b. 21

13. a. 140   b. 7
14. a. 120   b. 8

Chp. 2, Topic 3,
Problem Set 3
1. a $\frac{2}{3}$ b. $\frac{1}{3}$
2. a. $\frac{1}{3}$ b. $\frac{2}{9}$ c. $\frac{7}{9}$
3. $\frac{2}{3}$
4. a. $\frac{4}{7}$ b. $\frac{5}{7}$
5. a. $\frac{1}{5}$ b. $\frac{2}{5}$ c. 1   d. 0
6. a. 1   b. $\frac{1}{4}$ c. $\frac{1}{2}$ d. $\frac{1}{2}$
   e. $\frac{3}{4}$
7. a. 1   b. $\frac{1}{8}$ c. $\frac{3}{8}$ d. $\frac{1}{2}$
8. a. $S = \{(1,1), (1,2), (1,3), (2,1), (2,2), (2,3), (3,1), (3,2), (3,3)\}$
   b. $\frac{1}{3}$ c. $\frac{5}{9}$ d. $\frac{2}{9}$
9. a. $S = \{(1,2), (1,3), (2,1), (2,3), (3,1), (3,2)\}$
   b. $\frac{1}{3}$
10. $\frac{3}{8}$
11. a. $\frac{4}{7}$ b. $3:4$ c. $4:3$
12. $1:4$
13. $\frac{1}{10001}$
14. $\frac{7}{11}$
15. 0
16. 1
17. $\frac{7}{8}$
18. 0.75
19. $\frac{6}{7}$
20. 1
21. a. $\frac{2}{3}$ b. 0
22. 0.45

23. a. $\frac{4}{5}$ b. $\frac{2}{5}$ c. $\frac{1}{5}$ d. $\frac{3}{5}$

24. $\frac{1}{8}$

25. $\frac{1}{16}$

26. a. $\frac{1}{5}$ b. $\frac{1}{20}$ c. $\frac{1}{120}$

27. a. $\frac{8}{15}$ b. $\frac{1}{15}$ c. $\frac{2}{5}$

28. a. $\frac{1}{22}$ b. $\frac{7}{44}$ c. $\frac{21}{44}$

29. a. $\frac{80}{429}$ b. $\frac{160}{3003}$ c. $\frac{1}{3003}$ d. $\frac{140}{3003}$

Chp. 2, Topic 4, Problem Set 4

1. a. $\frac{3}{10} + \frac{2}{10} = \frac{1}{2}$ b. $\frac{5}{10} + \frac{2}{10} = \frac{7}{10}$
   c. $\frac{3}{10}$

2. a. $\frac{5}{6}$ b. 1

3. 0.6

4. a. $\frac{5}{26}$ b. $\frac{6}{13}$ c. $\frac{7}{13}$

5. 0.7

6. 0.5

7. a. 0.8   b. 0.2

8. $\frac{31}{100}$ or 0.31

9. $\frac{33}{100}$ or 0.33

10. $\frac{67}{100}$ or 0.67

11. 136

12. 268

13. $\frac{14}{50}$ or 0.28

14. 1

15. 0.40

16. 0.28

17. 0.54

18. 0.20

19. $\frac{23}{60}$

20. 0.30

21. $\frac{9}{23}$

22. 1

Chp. 2, Topic 5, Problem Set 5

1. $\frac{5}{8} \cdot \frac{1}{2} = \frac{5}{16}$

2. a. $\frac{7}{12} \cdot \frac{5}{11} = \frac{35}{132}$ b. $\frac{5}{12} \cdot \frac{4}{11} = \frac{5}{33}$
   c. $\frac{7}{12} \cdot \frac{6}{11} = \frac{7}{22}$

3. a. $\frac{7}{10} \cdot \frac{6}{9} = \frac{7}{15}$ b. $\frac{3}{10} \cdot \frac{2}{9} = \frac{1}{15}$

4. a. $\frac{2}{3} \cdot \frac{3}{8} = \frac{1}{4}$ b. $\frac{2}{3} + \frac{3}{8} - \frac{1}{4} = \frac{19}{24}$

5. a. $\frac{1}{2}$ b. $\frac{1}{36}$ c. $\frac{25}{216}$

6. 0.48

7. a. 0.28   b. 0.18   c. 0.42

8. 0.35

9. $\frac{7}{15}$

10. a. $\frac{1}{100}$ b. $\frac{19}{100}$

11. a. $\frac{1}{45}$ b. $\frac{17}{45}$

12. $\frac{4}{9}$

Chp. 2, Topic 6, Problem Set 6

1. c
2. c
3. 100, 93, 81, 65, 40, 21, 8
4. a. 46%   b. 13%
5. a. 64%   b. 31%
   c. $50,000   d. $79,999
6. d
7. d
8. a. 350   b. 1971 and 1972
   c. 1971 and 1975   d. 400
9. c
10. $2,000
11. d
12. a. 15%   b. 8.7%
13. b

Answers

Chp. 2, Topic 7, Problem Set 7

1. $9, 7, 6\frac{4}{5}$

2. $8 \text{ and } 5, 5\frac{1}{2}, 5\frac{3}{4}$

3. a. $513\frac{1}{3}$ b. 520   c. 400

4. c

5. a

6. c

7. b

8. c

9. b

10. c

11. d

12. 4, 4, 4.13

13. a. 3, 3   b. 2, 2   c. 2.38, 2.74

14. She reports only the mode which in this case is a poor reflection of central tendency.

Chp. 2, Topic 8, Problem Set 8

1. $13, 7, \sqrt{6}$

2. 13, 11, 4

3. $\sqrt{3.33}$

4. $\sqrt{7.25}$

5. b

6. c

7. Group 1

Chp. 2, Topic 9, Problem Set 9

1. a. T   b. F   c. F   d. T
      e. T   f. T   g. F   h. T
      i. T   j. F

2. a. 84%   b. 0.84   c. 16%   d. 0.16
      e. 13.5%   f. 0.135   g. 68%   h. 0.68

3. a. 680   b. 160

4. a. 0.6%   b. 24.1%   c. 0.669   d. 66, 900
      e. 69.2%

5. a. 6.7%   b. 60   c. 63   d. 88.8%

6. a. 625   b. 30.8%   c. 241

7. 2.5

Sample Examination — Probability and Statistics

1. e		34. d
2. c		35. a
3. a		36. a
4. c		37. c
5. b		38. c
6. c		39. a
7. b		40. a
8. c		41. c
9. a		42. b
10. c		43 d
11. b		44. a
12. e		45. b
13. c		46. c
14. b		47. c
15. d		48. c
16. b		49. b
17. a		50. c
18. b		51. d
19. c		52. b
20. b		53. b
21. b		54. b
22. d		55. d
23. c		56. a
24. c		57. a
25. a		58. a
26. c		59. a
27. b		60. b
28. d		61. c
29. a		62. c
30. c		63. b
31. c		64. d
32. b		65. d
33. a		

Answers for Chapter 3

Chp. 3, Topic 1,
Problem Set 1

1. 20 in
2. a. 3,700 b. 520 c. 91 d. 0.0048
3. 1,670 m = 1.67 km
4. $2,000
5. 128.4 ft
6. $133.33
7. W = 10, L = 20
8. W = 4, L = 11
9. a. 9 yd b. 5 yd c. 4 ft d. 4 yd
   e. 7 in f. 38 cm g. 6 km
   h. 2,501 km i. 2.7 km
   j. 24.27 cm k. 62.302 m
   l. 5,500 ft
10. a. 4 in b. $3\frac{1}{2}$ in c. $3\frac{3}{4}$ in d. $3\frac{5}{8}$ in
    e. 4 in f. 4 in
    g. 4 in h. $4\frac{1}{8}$ in
11. a. 35 grams b. 30 grams
    c. 33 grams
12. a. 7 lb b. 14 lb c. 6 gallons
    d. 17 gallons e. 4 gallons
    f. 3 minutes

Chp. 3, Topic 2,
Problem Set 2

1. $\angle$ ABC, $\angle$ CBA, $\angle$ B, $\angle$ 1
2. a. acute b. right
   c. obtuse d. straight
3. 12°
4. 102°
5. a. $\angle$ 2 and $\angle$ 4 b. $\angle$ 3
   c. $\angle$ 3 and $\angle$ 1
6. 2x + 50 + 4x + 10 = 90, x = 5°: 30°, 60°
7. 3x + 134 + 6x + 10 = 180, x = 4°: 34°, 146°
8. 65°
9. 167°
10. 40°, acute

11. 110°, obtuse
12. 180°, straight
13. 90°, right
14. 55°

Chp. 3, Topic 3,
Problem Set 3

1. $\angle$ 1, $\angle$ 8, $\angle$ 6
2. $\angle$ 6, $\angle$ 8, $\angle$ 3, $\angle$ 1
3. $\angle$ 4, $\angle$ 5, $\angle$ 7
4. $\angle$ 6, $\angle$ 8, $\angle$ 1, $\angle$ 3
5. m $\angle$ 2 = 12°, m $\angle$ 5 = 12°, m $\angle$ 6 = 12°,
   m $\angle$ 1 = 168°, m $\angle$ 3 = 168°, m $\angle$ 4 = 168°,
   m $\angle$ 7 = 168°
6. 140°
7. 45°
8. x = 25; The corresponding angles are each 125°.
9. b
10. c
11. d
12. m $\angle$ A = 35°, m $\angle$ B = 145°, m $\angle$ C = 145°,
    m $\angle$ D = 50°, m $\angle$ E = 130°, m $\angle$ F = 130°,
    m $\angle$ G = 50°, m $\angle$ H = 35°, m $\angle$ I = 95°,
    m $\angle$ J = 50°, m $\angle$ K = 95°, m $\angle$ L = 35°
13. x = 3°; 20°
14. 125°
15. 52°
16. b
17. 118°
18. 61°, 43°, 76°
19. 79°
20. 130°
21. 53°
22. a. 65° b. 10°
23. a. true b. true c true
    d. false e. true
24. c
25. 70°

Answers

Chp. 3, Topic 4,
Problem Set 4

1. ASA; definition of a congruence between triangles; The diagonals bisect.
2. SAS; Diagonals are congruent.
3. SSS; m∠AMD = m∠CMD = 90°; Diagonals are perpendicular.
4. SAS
5. $\overline{KM} \cong \overline{KN}$ because the triangles at both ends are congruent by SAS.
6. c
7. d

Chp. 3, Topic 5,
Problem Set 5

1. 4
2. 10
3. c
4. d
5. 21 ft
6. Two angles of one triangle are congruent to two angles of the other triangle (vertical angles and right angles).
7. 20 cm
8. 4 ft
9. 24
10. d
11. c
12. no; m∠CPQ ≠ m∠CAB since similar triangles cannot be established.
13. $\frac{x-3}{4x-22} = \frac{4}{x}$; x = 8 or x = 11
14. 24

Chp. 3, Topic 6,
Problem Set 6

1. a. 17 in   b. 7 ft   c. 8 yds
   d. 2 cm   e. 7 m   f. 1 in
2. a. 15 miles   b. 24 ft
   c. 25 ft   d. 20 ft
   e. 25 ft   f. yes

3. $2,640,000
4. b
5. 30 ft.
6. 21 ft.
7. 48 in.

Chp. 3, Topic 7,
Problem Set 7

1. 720°, 1,080°
2. 18°
3. 140°
4. 1,800°
5. 60°
6. a. rectangle, square   b. rhombus, square
   c. rectangle, square   d. rhombus, square
   e. parallelogram, rectangle, rhombus, square
   f. trapezoid   g. rectangle, square
   h. square
7. c
8. c
9. 12K
10. 2A + 2B + 2C + 2D
11. 38 ft
12. b
13. a
14. 125°, 55°
15. d
16. a
17. c
18. d
19. x = 21; m∠B = m∠D = 99°, m∠A = m∠C = 81°
20. x = 70; 100°, 80°, 100°, 80°
21. ASA establishes congruent triangles.
22. a : 48°   b : 42°   c : 138°   d : 56°
    e : 138°   f : 82 °   g : 42°   h : 56°
    i : 138°   k : 18°
23. m∠D + m∠R = 180°, ∠R ≅ ∠C
25. BD = 5, EF = 10, DE = 6, AC = 9

Chp. 3, Topic 8,
Problem Set 8
1. $272.58
2. 900 ft^2
3. 18 ft^2
4. 16π cm^2
5. 108 ft^2
6. 84 cm^2
7. 26 m^2
8. $3\frac{2}{3}$ ft^2
9. c
10. 21 cm^2
11. 6π yd
12. sh + 3bs
13. $\frac{\pi r^2}{4}$
14. 92.52 cm^2
15. 42.14 ft^2
16. a. It is multiplied by 4.   b. $6
17. 757 ft^2
18. 307 in^2
19. $44
20. 174 in^2
21. 25 ft^2
22. 675 m^2
23. 32 in^2
24. $\frac{1}{36}$
25. a. 2,500 cm^2 b. 76 m^2
    c. 27.5 cm^2

Chp. 3, Topic 9,
Problem Set 9
1. 8 yd^3
2. yes
3. three 4-inch cubes
4. 64 yd^3; 96 yd^2
5. $\frac{35}{48}$ ft^3
6. a. cm   b. cm^2 c. cm^3
7. 207,360 pounds

8. 360 yd^3
9. 864π gallons
10. 1,170 pounds
11. 288π m^3
12. $750
13. $72
14. $8
15. 9B^3
16. 2πr^2 + 2πrh
17. a. 19 yd^3 b. 2,400 cm^3
    c. 3,000 cm^3 d. 17.4 m^3
18. 8,620 cm^3

Sample Examination — Geometry

1. a
2. d
3. a
4. a
5. d
6. b
7. b
8. a
9. d
10. c
11. b
12. c
13. c
14. b
15. a
16. a
17. c
18. a
19. d
20. d
21. c
22. d
23. c
24. d
25. c

26. a
27. a
28. c
29. d
30. b
31. c
32. c
33. a
34. c
35. c
36. a
37. d
38. b
39. c
40. c
41. b
42. b
43. a
44. c
45. c
46. c
47. a
48. b
49. c
50. a

447

Answers for Chapter 4

Chp. 4, Topic 1,
Problem Set 1

1. two (19 and 23)
2. $2 \cdot 3^2 \cdot 5 \cdot 7$
3. two (2 and 3)
4. 35
5. one (6)
6. 28
7. c
8. $\frac{10}{2}, \frac{10}{3}$
9. b
10. d
11. $2\frac{4}{15}$
12. 20
13. 5.4
14. 160
15. $-\frac{8}{3}$
16. a. Associative property of multiplication
    b. Zero is the identity of addition.
    c. Distributive property
    d. Commutative property of multiplication
    e. Inverses of addition
    f. 1 is the identity of multiplication.
    g. Inverses of multiplication
    h. Distributive property
    i. Inverses of multiplication
    j. Commutative property of addition
    k. Commutative property of multiplication
17. T
18. F
19. T
20. T
21. F
22. T
23. F
24. F
25. T
26. F
27. T
28. T
29. F
30. -10
31. -36
32. $7\frac{3}{5}$
33. -6
34. $-\frac{8}{15}$
35. -14
36. 5
37. -16
38. $-11\frac{3}{4}$
39. $-7\frac{1}{3}$
40. 35
41. -2
42. 1
43. 2
44. 100
45. 17
46. -7.5
47. $14,250
48. 10°
49. $16.80
50. 123 miles per hour
51. -12
52. 12
53. 23
54. -42
55. d
56. $C = \frac{A^2}{B}$
57. 60 mm of mercury
58. 46
59. 119.7 ft.
60. 112.5%
61. $7 - 3x + 6y$
62. $7y - 6y^2$
63. $8a - 6a^2$
64. $4t^2 - 5t$
65. $5x - 15y$
66. $9x - 12$
67. $5x - 10$
68. $2x^2y - 6xy^2$
69. $-24x^2 - 20x$
70. 0

Chp. 4, Topic 2,
Problem Set 2

1. $5\sqrt{2}$
2. $2\sqrt{3}$
3. $6\sqrt{3}$
4. $12\sqrt{3} - 5\sqrt{2}$
5. $7\sqrt{2}$
6. $2\sqrt{6}$
7. $2\sqrt{2}$
8. 6
9. $4\sqrt{5}$
10. $2\sqrt{6}$
11. -48
12. $30\sqrt{11}$
13. $30\sqrt{2} + 40\sqrt{3}$
14. $6\sqrt{5} - 12$
15. 5
16. $2\sqrt{2}$
17. $\frac{3\sqrt{7}}{7}$
18. $\frac{\sqrt{2}}{2}$
19. $\frac{\sqrt{6}}{2}$
20. $\frac{\sqrt{2}}{10}$
21. $\frac{\sqrt{14}}{7}$
22. $\frac{3\sqrt{2}}{4}$
23. $\frac{\sqrt{2}}{2}$

Chp. 4, Topic 3,
Problem Set 3

1. a. a^{11}
   b. x^6
   c. $2x^9$
   d. $6x^7$
   e. $\frac{1}{y^3}$
   f. $\frac{1}{x^7}$
   g. x^3
   h. 1
   i. $\frac{1}{x^7}$
   j. $-3x^4$
   k. $\frac{1}{x^{18}}$
   l. $16a^4$
   m. $\frac{x^3}{y^3}$
2. no, $a^x \cdot a^y = a^{x+y}$
3. no, $2^2 \cdot 2^3 = 2^5$
4. a. $x^{20}y^{12}$
   b. $\frac{x^6}{y^{14}}$
   c. $64y^6$
   d. y^6
   e. $40y^{11}$
   f. $27b^2$
5. d
6. d
7. c
8. b
9. 532.36
10. 804.03
11. 0.367
12. 0.0354
13. d
14. a
15. a. $(3.76)(10^2)$
    b. $(5.7)(10^{-3})$
    c. $(1.4)(10^0)$
    d. $(5.7)(10^{-2})$
    e. $(5.7)(10^0)$
    f. $(3.76)(10^4)$
16. $(2.1)(10^3)$
17. $(2.2)(10^{-3})$
18. $(4.324)(10^3)$
19. $(2)(10^8)$
20. $(4)(10^{-12})$
21. $(5.964)(10^{-7})$
22. $(2.5)(10^5)$
23. $(5)(10^{-4})$
24. b
25. $1.\overline{1} \cdot 10^{24}$ times greater
26. $2.5344 \cdot 10^3$ cm/sec
27. $5 \cdot 10^2$ seconds ago
28. approximately $2.47 \cdot 10^4$ seconds (or 6 hr. 52 min.)
29. b
30. b

Chp. 4, Topic 4,
Problem Set 4

1. {4}
2. {$-\frac{13}{2}$}
3. {$-\frac{8}{3}$}
4. {-2}
5. {2}
6. {3}
7. {1}
8. {19}
9. {$\frac{1}{2}$}
10. {$\frac{1}{2}$}
11. b
12. a

Chp. 4, Topic 5,
Problem Set 5

1. 8
2. 45
3. 17
4. 9
5. 8
6. 12 and 24
7. 10 and 13
8. 500
9. 40%
10. 3; 12
11. $2050
12. a
13. 9, 10, 11
14. 77, 78, 79
15. 64, 66, 68
16. 15, 17, 19
17. 51, 53, 55, 57
18. 42, 44, 46, 48
19. No integers satisfy these conditions.
20. No odd integers satisfy these conditions.
21. 10, 12, 14
22. 17, 19, 21
23. 8, 10, 12
24. 17, 19, 21
25. The conditions are true for any three consecutive even integers.
26. No three consecutive odd integers satisfy these conditions.
27. d
28. 9
29. 13
30. 72
31. 59
32. 64
33. 93
34. c
35. d
36. 186
37. b
38. 1
39. d
40. 279-2013
41. 40
42. 240
43. $29
44. $3
45. 9 pounds
46. $54
47. 10
48. 84
49. 36

Chp. 4, Topic 6,
Problem Set 6

1. a. > b. <
   c. < d. <
   e. < f. <
   g. > h. =
   i. > j. <
2. $x > 1$

3. $x > -4$

4. $x \le -13\frac{1}{2}$

5. $x < -2$

6. $x \ge 0$

Answers

7. $2 < x \le 5$
8. $0 \le x < 4$
9. $y > 4$
10. $a \le 3$
11. b
12. a
13. d
14. c
15. a
16. c
17. b
18. a
19. d
20. b
21. 21 years
22. more than 80 hours
23. b
24. c
25. c
26. a
27. b
28. b
29. c
30. a

Chp. 4, Topic 7, Problem Set 7

1. $x = 11\frac{2}{3}$
2. $x = 1\frac{113}{195}$
3. 400 miles
4. $\frac{\text{width}}{\text{height}}$ $\frac{4}{7} = \frac{x}{10}$ $x = 5\frac{5}{7}$ in.
5. $\frac{\text{tagged bass}}{\text{total number}}$ $\frac{135}{x} = \frac{30}{140}$ $x = 630$
6. $\frac{\text{tagged deer}}{\text{total number}}$ $\frac{27}{108} = \frac{50}{x}$ $x = 200$
7. 180 kg
8. a. 6 days   b. 12 days
9. b
10. 12

11. 8
12. 20.8 pounds
13. b

Chp. 4, Topic 8, Problem Set 8

1. 35
2. $\frac{1}{2}$
3. 27
4. $\frac{4}{25}$
5. $10\frac{6}{25}$
6. 16 amps
7. 15 days
8. approximately 555.6 ft
9. 1600 ft
10. 6.4 pounds
11. approximately 11.1 foot candles
12. approximately 71 pounds
13. 15 m^3
14. 70

Chp. 4, Topic 9, Problem Set 9

1. $(3x + 5)(x + 1)$
2. $(2x + 7)(x + 1)$
3. $(5x + 1)(x + 11)$
4. $(4x + 1)(x + 2)$
5. $(2x + 1)(4x + 3)$
6. $(6x - 5)(x - 3)$
7. $(8x + 9)(2x - 3)$
8. $(4x - 3)(2x - 3)$
9. $(4x - 3)(x - 6)$
10. $(4x + 3)(3x - 7)$
11. $(4x - 9)((x + 2)$
12. $(3x + 1)(2x + 3)$
13. $(2x - 3)^2$

14. $(4x - 7)(2x - 3)$
15. $(3x - 1)(2x + 7)$

Chp. 4, Topic 10, Problem Set 10

1. $\frac{2}{3}$ or -4
2. $-\frac{1}{2}$ or 3
3. $\frac{3}{5}$ or 1
4. $\frac{2}{7}$ or 4
5. 2 or -1
6. -5 or -3
7. $\frac{2}{3}$ or 5
8. $\frac{3}{4}$ or 2
9. 9 or -6
10. $\frac{3}{2}$ or 1
11. $-\frac{3}{2}$ or 1
12. 8 or -2
13. 5 or 3
14. 1 or $-\frac{5}{7}$
15. -1 or $-\frac{4}{5}$
16. $\frac{1}{4}$ or $-\frac{1}{3}$
17. $-1 + \sqrt{5}$ or $-1 - \sqrt{5}$
18. $\frac{1 + \sqrt{7}}{3}$ or $\frac{1 - \sqrt{7}}{3}$
19. $\frac{3 + \sqrt{41}}{8}$ or $\frac{3 - \sqrt{41}}{8}$
20. $\frac{-7 + \sqrt{53}}{2}$ or $\frac{-7 - \sqrt{53}}{2}$
21. $\frac{-1 + \sqrt{5}}{2}$ or $\frac{-1 - \sqrt{5}}{2}$
22. 7 or -1
23. 9 or -5
24. $-\frac{1}{5}$
25. a

**Chp. 4, Topic 11,
Problem Set 11**

1.
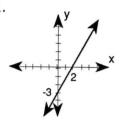

2.

3.

4.
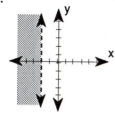

5.

6.
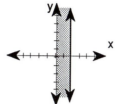

7.

8.

9.

10.

11.
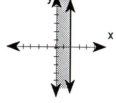
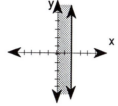

12.
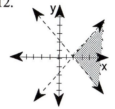
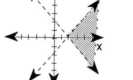

13. b
14. d
15. $x \geq 0$ and $y \geq 0$
    and $y \leq 2$
16. a
17. d

**Chp. 4, Topic 12,
Problem Set 12**
1. $\{(-31, -13)\}$
2. $\{(3, \frac{5}{2})\}$
3. $\{(2, -3)\}$
4. $\{(4, 0)\}$
5. $\{(5, -5)\}$
6. $\{(-2, -5)\}$
7. $\{(5, 4)\}$
8. $\{(5, 2)\}$
9. $\{(2, -1)\}$
10. $\{(2, -3)\}$
11. $\{(-4, 11)\}$
12. $\{(-1, -3)\}$
13. $\{(3, -1)\}$
14. $\{(4, \frac{1}{3})\}$

15. $\{(4, 2)\}$
16. $\{(-2, -1)\}$
17. $\{(7, 4)\}$
18. $\{(1, -2)\}$
19. $\{(0, 4)\}$
20. dependent
21. inconsistent
22. inconsistent
23. inconsistent
24. inconsistent
25. inconsistent
26. dependent

**Sample Examination —
Algebra**

1. a
2. a
3. c
4. e
5. e
6. d
7. b
8. e
9. d
10. d
11. c
12. c
13. a
14. d
15. b
16. c
17. c
18. a
19. c
20. a
21. c
22. b
23. d
24. d

451

Answers

25. b
26. c
27. b
28. b
29. c
30. b
31. a
32. a
33. d
34. b
35. a
36. c
37. d
38. b
39. c
40. a
41. d
42. b
43. c
44. a
45. a
46. d
47. b
48. c
49. b
50. c
51. d
52. b
53. d
54. c
55. a
56. a
57. d
58. b
59. d

60. a
61. a
62. d
63. c
64. c
65. a
66. c
67. b
68. b
69. b
70. b
71. c
72. d
73. c
74. a
75. a
76. c
77. c
78. b
79. d
80. c
81. d
82. d
83. c
84. d
85. c
86. b
87. c
88. a
89. d
90. b
91. c
92. c
93. d

Answers for Appendix I
Practice Arithmetic
Problems

1. $8\frac{11}{30}$
2. $20\frac{23}{30}$
3. $14\frac{2}{11}$
4. $13\frac{1}{8}$
5. $3\frac{7}{20}$
6. $57\frac{1}{2}$
7. 3
8. $\frac{7}{60}$
9. $3\frac{3}{25}$
10. 24.465
11. 0.0192
12. 12.421
13. 0.212998
14. 1.64615
15. 4,000
16. 12,000
17. 0.375
18. $0.3\overline{8}$
19. 3.6
20. 8.69
21. 23.90
22. 8.695
23. 317.236
24. a. 72.95%
    b. 0.6%
    c. 230%
25. a. 0.23
    b. 0.009
    c. 0.974
    d. 0.04125

26. a. 80%
    b. $33\frac{1}{3}$%
    c. 87.5%
27. a. $\frac{3}{4}$
    b. $\frac{1}{8}$
    c. $\frac{7}{8}$
    d. $\frac{2}{3}$
28. $104
29. $25.30
30. 10%
31. c
32. $200
33. 35
34. $270.50
35. $1.20
36. 2,000
37. c
38. d
39. $1,055
40. $2,588.93
41. $700
42. 45 cents
43. $\frac{1}{7}$
44. $62.50
45. 81
46. $97.20
47. $350
48. 2:45 P.M.
49. $4,770
50. $909.45